Oxford Paperback English Texts   General Editor **John Buxton**

John Dryden

Selected Criticism

John Dryden
Selected Criticism

Edited by **James Kinsley** and **George Parfitt**

1970 Clarendon Press · Oxford

Oxford University Press   *Ely House, London W.1*

Glasgow	Bombay
New York	Calcutta
Toronto	Madras
Melbourne	Karachi
Wellington	Lahore
	Dacca

Cape Town	
Salisbury	Kuala Lumpur
Ibadan	Singapore
Nairobi	Hong Kong
Dar es Salaam	Tokyo
Lusaka	
Addis Ababa	

Made and printed in Great Britain by
William Clowes and Sons, Limited
London and Beccles

Contents

Introduction

I A glance at the Chronological Table reminds us that from 1659 until his death in 1700 Dryden produced a substantial work almost every year; a glance at a chronological list of his critical writings would remind us that his 'critical' and 'creative' outputs march step for step. From the 1664 Preface to *The Rival Ladies* until the 1700 Preface to the *Fables* Dryden consistently comments upon his own creative work, or develops from it a general literary discussion of some kind; he explains, justifies, educates, attacks—but whatever he is doing at any moment in any of his critical essays, his own creative work is never far from the discussion. Several important points relevant to Dryden's criticism are implied by these opening remarks: his professionalism, his public role and situation, his range, and the close relationship between his critical and creative faculties.

The sheer bulk of Dryden's output and the consistency of annual production may suggest to post-Romantic tastes either that much of his work is 'hack', in the most pejorative sense, or that it is the rubble of collapsed inspiration. It is true—as he tells us often enough—that Dryden was a professional who was frequently writing for money rather than for his own satisfaction, and it is easy to assume that the man who glumly translated Maimbourg's *Histoire de la Ligue* and cobbled the mediocre 'Parallel of Poetry and Painting' to preface his translation of du Fresnoy spent most of his life pouring out substandard ephemera. But Dryden is professional in another, altogether worthier sense: he is a conscientious craftsman. Like Ben Jonson, Dryden is not a 'maker', if that term suggests a writer concerned with form rather than content, but nevertheless (again like Jonson) he seeks as a craftsman to make a durable object, to achieve a standard of real competence in whatever he attempts. Dryden lacks Jonson's broad integrity, is readier to sacrifice principle to expediency, readier to cater to public taste and then to denigrate his own work. Jonson refused in his drama to bend or apologize to his public, whereas Dryden did both, playing the whore while pretending still to be a virgin. But Dryden's *literary* integrity remains. Whether he is knocking out another comedy for the Restoration theatre, or celebrating the birth of the baby who was to be the Old Pretender, or writing the Preface to *Sylvae*, he remains concerned with the quality of his writing (even where his commitment to *genre* or addressee may be in doubt) and committed to the profession of poet, concerned with the present state of literature, with its past and with its future.

The fact that Dryden was a professional writer who earned his living by keeping his pen fluent and adaptable helps, of course, to explain his wide range. He was perhaps a little inert, a little too easily diverted by offers of commissions from the writing he wanted to do. But it is easy—and futile—to overemphasize this, and more profitable to stress that the pressure of earning a literary living works, with Dryden's interest in literature's many forms, to produce a solid and large-scale achievement in four major kinds—drama, poetry, translation, and criticism. But it is also important to note that it is Dryden's pride and interest in his profession, his awareness of being an heir to the great classical, Continental, and native writers, which make him a critic. Obviously enough Dryden is a poet-critic; not a critic who turned to creation because he believed that his analysis of other people's creations had given him the key to writing some of his own, but a poet who in the course of his creative writing found a need to explain what he was doing and why, and to justify himself in terms of what he saw as the literary tradition. This is why almost all of Dryden's criticism is connected with creative texts: the most famous of his essays—'Of Dramatic Poesy'—is part of his running battle with Sir Robert Howard, but the battle arose over the practice of the two men when they wrote drama in verse; the long 'Discourse concerning . . . Satire' is written to educate the readers of his translations from Juvenal and Persius; his well-known account of Chaucer is his justification of his modernization of that poet. This close link between creation and criticism is important, not only in indicating that Dryden usually has some particular purpose in writing criticism, but also in explaining his inconsistencies, for what Dryden argues at any particular point is likely to depend at least as much upon local demands (e.g. upon demands relevant to a particular addressee or text) as upon what may have been said at some other time.

II The opening remarks of Dryden's first critical essay ('To the Right Honourable Roger, Earl of Orrery', prefixed to *The Rival Ladies*) will help to define the nature and framework of his criticism:

This worthless present was designed you long before it was a play; when it was only a confused mass of thoughts, tumbling over one another in the dark; when the fancy was yet in its first work, moving the sleeping images of things towards the light, there to be distinguished, and then either chosen or rejected by the judgement: it was yours, my Lord, before I could call it mine.

Dryden is writing about his own play, and anything of general interest which he may go on to say will be conditioned by this fact. But he is also writing a Dedication, having to bear in mind the need to flatter and retain his patrons; and the framework—here and else-where—leads to uncritical excess, that unhappy exaggeration of Orrery's own importance as a writer which occurs later in this essay. It might be said that Dryden only seems to overestimate Orrery be-cause of the need to flatter, but the fact remains that Dryden is prepared to do this and it affects the nature and quality of his essay. But even these opening remarks become more than a gracefully self-abasing compliment to Orrery, for Dryden includes a fine statement about literary creation, a statement which is convincing as psycho-logy, brilliantly expressed, and which—in its doctrine of the control of fancy by judgement—reveals something of the Augustan view of the creative process. But we need to notice how this fine statement comes about: it arises from a context of flattery and not as a general conclusion based on careful analysis of particular cases. It is an example of intuitive criticism rather than an illustration of critical method. If criticism must reflect 'close reading', with as few pre-conceptions as possible and with a strong sense of the autonomy of the individual work, we shall find little of value in Dryden. His criticism shows the operation of general common sense upon litera-ture, upon the *genre* moreover, rather than the particular case: 'For the stage being the representation of the world, and the actions in it, how can it be imagined that the picture of human life can be more exact than life itself is?' The point is a general one, based on a dog-matic definition of drama, and is made in terms of common sense ('how can it be imagined?') rather than philosophically or scientific-ally. The famous 'examen' of Jonson's *Epicoene* in 'Of Dramatic Poesy' is often cited as the first sustained piece of close reading in English, but the analysis is only undertaken to make a general point; it is not án enquiry, with as few preconceptions as possible, into a particular work of art, but the demonstration of a general tenet in terms of an example chosen to strengthen the generalization, the analysis being organized to serve this function.

This reliance on the general rather than the particular relates to another important feature of Dryden's criticism: its reliance on authority. A simple illustration of this comes in another remark in the Preface to *The Rival Ladies*. Dryden is saying that it is proper for Orrery to write verse: 'Neither would I have justified your Lordship in it, if examples of it had not been in the world before you; if Xenophon had not written a romance, and a certain Roman called Augustus Caesar a tragedy and epigrams.' Dryden is being gracefully complimentary here rather than critically serious, yet the habit of reliance on authority can be dangerous if our 'guides' become our 'commanders'.

1*

In Dryden's case the authority is usually classical; you can track Horace's *Ars Poetica* from beginning to end of Dryden's critical career. But it is often also Italian or French. Dryden was always liable to be impressed by criticism that was classical, or based on the classics, and that was expressed with authority (hence the deference to Rymer), and his criticism can be viewed in part as his account of a battle between respect for authority and his own common sense. He seems at times to be working mechanically from a rule-book, as he comments upon Shakespeare's failures to adhere to unities he may never have heard of, or apologizes for his own errors in this kind, or ties himself in knots over the propriety of representing non-human characters on the stage. But when we grow impatient with Dryden's respect for authority we tend to forget both how frequently common sense leads Dryden to qualify excesses in neo-classical criticism and how sustaining authority is for Dryden's major achievements. The radical element in Dryden, the element that leads him to qualify or even reject particular aspects of critical authority, is strongest, perhaps, in the 'unbuttoned' notes which make up the 'Heads of an Answer to Rymer', where Dryden comes close to a heresy that appeals enormously to modern taste:

. . . consider whether Aristotle has made a just definition of tragedy, of its parts, of its ends, of its beauties; and whether he, having not seen any others but those of Sophocles, Euripides etc., had or truly could determine what all the excellencies of tragedy are, and wherein they consist.

Two things happen here. The greatest of authorities is about to be brought into question (and, ironically, Aristotle might well have approved of this more than of the mechanical application of his 'rules') as Dryden wonders whether the practical experience had been sufficient to validate the definition. Secondly, what Dryden says here implies that 'rules' should be defined by cases rather than that cases should be judged by rules which have been given a kind of Platonic ideal validity. For a moment, consciously or accidentally, Dryden trembles on the brink, looks likely to break with neo-classicism and move to a recognizably modern position, where the individual work defines the valid approach to that work. But it would be a mistake to 'modernize' Dryden on the strength of a single remark in an informal set of notes. Dryden's critical output as a whole suggests that he is here wondering not so much whether rules are possible as whether a particular set of rules is adequate. Yet the tension between authority and sound sense, reflecting upon direct experience of literary works, is present, and it is fruitful, for it gives pause to authoritarianism, makes room for some freedom of movement, allows the fresh response of this:

The French poets ... would not, for example, have suffered Cleopatra and Octavia to have met; or, if they had met, there must have only passed betwixt them some cold civilities, but no eagerness of repartee, for fear of offending against the greatness of their characters, and the modesty of their sex. This objection I foresaw, and at the same time contemned; for I judged it both natural and probable that Octavia, proud of her new-gained conquest, would search out Cleopatra to triumph over her; and that Cleopatra, thus attacked, was not of a spirit to shun the encounter: and 'tis not unlikely that two exasperated rivals should use such satire as I have put into their mouths; for after all, though the one were a Roman, and the other a queen, they were both women (Preface to *All for Love*).

Dryden's attitude here is a sensible reassertion of reason over regulation, and it sums up one of his distinctive qualities as a critic for he gives us the sense of an alert, interested, well-informed mind reacting to literature and caring for his subject.

This sense that Dryden cares about literature is, however, more than merely attractive, for it helps explain his respect for rules. While being capable on occasions of rejecting certain rules or extensions of them, Dryden never becomes, or looks remotely like becoming, a pragmatic critic. This can be 'explained' in terms of the history of critical thought, but such explanations tend to invoke an ineluctable abstract process rather than to indicate why a particular individual made certain choices, adopted certain attitudes at some specific point in time. Dryden was too intelligent, too much a first-rate literary practitioner, to be simply swamped by critical tradition: his critical classicism must be viewed, at least in part, as a conscious stance adopted of his own free will. It is true that at times he seems to accept traditional attitudes rather uncritically because of pressure of time: the long 'Discourse concerning ... Satire', for example, draws heavily and in detail upon a group of great Continental editors and is only intermittently enlivened by that tension and commitment spoken of earlier. But it is more to the point to stress Dryden's deep love of classical literature and his ambition for that of his own time. Dryden's feeling for classical literature and for the quality of its achievement is shown not so much by the fact that he translates from it but by how well he translates it, and, critically, by how well he distinguishes between, say, Virgil and Lucan. He was in touch with the classics in a way difficult for us to appreciate now; and he was genuinely in accord with a tradition which held that literary greatness lay in imitation of Nature and that the great Greek and Roman writers had imitated Nature to perfection, with the consequence that modern literature must succeed either by following classical precedent or by finding *genres* in which major classical writers had not worked. Such attitudes may seem strange to us, but before we smile indulgently we should remember that they lie behind *The Faerie Queene, Paradise Lost,* and the whole of Jonson's achievement. Granted that Virgil had, following Homer, perfected the epic, it would follow that his practice could be used to formulate rules for later would-be writers of epic, rules which should be seen less as arbitrary impositions than as guides to success based on the best precedent conceivable. It is easily remembered that over-emphasis on rules can produce an art which is appallingly formal, circumscribed and dead; and easily forgotten that an awareness of rules—in the sense of a sensitive understanding of earlier achievement—can produce an art which is classical in all the best senses of that word, the art of a Virgil, a Horace, a Milton, a Jonson. The key to this kind of classicism is a respect which is not subservience, an understanding which is not self-abasing, and it is precisely this that Dryden's best criticism manifests. When Dryden discusses Juvenal and Persius as models for satire he is not being pedantic or blindly sycophantic. The record of Elizabethan satire and of that written during the Civil War (even by such a gifted poet as Marvell) amply demonstrates that real understanding of what satire is and can do was most important if any serious attempt to establish formal satire in English was to succeed. The satires of Dryden and Pope fully vindicate Dryden's interest in Latin precedent and are major examples of how a respect for authority can be enlivening rather than deadening. Dryden wants to examine, understand, and vindicate the 'rules' not for some scholarly satisfaction of his own, but to enable himself and his contemporaries to write better, and it is this concern which sustains a modern reader, even when Dryden appears to be perverse about Shakespeare or hopelessly over-enthusiastic about Waller and Denham.

Dryden as critic, then, is concerned in part to understand the past for present purposes. But he is also a critic because he believes in reason. At times he uses invective (which critics don't?) as a substitute for reason, and he is not consciously a teacher about literature and taste as Ben Jonson had been and Samuel Johnson was to be; but a fundamental premiss of his criticism is that readers can be educated to understand and appreciate what he, as creative writer, is doing, and that objections to his work can be argued with to some purpose. However general or perverse Dryden may seem to be, there remains the overruling anxiety to explain, to lead readers to understand and to enjoy.

III I have tried to indicate certain prominent features of Dryden's criticism and to suggest how these may have come about. I have also tried to avoid a condescendingly modern attitude to the critical writings of a man who was working, as critic, with little valuable native precedent to help him. But, eventually, one has to face the central issue: why read Dryden-as-critic now?

The obvious answers are that Dryden's criticism tells us something about literary values and attitudes in the second half of the seventeenth century, and that it tells us something about Dryden's creative work. Neither reason is contemptible.

Clearly, reading Dryden to learn something of seventeenth-century attitudes to literature will be, on its own terms, productive. Dryden is the dominant literary figure of the period and he reflects and takes part in important literary controversies of the time. He is concerned about the relative merits of rhyme and blank verse in drama, about the issue of the effect of drama on its audience, about the whole problem of drama's function and purpose, and about the discussion over methods of translation. Since Dryden's criticism covers a wide range of time and genre, it is inevitable that he conveys much valuable information, about attitudes, beliefs, even the state of literary knowledge. It is interesting to know that Dryden believed 'The Flower and the Leaf' was by Chaucer and that Shakespeare usually took his plots from Cinthio. But on these terms Dryden is more important than Rymer or Roscommon only because he wrote more. In fact, if we are looking for typical seventeenth-century attitudes, Spingarn's anthology will serve us better, because, by definition, the greater a writer is the less typical he can be.

There is also no reason why Dryden's criticism should not be read to illuminate his creative writing. We may never develop any real fondness for heroic drama, but we shall be better able to make some sense of it if we have read 'Of Heroic Plays'; we shall grasp more clearly what kind of play *All for Love* is if we read Dryden's Preface; the Chaucerian adaptations begin to have an independence of Chaucer in the light of the Preface to the *Fables*. More generally, the function and nature of the translations are clearer if we have assimilated Dryden's ideas on the problems and possibilities of translation. This is all useful, all valid in itself, but it does not give Dryden real status as a critic.

Again, Dryden can be used as an awful warning of what criticism is when not conducted in the light of clearly defined awareness of its own nature and proper *modus operandi*. Dryden's limited ability to respond to Shakespeare and Donne may be used to demonstrate the folly of allowing rules to dominate the work of art, to show, that is, the Procrustean fallacy. Even this use of Dryden is, to an extent, proper—Dryden is inclined to allow rules to dominate, he does at times avoid permissiveness by becoming over-authoritarian. He is not a great close reader (this emerges at times as sloppiness over textual accuracy, even when quoting his own lines!), and he is neither careful enough nor knowledgeable enough to be a great literary historian, although at moments he foreshadows the future development of both close reading and literary history.

But if Dryden is more than an interesting critic in an historical or a cautionary sense, why is he? It is a question which puzzles George Watson in his book *The Literary Critics.* Having effectively demolished any claim Dryden may have to be any of various kinds of modern literary critic, Watson is bothered by a Dryden who is so assured in his criticism, and yet only fleetingly a critic in any modern sense that Watson can think of. But, natural though this puzzlement may be, I find it of little help when reading Dryden's criticism; so why is he a critic of stature?

One starts, I think, by reiterating an obvious fact, that Dryden is a critic in the tradition of Horace, a figure whose energies and interests are balanced between creation and criticism, not a critic like Arnold who became more critic than creator, or like Leavis whose creation is his criticism. This distinction is more than formal because the poet-critic works, as critic, from the inside, and, as relatively few major creators are also critics of any stature, the criticism of a James, a Coleridge, a Forster is likely to have a value of its own. Thus Dryden's remarks about rhyme in drama—indeed the best moments throughout his discussions of drama—are given an extra interest and have special value by being those of a practitioner. But even this only suggests that Dryden is an important critic at moments when his attitudes provide insights into the creative writer's world of problems and solutions.

More, however, can be said. A good critic is not one who is necessarily safe or (from our individual viewpoints) right. A critic operates valuably upon our minds when the operation of his mind upon his subject defines our own reactions more precisely, or augments them, or corrects them, or makes us re-examine them. One reason why Dryden is an important critic in an absolute sense is that he is involved, that he conveys a sense of literature as an important human activity. Another reason is that he is clear—his opinions and arguments have the clarity of confidence whenever Dryden is writing well, and consequently we are forced to think before we can disagree. Another is that he is stimulating—when we are told that Denham and Waller refined the language or that Shakespeare often wrote rubbish, we may well differ violently with Dryden, but his views are argued—not merely asserted—and so we are forced to reconsider and define our own attitudes if we are to sustain our disagreement. And, finally, Dryden is a great critic because he is not a specialist.

Specialism has its great advantages and can produce great criticism, but it also involves great sacrifices: sacrifices of response (can Leavis, or Winters, or Brooks be called catholic?) and of influence (reading Frye or Kenneth Burke is a specialist's task). Dryden is not a great image-critic, nor a great critic of form, nor a great close reader: his appeal—paradoxically for so professional a writer—is that of the amateur. His tradition sees criticism as a natural extension of the experience of reading a poem or seeing a play, as—in fact—informed conversation. If such a tradition, which regards criticism as a general cultural activity, is limited in the depth to which it can go over any particular element of the complex activity of creation, it nevertheless has the positive virtues of breadth and ability to communicate. And if we have allowed this kind of criticism to fall to the current level of review journalism, that is not Dryden's fault.

George Parfitt

Chronological Table

1631   John Dryden born (9 August, at Aldwinkle All Saints, Northamptonshire).

1659   *Heroic Stanzas.*

1660   *Astraea Redux.* . . .

1663   *The Wild Gallant* (comedy; pub. 1669).

1664   *The Rival Ladies* (tragi-comedy).

1665   *The Indian Emperor* (heroic tragedy; pub. 1667).

1667   *The Tempest* (adaptation of Shakespeare, with Davenant; pub. 1670).

1668   'Of Dramatic Poesy'.
      Appointed Poet Laureate.

1669   *Tyrannic Love* (tragedy; pub. 1670).

1672   *Marriage -à-la-Mode* (comedy; pub. 1673).

1675   *Aureng-Zebe* (tragedy; pub. 1676).

1676?   *Mac Flecknoe.*

1677   *The State of Innocence* ('opera' based on *Paradise Lost*).
      All for Love (tragedy adapted from Shakespeare's *Antony and Cleopatra*; pub. 1678).

1680   *Ovid's Epistles. Translated* (Dryden contributed the Preface and two epistles).
      The Spanish Friar (tragi-comedy; pub. 1681).

1681   *Absalom and Achitophel.*

1682   *The Medal.*
      Religio Laici.

1684   *Miscellany Poems* (large contributions by Dryden for Tonson).

1685   *Sylvae, or The Second Part of Miscellany Poems* (with Dryden translations from Virgil, Lucretius, and Theocritus).
      Threnodia Augustalis.

1687   *The Hind and The Panther.*
      A Song for St. Cecilia's Day.

1688   *Britannia Rediviva.*

1690   *Don Sebastian* (tragedy).
      Amphitryon (comedy).

1691   *King Arthur* ('dramatic opera').

1692   *Cleomenes* (tragedy).

1693   *The Satires* (of Juvenal and Persius; mainly translated by Dryden).

1694   *Love Triumphant* (tragi-comedy).

1697   *The Works of Virgil* (translation).
      Alexander's Feast.

1700   *Fables, Ancient and Modern* (translations from Chaucer, Boccaccio, Homer, and Ovid).
      Death of Dryden (1 May).

A Note on the Texts

The texts of *Of Dramatic Poesy* and *A Defence of an Essay of Dramatic Poesy* are from J. T. Boulton's edition (Oxford 1964). Those of *An Account of the Ensuing Poem, prefixt to Annus Mirabilis*; the *Preface to Ovid's Epistles*; the *Preface to Sylvae*; *A Discourse concerning . . . Satire*; *To . . . Hugh Lord Clifford . . .*; and the *Preface to Fables, Ancient and Modern* are from James Kinsley's edition of the Poems (Oxford 1958). The remaining texts are modernized versions of the various first editions, with punctuation and typographical errors silently emended where necessary.

The editors would like to thank Professor Boulton for permission to make use of his texts and notes for the two essays mentioned above, and the Bodleian Library for supplying copies of the first editions of a number of essays.

Any point in the text on which there is a Note at the end of the book is marked with a superior 'n'.

Reading List

Early Editions
Works (4 vols.), 1695.
Works (3 vols.), 1701.
Works, ed. Sir Walter Scott (18 vols.), 1808, 1821 (revised by George Saintsbury, 1882–92).
Dramatic Works, ed. W. Congreve (6 vols.), 1717.
Poems, ed. Joseph and John Warton, 1811.
Poems, ed. G. Gilfillan, 1855.
The Critical and Miscellaneous Prose Works, ed. E. Malone (3 vols.), 1800.

Modern Editions
Works ed. E. N. Hooker and H. T. Swedenberg (edition in progress, 1956–   ).
Dramatic Works, ed. M. Summers (6 vols.), 1931–2.
Poetical Works, ed. G. R. Noyes, 1908.
Poems, ed. J. Kinsley (4 vols.), 1958.
Essays, ed. W. P. Ker (2 vols.), 1900.
Essays, ed. G. Watson (2 vols.), 1962.
Letters, ed. C. E. Ward, 1942.

Important Books
L. I. Bredvold, *The Intellectual Milieu of John Dryden*, 1934.
W. Frost, *Dryden and the Art of Translation*, 1955.
P. Harth, *Contexts of Dryden's Thought*, 1968.
J. W. Johnson, *The Formation of English Neo-Classical Thought*, 1967.
S. Johnson, 'Life of Dryden' in *Lives of the Poets*.
B. King, *Dryden's Major Plays*, 1966.
J. and H. Kinsley (eds.), *Dryden: The Critical Heritage* (a collection of criticism of Dryden, 1660–1808), 1970.
J. W. Krutch, *Comedy and Conscience after the Restoration*, 1924.
E. Miner, *Dryden's Poetry*, 1967.
M. Van Doren, *The Poetry of Dryden*, 1920, 1946.
C. E. Ward, *The Life of John Dryden*, 1961.
J. H. Wilson, *The Court Wits of the Restoration*, 1967.

Important Articles
Apart from T. S. Eliot's 'Homage to John Dryden' (1924) and 'The Age of Dryden' (1933), most of the major essays on Dryden can be found either in H. T. Swedenberg (ed.), *Essential Articles for the Study of John Dryden* (1966); or in B. Schilling (ed.), *John Dryden: A Collection of Critical Essays* (1963).

TO THE RIGHT HONOURABLE ROGER, EARL OF ORRERY[n]

PREFIXED TO *THE RIVAL LADIES*

1664

MY LORD

THIS worthless present was designed you long before it was a play; when it was only a confused mass of thoughts, tumbling over one another in the dark; when the fancy was yet in its first work, moving the sleeping images of things towards the light, there to be distinguished, and then either chosen or rejected by the judgement: it was yours, my Lord, before I could call it mine. And, I confess, in that first tumult of my thoughts there appeared a disorderly kind of beauty in some of them, which gave me hope something worthy my Lord of Orrery might be drawn from them. But I was then in that eagerness of imagination which, by overpleasing fanciful men, flatters them into the danger of writing; so that, when I had moulded it to that shape it now bears, I looked with such disgust upon it, that the censures of our severest critics are charitable to what I thought (and still think) of it myself: 'tis so far from me to believe this perfect, that I am apt to conclude our best plays are scarcely so. For the stage being the representation of the world, and the actions in it, how can it be imagined that the picture of human life can be more exact than life itself is? He may be allowed sometimes to err who undertakes to move so many characters and humours as are requisite in a play in those narrow channels which are proper to each of them; to conduct his imaginary persons through so many various intrigues and chances as the labouring audience shall think them lost under every billow; and then at length to work them so naturally out of their distresses that when the whole plot is laid open, the spectators may rest satisfied that every cause was powerful enough to produce the effect it had; and that the whole chain of them was with such due order linked together that the first accident would naturally beget the second, till they all rendered the conclusion necessary.

These difficulties, my Lord, may reasonably excuse the errors of my undertaking; but for this confidence of my dedication, I have an argument which is too advantageous for me not to publish it to the world. 'Tis the kindness your Lordship has continually shown to all my writings. You have been pleased, my Lord, they should sometimes cross the Irish seas to kiss your hands; which passage (contrary to the experience of others) I have found the least dangerous in the world. Your favour has shone upon me at a remote distance, without the least knowledge of my person; and (like the influence of the heavenly bodies) you have done good without knowing to whom you did it. 'Tis this virtue in your lordship which emboldens me to this attempt; for, did I not consider you as my patron, I have little reason to desire you for my judge; and should appear with as much awe before you in the reading, as I had when the full theatre sat upon the action. For who could so severely judge of faults as he who has given testimony he commits none? Your excellent poems having afforded that knowledge of it to the world, that your enemies are ready to up-braid you with it, as a crime for a man of business to write so well. Neither durst I have justified your Lordship in it, if examples of it had not been in the world before you; if Xenophon had not written a romance, and a certain Roman called Augustus Caesar a tragedy and epigrams. But their writing was the entertainment of their pleasure; yours is only a diversion of your pain. The Muses have seldom em-ployed your thoughts, but when some violent fit of the gout has snatched you from affairs of state; and, like the priestess of Apollo, you never come to deliver his oracles, but unwillingly and in torment. So that we are obliged to your Lordship's misery for our delight: you treat us with the cruel pleasure of a Turkish triumph, where those who cut and wound their bodies, sing songs of victory as they pass, and divert others with their own sufferings. Other men endure their diseases, your Lordship only can enjoy them. Plotting and writing in this kind are certainly more troublesome employments than many which signify more, and are of greater moment in the world: the fancy, memory, and judgement, are then extended (like so many limbs) upon the rack; all of them reaching with their utmost stress at nature; a thing so almost infinite and boundless as can never fully be comprehended but where the images of all things are always present. Yet I wonder not your Lordship succeeds so well in this attempt; the knowledge of men is your daily practice in the world; to work and bend their stubborn minds, which go not all after the same grain, but each of them so particular a way that the same common humours, in several persons, must be wrought upon by several means. Thus, my Lord, your sickness is but the imitation of your health; the poet but subordinate to the statesman in you; you still govern men with the same address, and manage business with the same prudence; allowing it here (as in the world) the due increase and growth, till it comes to the just height; and then turning it when it is fully ripe, and nature calls out, as it were, to be delivered. With this only advantage of ease

---

Xenophon: c. 430–355 B.C. The romance is his *Cyropaedia*.

Augustus: 63 B.C.–A.D. 14, first Roman Emperor, whose writings (including a tragedy *Ajax*) are lost.

to you in your poetry, that you have fortune here at your command; with which wisdom does often unsuccessfully struggle in the world. Here is no chance which you have not foreseen; all your heroes are more than your subjects, they are your creatures. And though they seem to move freely in all the sallies of their passions, yet you make destinies for them which they cannot shun. They are moved (if I may dare to say so) like the rational creatures of the Almighty Poet, who walk at liberty, in their own opinion, because their fetters are invisible; when indeed the prison of their will is the more sure for being large; and instead of an absolute power over their actions, they have only a wretched desire of doing that which they cannot choose but do.

I have dwelt, my Lord, thus long upon your writing, not because you deserve not greater and more noble commendations, but because I am not equally able to express them in other subjects. Like an ill swimmer, I have willingly stayed long in my own depth; and though I am eager of performing more, yet am loth to venture out beyond my knowledge. For beyond your poetry, my Lord, all is ocean to me. To speak of you as a soldier, or a statesman, were only to betray my own ignorance: and I could hope no better success from it than that miserable rhetorician had, who solemnly declaimed before Hannibal of the conduct of armies and the art of war. I can only say, in general, that the souls of other men shine out at little crannies; they understand some one thing, perhaps, to admiration, while they are darkened on all the other parts. But your Lordship's soul is an entire globe of light, breaking out on every side; and if I have only discovered one beam of it, 'tis not that the light falls unequally, but because the body which receives it is of unequal parts.

The acknowledgment of which is a fair occasion offered me to retire from the consideration of your Lordship to that of myself. I here present you, my Lord, with that in print which you had the goodness not to dislike upon the stage; and account it happy to have met you here in England; it being, at best, like small wines, to be drunk out upon the place, and has not body enough to endure the sea. I know not whether I have been so careful of the plot and language as I ought; but, for the latter, I have endeavoured to write English, as near as I could distinguish it from the tongue of pedants, and that of affected travellers. Only I am sorry that (speaking so noble a language as we do) we have not a more certain measure of it, as they have in France, where they have an Academy erected for that purpose, and

---

rhetorician: Phormio, a Peripatetic philosopher (see Cicero, *De Oratore*, II. xviii. 75).

endowed with large privileges by the present king. I wish we might at
length leave to borrow words from other nations, which is now a
wantonness in us, not a necessity; but so long as some affect to speak
them, there will not want others who will have the boldness to write
them.

But I fear lest, defending the received words, I shall be accused for
following the new way. I mean, of writing scenes in verse, though, to
speak properly, 'tis not so much a new way amongst us, as an old way
new revived; for many years before Shakespeare's plays was the
tragedy of Queen Gorboduc, in English verse, written by that famous
Lord Buckhurst, afterwards Earl of Dorset, and progenitor to that
excellent person who (as he inherits his soul and title) I wish may in-
herit his good fortune. But supposing our countrymen had not
received this writing till of late; shall we oppose ourselves to the most
polished and civilized nations of Europe? Shall we with the same
singularity oppose the world in this, as most of us do in pronouncing
Latin? Or do we desire that the brand, which Barclay has (I hope
unjustly) laid upon the English, should still continue? *Angli suos ac
sua omnia impense mirantur; caeteras nationes despectui habent.* All
the Spanish and Italian tragedies I have yet seen are writ in rhyme.
For the French, I do not name them, because it is the fate of our
countrymen to admit little of theirs among us but the basest of their
men, the extravagancies of their fashions, and the frippery of their
merchandise. Shakespeare (who, with some errors not to be avoided
in that age, had undoubtedly a larger soul of poesy than ever any of
our nation) was the first who, to shun the pains of continual rhyming,
invented that kind of writing which we call blank verse,[n] but the
French, more properly, *prose mesurée*; into which the English tongue
so naturally slides that in writing prose 'tis hardly to be avoided.
And therefore I admire some men should perpetually stumble in a
way so easy, and inverting the order of their words, constantly close
their lines with verbs; which though commended sometimes in writing Latin, yet we were whipped at Westminster if we used it twice
together. I know some, who, if they were to write in blank verse, *Sir,
I ask your pardon*, would think it sounded more heroically to write,
Sir, I your pardon ask. I should judge him to have little command of

in verse: in rhyme.
the tragedy of Queen Gorboduc: *Gorboduc* (1565) was mainly in blank verse, deal-
    ing with a *King* Gorboduc, and written by Buckhurst (Lord Sackville) with
    Thomas Norton.
'*Angli suos . . .*': a paraphrase of a passage in Jean Barclay's *Icon animorum*
    (1614): 'The English admire themselves and their writings keenly; they look
    down upon other nations.'

English whom the necessity of a rhyme should force often upon this rock; though sometimes it cannot easily be avoided; and indeed this is the only inconvenience with which rhyme can be charged. This is that which makes them say rhyme is not natural, it being only so when the poet either makes a vicious choice of words, or places them for rhyme's sake so unnaturally as no man would in ordinary speaking; but when 'tis so judiciously ordered that the first word in the verse seems to beget the second, and that the next, till that becomes the last word in the line which, in the negligence of prose, would be so; it must then be granted, rhyme has all the advantages of prose besides its own. But the excellence and dignity of it were never fully known till Mr Waller[n] taught it; he first made writing easily an art; first showed us to conclude the sense most commonly in distichs; which, in the verse of those before him, runs on for so many lines together that the reader is out of breath to overtake it. This sweetness of Mr Waller's lyric poesy was afterwards followed in the epic by Sir John Denham, in his *Cooper's Hill*, a poem which, your Lordship knows, for the majesty of the style is, and ever will be, the exact standard of good writing. But if we owe the invention of it to Mr Waller, we are acknowledging for the noblest use of it Sir William Davenant; who at once brought it upon the stage, and made it perfect, in *The Siege of Rhodes*.

The advantages which rhyme has over blank verse are so many that it were lost time to name them: Sir Philip Sidney, in his defence of poesy, gives us one which, in my opinion, is not the least considerable; I mean the help it brings to memory, which rhyme so knits up by the affinity of sounds that, by remembering the last word in one line, we often call to mind both the verses. Then, in the quickness of repartees (which in discursive scenes fall very often), it has so particular a grace, and is so aptly suited to them, that the sudden smartness of the answer and the sweetness of the rhyme set off the beauty of each other. But that benefit which I consider most in it, because I have not seldom found it, is that it bounds and circumscribes the fancy. For imagination in a poet is a faculty so wild and lawless that, like an high-ranging spaniel, it must have clogs tied to it, lest it outrun the judgement. The great easiness of blank verse renders the poet too luxuriant; he is tempted to say many things which might better be

Siege of Rhodes: acted in 1656 as an opera and published in 1663; one of the plays which established the vogue for heroic drama.

defence of poesy: *An Apology for Poetry* (1595): 'Now, that verse far exceedeth prose in the knitting up of the memory, the reason is manifest: the words . . . being so set as one word cannot be lost but the whole work fails . . .' (ed. G. Shepherd, p. 122).

omitted, or at least shut up in fewer words; but when the difficulty of artful rhyming is interposed, where the poet commonly confines his sense to his couplet, and must contrive that sense into such words that the rhyme shall naturally follow them, not they the rhyme; the fancy then gives leisure to the judgement to come in; which, seeing so heavy a tax imposed, is ready to cut off all unnecessary expenses. This last consideration has already answered an objection which some have made, that rhyme is only an embroidery of sense, to make that which is ordinary in itself pass for excellent with less examination. But, certainly, that which most regulates the fancy, and gives the judgement its busiest employment, is like to bring forth the richest and clearest thoughts. The poet examines that most which he produceth with the greatest leisure, and which he knows must pass the severest test of the audience, because they are aptest to have it ever in their memory; as the stomach makes the best concoction when it strictly embraces the nourishment, and takes account of every little particle as it passes through. But as the best medicines may lose their virtue by being ill applied, so is it with verse, if a fit subject be not chosen for it. Neither must the argument alone, but the characters and persons be great and noble; otherwise (as Scaliger says of Claudian) the poet will be *ignobiliore materia depressus*. The scenes which, in my opinion, most commend it, are those of argumentation and discourse, on the result of which the doing or not doing some considerable action should depend.

But, my Lord, though I have more to say upon this subject,[n] yet I must remember 'tis your Lordship to whom I speak; who have much better commended this way by your writing in it, than I can do by writing for it. Where my reasons cannot prevail, I am sure your Lordship's example must. Your rhetoric has gained my cause; at least the greatest part of my design has already succeeded to my wish, which was to interest so noble a person in the quarrel, and withal to testify to the world how happy I esteem myself in the honour of being,

MY LORD
Your Lordship's most humble, and most
obedient servant,

JOHN DRYDEN

as Scaliger says: J. C. Scaliger (1484–1558), *Poetices* (1561), vi: 'weighed down with inferior material'.

AN ACCOUNT OF THE ENSUING POEM (*ANNUS MIRABILIS*) IN A LETTER TO THE HONOURABLE SIR ROBERT HOWARD

1667

SIR,

I AM so many ways obliged to you, and so little able to return your favours, that, like those who owe too much, I can only live by getting farther into your debt. You have not only been careful of my fortune, which was the effect of your nobleness, but you have been solicitous of my reputation, which is that of your kindness. It is not long since I gave you the trouble of perusing a play for me, and now, instead of an acknowledgment, I have given you a greater, in the correction of a poem. But since you are to bear this persecution, I will at least give you the encouragement of a martyr, you could never suffer in a nobler cause. For I have chosen the most heroic subject which any poet could desire: I have taken upon me to describe the motives, the beginning, progress and successes of a most just and necessary war; in it, the care, management and prudence of our King; the conduct and valour of a royal admiral, and of two incomparable generals; the invincible courage of our captains and seamen, and three glorious victories, the result of all. After this I have, in the Fire, the most deplorable, but withal the greatest argument that can be imagined: the destruction being so swift, so sudden, so vast and miserable, as nothing can parallel in story. The former part of this poem, relating to the war, is but a due expiation for my not serving my King and country in it. All gentlemen are almost obliged to it: and I know no reason we should give that advantage to the commonalty of England to be foremost in brave actions, which the noblesse of France would never suffer in their peasants. I should not have written this but to a person who has been ever forward to appear in all employments, whither his honour and generosity have called him. The latter part of my poem, which describes the Fire, I owe first to the piety and fatherly affection of our Monarch to his suffering subjects; and, in the second place, to the courage, loyalty and magnanimity of the City: both which were so conspicuous, that I have wanted words to celebrate them as they deserve. I have called my poem *historical*, not *epic*, though both the actions and actors are as much heroic, as any poem can contain. But since the action is not properly one, nor that accomplished in the last successes, I have judged it too bold a title for

---

royal admiral: i.e. the Duke of York (later James II), Prince Rupert, the Duke of Albemarle.
the Fire: the Great Fire of London burned 2–6 September 1666.

a few stanzas, which are little more in number than a single Iliad, or
the longest of the Aeneids. For this reason (I mean not of length, but
broken action, tied too severely to the laws of history) I am apt to
agree with those who rank Lucan rather among historians in verse,
than epic poets:[n] in whose room, if I am not deceived, Silius
Italicus, though a worse writer, may more justly be admitted. I have
chosen to write my poem in quatrains or stanzas of four in alternate
rhyme, because I have ever judged them more noble, and of greater
dignity, both for the sound and number, than any other verse in use
amongst us; in which I am sure I have your approbation. The learned
languages have, certainly, a great advantage of us, in not being tied
to the slavery of any rhyme; and were less constrained in the quantity
of every syllable, which they might vary with spondees or dactyls,
besides so many other helps of grammatical figures, for the lengthening or abbreviation of them, than the modern are in the close of that
one syllable, which often confines, and more often corrupts the sense
of all the rest. But in this necessity of our rhymes, I have always found
the couplet verse most easy (though not so proper for this occasion)
for there the work is sooner at an end, every two lines concluding the
labour of the poet: but in quatrains he is to carry it farther on; and
not only so, but to bear along in his head the troublesome sense of
four lines together. For those who write correctly in this kind must
needs acknowledge, that the last line of the stanza is to be considered
in the composition of the first. Neither can we give ourselves the
liberty of making any part of a verse for the sake of rhyme, or concluding with a word which is not current English, or using the variety
of female rhymes, all which our fathers practised; and for the female
rhymes, they are still in use amongst other nations: with the Italian
in every line, with the Spaniard promiscuously, with the French
alternately, as those who have read the *Alaric*, the *Pucelle*, or any of
their latter poems, will agree with me. And besides this, they write in
alexandrines, or verses of six feet, such as amongst us is the old
translation of Homer, by Chapman; all which, by lengthening of
their chain, makes the sphere of their activity the larger. I have dwelt
too long upon the choice of my stanza, which you may remember is
much better defended in the preface to *Gondibert*, and therefore I will
hasten to acquaint you with my endeavours in the writing. In general

---

Silius Italicus: (A.D. 26–101); author of the epic *Punica* (see Pliny, *Epistles*, iii. 7).
the Pucelle: *Alaric*: *ou Rome vaincue* (1654), by Georges de Scudéry; *La Pucelle*:
    ou la France délivrée (1656), by Jean Chapelain.
Chapman: his *Iliad* and *Odyssey* (1611, 1615) are in seven- and five-feet lines
    respectively.
Gondibert: (1650) by Sir W. Davenant; see Spingarn, II, p. 19.

I will only say, I have never yet seen the description of any naval
fight in the proper terms which are used at sea; and if there be any
such in another language, as that of Lucan in the third of his
Pharsalia, yet I could not prevail myself of it in the English; the
terms of arts in every tongue bearing more of the idiom of it than any
other words. We hear, indeed, among our poets, of the thundering of
guns, the smoke, the disorder and the slaughter; but all these are
common notions. And certainly as those who, in a logical dispute,
keep in general terms, would hide a fallacy, so those who do it in any
poetical description would veil their ignorance.

> Descriptas servare vices operumque colores
> cur ego, si nequeo ignoroque, poeta salutor?

For my own part, if I had little knowledge of the sea, yet I have
thought it no shame to learn: and if I have made some few mistakes,
'tis only, as you can bear me witness, because I have wanted opportunity to correct them, the whole poem being first written, and
now sent you from a place, where I have not so much as the converse
of any seaman. Yet, though the trouble I had in writing it was great,
it was more than recompensed by the pleasure; I found myself so
warm in celebrating the praises of military men, two such especially
as the Prince and General, that it is no wonder if they inspired me
with thoughts above my ordinary level. And I am well satisfied, that
as they are incomparably the best subject I have ever had, excepting
only the Royal Family; so also, that this I have written of them is
much better than what I have performed on any other. I have been
forced to help out other arguments, but this has been bountiful to me;
they have been low and barren of praise, and I have exalted them, and
made them fruitful: but here—*Omnia sponte sua reddit justissima
tellus*. I have had a large, a fair and a pleasant field, so fertile, that,
without my cultivating, it has given me two harvests in a summer,
and in both oppressed the reaper. All other greatness in subjects is
only counterfeit, it will not endure the test of danger; the greatness of
arms is only real: other greatness burdens a nation with its weight,
this supports it with its strength. And as it is the happiness of the age,
so is it the peculiar goodness of the best of kings, that we may praise
his subjects without offending him: doubtless it proceeds from a just

---

Descriptas servare: Horace, *Ars Poetica*, ll. 86–7 ('Why, if through ignorance and
    inability I cannot keep up an assumed position and use rhetorical figures in my
    writing, should I be called a poet?').
Omnia sponte sua . . .: compound of Virgil, *Georgics*, ii. 460 and *Eclogues*,
    iv. 39, with Ovid, *Metamorphoses*, i. 416–17 and *Fasti*, iv. 370 ('The earth, with
    justice, returns everything freely').

confidence of his own virtue, which the lustre of no other can be so great as to darken in him: for the good or the valiant are never safely praised under a bad or a degenerate prince. But to return from this digression to a farther account of my poem, I must crave leave to tell you, that as I have endeavoured to adorn it with noble thoughts, so much more to express those thoughts with elocution. The composition of all poems is or ought to be of wit, and wit in the poet, or wit writing, (if you will give me leave to use a school distinction) is no other than the faculty of imagination in the writer, which, like a nimble spaniel, beats over and ranges through the field of memory, till it springs the quarry it hunted after; or, without metaphor, which searches over all the memory for the species or ideas of those things which it designs to represent. Wit written, is that which is well defined, the happy result of thought, or product of that imagination. But to proceed from wit in the general notion of it, to the proper wit of an heroic or historical poem, I judge it chiefly to consist in the delightful imaging of persons, actions, passions, or things. 'Tis not the jerk or sting of an epigram, nor the seeming contradiction of a poor antithesis, (the delight of an ill-judging audience in a play of rhyme) nor the jingle of a more poor paranomasia: neither is it so much the morality of a grave sentence, affected by Lucan, but more sparingly used by Virgil; but it is some lively and apt description, dressed in such colours of speech, that it sets before your eyes the absent object, as perfectly and more delightfully than nature. So then, the first happiness of the poet's imagination is properly invention, or finding of the thought; the second is fancy, or the variation, deriving or moulding of that thought, as the judgement represents it proper to the subject; the third is elocution, or the art of clothing and adorning that thought so found and varied, in apt, significant and sounding words: the quickness of the imagination is seen in the invention, the fertility in the fancy, and the accuracy in the expression. For the two first of these Ovid is famous amongst the poets, for the latter Virgil. Ovid images more often the movements and affections of the mind, either combating between two contrary passions, or extremely discomposed by one: his words therefore are the least part of his care, for he pictures nature in disorder, with which the study and choice of words is inconsistent. This is the proper wit of dialogue or discourse, and, consequently, of the drama, where all

school distinction: 'Dryden has in his mind that of *Natura naturans* and *Natura naturata*. So in the case of Wit he distinguishes between Wit the faculty and Wit the product' (Ker).
paranomasia: a form of pun.

that is said is to be supposed the effect of sudden thought; which, though it excludes not the quickness of wit in repartees, yet admits not a too curious election of words, too frequent allusions, or use of tropes, or, in fine, anything that shows remoteness of thought, or labour in the writer. On the other side, Virgil speaks not so often to us in the person of another, like Ovid, but in his own; he relates almost all things as from himself, and thereby gains more liberty than the other to express his thoughts with all the graces of elocution, to write more figuratively, and to confess, as well the labour as the force of his imagination. Though he describes his Dido well and naturally, in the violence of her passions, yet he must yield in that to the Myrrha, the Biblis, the Althaea, of Ovid; for, as great an admirer of him as I am, I must acknowledge, that, if I see not more of their souls than I see of Dido's, at least I have a greater concernment for them: and that convinces me that Ovid has touched those tender strokes more delicately than Virgil could. But when action or persons are to be described, when any such image is to be set before us, how bold, how masterly are the strokes of Virgil! We see the objects he represents us with in their native figures, in their proper motions; but we so see them, as our own eyes could never have beheld them so beautiful in themselves. We see the soul of the poet, like that universal one of which he speaks, informing and moving through all his pictures, *Totamque infusa per artus mens agitat molem, et magno se corpore miscet*; we behold him embellishing his images, as he makes Venus breathing beauty upon her son Aeneas.

> —lumenque juventae
> purpureum, et laetos oculis afflarat honores:
> quale manus addunt Ebori decus, aut ubi flavo
> argentum, Pariusve lapis circundatur auro.

See his tempest, his funeral sports, his combat of Turnus and Aeneas, and in his *Georgics*, which I esteem the divinest part of all his writings, the plague, the country, the battle of bulls, the labour of the bees, and those many other excellent images of nature, most of which are neither great in themselves, nor have any natural ornament to bear them up: but the words wherewith he describes them are so excellent, that it might be well applied to him which was said by Ovid,

---

Dido: see *Aeneid*, i and iii; for Myrrha, Biblis, Althea see *Metamorphoses*, x. 311 ff., ix. 454 ff., viii. 445 ff.

Totamque infusa . . .: *Aeneid*, vi. 726-7 ('and, pervading everything, mind moves the mass and mixes with its great bulk').

lumenque juventae . . .: *Aeneid*, i. 590-3 ('and the radiant light of youth and the eyes shone brightly, like the beauty given to ivory by the craftsman or when silver or Parian marble is set in gold').

Materiam superabat opus: the very sound of his words has often somewhat that is connatural to the subject, and while we read him, we sit, as in a play, beholding the scenes of what he represents. To perform this, he made frequent use of tropes, which you know change the nature of a known word, by applying it to some other signification; and this is it which Horace means in his *Epistle to the Pisos*.

> Dixeris egregie notum si callida verbum
> reddiderit junctura novum—

But I am sensible I have presumed too far, to entertain you with a rude discourse of that art, which you both know so well, and put into practice with so much happiness. Yet before I leave Virgil, I must own the vanity to tell you, and by you the world, that he has been my master in this poem: I have followed him everywhere, I know not with what success, but I am sure with diligence enough: my images are many of them copied from him, and the rest are imitations of him.[n] My expressions also are as near as the idioms of the two languages would admit of in translation. And this, Sir, I have done with that boldness, for which I will stand accountable to any of our little critics, who, perhaps, are not better acquainted with him than I am. Upon your first perusal of this poem, you have taken notice of some words which I have innovated (if it be too bold for me to say refined) upon his Latin; which, as I offer not to introduce into English prose, so I hope they are neither improper, nor altogether unelegant in verse; and, in this, Horace will again defend me.

> Et nova, fictaque nuper habebunt verba fidem, si
> Graeco fonte cadant, parce detorta—

The inference is exceeding plain; for if a Roman poet might have liberty to coin a word, supposing only that it was derived from the Greek, was put into a Latin termination, and that he used this liberty but seldom, and with modesty: how much more justly may I challenge that privilege to do it with the same prerequisites, from the best and most judicious of Latin writers? In some places, where either the fancy, or the words, were his, or any others, I have noted it in the margin, that I might not seem a plagiary: in others I have neglected it, to avoid as well the tediousness, as the affectation of doing it too often. Such descriptions or images, well wrought, which I promise

---

Materiam superabat opus: *Metamorphoses*, ii. 5 ('The workmanship is better than the material').

Dixeris egregie . . .: *Ars Poetica*, ll. 47–8 ('You will write well if skilful placing reanimates a well-known word').

Et nova . . .: *Ars Poetica*, ll. 52–3 ('and new and recently coined words will have credit if they come from a Greek source only slightly altered').

not for mine, are, as I have said, the adequate delight of heroic poesy, for they beget admiration, which is its proper object; as the images of the burlesque, which is contrary to this, by the same reason beget laughter; for the one shows nature beautified, as in the picture of a fair woman, which we all admire; the other shows her deformed, as in that of a lazar, or of a fool with distorted face and antique gestures, at which we cannot forbear to laugh, because it is a deviation from nature. But though the same images serve equally for the epic poesy, and for the historic and panegyric, which are branches of it, yet a several sort of sculpture is to be used in them: if some of them are to be like those of Juvenal, *Stantes in curribus Aemiliani*, heroes drawn in their triumphal chariots, and in their full proportion; others are to be like that of Virgil, *Spirantia mollius aera*: there is somewhat more of softness and tenderness to be shown in them. You will soon find I write not this without concern. Some who have seen a paper of verses which I wrote last year to her Highness the Duchess, have accused them of that only thing I could defend in them; they have said I did *humi serpere*, that I wanted not only height of fancy, but dignity of words to set it off; I might well answer with that of Horace, *Nunc non erat his locus*, I knew I addressed them to a lady, and accordingly I affected the softness of expression, and the smoothness of measure, rather than the height of thought; and in what I did endeavour, it is no vanity to say I have succeeded. I detest arrogance, but there is some difference betwixt that and a just defence. But I will not farther bribe your candour, or the readers. I leave them to speak for me, and, if they can, to make out that character, not pretending to a greater, which I have given them.

Verses to her Highness the Duchess, on the memorable victory gained by the Duke against the Hollanders, June the 3. 1665. and on her journey afterwards into the North

MADAM,

> WHEN, for our sakes, your *hero* you resigned
> To swelling seas, and every faithless wind;

Juvenal: *Satires*, viii. 3 ('stantis in curribus Aemilianos': 'Aemiliani standing in their chariots').
Virgil: *Aeneid*, vi. 847 ('give gentler lines to breathing bronze').
humi serpere: *Ars Poetica*, l. 28 ('serpit humi tutus nimium timidusque procellae': 'one crawls on the earth through excessive prudence and fear of the storm').
Horace: ibid. l. 19 ('this was not now the place for these things').

When you released his courage, and set free
A valour fatal to the enemy,
You lodged your country's cares within your breast;
(The mansion where soft love should only rest:)
And ere our foes abroad were overcome,
The noblest conquest you had gained at home.
Ah, what concerns did both your souls divide!
Your honour gave us what your love denied:
And 'twas for him much easier to subdue
Those foes he fought with, than to part from you.
That glorious day, which two such navies saw,
As each, unmatched, might to the world give law,
Neptune, yet doubtful whom he should obey,
Held to them both the trident of the sea:
The winds were hushed, the waves in ranks were cast,
As awfully as when God's people passed:
Those, yet uncertain on whose sails to blow,
These, where the wealth of nations ought to flow.
Then with the Duke your Highness ruled the day:
While all the brave did his command obey,
The fair and pious under you did pray.
How powerful are chaste vows! the wind and tide
You bribed to combat on the English side.
Thus to your much loved lord you did convey
An unknown succour, sent the nearest way.
New vigour to his wearied arms you brought;
(So Moses was upheld while Israel fought.)
While, from afar, we heard the cannon play,
Like distant thunder on a shiny day,
For absent friends we were ashamed to fear,
When we considered what you ventured there.
Ships, men and arms our country might restore,
But such a leader could supply no more.
With generous thoughts of conquest he did burn,
Yet fought not more to vanquish than return.
Fortune and victory he did pursue,
To bring them, as his slaves, to wait on you.
Thus beauty ravished the rewards of fame,
And the fair triumphed when the brave o'ercame.
Then, as you meant to spread another way
By land your conquests far as his by sea,
Leaving our southern clime, you marched along
The stubborn north, ten thousand Cupids strong.

Like commons the nobility resort
In crowding heaps, to fill your moving court:
To welcome your approach the vulgar run,
Like some new envoy from the distant sun.
And country beauties by their lovers go,
Blessing themselves, and wondering at the show.
So when the new-born Phoenix first is seen,
Her feathered subjects all adore their queen.
And, while she makes her progress through the east,
From every grove her numerous trains increase:
Each poet of the air her glory sings,
And round him the pleased audience clap their wings.

And now, sir, 'tis time I should relieve you from the tedious length of this account. You have better and more profitable employment for your hours, and I wrong the public to detain you longer. In conclusion, I must leave my poem to you with all its faults, which I hope to find fewer in the printing by your emendations. I know you are not of the number of those, of whom the younger Pliny speaks, *Nec sunt parum multi qui carpere amicos suos judicium vocant*; I am rather too secure of you on that side. Your candour in pardoning my errors may make you more remiss in correcting them; if you will not withall consider that they come into the world with your approbation, and through your hands. I beg from you the greatest favour you can confer upon an absent person, since I repose upon your management what is dearest to me, my fame and reputation; and therefore I hope it will stir you up to make my poem fairer by many of your blots. If not, you know the story of the gamester who married the rich man's daughter, and when her father denied the portion, christened all the children by his surname, that if, in conclusion, they must beg, they should do so by one name, as well as by the other. But since the reproach of my faults will light on you, 'tis but reason I should do you that justice to the readers, to let them know that if there be anything tolerable in this poem, they owe the argument to your choice, the writing to your encouragement, the correction to your judgement, and the care of it to your friendship, to which he must ever acknowledge himself to owe all things, who is,

> *SIR,*
> *The most obedient and most faithful of*
> *your servants,*
>
> JOHN DRYDEN

Pliny: *Epistles*, vii. 28 ('there is no lack of people who call it good judgement to criticize their friends').

To the Right Honourable,
Charles Lord Buckhurst[n]

MY LORD,

As I was lately reviewing my loose papers, amongst the rest I found this Essay, the writing of which in this rude and indigested manner wherein your Lordship now sees it, served as an amusement to me in the country, when the violence of the last plague[n] had driven me from the town. Seeing then our theatres shut up, I was engaged in these kind of thoughts with the same delight with which men think upon their absent mistresses: I confess I find many things in this discourse which I do not now approve; my judgement being not a little altered since the writing of it, but whether for the better or the worse I know not: neither indeed is it much material in an Essay, where all I have said is problematical. For the way of writing plays in verse, which I have seemed to favour, I have since that time laid the practice of it aside, till I have more leisure, because I find it troublesome and slow. But I am no way altered from my opinion of it, at least with any reasons which have opposed it. For your Lordship may easily observe that none are very violent against it, but those who either have not attempted it, or who have succeeded ill in their attempt. 'Tis enough for me to have your Lordship's example for my excuse in that little which I have done in it; and I am sure my adversaries can bring no such arguments against verse, as those with which the fourth act of *Pompey* will furnish me in its defence. Yet, my Lord, you must suffer me a little to complain of you, that you too soon withdraw from us a contentment, of which we expected the continuance, because you gave it us so early. 'Tis a revolt without occasion from your party, where your merits had already raised you to the highest commands, and where you have not the excuse of other men that you have been ill used, and therefore laid down arms. I know no other quarrel you can have to verse, than that which Spurina had to his beauty, when he tore and mangled the features of his face, only because they pleased too well the sight. It was an honour which seemed to wait for you, to lead out a new colony of writers from the mother nation: and upon the first spreading of your ensigns, there had been many in a

---

Pompey: Pierre Corneille's *La Mort de Pompée* (1644), translated (1664) by Buckhurst—who was presumably most concerned with Act IV—Sedley, Waller, and Godolphin.

Spurina: see Valerius Maximus, *De Verecundia*, iv. 5.

readiness to have followed so fortunate a leader; if not all, yet the better part of poets.

> Pars, indocili melior grege; mollis et expes
> inominata perprimat cubilia.

I am almost of opinion, that we should force you to accept of the command, as sometimes the Praetorian bands have compelled their captains to receive the Empire. The Court, which is the best and surest judge of writing, has generally allowed of verse; and in the Town it has found favourers of wit and quality. As for your own particular, my Lord, you have yet youth, and time enough to give part of them to the divertisement of the public, before you enter into the serious and more unpleasant business of the world. That which the French poet said of the Temple of Love, may be as well applied to the Temple of the Muses. The words, as near as I can remember them, were these:

> Le jeune homme, à mauvaise grace,
> N'ayant pas adoré dans le Temple d'Amour:
> Il faut qu'il entre, et pour le sage
> Si ce n'est pas son vray sejour
> C'est un giste sur son passage.

I leave the words to work their effect upon your Lordship in their own language, because no other can so well express the nobleness of the thought; and wish you may be soon called to bear a part in the affairs of the nation, where I know the world expects you, and wonders why you have been so long forgotten; there being no person amongst our young nobility, on whom the eyes of all men are so much bent. But in the mean time your Lordship may imitate the course of Nature, who gives us the flower before the fruit: that I may speak to you in the language of the Muses, which I have taken from an excellent poem to the King.

> As Nature, when she fruit designs, thinks fit
> By beauteous blossoms to proceed to it;
> And while she does accomplish all the spring,
> Birds to her secret operations sing.

I confess I have no greater reason, in addressing this Essay to your Lordship, than that it might awaken in you the desire of writing

---

Pars, indocili . . .: Horace, *Epodes*, xvi. 37–8 ('the part better than the ignorant mob; the weak and faint-hearted may stay on their unlucky beds').
Le jeune homme . . .: untraced.
As Nature . . .: Sir William Davenant, *Poem to the King's most Sacred Majesty* (1663).

something, in whatever kind it be, which might be an honour to our age and country. And methinks it might have the same effect on you, which Homer tells us the fight of the Greeks and Trojans before the fleet had on the spirit of Achilles, who though he had resolved not to engage, yet found a martial warmth to steal upon him, at the sight of blows, the sound of trumpets, and the cries of fighting men. For my own part, if, in treating of this subject, I sometimes dissent from the opinion of better wits, I declare it is not so much to combat their opinions, as to defend my own, which were first made public. Sometimes, like a scholar in a fencing-school, I put forth myself, and show my own ill play, on purpose to be better taught. Sometimes I stand desperately to my arms, like the foot when deserted by their horse, not in hope to overcome, but only to yield on more honourable terms. And yet, my Lord, this war of opinions, you well know, has fallen out among the writers of all ages, and sometimes betwixt friends. Only it has been prosecuted by some, like pedants, with violence of words, and managed by others like gentlemen, with candour and civility. Even Tully had a controversy with his dear Atticus; and in one of his dialogues makes him sustain the part of an enemy in philosophy, who in his letters is his confidant of state, and made privy to the most weighty affairs of the Roman Senate. And the same respect which was paid by Tully to Atticus, we find returned to him afterwards by Caesar on a like occasion, who answering his book in praise of Cato, made it not so much his business to condemn Cato, as to praise Cicero.

But that I may decline some part of the encounter with my adversaries, whom I am neither willing to combat, nor well able to resist; I will give your Lordship the relation of a dispute betwixt some of our wits on the same subject, in which they did not only speak of plays in verse, but mingled, in the freedom of discourse, some things of the ancient, many of the modern ways of writing; comparing those with these, and the wits of our nation with those of others: 'tis true, they differed in their opinions, as 'tis probable they would: neither do

---

Homer: *Iliad*, xvi, ll. 46 f.

to defend my own: in 'To the Right Honourable Roger, Earl of Orrery...' (1664).

candour: integrity, good nature.

in one of his dialogues: *De Legibus*. Cicero is frequently called Tully before and during the 17th century. Titus Pomponius Atticus (109–32 B.C.) withdrew from Rome to Athens in 88 B.C. (hence his cognomen Atticus) and began his correspondence with Cicero in 68 B.C. Their friendship continued up to Cicero's death in 43 B.C.

I take upon me to reconcile, but to relate them: and that as Tacitus professes of himself, *sine studio partium aut ira*: without passion or interest; leaving your Lordship to decide it in favour of which part you shall judge most reasonable, and withal, to pardon the many errors of,

Your Lordship's most obedient humble servant,

JOHN DRYDEN

TO THE READER

The drift of the ensuing discourse was chiefly to vindicate the honour of our English writers, from the censure of those who unjustly prefer the French before them. This I intimate, lest any should think me so exceeding vain, as to teach others an art which they understand much better than myself. But if this incorrect Essay, written in the country without the help of books, or advice of friends, should find any acceptance in the world, I promise to myself a better success of the second part, wherein I shall more fully treat of the virtues and faults of the English poets, who have written either in this, the epic, or the lyric way.

AN ESSAY OF DRAMATIC POESY

It was that memorable day, in the first summer of the late war, when our Navy engaged the Dutch: a day wherein the two most mighty and best appointed fleets which any age had ever seen, disputed the command of the greater half of the globe, the commerce of nations, and the riches of the universe. While these vast floating bodies, on either side, moved against each other in parallel lines, and our countrymen, under the happy conduct of his Royal Highness, went breaking, by little and little, into the line of the enemies, the noise of the cannon from both navies reached our ears about the City; so that all men, being alarmed with it, and in a dreadful suspense of the event, which they knew was then deciding, every one went following the sound as

---

sine studio . . .: *Annals*, **I. i** ('sine ira et studio, quorum causas procul habeo': Dryden's version means 'without anger or party spirit').

the second part: Dryden never formally carried out this promise.

that memorable day: 3 June 1665. The Treaty of Breda concluded the war in July 1667, so Dryden's reference to 'the late war' must represent a revision before the *Essay* was entered in the Stationers' Register in August 1667.

his Royal Highness: James, Duke of York; later James II.

his fancy led him; and leaving the town almost empty, some took towards the Park, some cross the river, others down it; all seeking the noise in the depth of silence.

Amongst the rest, it was the fortune of Eugenius, Crites, Lisideius and Neander,[n] to be in company together: three of them persons whom their wit and quality have made known to all the town: and whom I have chose to hide under these borrowed names, that they may not suffer by so ill a relation as I am going to make of their discourse.

Taking then a barge which a servant of Lisideius had provided for them, they made haste to shoot the bridge, and left behind them that great fall of waters which hindered them from hearing what they desired: after which, having disengaged themselves from many vessels which rode at anchor in the Thames, and almost blocked up the passage towards Greenwich, they ordered the watermen to let fall their oars more gently; and then every one favouring his own curiosity with a strict silence, it was not long ere they perceived the air to break about them like the noise of distant thunder, or of swallows in a chimney: those little undulations of sound, though almost vanishing before they reached them, yet still seeming to retain somewhat of their first horror which they had betwixt the fleets: after they had attentively listened till such time as the sound by little and little went from them; Eugenius lifting up his head, and taking notice of it, was the first who congratulated to the rest that happy omen of our nation's victory: adding, that we had but this to desire in confirmation of it, that we might hear no more of that noise which was now leaving the English coast. When the rest had concurred in the same opinion, Crites, a person of a sharp judgement, and somewhat too delicate a taste in wit, which the world have mistaken in him for ill nature, said, smiling to us, that if the concernment of this battle had not been so exceeding great, he could scarce have wished the victory at the price he knew he must pay for it, in being subject to the reading and hearing of so many ill verses as he was sure would be made on that subject. Adding, that no argument could scape some of those eternal rhymers, who watch a battle with more diligence than the ravens and birds of prey; and the worst of them surest to be first in upon the quarry, while the better able, either out of modesty writ not at all, or set that due value upon their poems, as to let them be often desired and long expected! There are some of those impertinent people of whom you speak, answered Lisideius, who to my know-

the Park: St. James's Park.

ledge are already so provided, either way, that they can produce not only a panegyric upon the victory, but, if need be, a funeral elegy on the Duke: wherein after they have crowned his valour with many laurels, they will at last deplore the odds under which he fell, concluding that his courage deserved a better destiny. All the company smiled at the conceit of Lisideius; but Crites, more eager than before, began to make particular exceptions against some writers, and said the public magistrate ought to send betimes to forbid them; and that it concerned the peace and quiet of all honest people, that ill poets should be as well silenced as seditious preachers. In my opinion, replied Eugenius, you pursue your point too far; for as to my own particular, I am so great a lover of poesy, that I could wish them all rewarded who attempt but to do well, at least I would not have them worse used than one of their brethren was by Sylla the dictator: *Quem in concione vidimus* (says Tully) *cum ei libellum malus poeta de populo subjecisset, quod epigramma in eum fecisset tantummodo alternis versibus longiusculis, statim ex iis rebus quas tunc vendebat jubere ei praemium tribui, sub ea conditione ne quid postea scriberet.* I could wish with all my heart, replied Crites; that many whom we know were as bountifully thanked upon the same condition, that they would never trouble us again. For amongst others, I have a mortal apprehension of two poets, whom this victory with the help of both her wings will never be able to escape; 'tis easy to guess whom you intend, said Lisideius, and without naming them, I ask you if one of them does not perpetually pay us with clenches upon words and a certain clownish kind of raillery? If now and then he does not offer at a catachresis or Clevelandism, wresting and torturing a word into another meaning: in fine, if he be not one of those whom the French would call *un mauvais buffon*; one who is so much a well-willer to the satire, that he intends at least, to spare no man; and though he cannot strike a blow to hurt any, yet he ought to be punished for the malice of the action; as our witches are justly hanged because they think themselves to be such: and suffer deservedly for believing they

---

Quem in concione . . .: Cicero, *Pro Archia poeta*, x. 25 ('Quem nos in contione . . .': 'We have seen him at a public meeting, when a bad poet in the crowd handed up an epigram on himself, written in rather unmetrical elegiacs. Immediately Sulla ordered him to be paid from the proceeds of the sale, on condition that he would never write again.')

two poets: probably Richard Wild (1609–79) and Richard Flecknoe (*c.* 1620–78), who had already written poems on the battle.

clenches: puns.

catachresis: the improper use of a word (Puttenham's 'figure of abuse'). Dryden associates this with John Cleveland (1613–58), the best known example of overzealous imitation of Donne's excesses.

2*

did mischief, because they meant it. You have described him, said Crites, so exactly, that I am afraid to come after you with my other extremity of poetry: he is one of those who having had some advantage of education and converse, knows better than the other what a poet should be, but puts it into practice more unluckily than any man; his style and matter are everywhere alike; he is the most calm, peaceable writer you ever read: he never disquiets your passions with the least concernment, but still leaves you in as even a temper as he found you; he is a very Leveller in poetry, he creeps along with ten little words in every line, and helps out his numbers with *For to*, and *Unto*, and all the pretty expletives he can find, till he drags them to the end of another line; while the sense is left tired half way behind it: he doubly starves all his verses, first for want of thought, and then of expression; his poetry neither has wit in it, nor seems to have it; like him in Martial.

Pauper videri Cinna vult, et est pauper:

He affects plainness, to cover his want of imagination: when he writes the serious way, the highest flight of his fancy is some miserable antithesis, or seeming contradiction; and in the comic he is still reaching at some thin conceit, the ghost of a jest, and that too flies before him, never to be caught; these swallows which we see before us on the Thames, are the just resemblance of his wit: you may observe how near the water they stoop, how many proffers they make to dip, and yet how seldom they touch it: and when they do, 'tis but the surface: they skim over it but to catch a gnat, and then mount into the air and leave it. Well gentlemen, said Eugenius, you may speak your pleasure of these authors; but though I and some few more about the town may give you a peaceable hearing, yet assure yourselves, there are multitudes who would think you malicious and them injured: especially him whom you first described; he is the very Withers of the City: they have bought more editions of his works than would serve to lay under all their pies at the Lord Mayor's Christmas. When his famous poem first came out in the year 1660, I have seen them reading it in the midst of change-time; nay so vehement they were at it, that they lost their bargain by the candles'

<hr>

Leveller: John Lilburne (?1614–57) and his followers were called Levellers because of the primitive communism of their social policies.

Pauper videri . . .: *Epigrams*, viii. 19 ('Cinna wants to seem poor; so he is poor').

Withers: George Withers (1588–1667) was an extraordinarily prolific Puritan poet of limited talent.

than would serve . . . Christmas: cf. Jonson, *Epigrams*, iii; and Horace, *Epistles*, II. i. 269–70.

ends: but what will you say, if he has been received amongst great persons; I can assure you he is, this day, the envy of one, who is lord in the art of quibbling; and who does not take it well, that any man should intrude so far into his province. All I would wish, replied Crites, is, that they who love his writings, may still admire him, and his fellow poet, *qui Bavium non odit*, etc. is curse sufficient. And farther, added Lisideius, I believe there is no man who writes well, but would think he had hard measure, if their admirers should praise anything of his: *Nam quos contemnimus eorum quoque laudes contemnimus.* There are so few who write well in this age, said Crites, that methinks any praises should be welcome; they neither rise to the dignity of the last age, nor to any of the Ancients; and we may cry out of the writers of this time, with more reason than Petronius of his, *Pace vestra liceat dixisse, primi omnium eloquentiam perdidistis*: you have debauched the true old poetry so far, that nature, which is the soul of it, is not in any of your writings.

If your quarrel (said Eugenius) to those who now write, be grounded only on your reverence to antiquity, there is no man more ready to adore those great Greeks and Romans than I am: but on the other side, I cannot think so contemptibly of the age in which I live or so dishonourably of my own country, as not to judge we equal the Ancients in most kinds of poesy, and in some surpass them; neither know I any reason why I may not be as zealous for the reputation of our age, as we find the Ancients themselves were in reference to those who lived before them. For you hear your Horace saying,

> Indignor quidquam reprehendi, non quia crasse
> compositum, illepideve putetur, sed quia nuper.

And after,

> Si meliora dies, ut vina, poemata reddit,
> scire velim pretium chartis quotus arroget annus?

candles' ends: a candle was lighted at an auction and bidding ceased when it burned out.

qui Bavium . . .: Virgil, *Eclogues*, iii. 90 ('Qui Bavium non odit, amet tua carmina, Maevius'; 'Let him who does not hate Bavius love your songs, Maevius').

Nam quos . . .: untraced ('We contemn praises given to those whom we contemn').

Petronius: *Satyricon*, ii ('If you will allow me, I must tell you that it is true that you [teachers] have killed real eloquence').

Horace: *Epistles*, II. i. 76-7 ('I get angry when anything is attacked, not for being coarse or inelegant, but just because it is modern'). Ibid. 34-5 ('If, like wine, poems improve as time passes, I should like to know the best year for literature').

But I see I am engaging in a wide dispute, where the arguments are not like to reach close on either side; for poesy is of so large an extent, and so many both of the Ancients and Moderns have done well in all kinds of it, that in citing one against the other, we shall take up more time this evening, than each man's occasions will allow him: therefore I would ask Crites to what part of poesy he would confine his arguments, and whether he would defend the general cause of the Ancients against the Moderns, or oppose any age of the Moderns against this of ours?

Crites a little while considering upon this demand, told Eugenius that if he pleased, he would limit their dispute to Dramatic Poesy; in which he thought it not difficult to prove, either that the Ancients were superior to the Moderns,[n] or the last age to this of ours.

Eugenius was somewhat surprised, when he heard Crites make choice of the subject; for aught I see, said he, I have undertaken a harder province than I imagined; for though I never judged the plays of the Greek or Roman poets comparable to ours; yet on the other side those we now seen acted, come short of many which were written in the last age: but my comfort is if we are overcome, it will be only by our own countrymen: and if we yield to them in this one part of poesy, we more surpass them in all the other; for in the epic or lyric way it will be hard for them to show us one such amongst them, as we have many now living, or who lately were. They can produce nothing so courtly writ, or which expresses so much the conversation of a gentleman, as Sir John Suckling; nothing so even, sweet, and flowing as Mr. Waller, nothing so majestic, so correct as Sir John Denham; nothing so elevated, so copious, and full of spirit, as Mr. Cowley; as for the Italian, French, and Spanish plays, I can make it evident, that those who now write, surpass them; and that the drama is wholly ours.

All of them were thus far of Eugenius' opinion, that the sweetness of English verse was never understood or practised by our fathers. Even Crites himself did not much oppose it: and every one was willing to acknowledge how much our poesy is improved, by the happiness of some writers yet living; who first taught us to mould our thoughts into easy and significant words, to retrench the superfluities of expression, and to make our rhyme so properly a part of the verse, that it should never mislead the sense, but itself be led and governed by it.

Eugenius was going to continue this discourse, when Lisideius told him that it was necessary, before they proceeded further, to take a standing measure of their controversy; for how was it possible to be decided who writ the best plays, before we know what a play should be? but, this once agreed on by both parties, each might have recourse to it, either to prove his own advantages, or to discover the failings of his adversary.

He had no sooner said this, but all desired the favour of him to give the definition of a play; and they were the more importunate, because neither Aristotle, nor Horace, nor any other, who had writ of that subject, had ever done it.

Lisideius, after some modest denials, as last confessed he had a rude notion of it; indeed rather a description than a definition, but which served to guide him in his private thoughts, when he was to make a judgement of what others writ: that he conceived a play ought to be, a just and lively image of human nature, representing its passions and humours, and the changes of fortune to which it is subject; for the delight and instruction of mankind.[n]

This definition, though Crites raised a logical objection against it; that it was only *a genere et fine*, and so not altogether perfect; was yet well received by the rest: and after they had given order to the watermen to turn their barge, and row softly, that they might take the cool of the evening in their return, Crites, being desired by the company to begin, spoke on behalf of the Ancients, in this manner:

If confidence presage a victory, Eugenius, in his own opinion, has already triumphed over the Ancients. Nothing seems more easy to him, than to overcome those whom it is our greatest praise to have imitated well: for we do not only build upon their foundations; but by their models. Dramatic poesy had time enough, reckoning from Thespis (who first invented it) to Aristophanes, to be born, to grow up, and to flourish in maturity. It has been observed of arts and sciences, that in one and the same century they have arrived to great perfection; and no wonder, since every age has a kind of universal genius, which inclines those that live in it to some particular studies: the work then being pushed on by many hands, must of necessity go forward.

Is it not evident, in these last hundred years (when the study of philosophy has been the business of all the virtuosi in Christendom) that almost a new nature has been revealed to us? that more errors of the school[n] have been detected, more useful experiments in philosophy have been made, more noble secrets in optics, medicine, anatomy, astronomy, discovered, than in all those credulous and doting ages from Aristotle to us? so true it is that nothing spreads more fast than science, when rightly and generally cultivated.

Add to this the more than common emulation that was in those

science: natural science.

times of writing well; which though it be found in all ages and all persons that pretend to the same reputation; yet poesy being then in more esteem than now it is, had greater honours decreed to the professors of it; and consequently the rivalship was more high between them; they had judges ordained to decide their merit, and prizes to reward it: and historians have been diligent to record of Aeschylus, Euripides, Sophocles, Lycophron, and the rest of them, both who they were that vanquished in these wars of the theatre, and how often they were crowned: while the Asian kings, and Grecian commonwealths scarce afforded them a nobler subject than the unmanly luxuries of a debauched court, or giddy intrigues of a factious city. *Alit aemulatio ingenia* (says Paterculus) *et nunc invidia, nunc admiratio incitationem accendit*: Emulation is the spur of wit, and sometimes envy, sometimes admiration quickens our endeavours.

But now since the rewards of honour are taken away, that virtuous emulation is turned into direct malice; yet so slothful, that it contents itself to condemn and cry down others, without attempting to do better. 'Tis a reputation too unprofitable, to take the necessary pains for it; yet wishing they had it, that desire is incitement enough to hinder others from it. And this, in short, Eugenius, is the reason, why you have now so few good poets; and so many severe judges. Certainly, to imitate the Ancients well, much labour and long study is required: which pains, I have already shown, our poets would want encouragement to take, if yet they had ability to go through the work. Those Ancients have been faithful imitators and wise observers of that nature which is so torn and ill represented in our plays; they have handed down to us a perfect resemblance of her; which we, like ill copiers, neglecting to look on, have rendered monstrous, and disfigured. But, that you may know how much you are indebted to those your masters, and be ashamed to have so ill requited them, I must remember you that all the rules by which we practise the drama at this day, (either such as relate to the justness and symmetry of the plot; or the episodical ornaments, such as descriptions, narrations, and other beauties, which are not essential to the play) were delivered to us from the observations which Aristotle made, of those poets, who either lived before him, or were his contemporaries: we have added nothing of our own, except we have the confidence to say our wit is better; of which none boast in this our age, but such as understand not theirs. Of that book which Aristotle has left us περὶ τῆς

Lycophron: Alexandrian poet, b. *c.* 320 B.C. at Chalcis; author of a number of tragedies which have not survived.
Paterculus: *Historia Romana*, i. 17.

Ποιητικῆς, Horace's *Art of Poetry* is an excellent comment, and, I believe, restores to us that second book of his concerning comedy, which is wanting in him.

Out of these two[n] have been extracted the famous rules which the French call, *Des Trois Unités*, or, the three unities, which ought to be observed in every regular play; namely, of time, place, and action.

The unity of time they comprehend in 24 hours, the compass of a natural day; or as near it as can be contrived. And the reason of it is obvious to every one; that the time of the feigned action, or fable of the play, should be proportioned as near as can be to the duration of that time in which it is represented; since therefore all plays are acted on the theatre in a space of time much within the compass of 24 hours, that play is to be thought the nearest imitation of nature, whose plot or action is confined within that time; and, by the same rule which concludes this general proportion of time, it follows, that all the parts of it are (as near as may be) to be equally sub-divided; namely, that one act take not up the supposed time of half a day, which is out of proportion to the rest, since the other four are then to be straitened within the compass of the remaining half. For it is unnatural that one act, which being spoke or written, is not longer than the rest, should be supposed longer by the audience. 'Tis therefore the poet's duty, to take care that no act should be imagined to exceed the time in which it is represented on the stage; and that the intervals and inequalities of time be supposed to fall out between the acts.

This rule of time how well it has been observed by the Ancients, most of their plays will witness. You see them in their tragedies (wherein to follow this rule, is certainly most difficult) from the very beginning of their plays, falling close into that part of the story which they intend for the action or principal object of it; leaving the former part to be delivered by narration: so that they set the audience, as it were, at the post where the race is to be concluded: and, saving them the tedious expectation of seeing the poet set out and ride the beginning of the course, they suffer you not to behold him, till he is in sight of the goal, and just upon you.

For the second unity, which is that of place, the Ancients meant by it, that the scene ought to be continued through the play, in the same place where it was laid in the beginning: for the stage, on which it is represented, being but one and the same place, it is unnatural to conceive it many; and those far distant from one another. I will not deny but by the variation of painted scenes, the fancy (which in these cases will contribute to its own deceit) may sometimes imagine it several places, with some appearance of probability; yet it still carries the greater likelihood of truth, if those places be supposed so near each other, as in the same town or city; which may all be comprehended under the larger denomination of one place: for a greater distance will bear no proportion to the shortness of time, which is allotted in the acting, to pass from one of them to another; for the observation of this, next to the Ancients, the French are to be most commended. They tie themselves so strictly to the unity of place, that you never see in any of their plays, a scene changed in the middle of an act: if the act begins in a garden, a street, or chamber, 'tis ended in the same place; and that you may know it to be the same, the stage is so supplied with persons that it is never empty all the time: he who enters second has business with him who was on before; and before the second quits the stage, a third appears who has business with him.

This Corneille calls *La liaison des scènes*, the continuity or joining of the scenes; and 'tis a good mark of a well contrived play when all the persons are known to each other, and every one of them has some affairs with all the rest.

As for the third unity, which is that of action, the Ancients meant no other by it than what the logicians do by their Finis, the end or scope of any action: that which is the first in intention, and last in execution. Now the poet is to aim at one great and complete action, to the carrying on of which all things in his play, even the very obstacles, are to be subservient; and the reason of this is as evident as any of the former.

For two actions equally laboured and driven on by the writer, would destroy the unity of the poem; it would be no longer one play, but two: not but that there may be many actions in a play, as Ben Jonson has observed in his *Discoveries*; but they must be all subservient to the great one, which our language happily expresses in the name of under-plots: such as in Terence's *Eunuch* is the difference and reconcilement of Thais and Phaedria, which is not the chief business of the play, but promotes the marriage of Charea and Chremes's sister, principally intended by the poet. There ought to be but one action, says Corneille, that is one complete action which leaves the mind of the audience in a full repose. But this cannot be brought to pass but by many other imperfect actions which conduce to it, and hold the audience in a delightful suspense of what will be.

If by these rules (to omit many other drawn from the precepts and practice of the Ancients) we should judge our modern plays, 'tis probable, that few of them would endure the trial. That which should be the business of a day, takes up in some of them an age; instead of

---

says Corneille: *Discours des Trois Unités* (1660).

one action they are the epitomes of a man's life; and for one spot of ground (which the stage should represent) we are sometimes in more countries than the map can show us.

But if we will allow the Ancients to have contrived well, we must acknowledge them to have written better; questionless we are deprived of a great stock of wit in the loss of Menander among the Greek poets, and of Caecilius, Affranius, and Varius, among the Romans: we may guess at Menander's excellency by the plays of Terence, who translated some of them: and yet wanted so much of him that he was called by C. Caesar the half-Menander; and may judge of Varius, by the testimonies of Horace, Martial, and Velleius Paterculus. 'Tis probable that these, could they be recovered, would decide the controversy; but so long as Aristophanes and Plautus are extant; while the tragedies of Euripides, Sophocles, and Seneca are in our hands, I can never see one of those plays which are now written, but it increases my admiration of the Ancients; and yet I must acknowledge further, that to admire them as we ought, we should understand them better than we do. Doubtless many things appear flat to us, the wit of which depended on some custom or story which never came to our knowledge, or perhaps on some criticism in their language, which being so long dead, and only remaining in their books, 'tis not possible they should make us understand perfectly. To read Macrobius, explaining the propriety and elegancy of many words in Virgil, which I had before passed over without considera-tion, as common things, is enough to assure me that I ought to think the same of Terence; and that in the purity of his style (which Tully so much valued that he ever carried his works about him) there is yet left in him great room for admiration, if I knew but where to place it. In the mean time I must desire you to take notice, that the greatest man of the last age (Ben Jonson) was willing to give place to them in all things. He was not only a professed imitator of Horace, but a learned plagiary of all the others. You track him everywhere in their snow. If Horace, Lucan, Petronius Arbiter, Seneca, and Juvenal, had their own from him, there are few serious thoughts which are new in him. You will pardon me therefore if I presume he loved their fashion when he wore their clothes. But since I have otherwise a great venera-tion for him, and you, Eugenius, prefer him above all other poets, I

Menander: see Horace, *Epistles*, II. i. 57–9; and Aulus Gellius, *Noctes Atticae*, ii. 23.

half-Menander: see Suetonius, *Vita Terentii*.

Horace, Martial: see Horace, *Odes*, i, 6; *Satires*, I. ix. 23, I. x. 44; *Ars Poetica* l. 55; Martial, *Epigrams*, VIII. xviii. 7. Velleius has no mention of Varius.

Macrobius: *Conviviorum Saturnaliorum libri septem* (c. A.D. 400), Bk. iv.

will use no farther argument to you than his example. I will produce
before you Father Ben, dressed in all the ornaments and colours of
the Ancients, you will need no other guide to our party if you follow
him; and whether you consider the bad plays of our age, or regard
the good plays of the last, both the best and worst of the modern
poets will equally instruct you to admire the Ancients.

Crites had no sooner left speaking, but Eugenius, who had waited
with some impatience for it, thus began:

I have observed in your speech that the former part of it is convincing as to what the Moderns have profited by the rules of the
Ancients, but in the latter you are careful to conceal how much they
have excelled them. We own all the helps we have from them, and
want neither veneration nor gratitude while we acknowledge that to
overcome them we must make use of the advantages we have received
from them; but to these assistances we have joined our own industry;
for (had we sat down with a dull imitation of them) we might then
have lost somewhat of the old perfection, but never acquired any that
was new. We draw not therefore after their lines, but those of nature;
and having the life before us, besides the experience of all they knew,
it is no wonder if we hit some airs and features which they have
missed. I deny not what you urge of arts and sciences, that they have
flourished in some ages more than others; but your instance in
philosophy makes for me; for if natural causes be more known now
than in the time of Aristotle, because more studied, it follows that
poesy and other arts may with the same pains arrive still nearer to
perfection, and, that granted, it will rest for you to prove that they
wrought more perfect images of human life than we; which, seeing
in your discourse you have avoided to make good, it shall now be my
task to show you some part of their defects, and some few excellencies
of the Moderns; and I think there is none among us can imagine I do
it enviously, or with purpose to detract from them; for what interest
of fame or profit can the living lose by the reputation of the dead?
On the other side, it is a great truth which Velleius Paterculus affirms,
*Audita visis libentius laudamus; et praesentia invidia, praeterita
admiratione prosequimur; et his nos obrui, illis instrui credimus*: That
praise or censure is certainly the most sincere which unbribed posterity shall give us.

Be pleased then in the first place to take notice, that the Greek

---

Velleius Paterculus: *Historia romana*, ii. 92 (for 'admiratione' read 'veneratione':
    'We tend to praise what we have heard more than what we have seen; we view
    the present with envy, the past with admiration, and we believe that the former
    eclipses us while the latter teaches').

poesy, which Crites has affirmed to have arrived to perfection in the
reign of the Old Comedy, was so far from it, that the distinction of it
into acts was not known to them; or if it were, it is yet so darkly
delivered to us that we cannot make it out.

All we know of it is from the singing of their chorus, and that too
is so uncertain that in some of their plays we have reason to conjecture they sung more than five times. Aristotle indeed divides the
integral parts of a play into four.[n] First, the protasis or entrance,
which gives light only to the characters of the persons, and proceeds
very little into any part of the action: secondly, the epitasis, or working up of the plot where the play grows warmer; the design or action
of it is drawing on, and you see something promising that it will come
to pass: thirdly, the catastasis, called by the Romans, status, the
heighth, and full growth of the play: we may call it properly the
counterturn, which destroys that expectation, embroils the action in
new difficulties, and leaves you far distant from that hope in which it
found you, as you may have observed in a violent stream resisted by
a narrow passage: it runs round to an eddy, and carries back the
waters with more swiftness than it brought them on. Lastly, the
catastrophe, which the Grecians called λύσις, the French *le dénoue-
ment*, and we the discovery or unravelling of the plot: there you see
all things settling again upon their first foundations, and the obstacles
which hindered the design or action of the play once removed, it ends
with that resemblance of truth and nature, that the audience are
satisfied with the conduct of it. Thus this great man delivered to us
the image of a play, and I must confess it is so lively that from thence
much light has been derived to the forming it more perfectly into acts
and scenes; but what poet first limited to five the number of the acts I
know not; only we see it so firmly established in the time of Horace,
that he gives it for a rule in comedy; *Neu brevior quinto, neu sit
productior actu*: So that you see the Grecians cannot be said to have
consummated this art; writing rather by entrances than by acts, and
having rather a general indigested notion of a play, than knowing
how and where to bestow the particular graces of it.

But since the Spaniards at this day allow but three acts, which they
call *jornadas*, to a play, and the Italians in many of theirs follow them,
when I condemn the Ancients, I declare it is not altogether because
they have not five acts to every play, but because they have not confined themselves to one certain number; 'tis building an house

---

Neu brevior . . .: *Ars Poetica*, l. 189 ('Neve minor neu sit quinto productior actu';
  'Let no play be longer or shorter than five acts').
jornadas: the term 'jornada' was made fashionable by Calderón, but the three-act
  structure was established in Spain mainly by Lope de Vega (1562-1635).

without a model: and when they succeeded in such undertakings, they ought to have sacrificed to Fortune, not to the Muses.

Next, for the plot, which Aristotle called τὸ μῦθος, and often τῶν πραγμάτων σύνθεσις, and from him the Romans *fabula*, it has already been judiciously observed by a late writer, that in their tragedies it was only some tale derived from Thebes or Troy, or at least something that happened in those two ages; which was worn so threadbare by the pens of all the epic poets, and even by tradition itself of the talkative Greeklings (as Ben Jonson calls them) that before it came upon the stage, it was already known to all the audience: and the people so soon as ever they heard the name of Oedipus, knew as well as the poet, that he had killed his father by a mistake, and committed incest with his mother, before the play; that they were now to hear of a great plague, an oracle, and the ghost of Laius: so that they sat with a yawning kind of expectation, till he was to come with his eyes pulled out, and speak a hundred or more verses in a tragic tone, in complaint of his misfortunes. But one Oedipus, Hercules, or Medea, had been tolerable; poor people they scaped not so good cheap: they had still the *chapon bouillé* set before them, till their appetites were cloyed with the same dish, and the novelty being gone, the pleasure vanished: so that one main end of dramatic poesy in its definition, which was to cause delight, was of consequence destroyed.

In their comedies, the Romans generally borrowed their plots from the Greek poets; and theirs was commonly a little girl stolen or wandered from her parents, brought back unknown to the city, there got with child by some lewd young fellow; who, by the help of his servant, cheats his father, and when her time comes, to cry *Juno Lucina fer opem*; one or other sees a little box or cabinet which was carried away with her, and so discovers her to her friends, if some God do not prevent it, by coming down in a machine, and taking the thanks of it to himself.

By the plot you may guess much of the characters of the persons. An old father who would willingly before he dies see his son well married; his debauched son, kind in his nature to his mistress, but miserably in want of money; a servant or slave, who has so much wit to strike in with him, and help to dupe his father, a braggadochio captain, a parasite, and a lady of pleasure.

Jonson: *Discoveries*, Herford and Simpson, VIII, 641.

so good cheap: i.e. so easily.

chapon bouillé: lit. 'boiled capon'.

Juno Lucina: Terence, *Andria*, III. i. 15 ('Goddess of childbirth, help me').

machine: the *deus ex machina* was 'brought on to the Greek stage by some mechanical device to resolve a complex dramatic situation' (Boulton).

As for the poor honest maid, on whom the story is built, and who ought to be one of the principal actors in the play, she is commonly a mute in it. She has the breeding of the old Elizabeth way, which was for maids to be seen and not to be heard; and it is enough you know she is willing to be married, when the fifth act requires it.

These are plots built after the Italian mode of houses, you see through them all at once; the characters are indeed the imitations of nature, but so narrow as if they had imitated only an eye or an hand, and did not dare to venture on the lines of a face, or the proportion of a body.

But in how straight a compass soever they have bounded their plots and characters, we will pass it by, if they have regularly pursued them, and perfectly observed those three unities of time, place, and action: the knowledge of which you say is derived to us from them. But in the first place give me leave to tell you, that the unity of place, however it might be practised by them, was never any of their rules. We neither find it in Aristotle, Horace, or any who have written of it, till in our age the French poets first made it a precept of the stage. The unity of time, even Terence himself (who was the best and most regular of them) has neglected. His *Heautontimoroumenos* or *Self-Punisher* takes up visibly two days; says Scaliger, the two first acts concluding the first day, the three last the day ensuing; and Euripides, in tying himself to one day, has committed an absurdity never to be forgiven him: for in one of his tragedies he has made Theseus go from Athens to Thebes, which was about 40 English miles, under the walls of it to give battle, and appear victorious in the next act; and yet from the time of his departure to the return of the Nuntius, who gives the relation of his victory, Aethra and the chorus have but 36 verses; which is not for every mile a verse.

The like error is as evident in Terence's *Eunuch*, when Laches, the old man, enters by mistake into the house of Thais, where betwixt his exit and the entrance of Pythias, who comes to give ample relation of the disorders he has raised within, Parmeno who was left upon the stage, has not above five lines to speak: *C'est bien employer un temps si court*, says the French poet, who furnished me with one of the

---

precept of the stage: Dryden is wrong: Castelvetro invented the 'rule' and Sidney (*Defence of Poesy*, 1595) remarks that 'the stage should always represent but one place'.

Scaliger: *Poetices*, VI. iii.

Euripides: Dryden is translating closely from Corneille's *Troisième Discours*.

C'est bien employer . . .: here, and in the following paragraph, Dryden again follows Corneille's *Troisième Discours* closely.

observations; and almost all their tragedies will afford us examples of the like nature.

'Tis true, they have kept the continuity, or as you called it, *liaison des scènes* somewhat better: two do not perpetually come in together, talk, and go out together; and other two succeed them, and do the same throughout the act, which the English call by the name of single scenes; but the reason is, because they have seldom above two or three scenes, properly so called, in every act; for it is to be accounted a new scene, not only every time the stage is empty, but every person who enters, though to others, makes it so; because he introduces a new business. Now the plots of their plays being narrow, and the persons few, one of their acts was written in a less compass than one of our well wrought scenes, and yet they are often deficient even in this. To go no further than Terence, you find in the *Eunuch* Antipho entering single in the midst of the third act, after Chremes and Pythias were gone off. In the same play you have likewise Dorias beginning the fourth act alone; and after she has made a relation of what was done at the soldiers' entertainment (which by the way was very inartificial) because she was presumed to speak directly to the audience, and to acquaint them with what was necessary to be known, but yet should have been so contrived by the poet as to have been told by persons of the drama to one another (and so by them to have come to the knowledge of the people) she quits the stage, and Phaedria enters next, alone likewise. He also gives you an account of himself, and of his returning from the country, in monologue, to which unnatural way of narration Terence is subject in all his plays: In his *Adelphi* or Brothers, Syrus and Demea enter; after the scene was broken by the departure of Sostrata, Geta and Canthara; and indeed you can scarce look into any of his comedies, where you will not presently discover the same interruption.

But as they have failed both in laying of their plots, and in the management, swerving from the rules of their own art, by misrepresenting nature to us, in which they have ill-satisfied one intention of a play, which was delight, so in the instructive part they have erred worse: instead of punishing vice and rewarding virtue, they have often shown a prosperous wickedness, and an unhappy piety. They have set before us a bloody image of revenge in *Medea*, and given her dragons to convey her safe from punishment. A Priam and Astyanax murdered, and Cassandra ravished, and the lust and murder ending in the victory of him who acted them. In short, there

---

inartificial: clumsy.
Medea: Dryden is referring to Euripides's play rather than Seneca's.

is no indecorum in any of our modern plays, which if I would excuse, I could not shadow with some authority from the Ancients.

And one farther note of them let me leave you. Tragedies and comedies were not writ then as they are now, promiscuously, by the same person; but he who found his genius bending to the one, never attempted the other way. This is so plain, that I need not instance to you, that Aristophanes, Plautus, Terence, never any of them writ a tragedy; Aeschylus, Euripides, Sophocles, and Seneca, never meddled with comedy: the sock and buskin were not worn by the same poet: having then so much care to excel in one kind, very little is to be pardoned them if they miscarried in it; and this would lead me to the consideration of their wit, had not Crites given me sufficient warning not to be too bold in my judgement of it; because the languages being dead, and many of the customs and little accidents on which it depended, lost to us, we are not competent judges of it. But though I grant that here and there we may miss the application of a proverb or a custom, yet a thing well said will be wit in all languages; and though it may lose something in the translation, yet to him who reads it in the original, 'tis still the same; he has an idea of its excellency, though it cannot pass from his mind into any other expression or words than those in which he finds it. When Phaedria, in the *Eunuch*, had a command from his mistress to be absent two days; and encouraging himself to go through with it, said; *Tandem ego non illa caream, si opus sit, vel totum triduum?* Parmeno to mock the softness of his master, lifting up his hands and eyes, cries out as it were in admiration; *Hui! universum triduum!* the elegancy of which *universum*, though it cannot be rendered in our language, yet leaves an impression on our souls: but this happens seldom in him, in Plautus oftener; who is infinitely too bold in his metaphors and coining words; out of which many times his wit is nothing, which questionless was one reason why Horace falls upon him so severely in those verses:

> Sed proavi nostri Plautinos et numeros, et
> laudavere sales, nimium patienter utrumque
> ne dicam stolide.

Comedy: Euripides's *Cyclops* and Sophocles's *Ichneutai* would now be considered comedies.

sock and buskin: symbols of comedy and tragedy respectively.

Tandem ego: Terence, *Eunuch*, II. i. 17–18 ('But can't I manage without her, if necessary, for three days together?' Parmeno replies 'Three whole days!').

sed proavi . . .: *Ars Poetica*, ll. 270–2 ('At vestri proavi Plautinos . . . ne dicam stulte': 'But our forebears praised Plautus's verse and his wit, being over tolerant, not to say stupid').

For Horace himself was cautious to obtrude a new word on his
readers, and makes custom and common use the best measure of receiving it into our writings.

> Multa renascentur quae nunc cecidere, cadentque
> quae nunc sunt in honore vocabula, si volet usus,
> quem penes, arbitrium est, et jus, et norma loquendi.

The not observing this rule is that which the world has blamed in
our satirist Cleveland; to express a thing hard and unnaturally, is his
new way of elocution. 'Tis true, no poet but may sometimes use a
catachresis, Virgil does it;

> Mistaque ridenti colocasia fundet acantho.

In his Eclogue of Pollio, and in his 7th *Æneid*.

> Mirantur et undae,
> miratur nemus, insuetum fulgentia longe,
> scuta virum fluvio, pictasque, innare carinas.

And Ovid once so modestly, that he asks leave to do it;

> Si verbo audacia detur
> haud metuam summi dixisse Palatia coeli.

Calling the court of Jupiter by the name of Augustus his palace,
though in another place he is more bold, where he says, *et longas
visent capitolia pompas*. But to do this always, and never be able to
write a line without it, though it may be admired by some few
pedants, will not pass upon those who know that wit is best conveyed
to us in the most easy language; and is most to be admired when a
great thought comes dressed in words so commonly received that it is
understood by the meanest apprehensions, as the best meat is the
most easily digested: but we cannot read a verse of Cleveland's without making a face at it, as if every word were a pill to swallow. He
gives us many times a hard nut to break our teeth, without a kernel
for our pains. So that there is this difference between his satires and
Doctor Donne's, that the one gives us deep thoughts in common

---

Multa renascentur . . .: ibid. ll. 70–2 ('. . . quae iam cecidere . . .': 'Many terms
  now obsolete shall be reborn, and those now in favour shall fall, if usage so
  decrees, in whose hands lies the judgement, the law, and the rule of speech').
Mistaque . . .: *Eclogues*, iv. 20 ('The Egyptian bean, mixed with the joyful
  acanthus, will grow abundantly').
Mirantur et undae: *Aeneid*, viii. 91–3 ('The waves and the woods marvel, shocked
  by the flashing shields of the warriors and by the painted ships').
Si verbo . . .: *Metamorphoses*, i. 175–6 ('Si verbis . . . haud timeam magni
  dixisse . . .': 'If I may be so bold, I would not fear to call it the Palatia of
  Heaven itself').
et longas: ibid. 561 ('and Capitols witness long processions').

language, though rough cadence; the other gives us common thoughts in abstruse words: 'tis true, in some places his wit is independent of his words, as in that of the *Rebel Scot*:

> Had Cain been Scot God would have changed his doom;
> Not forced him wander, but confined him home,

Si sic omnia dixisset! This is wit in all languages: 'tis like Mercury, never to be lost or killed; and so that other:

> For beauty like white-powder makes no noise,
> And yet the silent hypocrite destroys.

You see the last line is highly metaphorical, but it is so soft and gentle that it does not shock us as we read it.

But, to return from whence I have digressed, to the consideration of the Ancients' writing and their wit, (of which by this time you will grant us in some measure to be fit judges,) though I see many excellent thoughts in Seneca, yet he, of them who had a genius most proper for the stage, was Ovid; he had a way of writing so fit to stir up a pleasing admiration and concernment, which are the objects of a tragedy, and to show the various movements of a soul combating between two different passions, that, had he lived in our age, or in his own could have writ with our advantages, no man but must have yielded to him; and therefore I am confident the *Medea* is none of his: for, though I esteem it for the gravity and sententiousness of it, which he himself concludes to be suitable to a tragedy, *Omne genus scripti gravitate tragaedia vincit*, yet it moves not my soul enough to judge that he, who in the epic way wrote things so near the drama, as the story of Myrrha, of Caunus and Biblis, and the rest, should stir up no more concernment where he most endeavoured it. The masterpiece of Seneca I hold to be that scene in the *Troades*, where Ulysses is seeking for Astyanax to kill him. There you see the tenderness of a mother, so represented in Andromache, that it raises compassion to a high degree in the reader, and bears the nearest resemblance of anything in the tragedies of the Ancients, to the excellent scenes of passion in Shakespeare, or in Fletcher. For love-scenes you will find few among them, their tragic poets dealt not with that soft passion, but with lust, cruelty, revenge, ambition, and those bloody actions

---

Had Cain...: Cleveland, *The Rebel Scot*, ll. 63–4.
Si sic ...: Juvenal, *Satires*, X. 123–4 ('If only he had always spoken like this').
For beauty...: *To P. Rupert*, ll. 39–40; 'white-powder' is arsenic.
Omne genus ...: *Tristia*, ii. 381 ('Tragedy surpasses in solemnity all other kinds of writing').
Myrrha, etc.: *Metamorphoses*, x. 312 ff.; ix. 453 ff.

they produced; which were more capable of raising horror than compassion in an audience: leaving love untouched, whose gentleness would have tempered them, which is the most frequent of all the passions, and which being the private concernment of every person, is soothed by viewing its own image in a public entertainment.

Among their comedies, we find a scene or two of tenderness, and that where you would least expect it, in Plautus; but to speak generally, their lovers say little, when they see each other, but *anima mea, vita mea*; ζωὴ καὶ ψυχή, as the women in Juvenal's time used to cry out in the fury of their kindness. Any sudden gust of passion (as an ecstasy of love in an unexpected meeting) cannot better be expressed than in a word and a sigh, breaking one another. Nature is dumb on such occasions, and to make her speak, would be to represent her unlike herself. But there are a thousand other concernments of lovers, as jealousies, complaints, contrivances and the like, where not to open their minds at large to each other, were to be wanting to their own love, and to the expectation of the audience who watch the movements of their minds, as much as the changes of their fortunes. For the imaging of the first is properly the work of a poet, the latter he borrows from the historian.

Eugenius was proceeding in that part of his discourse, when Crites interrupted him. I see, said he, Eugenius and I are never like to have this question decided betwixt us; for he maintains the Moderns have acquired a new perfection in writing; I can only grant they have altered the mode of it. Homer described his heroes men of great appetites, lovers of beef broiled upon the coals, and good fellows; contrary to the practice of the French romances, whose heroes neither eat, nor drink, nor sleep, for love. Virgil makes Aeneas a bold avower of his own virtues,

> Sum pius Aeneas fama super aethera notus;

which in the civility of our poets is the character of a fanfaron or Hector: for with us the knight takes occasion to walk out, or sleep, to avoid the vanity of telling his own story, which the trusty squire is ever to perform for him. So in their love scenes, of which Eugenius spoke last, the Ancients were more hearty, we more talkative: they writ love as it was then the mode to make it, and I will grant thus

---

anima mea, . . .: Juvenal, *Satires*, vi. 195 ('my life and my soul').
Sum pius . . .: *Aeneid* i. 378–9 (compressed; 'I am the faithful Aeneas, renowned throughout the world').
fanfaron: braggart.

much to Eugenius, that perhaps one of their poets, had he lived in our age,

> Si foret hoc nostrum fato delapsus in aevum,

(as Horace says of Lucilius) he had altered many things; not that they were not natural before, but that he might accommodate himself to the age in which he lived; yet in the mean time we are not to conclude anything rashly against those great men, but preserve to them the dignity of masters, and give that honour to their memories, (*Quos libitina sacravit*;) part of which we expect may be paid to us in future times.

This moderation of Crites, as it was pleasing to all the company, so it put an end to that dispute; which, Eugenius, who seemed to have the better of the argument, would urge no farther: but Lisideius after he had acknowledged himself of Eugenius's opinion concerning the Ancients, yet told him he had forborne, till his discourse were ended, to ask him why he preferred the English plays above those of other nations? and whether we ought not to submit our stage to the exactness of our next neighbours?

Though, said Eugenius, I am at all times ready to defend the honour of my country against the French, and to maintain, we are as well able to vanquish them with our pens as our ancestors have been with their swords, yet, if you please, added he, looking upon Neander, I will commit this cause to my friend's management; his opinion of our plays is the same with mine: and besides, there is no reason, that Crites and I, who have now left the stage, should re-enter so suddenly upon it; which is against the laws of comedy.

If the question had been stated, replied Lisideius, who had writ best, the French or English forty years ago, I should have been of your opinion, and adjudged the honour to our own nation; but since that time (said he, turning towards Neander) we have been so long together bad Englishmen, that we had not leisure to be good poets; Beaumont, Fletcher, and Jonson (who were only capable of bringing us to that degree of perfection which we have) were just then leaving the world; as if in an age of so much horror, wit and those milder studies of humanity, had no farther business among us. But the Muses, who ever follow peace, went to plant in another country; it was then, that the great Cardinal of Richelieu began to take them

---

Si foret . . .: *Satires*, I. x. 68 (for 'delapsus' read 'dilatus'; 'if Fate had had him born in this age of ours').

Quos libitina sacravit: Horace, *Epistles*, II. i. 49 ('quod . . .'; 'whom the Funeral Goddess has consecrated').

Beaumont . . . *world*: Beaumont died 1616, Fletcher 1625, Jonson 1637.

into his protection; and that, by his encouragement, Corneille and
some other Frenchmen reformed their theatre,[n] (which before was as
much below ours as it now surpasses it and the rest of Europe); but
because Crites, in his discourse for the Ancients, has prevented me,
by observing many rules of the stage, which the Moderns have
borrowed from them, I shall only, in short, demand of you, whether
you are not convinced that of all nations the French have best
observed them? In the unity of time you find them so scrupulous, that
it yet remains a dispute among their poets, whether the artificial day
of twelve hours more or less, be not meant by Aristotle, rather than
the natural one of twenty-four; and consequently whether all plays
ought not to be reduced into that compass? This I can testify, that in
all their dramas writ within these last 20 years and upwards, I have
not observed any that have extended the time to thirty hours: in the
unity of place they are full as scrupulous, for many of their critics
limit it to that very spot of ground where the play is supposed to
begin; none of them exceed the compass of the same town or
city.

The unity of action in all their plays is yet more conspicuous, for
they do not burden them with under-plots, as the English do, which
is the reason why many scenes of our tragi-comedies carry on a design
that is nothing of kin to the main plot; and that we see two distinct
webs in a play, like those in ill-wrought stuffs; and two actions, that
is, two plays carried on together, to the confounding of the audience,
who, before they are warm in their concernments for one part, are
diverted to another; and by that means espouse the interest of neither.
From hence likewise it arises that the one half of our actors are not
known to the other. They keep their distances as if they were
Montagues and Capulets, and seldom begin an acquaintance till the
last scene of the fifth act, when they are all to meet upon the stage.
There is no theatre in the world has anything so absurd as the English
tragi-comedy, 'tis a drama of our own invention, and the fashion of
it is enough to proclaim it so; here a course of mirth, there another
of sadness and passion; and a third of honour, and a duel. Thus in
two hours and a half we run through all the fits of Bedlam. The
French afford you as much variety on the same day, but they do it
not so unseasonably, or *mal à propos* as we. Our poets present you the

---

... *into that compass*: cf. Corneille, *Discours des Trois Unités*. Scaliger and La
    Mesnardière argued for a minimum of twenty-four hours, but d'Aubignac
    wanted no more than twelve.
tragi-comedy: cf. *A Parallel of Poetry and Painting* (Watson, II, p. 202), and for
    refutation Neander's comments and the Preface to *Don Sebastian* (Watson, II,
    p. 49).

play and the farce together, and our stages still retain somewhat of the original civility of the Red Bull;

> Atque ursum et pugiles media inter carmina poscunt.

The end of tragedies or serious plays, says Aristotle, is to beget admiration, compassion, or concernment; but are not mirth and compassion things incompatible? and is it not evident that the poet must of necessity destroy the former by intermingling of the latter? that is, he must ruin the sole end and object of his tragedy to introduce somewhat that is forced in to it; and is not of the body of it. Would you not think that physician mad, who having prescribed a purge, should immediately order you to take restringents?

But to leave our plays, and return to theirs, I have noted one great advantage they have had in the plotting of their tragedies; that is, they are always grounded upon some known history: according to that of Horace, *ex noto fictum carmen sequar*; and in that they have so imitated the Ancients, that they have surpassed them. For the Ancients, as was observed before, took for the foundation of their plays some poetical fiction, such as under that consideration could move but little concernment in the audience, because they already knew the event of it.[n] But the French goes farther;

> Atque ita mentitur; sic veris falsa remiscet,
> primo ne medium, medio ne discrepet imum.

He so interweaves truth with probable fiction, that he puts a pleasing fallacy upon us; mends the intrigues of fate, and dispenses with the severity of history, to reward that virtue which has been rendered to us there unfortunate. Sometimes the story has left the success so doubtful, that the writer is free, by the privilege of a poet, to take that which of two or more relations will best suit with his design. As for example, in the death of Cyrus, whom Justin and some others report to have perished in the Scythian war, but Xenophon affirms to have died in his bed of extreme old age. Nay more, when

---

Red Bull: this theatre was built *c.* 1605 in Clerkenwell and rebuilt *c.* 1624. It was known for popular productions and general disorder.

Atque ursum . . .: Horace, *Epistles*, II. i. 185–6 ('media inter carmina poscunt/aut ursum aut pugiles': 'and the mob are capable of demanding boxers or a bear in the middle of the play').

Aristotle: Aristotle mentions only 'compassion' (pity) and 'concernment' (fear) (*Poetics*, vi). 'Admiration' is a 16th-century addition.

Horace: *Ars Poetica*, l. 240 ('I shall create from familiar matter').

Atque ita . . .: ibid., ll. 151–2 ('And so [Homer] invents, so closely mixes fiction and fact, that the middle is never out of harmony with the beginning, nor the end with the middle').

Cyrus: Justinus, i. 8; Xenophon, *Cyropaedia*, viii. 7.

the event is past dispute, even then we are willing to be deceived, and
the poet, if he contrives it with appearance of truth, has all the
audience of his party; at least during the time his play is acting: so
naturally we are kind to virtue, when our own interest is not in
question, that we take it up as the general concernment of mankind.
On the other side, if you consider the historical plays of Shakespeare,
they are rather so many chronicles of kings, or the business many
times of thirty or forty years, cramped into a representation of two
hours and an half, which is not to imitate or paint nature, but rather
to draw her in miniature, to take her in little, to look upon her through
the wrong end of a perspective, and receive her images not only much
less, but infinitely more imperfect than the life: this, instead of making
a play delightful, renders it ridiculous.

> Quodcumque ostendis mihi sic, incredulus odi.

For the spirit of man cannot be satisfied but with truth, or at least
verisimility; and a poem is to contain, if not τὰ ἔτυμα, yet ἐτύμοισιν
ὁμοῖα, as one of the Greek poets has expressed it.

Another thing in which the French differ from us and from the
Spaniards, is that they do not embarrass, or cumber themselves with
too much plot: they only represent so much of a story as will constitute one whole and great action sufficient for a play; we, who
undertake more, do but multiply adventures; which, not being produced from one another, as effects from causes, but barely following,
constitute many actions in the drama, and consequently make it
many plays.

But by pursuing closely one argument, which is not cloyed with
many turns, the French have gained more liberty for verse, in which
they write: they have leisure to dwell on a subject which deserves it;
and to represent the passions (which we have acknowledged to be the
poet's work) without being hurried from one thing to another, as we
are in the plays of Calderón, which we have seen lately upon our
theatres, under the name of Spanish plots. I have taken notice but of
one tragedy of ours, whose plot has that uniformity and unity of
design in it which I have commended in the French; and that is *Rollo*,

---

perspective: telescope.
Quodcumque . . .: *Ars Poetica*, l. 188 ('Whatever you show me thus, I hate and
  disbelieve').
Greek poets: Hesiod, *Theogony*, l. 27; Homer, *Odyssey*, xix. 203 ('if not "the
  truth" yet "resembling the truth" ').
Calderón: The best-known examples of adaptations from Calderón are Dryden's
  own *An Evening's Love* (1668) and the Earl of Bristol's *Elvira* (1663).

or rather, under the name of *Rollo*, the story of Bassianus and Geta
in Herodian; there indeed the plot is neither large nor intricate, but
just enough to fill the minds of the audience, not to cloy them. Besides, you see it founded upon the truth of history, only the time of
the action is not reducible to the strictness of the rules; and you see
in some places a little farce mingled, which is below the dignity of the
other parts; and in this all our poets are extremely peccant, even Ben
Jonson himself in *Sejanus* and *Catiline* has given us this oleo of a
play: this unnatural mixture of comedy and tragedy, which to me
sounds just as ridiculously as the history of David with the merry
humours of Golia. In *Sejanus* you may take notice of the scene
betwixt Livia and the physician, which is a pleasant satire upon the
artificial helps of beauty. In *Catiline* you may see the parliament of
women; the little envies of them to one another; and all that passes
betwixt Curio and Fulvia, scenes admirable in their kind, but of an
ill mingle with the rest.

But I return again to the French writers who, as I have said, do not
burden themselves too much with plot, which has been reproached
to them by an ingenious person of our nation as a fault, for he says
they commonly make but one person considerable in a play; they
dwell on him, and his concernments, while the rest of the persons are
only subservient to set him off. If he intends this by it, that there is
one person in the play who is of greater dignity than the rest, he must
tax, not only theirs, but those of the Ancients, and which he would
be loth to do, the best of ours; for 'tis impossible but that one person
must be more conspicuous in it than any other, and consequently the
greatest share in the action must devolve on him. We see it so in the
management of all affairs; even in the most equal aristocracy, the
balance cannot be so justly poised, but someone will be superior to
the rest, either in parts, fortune, interest, or the consideration of some
glorious exploit, which will reduce the greatest part of business into
his hands.

But, if he would have us to imagine that in exalting one character
the rest of them are neglected, and that all of them have not some
share or other in the action of the play, I desire him to produce any

---

Rollo: the play was first published as *The Bloody Brother* (1639), and may be the
   co-operative work of Chapman, Fletcher, Jonson, and Massinger.
oleo: corruption of 'olla podrida', a Spanish stew: hence 'mixture'.
Golia: a comic figure in medieval literature. The *Confessio Goliae* is doubtfully
   attributed to Walter Map (fl. 1200).
In Sejanus . . . In Catiline: *Sejanus* II. i; *Cataline* III. iii; II. i.
ingenious person: probably Thomas Sprat, *Observations on M. de Sorbier's
   Voyage into England* (1665).

of Corneille's tragedies, wherein every person (like so many servants in a well governed family) has not some employment, and who is not necessary to the carrying on of the plot, or at least to your understanding it.

There are indeed some protatic persons in the Ancients, whom they make use of in their plays, either to hear, or give the relation: but the French avoid this with great address, making their narrations only to, or by such, who are some way interested in the main design. And now I am speaking of relations, I cannot take a fitter opportunity to add this in favour of the French, that they often use them with better judgement and more *à propos* than the English do. Not that I commend narrations in general, but there are two sorts of them; one of those things which are antecedent to the play, and are related to make the conduct of it more clear to us, but, 'tis a fault to choose such subjects for the stage as will force us on that rock; because we see they are seldom listened to by the audience, and that is many times the ruin of the play: for, being once let pass without attention, the audience can never recover themselves to understand the plot; and indeed it is somewhat unreasonable that they should be put to so much trouble as, that to comprehend what passes in their sight, they must have recourse to what was done, perhaps, ten or twenty years ago.

But there is another sort of relations, that is, of things happening in the action of the play, and supposed to be done behind the scenes, and this is many times both convenient and beautiful: for, by it the French avoid the tumult, to which we are subject in England, by representing duels, battles, and the like, which renders our stage too like the theatres where they fight prizes. For what is more ridiculous than to represent an army with a drum and five men behind it; all which, the hero of the other side is to drive in before him, or to see a duel fought, and one slain with two or three thrusts of the foil, which we know are so blunted, that we might give a man an hour to kill another in good earnest with them.

I have observed that in all our tragedies, the audience cannot forbear laughing when the actors are to die; 'tis the most comic part of the whole play. All passions may be lively represented on the stage, if to the well-writing of them the actor supplies a good commanded voice, and limbs that move easily, and without stiffness; but there are many actions which can never be imitated to a just height: dying

---

protatic: i.e. characters who appear only in a play's introductory part.
interested: concerned.
fight prizes: have public fights.

especially is a thing which none but a Roman gladiator could naturally perform on the stage when he did not imitate or represent, but do it; and therefore it is better to omit the representation of it.

The words of a good writer which describe it lively, will make a deeper impression of belief in us than all the actor can insinuate into us, when he seems to fall dead before us; as a poet in the description of a beautiful garden, or a meadow, will please our imagination more than the place itself can please our sight. When we see death represented we are convinced it is but fiction; but when we hear it related, our eyes (the strongest witnesses) are wanting, which might have undeceived us; and we are all willing to favour the sleight when the poet does not too grossly impose on us. They therefore who imagine these relations would make no concernment in the audience, are deceived, by confounding them with the other, which are of things antecedent to the play; those are made often in cold blood (as I may say) to the audience; but these are warmed with our concernments, which were before awakened in the play. What the philosophers say of motion, that, when it is once begun, it continues of itself, and will do so to eternity without some stop put to it, is clearly true on this occasion; the soul being already moved with the characters and fortunes of those imaginary persons, continues going of its own accord, and we are no more weary to hear what becomes of them when they are not on the stage, than we are to listen to the news of an absent mistress. But it is objected, that if one part of the play may be related, then why not all? I answer, some parts of the action are more fit to be represented, some to be related. Corneille says judiciously, that the poet is not obliged to expose to view all particular actions which conduce to the principal: he ought to select such of them to be seen which will appear with the greatest beauty, either by the magnificence of the show, or the vehemence of passions which they produce, or some other charm which they have in them, and let the rest arrive to the audience by narration. 'Tis a great mistake in us to believe the French present no part of the action on the stage: every alteration or crossing of a design, every new sprung passion, and turn of it, is a part of the action, and much the noblest, except we conceive nothing to be action till the players come to blows; as if the painting of the hero's mind were not more properly the poet's work than the

---

philosophers: Watson quotes from the first English edition (1664) of Descartes' *Principia Philosophiae* (1644) to show that Dryden is here echoing a principle of Cartesian physics.

Corneille: Dryden is again following Corneille's *Discours des Trois Unités*.

3+s.c.

strength of his body. Nor does this anything contradict the opinion of Horace, where he tells us,

> Segnius irritant animos demissa per aurem,
> quam quae sunt oculis subjecta fidelibus.—

For he says immediately after,

> Non tamen intus
> digna geri promes in scenam, multaque tolles
> ex oculis, quae mox narret facundia praesens.

Among which many he recounts some.

> Nec pueros coram populo Medea trucidet,
> aut in avem Progne mutetur, Cadmus in anguem, etc.

That is, those actions which by reason of their cruelty will cause aversion in us, or by reason of their impossibility unbelief, ought either wholly to be avoided by a poet, or only delivered by narration. To which, we may have leave to add such as to avoid tumult, (as was before hinted) or to reduce the plot into a more reasonable compass of time, or for defect of beauty in them, are rather to be related than presented to the eye. Examples of all these kinds are frequent, not only among all the Ancients, but in the best received of our English poets. We find Ben Jonson using them in his *Magnetic Lady*, where one comes out from dinner, and relates the quarrels and disorders of it to save the indecent appearance of them on the stage, and to abbreviate the story: and this in express imitation of Terence, who had done the same before him in his *Eunuch*, where Pythius makes the like relation of what had happened within at the soldiers' entertainment. The relations likewise of Sejanus's death, and the prodigies before it are remarkable; the one of which was hid from sight to avoid the horror and tumult of the representation; the other to shun the introducing of things impossible to be believed. In that excellent play the *King and no King*, Fletcher goes yet farther; for the whole unravelling of the plot is done by narration in the fifth act, after the

---

Horace: *Ars Poetica* ll. 180–7 (after 'trucidet' a line is omitted; '. . . Procne vertatur . . .'; 'The mind is less strongly stirred by what comes through the ears than by what is brought before its faithful eyes, and by what the spectator sees for himself. But do not stage what should be performed off-stage, and keep much to be narrated by an actor's ready tongue. Medea must not slaughter her boys in front of the audience . . . nor Procne be turned into a bird, Cadmus into a snake').

Magnetic Lady: see esp. III. ii (the play licensed 1632, printed 1640).

Eunuch: IV, iii.

Sejanus: *Sejanus*, V. x.

Fletcher: joint work of Beaumont and Fletcher (1611).

manner of the Ancients; and it moves great concernment in the audience, though it be only a relation of what was done many years before the play. I could multiply other instances, but these are sufficient to prove that there is no error in choosing a subject which requires this sort of narrations; in the ill-management of them, there may.

But I find I have been too long in this discourse since the French have many other excellencies not common to us; as that you never see any of their plays end with a conversion, or simple change of will, which is the ordinary way which our poets use to end theirs. It shows little art in the conclusion of a dramatic poem, when they who have hindered the felicity during the four acts, desist from it in the fifth without some powerful cause to take them off their design; and though I deny not but such reasons may be found, yet it is a path that is cautiously to be trod, and the poet is to be sure he convinces the audience that the motive is strong enough. As for example, the conversion of the usurer in *The Scornful Lady*, seems to me a little forced; for being a usurer, which implies a lover of money to the highest degree of covetousness, (and such the poet has represented him) the account he gives for the sudden change is that he has been duped by the wild young fellow, which in reason might render him more wary another time, and make him punish himself with harder fare and coarser clothes to get up again what he had lost: but that he should look on it as a judgement, and so repent, we may expect to hear in a sermon, but I should never endure it in a play.

I pass by this; neither will I insist on the care they take, that no person after his first entrance shall ever appear, but the business which brings him upon the stage shall be evident: which rule if observed, must needs render all the events in the play more natural; for there you see the probability of every accident, in the cause that produced it; and that which appears chance in the play will seem so reasonable to you, that you will there find it almost necessary; so that in the exit of the actor you have a clear account of his purpose and design in the next entrance: (though, if the scene be well wrought, the event will commonly deceive you) for there is nothing so absurd, says Corneille, as for an actor to leave the stage, only because he has no more to say.

I should now speak of the beauty of their rhyme, and the just reason I have to prefer that way of writing in tragedies before ours in

Scornful Lady: again Beaumont and Fletcher's joint work (1609–10).
evident: inevitable.
Corneille: cf., again, Corneille's *Discours des Trois Unités*.

blank verse; but because it is partly received by us, and therefore not altogether peculiar to them, I will say no more of it in relation to their plays. For our own I doubt not but it will exceedingly beautify them, and I can see but one reason why it should not generally obtain, that is, because our poets write so ill in it. This indeed may prove a more prevailing argument than all others which are used to destroy it, and therefore I am only troubled when great and judicious poets, and those who are acknowledged such, have writ or spoke against it; as for others they are to be answered by that one sentence of an ancient author.

Sed ut primo ad consequendos eos quos priores ducimus accendimur, ita ubi aut praeteriri, aut aequari eos posse desperavimus, studium cum spe senescit: quod, scilicet, assequi non potest, sequi desinit; praeteritoque eo in quo eminere non possumus, aliquid in quo nitamur conquirimus.

Lisideius concluded in this manner; and Neander after a little pause thus answered him.

I shall grant Lisideius, without much dispute, a great part of what he has urged against us; for I acknowledge that the French contrive their plots more regularly, and observe the laws of comedy, and decorum of the stage (to speak generally) with more exactness than the English. Farther, I deny not but he has taxed us justly in some irregularities of ours which he has mentioned; yet, after all, I am of opinion that neither our faults nor their virtues are considerable enough to place them above us.

For the lively imitation of nature being in the definition of a play, those which best fulfil that law ought to be esteemed superior to the others. 'Tis true, those beauties of the French poesy are such as will raise perfection higher where it is, but are not sufficient to give it where it is not: they are indeed the beauties of a statue, but not of a man, because not animated with the soul of poesy, which is imitation of humour and passions: and this Lisideius himself, or any other, however biased to their party, cannot but acknowledge, if he will either compare the humours of our comedies, or the characters of our serious plays with theirs. He who will look upon theirs which have been written till these last ten years or thereabouts, will find it an hard matter to pick out two or three passable humours amongst them. Corneille himself, their arch-poet, what has he produced

---

Sed ut primo . . .: Velleius Paterculus, *Historia Romana*, i. 17 ('Et ut primo consequendos quos . . . senescit, et quod adsequi non potest . . .': 'But as at first we burn to surpass those whom we think of as leaders, so, when we have despaired of being able to equal, let alone surpass them, our zeal decreases with our hopes; it stops following when it cannot overtake . . . and leaving aside those things in which we cannot excel, we seek a new object for our effort').

except *The Liar*, and you know how it was cried up in France; but when it came upon the English stage, though well translated, and that part of Dorant acted to so much advantage as I am confident it never received in its own country, the most favourable to it would not put it in competition with many of Fletcher's or Ben Jonson's. In the rest of Corneille's comedies you have little humour; he tells you himself his way is first to show two lovers in good intelligence with each other; in the working up of the play to embroil them by some mistake, and in the latter end to clear it, and reconcile them.

But of late years Molière, the younger Corneille, Quinault, and some others, have been imitating afar off the quick turns and graces of the English stage. They have mixed their serious plays with mirth, like our tragi-comedies, since the death of Cardinal Richelieu, which Lisideius and many others not observing, have commended that in them for a virtue which they themselves no longer practise. Most of their new plays are like some of ours, derived from the Spanish novels. There is scarce one of them without a veil, and a trusty Diego, who drolls much after the rate of the *Adventures*. But their humours, if I may grace them with that name, are so thin sown that never above one of them comes up in any play. I dare take upon me to find more variety of them in some one play of Ben Jonson's than in all theirs together: as he who has seen the *Alchemist*, *The Silent Woman*, or *Bartholomew Fair*, cannot but acknowledge with me.

I grant the French have performed what was possible on the ground-work of the Spanish plays; what was pleasant before, they have made regular; but there is not above one good play to be writ on all those plots; they are too much alike to please often, which we need not the experience of our own stage to justify. As for their new way of mingling mirth with serious plot, I do not with Lisideius condemn the thing, though I cannot approve their manner of doing it. He tells us we cannot so speedily recollect ourselves after a scene of great passion and concernment, as to pass to another of mirth and humour, and to enjoy it with any relish: but why should he imagine the soul of man more heavy than his senses? Does not the eye pass from an unpleasant object to a pleasant in a much shorter time than is required to this? and does not the unpleasantness of the first

The Liar: *Le Menteur* (1643) was translated and produced in London as *The Mistaken Beauty; or The Liar*.

younger Corneille: Thomas Corneille (1625–1709), younger brother of Pierre, and a confessed user of Spanish material.

Quinault: Philippe Quinault (1635–88), a very popular dramatist of his day.

some of ours: e.g. Dryden's own *Wild Gallant* (1663) and *Rival Ladies* (1664).

Diego: the cowardly servant of Sir Samuel Tuke's *Adventures of Five Hours*.

commend the beauty of the latter? The old rule of logic might have convinced him, that contraries when placed near, set off each other. A continued gravity keeps the spirit too much bent; we must refresh it sometimes, as we bait in a journey, that we may go on with greater ease. A scene of mirth mixed with tragedy has the same effect upon us which our music has betwixt the acts, which we find a relief to us from the best plots and language of the stage, if the discourses have been long. I must therefore have stronger arguments ere I am convinced, that compassion and mirth in the same subject destroy each other, and in the mean time cannot but conclude, to the honour of our nation, that we have invented, increased and perfected a more pleasant way of writing for the stage than was ever known to the Ancients or Moderns of any nation, which is tragi-comedy.

And this leads me to wonder why Lisideius and many others should cry up the barrenness of the French plots above the variety and copiousness of the English. Their plots are single, they carry on one design which is pushed forward by all the actors, every scene in the play contributing and moving towards it. Our plays besides the main design, have under-plots or by-concernments, of less considerable persons, and intrigues, which are carried on with the motion of the main plot: as they say the orb of the fixed stars, and those of the planets, though they have motions of their own, are whirled about by the motion of the *primum mobile*, in which they are contained: that similitude expresses much of the English stage, for if contrary motions may be found in nature to agree; if a planet can go east and west at the same time, one way by virtue of his own motion, the other by the force of the first mover, it will not be difficult to imagine how the under-plot, which is only different, not contrary to the great design, may naturally be conducted along with it.

Eugenius has already shown us, from the confession of the French poets, that the unity of action is sufficiently preserved if all the imperfect actions of the play are conducing to the main design: but when those pretty intrigues of a play are so ill ordered, that they have no coherence with the other, I must grant that Lisideius has reason to tax that want of due connexion; for co-ordination in a play is as

---

rule of logic: Watson quotes Burgersdijck, *Institutionum logicarum libri duo* (1626), I, xxii, Theorem V ('Contraries, placed together shine more greatly').
bait: rest.
primum mobile: Dryden is using the out-of-date Ptolemaic astronomy, in which the 'primum mobile' is the ninth sphere, which gives motion to the eight inner spheres.
Eugenius: an error for 'Crites'.
co-ordination: equality of rank.

dangerous and unnatural as in a state. In the mean time he must acknowledge our variety, if well ordered, will afford a greater pleasure to the audience.

As for his other argument, that by pursuing one single theme they gain an advantage to express and work up the passions, I wish any example he could bring from them would make it good: for I confess their verses are to me the coldest I have ever read. Neither indeed is it possible for them, in the way they take, so to express passion, as that the effects of it should appear in the concernment of an audience, their speeches being so many declamations, which tire us with the length; so that instead of persuading us to grieve for their imaginary heroes, we are concerned for our own trouble, as we are in tedious visits of bad company; we are in pain till they are gone. When the French stage came to be reformed by Cardinal Richelieu, those long harangues were introduced, to comply with the gravity of a church-man. Look upon the *Cinna* and the *Pompey*, they are not so properly to be called plays, as long discourses of reason of state: and *Polyeucte* in matters of religion is as solemn as the long stops upon our organs. Since that time it is grown into a custom, and their actors speak by the hourglass, like our parsons; nay, they account it the grace of their parts, and think themselves disparaged by the poet, if they may not twice or thrice in a play entertain the audience with a speech of an hundred lines. I deny not but this may suit well enough with the French; for as we, who are a more sullen people, come to be diverted at our plays; so they who are of an airy and gay temper come thither to make themselves more serious. And this I conceive to be one reason why comedies are more pleasing to us, and tragedies to them. But to speak generally, it cannot be denied that short speeches and replies are more apt to move the passions, and beget concernment in us than the other: for it is unnatural for any one in a gust of passion to speak long together, or for another in the same condition, to suffer him, without interruption. Grief and passion are like floods raised in little brooks by a sudden rain; they are quickly up, and if the concern-ment be poured unexpectedly in upon us, it overflows us. But a long sober shower gives them leisure to run out as they came in, without troubling the ordinary current. As for comedy, repartee is one of its chiefest graces; the greatest pleasure of the audience is a chase of wit kept up on both sides, and swiftly managed. And this our fore-fathers, if not we, have had in Fletcher's plays, to a much higher degree of perfection than the French poets can, reasonably, hope to reach.

Cinna ... *Polyeucte*: *Cinna* (1640), *La Mort de Pompée* (1644), *Polyeucte* (1641 ?): all early plays of Pierre Corneille.

There is another part of Lisideius's discourse, in which he has
rather excused our neighbours than commended them; that is, for
aiming only to make one person considerable in their plays. 'Tis very
true what he has urged, that one character in all plays, even without
the poet's care, will have advantage of all the others; and that the
design of the whole drama will chiefly depend on it. But this hinders
not that there may be more shining characters in the play: many
persons of a second magnitude, nay, some so very near, so almost
equal to the first, that greatness may be opposed to greatness, and all
the persons be made considerable, not only by their quality, but their
action. 'Tis evident that the more the persons are, the greater will be
the variety of the plot. If then the parts are managed so regularly that
the beauty of the whole be kept entire, and that the variety become
not a perplexed and confused mass of accidents, you will find it infinitely pleasing to be led in a labyrinth of design, where you see some
of your way before you, yet discern not the end till you arrive at it.
And that all this is practicable, I can produce for examples many of
our English plays: as *The Maid's Tragedy, The Alchemist, The Silent
Woman*: I was going to have named *The Fox*, but that the unity of
design seems not exactly observed in it; for there appear two actions
in the play; the first naturally ending with the fourth act; the second
forced from it in the fifth: which yet is the less to be condemned in
him, because the disguise of Volpone, though it suited not with his
character as a crafty or covetous person, agreed well enough with
that of a voluptuary: and by it the poet gained the end at which he
aimed, the punishment of vice, and the reward of virtue, both which
that disguise produced. So that to judge equally of it, it was an
excellent fifth act, but not so naturally proceeding from the former.

But to leave this, and pass to the latter part of Lisideius's discourse,
which concerns relations, I must acknowledge with him, that the
French have reason to hide that part of the action which would
occasion too much tumult on the stage, and to choose rather to have
it made known by narration to the audience. Farther I think it very
convenient, for the reasons he has given, that all incredible actions
were removed; but, whether custom has so insinuated itself into our
countrymen, or nature has so formed them to fierceness, I know not;
but they will scarcely suffer combats and other objects of horror to
be taken from them. And indeed, the indecency of tumults is all

---

The Maid's Tragedy . . .: *The Maid's Tragedy* (1619) is by Beaumont and Fletcher,
the other three by Jonson, *The Fox* being *Volpone's* sub-title. Dryden's
criticism of *Volpone* is misplaced, the play being held as a firm single action
by the title-character's pervasive lust and greed.

which can be objected against fighting. For why may not our imagination as well suffer itself to be deluded with the probability of it, as with any other thing in the play? For my part, I can with as great ease persuade myself that the blows are given in good earnest, as I can, that they who strike them are kings or princes, or those persons which they represent. For objects of incredibility I would be satisfied from Lisideius, whether we have any so removed from all appearance of truth as are those of Corneille's *Andromède*? A play which has been frequented the most of any he has writ? If the Perseus, or the son of an heathen god, the Pegasus and the monster were not capable to choke a strong belief, let him blame any representation of ours hereafter. Those indeed were objects of delight; yet the reason is the same as to the probability: for he makes it not a ballet or masque, but a play, which is to resemble truth. But for death, that it ought not to be represented, I have besides the arguments alleged by Lisideius, the authority of Ben Jonson, who has forborne it in his tragedies; for both the death of Sejanus and Catiline are related: though in the latter I cannot but observe one irregularity of that great poet: he has removed the scene in the same act, from Rome to Catiline's army, and from thence again to Rome; and besides, has allowed a very inconsiderable time, after Catiline's speech, for the striking of the battle, and the return of Petreius, who is to relate the event of it to the Senate: which I should not animadvert on him, who was otherwise a painful observer of τὸ πρέπον, or the decorum of the stage, if he had not used extreme severity in his judgement on the incomparable Shakespeare for the same fault. To conclude on this subject of relations, if we are to be blamed for showing too much of the action, the French are as faulty for discovering too little of it: a mean betwixt both should be observed by every judicious writer, so as the audience may neither be left unsatisfied by not seeing what is beautiful, or shocked by beholding what is either incredible or indecent. I hope I have already proved in this discourse, that though we are not altogether so punctual as the French, in observing the laws of comedy; yet our errors are so few and little, and those things wherein we excel them so considerable, that we ought of right to be preferred before them. But what will Lisideius say if they themselves acknowledge they are too strictly bounded by those laws, for breaking which he has blamed the English? I will allege Corneille's words, as I find them in the end of his Discourse of the three unities; *Il est*

Andromède: (1650) the first of Corneille's plays to use elaborate stage-effects.
ballet: the newness of the word is indicated by Dryden's concern to gloss it ('or masque'): the ballet grew in Louis XIV's Court in the 1650s.
fault: see Jonson's prologue to *Every Man in His Humour* (1616).

3*

facile aux speculatifs d'estre sevères, etc. ' 'Tis easy for speculative
persons to judge severely; but if they would produce to public view
ten or twelve pieces of this nature, they would perhaps give more
latitude to the rules than I have done, when by experience they had
known how much we are limited and constrained by them, and how
many beauties of the stage they banished from it.' To illustrate a little
what he has said; by their servile observations of the unities of time
and place, and integrity of scenes, they have brought on themselves
that dearth of plot, and narrowness of imagination, which may be
observed in all their plays. How many beautiful accidents might
naturally happen in two or three days, which cannot arrive with any
probability in the compass of 24 hours? There is time to be allowed
also for maturity of design, which amongst great and prudent persons,
such as are often represented in tragedy, cannot, with any likelihood
of truth, be brought to pass at so short a warning. Farther, by tying
themselves strictly to the unity of place, and unbroken scenes, they
are forced many times to omit some beauties which cannot be shown
where the act began; but might, if the scene were interrupted, and the
stage cleared for the persons to enter in another place; and therefore
the French poets are often forced upon absurdities: for if the act
begins in a chamber, all the persons in the play must have some
business or other to come thither, or else they are not to be shown
that act, and sometimes their characters are very unfitting to appear
there; as, suppose it were the king's bedchamber, yet the meanest
man in the tragedy must come and dispatch his business there, rather
than in the lobby or courtyard, (which is fitter for him) for fear the
stage should be cleared, and the scenes broken. Many times they fall
by it into a greater inconvenience; for they keep their scenes un-
broken, and yet change the place; as in one of their newest plays
where the act begins in the street. There a gentleman is to meet his
friend; he sees him with his man, coming out from his father's house;
they talk together, and the first goes out: the second, who is a lover,
has made an appointment with his mistress; she appears at the
window, and then we are to imagine the scene lies under it. This
gentleman is called away, and leaves his servant with his mistress:
presently her father is heard from within; the young lady is afraid the
serving-man should be discovered, and thrusts him into a place of
safety, which is supposed to be her closet. After this, the father enters
to the daughter, and now the scene is in a house: for he is seeking
from one room to another for this poor Philipin, or French Diego,
who is heard from within, drolling and breaking many a miserable

newest plays: Thomas Corneille's *L'Amour à la mode* (1651).

conceit on the subject of his sad condition. In this ridiculous manner the play goes forward, the stage being never empty all the while: so that the street, the window, the two houses, and the closet, are made to walk about, and the persons to stand still. Now what, I beseech you, is more easy than to write a regular French play, or more difficult than to write an irregular English one, like those of Fletcher, or of Shakespeare?

If they content themselves as Corneille did, with some flat design, which, like an ill riddle, is found out ere it be half proposed, such plots we can make every way regular as easily as they: but whenever they endeavour to rise to any quick turns and counterturns of plot, as some of them have attempted, since Corneille's plays have been less in vogue, you see they write as irregularly as we, though they cover it more speciously. Hence the reason is perspicuous, why no French plays, when translated, have, or ever can, succeed on the English stage. For, if you consider the plots, our own are fuller of variety; if the writing, ours are more quick and fuller of spirit: and therefore 'tis a strange mistake in those who decry the way of writing plays in verse, as if the English therein imitated the French. We have borrowed nothing from them; our plots are weaved in English looms: we endeavour therein to follow the variety and greatness of characters which are derived to us from Shakespeare and Fletcher. The copiousness and well-knitting of the intrigues we have from Jonson, and for the verse itself we have English precedents of elder date than any of Corneille's plays (not to name our old comedies before Shakespeare, which were all writ in verse of six feet, or Alexandrines, such as the French now use). I can show in Shakespeare, many scenes of rhyme together, and the like in Ben Jonson's tragedies: in *Catiline* and *Sejanus* sometimes thirty or forty lines; I mean besides the chorus, or the monologues, which by the way, showed Ben no enemy to this way of writing, especially if you read his *Sad Shepherd*, which goes sometimes on rhyme, sometimes on blank verse, like an horse who eases himself on trot and amble. You find him likewise commending Fletcher's pastoral of *The Faithful Shepherdess*; which is for the most part rhyme, though not refined to that purity to which it hath since been brought. And these examples are enough to clear us from a servile imitation of the French.

English looms: as both Watson and Boulton note, this is a rather wild statement, considering how many Restoration plays are French-based.
French now use: in fact some early Elizabethan comedies (e.g. Peele's *Old Wives, Tale* and Greene's *Friar Bacon and Friar Bungay*) use pentameters.
Sad Shepherd: this—Jonson's last and unfinished play—was written *c.* 1635.
Faithful Shepherdess: (*c.* 1608–9).

But to return whence I have digressed, I dare boldly affirm these two things of the English drama: first, that we have many plays of ours as regular as any of theirs; and which, besides, have more variety of plot and characters: and secondly, that in most of the irregular plays of Shakespeare or Fletcher (for Ben Jonson's are for the most part regular) there is a more masculine fancy and greater spirit in the writing, than there is in any of the French. I could produce even in Shakespeare's and Fletcher's works, some plays which are almost exactly formed; as *The Merry Wives of Windsor*, and *The Scornful Lady*: but because (generally speaking) Shakespeare, who writ first, did not perfectly observe the laws of comedy, and Fletcher, who came nearer to perfection, yet through carelessness made many faults, I will take the pattern of a perfect play from Ben Jonson, who was a careful and learned observer of the dramatic laws, and from all his comedies I shall select *The Silent Woman*; of which I will make a short examen, according to those rules which the French observe.

As Neander was beginning to examine *The Silent Woman*, Eugenius, earnestly regarding him; I beseech you, Neander, said he, gratify the company and me in particular so far, as before you speak of the play, to give us a character of the author; and tell us frankly your opinion, whether you do not think all writers, both French and English, ought to give place to him?

I fear, replied Neander, that in obeying your commands I shall draw some envy on myself. Besides, in performing them, it will be first necessary to speak somewhat of Shakespeare and Fletcher, his rivals in poesy, and one of them, in my opinion, at least his equal, perhaps his superior.

To begin with Shakespeare; he was the man who of all modern, and perhaps ancient poets, had the largest and most comprehensive soul. All the images of nature were still present to him, and he drew them not laboriously, but luckily: when he describes anything, you more than see it, you feel it too. Those who accuse him to have wanted learning,[n] give him the greater commendation: he was naturally learned; he needed not the spectacles of books to read nature; he looked inwards, and found her there. I cannot say he is everywhere alike; were he so, I should do him injury to compare him with the greatest of mankind. He is many times flat, insipid; his comic wit degenerating into clenches, his serious swelling into bom-

---

Scornful Lady: the action of Shakespeare's *Merry Wives* (1602) is confined to two days and the environs of Windsor; Beaumont and Fletcher's *Scornful Lady* (1616) has a similar time-restriction and is set in London.
examen: critical analysis and evaluation.

bast. But he is always great, when some great occasion is presented
to him: no man can say he ever had a fit subject for his wit, and did
not then raise himself as high above the rest of poets,

Quantum lenta solent inter viburna cupressi.

The consideration of this made Mr. Hales of Eton say that there
was no subject of which any poet ever writ, but he would produce it
much better done in Shakespeare; and however others are now
generally preferred before him, yet the age wherein he lived, which
had contemporaries with him, Fletcher and Jonson, never equalled
them to him in their esteem. And in the last king's Court, when Ben's
reputation was at highest, Sir John Suckling, and with him the greater
part of the courtiers, set our Shakespeare far above him.

Beaumont and Fletcher of whom I am next to speak, had with the
advantage of Shakespeare's wit, which was their precedent, great
natural gifts, improved by study, Beaumont especially being so
accurate a judge of plays, that Ben Jonson while he lived, submitted
all his writings to his censure, and 'tis thought, used his judgement in
correcting, if not contriving all his plots. What value he had for him,
appears by the verses he writ to him; and therefore I need speak no
farther of it. The first play that brought Fletcher and him in esteem
was their *Philaster*, for before that, they had written two or three very
unsuccessfully: as the like is reported of Ben Jonson, before he writ
Every Man in his Humour.[n] Their plots were generally more regular
than Shakespeare's, especially those which were made before Beaumont's death; and they understood and imitated the conversation of
gentlemen much better; whose wild debaucheries, and quickness of
wit in repartees, no poet before them could paint as they have done.
Humour which Ben Jonson derived from particular persons, they
made it not their business to describe. They represented all the
passions very lively, but above all, love. I am apt to believe the
English language in them arrived to its highest perfection; what
words have since been taken in, are rather superfluous than ornamental. Their plays are now the most pleasant and frequent entertainments of the stage, two of theirs being acted through the year for
one of Shakespeare's or Jonson's: the reason is, because there is a

---

Quantum . . .: Virgil, *Eclogues*, i. 25 ('as cypresses often do among bending
  osiers').

Hales: John Hales (1584–1656), Fellow of Eton from 1613.

king's Court: Charles I (reigned 1625–49).

the verses: *Epigrammes*, LV.

Philaster: first produced between 1608 and 1610. The failures referred to (which
  may not all be joint works) are presumably *The Woman Hater*, *The Knight of
  the Burning Pestle*, and *Cupid's Revenge*.

certain gaiety in their comedies, and pathos in their more serious
plays, which suits generally with all men's humours. Shakespeare's
language is likewise a little obsolete, and Ben Jonson's wit comes
short of theirs.

As for Jonson, to whose character I am now arrived, if we look
upon him while he was himself, (for his last plays were but his
dotages) I think him the most learned and judicious writer which any
theatre ever had. He was a most severe judge of himself as well as
others. One cannot say he wanted wit, but rather that he was frugal
of it. In his works you find little to retrench or alter. Wit and language, and humour also in some measure we had before him; but
something of art was wanting to the drama till he came. He managed
his strength to more advantage than any who preceded him. You
seldom find him making love in any of his scenes, or endeavouring to
move the passions; his genius was too sullen and saturnine to do it
gracefully, especially when he knew he came after those who had
performed both to such an height. Humour was his proper sphere,
and in that he delighted most to represent mechanic people. He was
deeply conversant in the Ancients, both Greek and Latin, and he
borrowed boldly from them. There is scarce a poet or historian
among the Roman authors of those times whom he has not translated
in *Sejanus* and *Catiline*. But he has done his robberies so openly, that
one may see he fears not to be taxed by any law. He invades authors
like a monarch, and what would be theft in other poets, is only
victory in him. With the spoils of these writers he so represents old
Rome to us, in its rites, ceremonies and customs, that if one of their
poets had written either of his tragedies, we had seen less of it than
in him. If there was any fault in his language, 'twas that he weaved it
too closely and laboriously, in his comedies especially: perhaps too,
he did a little too much Romanize our tongue,[n] leaving the words
which he translated almost as much Latin as he found them: wherein
though he learnedly followed their language, he did not enough
comply with the idiom of ours. If I would compare him with Shakespeare, I must acknowledge him the more correct poet, but Shakespeare the greater wit. Shakespeare was the Homer, or father of our
dramatic poets; Jonson was the Virgil, the pattern of elaborate
writing. I admire him, but I love Shakespeare. To conclude of him,
as he has given us the most correct plays, so in the precepts which he
has laid down in his *Discoveries*, we have as many and profitable
rules for perfecting the stage as any wherewith the French can
furnish us.

mechanic: vulgar, base.

Having thus spoken of the author, I proceed to the examination of his comedy, *The Silent Woman*.

EXAMEN OF THE SILENT WOMAN

To begin first with the length of the action, it is so far from exceeding the compass of a natural day, that it takes not up an artificial one. 'Tis all included in the limits of three hours and an half, which is no more than is required for the presentment on the stage. A beauty perhaps not much observed; if it had, we should not have looked on the Spanish translation of *Five Hours* with so much wonder. The scene of it is laid in London; the latitude of place is almost as little as you can imagine, for it lies all within the compass of two houses, and after the first act, in one. The continuity of scenes is observed more than in any of our plays, except his own *Fox* and *Alchemist*. They are not broken above twice or thrice at most in the whole comedy, and in the two best of Corneille's plays, the *Cid* and *Cinna*, they are interrupted once. The action of the play is entirely one; the end or aim of which is the settling Morose's estate on Dauphine. The intrigue of it is the greatest and most noble of any pure unmixed comedy in any language: you see in it many persons of various characters and humours, and all delightful; as first, Morose, or an old man, to whom all noise but his own talking is offensive. Some who would be thought critics, say this humour of his is forced: but to remove that objection, we may consider him first to be naturally of a delicate hearing, as many are to whom all sharp sounds are unpleasant; and secondly, we may attribute much of it to the peevishness of his age, or the wayward authority of an old man in his own house, where he may make himself obeyed; and to this the poet seems to allude in his name, Morose. Beside this, I am assured from divers persons, that Ben Jonson was actually acquainted with such a man, one altogether as ridiculous as he is here represented. Others say it is not enough to find one man of such an humour; it must be common to more, and the more common the more natural. To prove this, they instance in the best of comical characters, Falstaff. There are many men resembling him; old, fat, merry, cowardly, drunken, amorous, vain, and lying. But to convince these people, I need but

---

artificial one: the action, in fact, covers a minimum of twelve hours.

Five Hours: Tuke's play, mentioned above (p. 49).

scene: in fact the play involves six different scenes.

they are not broken . . . : as just hinted, there are several breaks between scenes.

Cid: Ker points out that this is not really accurate, there being several breaks in *Le Cid*.

tell them, that humour is the ridiculous extravagance of conversation, wherein one man differs from all others. If then it be common, or communicated to many, how differs it from other men's? or what indeed causes it to be ridiculous so much as the singularity of it? As for Falstaff, he is not properly one humour, but a miscellany of humours or images, drawn from so many several men; that wherein he is singular is his wit, or those things he says, *praeter expectatum*, unexpected by the audience; his quick evasions when you imagine him surprised, which as they are extremely diverting of themselves, so receive a great addition from his person; for the very sight of such an unwieldy old debauched fellow is a comedy alone. And here having a place so proper for it, I cannot but enlarge somewhat upon this subject of humour into which I am fallen. The Ancients had little of it in their comedies; for the τὸ γελοῖον, of the Old Comedy, of which Aristophanes was chief, was not so much to imitate a man, as to make the people laugh at some odd conceit, which had commonly somewhat of unnatural or obscene in it. Thus when you see Socrates brought upon the stage you are not to imagine him made ridiculous by the imitation of his actions, but rather by making him perform something very unlike himself, something so childish and absurd, as by comparing it with the gravity of the true Socrates, makes a ridiculous object for the spectators. In their New Comedy which succeeded, the poets sought indeed to express the ἦθος, as in their tragedies the πάθος of mankind. But this ἦθος contained only the general characters of men and manners; as old men, lovers, serving-men, courtesans, parasites, and such other persons as we see in their comedies; all which they made alike: that is, one old man or father; one lover, one courtesan so like another, as if the first of them had begot the rest of every sort: *ex homine hunc natum dicas*. The same custom they observed likewise in their tragedies. As for the French, though they have the word *humeur* among them, yet they have small use of it in their comedies, or farces;[n] they being but ill imitations of the *ridiculum*, or that which stirred up laughter in the Old Comedy. But among the English 'tis otherwise, whereby humour is meant some extravagant habit, passion, or affection, particular (as I said before) to some one person, by the oddness of which, he is immediately distinguished from the rest of men; which being lively and naturally represented, most frequently begets that malicious pleasure

τὸ γελοῖον: Aristotle, *Poetics*, V ('the ludicrous').
Socrates . . . spectators: the reference is to Aristophanes's *Clouds*.
ἦθος: 'character', 'natural disposition'.
πάθος: 'emotion', 'transient mood'.
ex homine . . .: Terence, *Eunuch*, l. 460 ('one the precise image of the other').

in the audience which is testified by laughter, as all things which are deviations from customs are ever the aptest to produce it, though by the way this laughter is only accidental, as the person represented is fantastic or bizarre. But pleasure is essential to it, as the imitation of what is natural. The description of these humours, drawn from the knowledge and observation of particular persons, was the peculiar genius and talent of Ben Jonson; to whose play I now return.

Besides Morose, there are at least nine or ten different characters and humours in *The Silent Woman*, all which persons have several concernments of their own, yet are all used by the poet, to the conducting of the main design to perfection. I shall not waste time in commending the writing of this play, but I will give you my opinion, that there is more wit and acuteness of fancy in it than in any of Ben Jonson's. Besides, that he has here described the conversation of gentlemen in the persons of Truewit, and his friends, with more gaiety, air and freedom, than in the rest of his comedies. For the contrivance of the plot, 'tis extreme elaborate, and yet withal easy; for the λύσις, or untying of it, 'tis so admirable, that when it is done, no one of the audience would think the poet could have missed it; and yet it was concealed so much before the last scene, that any other way would sooner have entered into your thoughts. But I dare not take upon me to commend the fabric of it, because it is altogether so full of art, that I must unravel every scene in it to commend it as I ought. And this excellent contrivance is still the more to be admired, because 'tis comedy where the persons are only of common rank, and their business private, not elevated by passions or high concernments as in serious plays. Here everyone is a proper judge of all he sees; nothing is represented but that with which he daily converses: so that by consequence all faults lie open to discovery, and few are pardonable. 'Tis this which Horace has judiciously observed:

> Creditur ex medio quia res arcessit habere
> sudoris minimum, sed habet Comedia tanto
> plus oneris, quanto veniae minus.—

But our poet, who was not ignorant of these difficulties, has made use of all advantages, as he who designs a large leap takes his rise from the highest ground. One of these advantages is that which Corneille has laid down as the greatest which can arrive to any poem, and which he himself could never compass above thrice in all his

Creditur . . .: *Epistles*, II. i. 168–70 ('It is thought that comedy, drawing its subjects from daily life, requires less labour; but proportionately it requires more as less indulgence is allowed').
Corneille: *Discours des Trois Unités*.

plays, *viz.* the making choice of some signal and long-expected day, whereon the action of the play is to depend. This day was that designed by Dauphine for the settling of his uncle's estate upon him; which to compass he contrives to marry him. That the marriage had been plotted by him long beforehand is made evident by what he tells Truewit in the second act, that in one moment he had destroyed what he had been raising many months.

There is another artifice of the poet, which I cannot here omit, because by the frequent practice of it in his comedies, he has left it to us almost as a rule, that is, when he has any character or humour wherein he would show a *coup de maistre*, or his highest skill; he recommends it to your observation by a pleasant description of it before the person first appears. Thus, in *Bartholomew Fair* he gives you the pictures of Numps and Cokes, and in this those of Daw, Lafoole, Morose, and the Collegiate Ladies; all which you hear described before you see them. So that before they come upon the stage you have a longing expectation of them, which prepares you to receive them favourably; and when they are there, even from their first appearance you are so far acquainted with them, that nothing of their humour is lost to you.

I will observe yet one thing further of this admirable plot; the business of it rises in every act. The second is greater than the first, the third than the second, and so forward to the fifth. There too you see, till the very last scene, new difficulties arising to obstruct the action of the play; and when the audience is brought into despair that the business can naturally be effected, then, and not before, the discovery is made. But that the poet might entertain you with more variety all this while, he reserves some new characters to show you, which he opens not till the second and third act. In the second Morose, Daw, the Barber and Otter; in the third the Collegiate Ladies, all which he moves afterwards in by-walks, or under-plots, as diversions to the main design, lest it should grow tedious, though they are still naturally joined with it, and somewhere or other subservient to it. Thus, like a skilful chess-player, by little and little he draws out his men, and makes his pawns of use to his greater persons.

If this comedy, and some others of his, were translated into French prose (which would now be no wonder to them, since Molière has lately given them plays out of verse which have not displeased them)

---

many months: see II. iv. 37–9.

Molière: probably a reference to *Don Juan* (1665) and perhaps to *L'Impromptu de Versailles* (1663).

I believe the controversy would soon be decided betwixt the two nations, even making them the judges. But we need not call our heroes to our aid. Be it spoken to the honour of the English, our nation can never want in any age such who are able to dispute the empire of wit with any people in the universe. And though the fury of a civil war, and power, for twenty years together, abandoned to a barbarous race of men, enemies of all good learning, had buried the muses under the ruins of monarchy, yet with the restoration of our happiness, we see revived poesy lifting up its head, and already shaking off the rubbish which lay so heavy on it. We have seen since his majesty's return, many dramatic poems which yield not to those of any foreign nation, and which deserve all laurels but the English. I will set aside flattery and envy. It cannot be denied but we have had some little blemish either in the plot or writing of all those plays which have been made within these seven years: (and perhaps there is no nation in the world so quick to discern them, or so difficult to pardon them, as ours:) yet if we can persuade ourselves to use the candour of that poet, who (though the most severe of critics) has left us this caution by which to moderate our censures;

—Ubi plura nitent in carmine non ego paucis offendar maculis.

If in consideration of their many and great beauties, we can wink at some slight, and little imperfections; if we, I say, can be thus equal to ourselves, I ask no favour from the French. And if I do not venture upon any particular judgement of our late plays, 'tis out of the consideration which an ancient writer gives me; *Vivorum, ut magna admiratio, ita censura difficilis*: betwixt the extremes of admiration and malice, 'tis hard to judge uprightly of the living. Only I think it may be permitted me to say, that as it is no lessening to us to yield to some plays, and those not many of our own nation in the last age, so can it be no addition to pronounce of our present poets that they have far surpassed all the Ancients, and the modern writers of other countries.

This was the substance of what was then spoke on that occasion; and Lisideius, I think was going to reply, when he was prevented thus by Crites. I am confident, said he, that the most material things that can be said, have been already urged on either side; if they have not,

---

Ubi plura . . .: Horace, *Ars Poetica* ll. 351–2 ('When a poem has many beauties, I shall not carp at its few faults').
equal: impartial.
Vivorum, ut magna . . .: Velleius Paterculus, *Historia Romana*, ii. 36.

I must beg of Lisideius that he will defer his answer till another time, for I confess I have a joint quarrel to you both, because you have concluded, without any reason given for it, that rhyme is proper for the stage. I will not dispute how ancient it hath been among us to write this way; perhaps our ancestors knew no better till Shakespeare's time. I will grant it was not altogether left by him, and that Fletcher and Ben Jonson used it frequently in their pastorals, and sometimes in other plays. Farther, I will not argue whether we received it originally from our own countrymen, or from the French; for that is an inquiry of as little benefit, as theirs who in the midst of the late plague[n] were not so solicitous to provide against it, as to know whether we had it from the malignity of our own air, or by transportation from Holland. I have therefore only to affirm, that it is not allowable in serious plays; for comedies I find you already concluding with me. To prove this, I might satisfy myself to tell you, how much in vain it is for you to strive against the stream of the people's inclination; the greatest part of which are prepossessed so much with those excellent plays of Shakespeare, Fletcher, and Ben Jonson, (which have been written out of rhyme) that except you could bring them such as were written better in it, and those too by persons of equal reputation with them, it will be impossible for you to gain your cause with them, who will still be judges. This it is to which in fine all your reasons must submit. The unanimous consent of an audience is so powerful, that even Julius Caesar (as Macrobius reports of him) when he was perpetual dictator, was not able to balance it on the other side. But when Laberius, a Roman knight, at his request contended in the mime with another poet, he was forced to cry out, *etiam favente me victus es Laberi.* But I will not on this occasion, take the advantage of the greater number, but only urge such reasons against rhyme,[n] as I find in the writings of those who have argued for the other way. First then I am of opinion, that rhyme is unnatural in a play, because dialogue there is presented as the effect of sudden thought. For a play is the imitation of nature; and since no man, without premeditation speaks in rhyme, neither ought he to do it on the stage. This hinders not but the fancy may be there elevated to an higher pitch of thought than it is in ordinary discourse: for there is a probability that men of excellent and quick parts may speak noble things *ex tempore*: but those thoughts are never fettered with the numbers or sound of verse without study, and therefore it cannot be but unnatural to present the most free way of speaking, in

---

etiam favente . . .: *Saturnalia.* ii. 7 ('You have been beaten, Laberius, although I favoured you').

that which is the most constrained. For this reason, says Aristotle,
'tis best to write tragedy in that kind of verse which is the least such,
or which is nearest prose: and this amongst the Ancients was the
iambic, and with us is blank verse, or the measure of verse, kept
exactly without rhyme. These numbers therefore are fittest for a play;
the others for a paper of verses, or a poem. Blank verse being as much
below them, as rhyme is improper for the drama. And if it be
objected that neither are blank verses made *ex tempore*, yet as nearest
nature, they are still to be preferred. But there are two particular
exceptions which many besides myself have had to verse, by which it
will appear yet more plainly, how improper it is in plays. And the
first of them is grounded on that very reason for which some have
commended rhyme. They say the quickness of repartees in argumentative scenes receives an ornament from verse. Now what is more
unreasonable than to imagine that a man should not only light upon
the wit, but the rhyme too upon the sudden? This nicking of him
who spoke before both in sound and measure, is so great an happiness, that you must at least suppose the persons of your play to be
born poets, *Arcades omnes et cantare pares et respondere parati*, they
must have arrived to the degree of *quicquid conabar dicere*: to make
verses almost whether they will or no: if they are anything below
this, it will look rather like the design of two, than the answer of one:
it will appear that your actors hold intelligence together, that they
perform their tricks like fortune-tellers, by confederacy. The hand of
art will be too visible in it against that maxim of all professions; *Ars
est celare artem*, that it is the greatest perfection of art to keep itself
undiscovered. Nor will it serve you to object, that however you
manage it, 'tis still known to be a play; and consequently the dialogue
of two persons understood to be the labour of one poet. For a play is
still an imitation of nature; we know we are to be deceived, and we
desire to be so; but no man ever was deceived but with a probability
of truth, for who will suffer a gross lie to be fastened on him? Thus
we sufficiently understand that the scenes which represent cities and
countries to us, are not really such, but only painted on boards and
canvas. But shall that excuse the ill painture or designment of them?

Aristotle: *Poetics*, iv.

nicking: matching.

Arcades omnes . . .: Virgil, *Eclogues*, vii. 4–5 ('Arcades ambo . . .': 'all Ar-
cadians, equally ready to sing and to make reply').

quicquid . . .: Boulton points out that Sidney's *Apology* has the same quotation,
attributed to Ovid, the remembered line perhaps being *Tristia*, IV. x. 26 ('Et
quod tentabam dicere versus erat': 'And whatever I tried to say was poetry').

Ars est . . .: (anonymous).

Nay rather ought they not to be laboured with so much the more diligence and exactness to help the imagination? since the mind of man does naturally tend to truth: and therefore the nearer anything comes to the imitation of it, the more it pleases.

Thus, you see, your rhyme is incapable of expressing the greatest thoughts naturally, and the lowest it cannot with any grace: for what is more unbefitting the majesty of verse, than to call a servant, or bid a door be shut in rhyme? And yet you are often forced on this miserable necessity. But verse, you say, circumscribes a quick and luxuriant fancy, which would extend itself too far on every subject, did not the labour which is required to well turned and polished rhyme, set bounds to it. Yet this argument, if granted, would only prove that we may write better in verse, but not more naturally. Neither is it able to evince that; for he who wants judgement to confine his fancy in blank verse, may want it as much in rhyme; and he who has it will avoid errors in both kinds. Latin verse was as great a confinement to the imagination of those poets, as rhyme to ours: and yet you find Ovid saying too much on every subject. *Nescivit* (says Seneca) *quod bene cessit relinquere*: of which he gives you one famous instance in his description of the deluge.

> Omnia pontus erant, deerant quoque litora ponto.

Now all was sea, nor had that sea a shore. Thus Ovid's fancy was not limited by verse, and Virgil needed not verse to have bounded his.

In our own language we see Ben Jonson confining himself to what ought to be said, even in the liberty of blank verse; and yet Corneille, the most judicious of the French poets, is still varying the same sense an hundred ways, and dwelling eternally on the same subject, though confined by rhyme. Some other exceptions I have to verse, but since these I have named are for the most part already public; I conceive it reasonable they should first be answered.

It concerns me less than any, said Neander, (seeing he had ended) to reply to this discourse; because when I should have proved that verse may be natural in plays, yet I should always be ready to confess, that those which I have written in this kind come short of that perfection which is required. Yet since you are pleased I should undertake this province, I will do it, though with all imaginable respect and deference, both to that person from whom you have borrowed your

---

Seneca: the rhetorician Marcus Seneca says of Ovid 'nescit quod bene . . .' ('he does not know when to leave well alone . . .': *Controversiae*, ix. 5) but it was the philosopher Lucius Seneca who (*Quaestiones Naturales*, iii. 27) quoted the line 'Omnia pontus erant . . .' from *Metamorphoses*, i. 292.

strongest arguments, and to whose judgement when I have said all, I finally submit. But before I proceed to answer your objections, I must first remember you, that I exclude all comedy from my defence; and next that I deny not but blank verse may be also used, and content myself only to assert, that in serious plays where the subject and characters are great, and the plot unmixed with mirth, which might allay or divert these concernments which are produced, rhyme is there as natural and more effectual than blank verse.

And now having laid down this as a foundation, to begin with Crites, I must crave leave to tell him, that some of his arguments against rhyme reach no farther than from the faults or defects of ill rhyme, to conclude against the use of it in general. May not I conclude against blank verse by the same reason? If the words of some poets who write in it are either ill chosen, or ill placed (which makes not only rhyme, but all kind of verse in any language unnatural) shall I, for their vicious affectation condemn those excellent lines of Fletcher, which are written in that kind? Is there anything in rhyme more constrained than this line in blank verse? *I Heaven invoke, and strong resistance make*; where you see both the clauses are placed unnaturally; that is, contrary to the common way of speaking, and that without the excuse of a rhyme to cause it: yet you would think me very ridiculous if I should accuse the stubbornness of blank verse for this, and not rather the stiffness of the poet. Therefore, Crites, you must either prove that words, though well chosen, and duly placed, yet render not rhyme natural in itself; or that however natural and easy the rhyme may be, yet it is not proper for a play. If you insist on the former part, I would ask you what other conditions are required to make rhyme natural in itself, besides an election of apt words, and a right disposition of them? For the due choice of your words expresses your sense naturally, and the due placing them adapts the rhyme to it. If you object that one verse may be made for the sake of another, though both the words and rhyme be apt, I answer it cannot possibly so fall out, for either there is a dependence of sense betwixt the first line and the second, or there is none: if there be that connection, then in the natural position of the words, the latter line must of necessity flow from the former: if there be no dependence, yet still the due ordering of words makes the last line as natural in itself as the other, so that the necessity of a rhyme never forces any but bad or lazy writers to say what they would not otherwise. 'Tis true, there is both care and art required to write in verse. A good poet never establishes the first line, till he has sought out such a rhyme as may

I Heaven invoke, . . .: source unknown.

fit the sense, already prepared to heighten the second. Many times the close of the sense falls into the middle of the next verse, or farther off, and he may often prevail himself of the same advantages in English which Virgil had in Latin; he may break off in the hemistich, and begin another line: indeed, the not observing these two last things, makes plays which are writ in verse, so tedious: for though, most commonly, the sense is to be confined to the couplet, yet nothing that does *perpetuo tenore fluere*, run in the same channel, can please always. 'Tis like the murmuring of a stream, which not varying in the fall, causes at first attention, at last drowsiness. Variety of cadences is the best rule, the greatest help to the actors, and refreshment to the audience.

If then verse may be made natural in itself, how becomes it unnatural in a play? You say the stage is the representation of nature, and no man in ordinary conversation speaks in rhyme. But you foresaw when you said this, that it might be answered; neither does any man speak in blank verse, or in measure without rhyme. Therefore you concluded, that which is nearest nature is still to be preferred. But you took no notice that rhyme might be made as natural as blank verse, by the well placing of the words, etc. all the difference between them when they are both correct, is the sound in one, which the other wants; and if so, the sweetness of it, and all the advantage resulting from it, which are handled in the preface to *The Rival Ladies*, will yet stand good. As for that place of Aristotle, where he says plays should be writ in that kind of verse which is nearest prose; it makes little for you, blank verse being properly but measured prose. Now measure alone in any modern language, does not constitute verse; those of the Ancients in Greek and Latin, consisted in quantity of words, and a determinate number of feet. But when, by the inundation of the Goths and Vandals into Italy new languages were introduced, and barbarously mingled with the Latin (of which the Italian, Spanish, French, and ours, (made out of them and the Teutonic) are dialects:) a new way of poesy was practised; new, I say in those countries, for in all probability it was that of the conquerors in their own nations: at least we are able to prove, that the eastern people have used it from all antiquity, *vide* Daniel's *Defence of Rhyme*. This new way consisted in measure or number of feet and rhyme. The sweetness of rhyme, and observation of accent, supplying the place of quantity in words, which could neither exactly be observed by those barbarians who knew not the rules of it, neither was it suitable to their tongues

perpetuo . . .: Cicero, *De Oratore*, vi. 21 ('uno tenore . . . fluit').
Defence of Rhyme: published in 1603.

as it had been to the Greek and Latin. No man is tied in modern poesy to observe any farther rule in the feet of his verse, but that they be disyllables; whether spondee, trochee, or iambic, it matters not; only he is obliged to rhyme. Neither do the Spanish, French, Italian or Germans acknowledge at all, or very rarely, any such kind of poesy as blank verse amongst them. Therefore at most 'tis but a poetic prose, a *sermo pedestris*, and as such most fit for comedies, where I acknowledge rhyme to be improper. Farther, as to that quotation of Aristotle, our couplet verses may be rendered as near prose as blank verse itself, by using those advantages I lately named, as breaks in an hemistich, or running the sense into another line, thereby making art and order appear as loose and free as nature; or not tying ourselves to couplets strictly, we may use the benefit of the Pindaric way practised in *The Siege of Rhodes*; where the numbers vary and the rhyme is disposed carelessly, and far from often chiming. Neither is that other advantage of the Ancients to be despised, of changing the kind of verse when they please with the change of the scene, or some new entrance: for they confine not themselves always to iambics, but extend their liberty to all lyric numbers, and sometimes even to hexameter. But I need not go so far to prove that rhyme, as it succeeds to all other offices of Greek and Latin verse, so especially to this of plays, since the custom of nations at this day confirms it, the French, Italian and Spanish tragedies are generally writ in it, and sure the universal consent of the most civilized parts of the world, ought in this, as it doth in other customs, to include the rest.

But perhaps you may tell me I have proposed such a way to make rhyme natural, and consequently proper to plays, as is unpracticable, and that I shall scarce find six or eight lines together in any play, where the words are so placed and chosen as is required to make it natural. I answer, no poet need constrain himself at all times to it. It is enough he makes it his general rule; for I deny not but sometimes there may be a greatness in placing the words otherwise; and sometimes they may sound better, sometimes also the variety itself is excuse enough. But if, for the most part, the words be placed as they are in the negligence of prose, it is sufficient to denominate the way practicable; for we esteem that to be such, which in the trial oftener succeeds than misses. And thus far you may find the practice made

---

Italian ... blank verse: Ker points out that Dryden is forgetting some Italian tragedies and Tasso's *Amintas*.

Siege of Rhodes: see 'To the Right Honourable Roger, Earl of Orrery', p. 5 above, and footnote.

good in many plays; where you do not, remember still, that if you cannot find six natural rhymes together, it will be as hard for you to produce as many lines in blank verse, even among the greatest of our poets, against which I cannot make some reasonable exception.

And this, Sir, calls to my remembrance the beginning of your discourse, where you told us we should never find the audience favourable to this kind of writing, till we could produce as good plays in rhyme, as Ben Jonson, Fletcher, and Shakespeare, had writ out of it. But it is to raise envy to the living, to compare them with the dead. They are honoured, and almost adored by us, as they deserve; neither do I know any so presumptuous of themselves as to contend with them. Yet give me leave to say thus much, without injury to their ashes, that not only we shall never equal them, but they could never equal themselves, were they to rise and write again. We acknowledge them our fathers in wit, but they have ruined their estates themselves before they came to their children's hands. There is scarce an humour, a character, or any kind of plot, which they have not used. All comes sullied or wasted to us: and were they to entertain this age, they could not now make so plenteous treatments out of such decayed fortunes. This therefore will be a good argument to us either not to write at all, or to attempt some other way. There is no bays to be expected in their walks; *Tentanda via est qua me quoque possum tollere humo.*

This way of writing in verse, they have only left free to us; our age is arrived to a perfection in it, which they never knew; and which (if we may guess by what of theirs we have seen in verse as *The Faithful Shepherdess*, and *Sad Shepherd*): 'tis probable they never could have reached. For the genius of every age is different; and though ours excel in this, I deny not but that to imitate nature in that perfection which they did in prose, is a greater commendation than to write in verse exactly. As for what you have added, that the people are not generally inclined to like this way; if it were true, it would be no wonder, that betwixt the shaking off an old habit, and the introducing of a new, there should be difficulty. Do we not see them stick to Hopkins and Sternhold's Psalms, and forsake those of David, I mean Sandys's translation of them? If by the people you understand

Tentanda via . . .: Virgil, *Georgics*, iii. 8–9 ('temptanda . . . possim . . .': 'I must try a way whereby I may also rise from the earth').

Faithful Shepherdess: Fletcher's *Faithful Shepherdess* and Jonson's unfinished *Sad Shepherd* are both partly in rhyme.

Sandys: George Sandys's verse *Paraphrase upon the Psalms* (1636) never became as popular as the inferior versification of Thomas Sternhold and John Hopkins (pub. 1549).

the multitude, the οἱ πολλοί. 'Tis no matter what they think; they are sometimes in the right, sometimes in the wrong; their judgement is a mere lottery. *Est ubi plebs recte putat, est ubi peccat.* Horace says it of the vulgar, judging poesy. But if you mean the mixed audience of the populace, and the noblesse, I dare confidently affirm that a great part of the latter sort, are already favourable to verse; and that no serious plays written since the king's return have been more kindly received by them, than *The Siege of Rhodes*, the *Mustapha*, the *Indian Queen*, and *Indian Emperor*.

But I come now to the inference of your first argument. You said that the dialogue of plays is presented as the effect of sudden thought, but no man speaks suddenly, or *ex tempore* in rhyme: and you inferred from thence, that rhyme, which you acknowledge to be proper to epic poesy cannot equally be proper to dramatic, unless we could suppose all men born so much more than poets, that verses should be made in them, not by them.

It has been formerly urged by you, and confessed by me, that since no man spoke any kind of verse *ex tempore*, that which was nearest nature was to be preferred. I answer you therefore, by distinguishing betwixt what is nearest to the nature of comedy, which is the imitation of common persons and ordinary speaking, and what is nearest the nature of a serious play: this last is indeed the representation of nature, but 'tis nature wrought up to an higher pitch. The plot, the characters, the wit, the passions, the descriptions, are all exalted above the level of common converse, as high as the imagination of the poet can carry them, with proportion to verisimility. Tragedy we know is wont to image to us the minds and fortunes of noble persons, and to portray these exactly; heroic rhyme is nearest nature, as being the noblest kind of modern verse.

> Indignatur enim privatis, et prope socco,
> dignis carminibus, narrari caena Thyestae. (Says Horace.)

And in another place,

> Effutire leves indigna tragoedia versus.

Blank verse is acknowledged to be too low for a poem; nay more,

---

Est ubi plebs . . .: Horace, *Epistles*, II. i. 63 ('Interdum vulgus rectum videt, est ubi peccat'.)

Mustapha: *The Tragedy of Mustapha* by Roger Boyle, Earl of Orrery, was produced in 1665.

Indignatur . . .: *Ars Poetica*, ll. 90–1, 231 (for 'enim' read 'item', and for 'leves' read 'levis': 'For the feast of Thyestes scorns to be told in everyday language which is almost fit for comedy'; 'Tragedy scorns to babble silly verses').

for a paper of verses; but if too low for an ordinary sonnet, how much more for tragedy, which is by Aristotle in the dispute betwixt the epic poesy and the dramatic, for many reasons he there alleges, ranked above it?

But setting this defence aside, your argument is almost as strong against the use of rhyme in poems as in plays; for the epic way is everywhere interlaced with dialogue, or discoursive scenes; and therefore you must either grant rhyme to be improper there, which is contrary to your assertion, or admit it into plays by the same title which you have given it to poems. For though tragedy be justly preferred above the other, yet there is a great affinity between them, as may easily be discovered in that definition of a play which Lisideius gave us. The genus of them is the same, a just and lively image of human nature, in its actions, passions, and traverses of fortune. So is the end, namely for the delight and benefit of mankind. The characters and persons are still the same, *viz.* the greatest of both sorts, only the manner of acquainting us with those actions, passions and fortunes is different. Tragedy performs it *viva voce*, or by action, in dialogue, wherein it excels the epic poem which does it chiefly by narration, and therefore is not so lively an image of human nature. However, the agreement betwixt them is such, that if rhyme be proper for one, it must be for the other. Verse 'tis true is not the effect of sudden thought; but this hinders not that sudden thought may be represented in verse, since those thoughts are such as must be higher than nature can raise them without premeditation, especially to a continuance of them even out of verse, and consequently you cannot imagine them to have been sudden either in the poet, or the actors. A play, as I have said to be like nature, is to be set above it; as statues which are placed on high are made greater than the life, that they may descend to the sight in their just proportion.

Perhaps I have insisted too long on this objection; but the clearing of it will make my stay shorter on the rest. You tell us Crites, that rhyme appears most unnatural in repartees, or short replies: when he who answers (it being presumed he knew not what the other would say, yet) makes up that part of the verse which was left incomplete, and supplies both the sound and measure of it. This you say looks rather like the confederacy of two, than the answer of one.

This, I confess, is an objection which is in every man's mouth who loves not rhyme: but suppose, I beseech you, the repartee were made only in blank verse, might not part of the same argument be turned

---

sonnet: here simply a short poem, as in Donne's 'Songs and Sonnets'.
Aristotle: see *Poetics*, xxvi.

against you? for the measure is as often supplied there as it is in rhyme. The latter half of the hemistich as commonly made up, or a second line subjoined as a reply to the former; which any one leaf in Jonson's plays will sufficiently clear to you. You will often find in the Greek tragedians, and in Seneca, that when a scene grows up into the warmth of repartees (which is the close fighting of it) the latter part of the trimeter is supplied by him who answers; and yet it was never observed as a fault in them by any of the ancient or modern critics. The case is the same in our verse as it was in theirs, rhyme to us being in lieu of quantity to them. But if no latitude is to be allowed a poet, you take from him not only his license of *quidlibet audendi*, but you tie him up in a straighter compass than you would a philosopher. This is indeed *Musas colere severiores*. You would have him follow nature, but he must follow her on foot: you have dismounted him from his Pegasus. But you tell us this supplying the last half of a verse, or adjoining a whole second to the former, looks more like the design of two than the answer of one. Suppose we acknowledge it, how comes this confederacy to be more displeasing to you than in a dance which is well contrived? You see there the united design of many persons to make up one figure: after they have separated themselves in many petty divisions, they rejoin one by one into a gross. The confederacy is plain amongst them; for chance could never produce anything so beautiful, and yet there is nothing in it, that shocks your sight. I acknowledge the hand of art appears in repartee, as of necessity it must in all kind of verse. But there is also the quick and poignant brevity of it (which is an high imitation of nature in those sudden gusts of passion) to mingle with it: and this joined with the cadency and sweetness of the rhyme, leaves nothing in the soul of the hearer to desire. 'Tis an art which appears; but it appears only like the shadowings of painture, which being to cause the rounding of it, cannot be absent; but while that is considered they are lost: so while we attend to the other beauties of the matter, the care and labour of the rhyme is carried from us, or at least drowned in its own sweetness, as bees are sometimes buried in their honey. When a poet has found the repartee, the last perfection he can add to it, is to put it into verse. However good the thought may be; however apt the words in which 'tis couched, yet he finds himself at a little unrest while rhyme is wanting: he cannot leave it till that comes naturally, and then is at ease, and sits down contented.

---

quidlibet audendi: Horace, *Ars Poetica*, l. 10 ('daring anything').

Musas colere severiores: Martial *Epigrams* IX. xi. 17: ('to cultivate the stricter muses').

From replies, which are the most elevated thoughts of verse, you pass to those which are most mean and which are common with the lowest of household conversation. In these, you say, the majesty of verse suffers. You instance in the calling of a servant, or commanding a door to be shut in rhyme. This, Crites, is a good observation of yours, but no argument: for it proves no more but that such thoughts should be waived, as often as may be, by the address of the poet. But suppose they are necessary in the places where he uses them, yet there is no need to put them into rhyme. He may place them in the beginning of a verse, and break it off, as unfit, when so debased for any other use: or granting the worst, that they require more room than the hemistich will allow; yet still there is a choice to be made of the best words, and least vulgar (provided they be apt) to express such thoughts. Many have blamed rhyme in general, for this fault, when the poet, with a little care, might have redressed it. But they do it with no more justice, than if English poesy should be made ridiculous for the sake of the Water Poet's rhymes. Our language is noble, full and significant; and I know not why he who is master of it may not clothe ordinary things in it as decently as the Latin; if he use the same diligence in his choice of words.

> Delectus verborum origo est eloquentiae.

It was the saying of Julius Caesar, one so curious in his, that none of them can be changed but for a worse. One would think 'unlock the door' was a thing as vulgar as could be spoken; and yet Seneca could make it sound high and lofty in his Latin.—

> Reserate clusos regii postes laris.
> Set wide the palace gates.

But I turn from this exception, both because it happens not above twice or thrice in any play that those vulgar thoughts are used; and then too (were there no other apology to be made, yet) the necessity of them (which is alike in all kind of writing) may excuse them. For if they are little and mean in rhyme, they are of consequence such in blank verse. Besides that the great eagerness and precipitation with which they are spoken makes us rather mind the substance than the dress; that for which they are spoken, rather than what is spoke. For they are always the effect of some hasty concernment, and something of consequence depends on them.

Water Poet: John Taylor (1578?–1653) was a Thames waterman who wrote reams of amiable doggerel.

Delectus . . .: Cicero, *Brutus*, lxxii. 253 ('verborum delectum originem esse eloquentiae': 'the choice of words is the foundation of eloquence').

Reserate . . .: *Hippolytus*, l. 863 ('Reserate clausas . . .').

Thus, Crites, I have endeavoured to answer your objections. It remains only that I should vindicate an argument for verse, which you have gone about to overthrow. It had formerly been said, that the easiness of blank verse, renders the poet too luxuriant, but that the labour of rhyme bounds and circumscribes an over-fruitful fancy; the sense there being commonly confined to the couplet, and the words so ordered that the rhyme naturally follows them, not they the rhyme. To this you answered, that it was no argument to the question in hand, for the dispute was not which way a man may write best; but which is most proper for the subject on which he writes.

First, give me leave, Sir, to remember you that the argument against which you raised this objection, was only secondary: it was built on this hypothesis, that to write in verse was proper for serious plays, which supposition being granted (as it was briefly made out in that discourse, by showing how verse might be made natural) it asserted, that this way of writing was an help to the poet's judgement, by putting bounds to a wild overflowing fancy. I think therefore it will not be hard for me to make good what it was to prove on that supposition. But you add, that were this let pass, yet he who wants judgement in the liberty of his fancy, may as well show the defect of it when he is confined to verse: for he who has judgement will avoid errors, and he who has it not, will commit them in all kinds of writing.

This argument, as you have taken it from a most acute person, so I confess it carries much weight in it. But by using the word judgement here indefinitely, you seem to have put a fallacy upon us. I grant he who has judgement, that is, so profound, so strong, or rather so infallible a judgement, that he needs no helps to keep it always poised and upright, will commit no faults either in rhyme or out of it. And on the other extreme, he who has a judgement so weak and crazed that no helps can correct or amend it, shall write scurvily out of rhyme, and worse in it. But the first of these judgements is nowhere to be found, and the latter is not fit to write at all. To speak therefore of judgement as it is in the best poets: they who have the greatest proportion of it, want other helps than from it within. As for example, you would be loth to say, that he who is indued with a sound judgement has no need of history, geography, or moral philosophy, to write correctly. Judgement is indeed the master-workman in a play: but he requires many subordinate hands, many tools to his assistance. And verse I affirm to be one of these. 'Tis a rule and line by which he keeps his building compact and even, which

acute person: presumably Howard.

otherwise lawless imagination would raise either irregularly or loosely. At least if the poet commits errors with this help, he would make greater and more without it: 'tis (in short) a slow and painful, but the surest kind of working. Ovid whom you accuse for luxuriancy in verse, had perhaps been farther guilty of it had he writ in prose. And for your instance of Ben Jonson, who you say, writ exactly without the help of rhyme; you are to remember 'tis only an aid to a luxuriant fancy, which his was not. As he did not want imagination, so none ever said he had much to spare. Neither was verse then refined so much to be an help to that age as it is to ours. Thus then the second thoughts being usually the best, as receiving the maturest digestion from judgement, and the last and most mature product of those thoughts being artful and laboured verse, it may well be inferred, that verse is a great help to a luxuriant fancy; and this is what that argument which you opposed was to evince.

Neander was pursuing this discourse so eagerly, that Eugenius had called to him twice or thrice ere he took notice that the barge stood still, and that they were at the foot of Somerset-Stairs, where they had appointed it to land. The company were all sorry to separate so soon, though a great part of the evening was already spent; and stood a while looking back on the water, upon which the moonbeams played, and made it appear like floating quicksilver. At last they went up through a crowd of French people who were merrily dancing in the open air, and nothing concerned for the noise of guns which had alarmed the Town that afternoon. Walking thence together to the Piazze they parted there; Eugenius and Lisideius to some pleasant appointment they had made, and Crites and Neander to their several lodgings.

Somerset-Stairs: this landing-place was destroyed when the original Somerset
   House was demolished in 1775.
Piazze: a fashionable part of the city.

A DEFENCE OF AN ESSAY
OF DRAMATIC POESY[n]   *1668*

BEING AN ANSWER TO THE PREFACE OF
THE GREAT FAVOURITE, OR THE DUKE
OF LERMA

THE former edition of *The Indian Emperor* being full of faults which
had escaped the printer, I have been willing to overlook this second
with more care: and though I could not allow myself so much time
as was necessary, yet by that little I have done, the press is freed from
some gross errors which it had to answer for before. As for the more
material faults of writing, which are properly mine, though I see
many of them, I want leisure to amend them. 'Tis enough for those
who make one poem the business of their lives, to leave that correct;
yet, excepting Virgil, I never met with any which was so in any
language.

But while I was thus employed about this impression, there came
to my hands a new printed play, called, *The Great Favourite, or the
Duke of Lerma*, the author of which, a noble and most ingenious
person, has done me the favour to make some observations and
animadversions upon my *Dramatic Essay*. I must confess he might
have better consulted his reputation, than by matching himself with
so weak an adversary. But if his honour be diminished in the choice
of his antagonist, it is sufficiently recompensed in the election of his
cause: which being the weaker, in all appearance, as combating the
received opinions of the best ancient and modern authors, will add to
his glory, if he overcome; and to the opinion of his generosity, if he
be vanquished, since he engages at so great odds; and, so like a
cavalier, undertakes the protection of the weaker party. I have only
to fear on my own behalf, that so good a cause as mine may not
suffer by my ill management, or weak defence; yet I cannot in honour
but take the glove when 'tis offered me, though I am only a champion
by succession; and no more able to defend the right of Aristotle
and Horace, than an infant Dymoke to maintain the title of a
king.

For my own concernment in the controversy, it is so small, that I
can easily be contented to be driven from a few notions of dramatic
poesy, especially by one, who has the reputation of understanding all

---

Dymoke: the Dymoke family of Scrivelsby, Lincs., have held the hereditary title
of King's Champion since at least the reign of Richard II.
understanding all things: Dryden's sarcasm: Howard had a know-all's reputation.
4+S.C.

things: and I might justly make that excuse for my yielding to him, which the philosopher made to the emperor; why should I offer to contend with him who is master of more than twenty legions of arts and sciences? But I am forced to fight, and therefore it will be no shame to be overcome.

Yet I am so much his servant as not to meddle with anything which does not concern me in his preface: therefore I leave the good sense and other excellencies of the first twenty lines to be considered by the critics. As for the play of *The Duke of Lerma*, having so much altered and beautified it, as he has done, it can justly belong to none but him. Indeed they must be extreme ignorant as well as envious, who would rob him of that honour; for you see him putting in his claim to it, even in the first two lines.

> Repulse upon repulse like waves thrown back,
> That slide to hang upon obdurate rocks.

After this let detraction do its worst; for if this be not his, it deserves to be. For my part I declare for distributive justice, and from this and what follows he certainly deserves those advantages, which he acknowledges to have received from the opinion of sober men.

In the next place I must beg leave to observe his great address in courting the reader to his party. For intending to assault all poets, both ancient and modern, he discovers not his whole design at once, but seems only to aim at me, and attacks me on my weakest side, my defence of verse.

To begin with me, he gives me the compellation of The Author of a Dramatic Essay, which is a little discourse in dialogue, for the most part borrowed from the observations of others: therefore, that I may not be wanting to him in civility, I return his compliment by calling him The Author of the Duke of Lerma.

But (that I may pass over his salute) he takes notice of my great pains to prove rhyme as natural in a serious play, and more effectual than blank verse. Thus indeed I did state the question; but he tells me, I pursue that which I call natural in a wrong application: for 'tis not the question whether rhyme or not rhyme be best or most natural for a serious subject, but what is nearest the nature of that it represents.

If I have formerly mistaken the question, I must confess my ignorance so far, as to say I continue still in my mistake. But he ought

---

overcome: the philosopher Favorinus is supposed to have said this to the Emperor Hadrian (Spartianus, *Vita Hadriani*, 15).

to have proved that I mistook it; for 'tis yet but *gratis dictum*; I still shall think I have gained my point if I can prove that rhyme is best or most natural for a serious subject. As for the question as he states it, whether rhyme be nearest the nature of what it represents, I wonder he should think me so ridiculous as to dispute whether prose or verse be nearest to ordinary conversation?

It still remains for him to prove his inference; that since verse is granted to be more remote than prose from ordinary conversation, therefore no serious plays ought to be writ in verse: and when he clearly makes that good, I will acknowledge his victory as absolute as he can desire it.

The question now is which of us two has mistaken it, and if it appear I have not, the world will suspect what gentleman that was, who was allowed to speak twice in Parliament, because he had not yet spoken to the question; and perhaps conclude it to be the same, who, as 'tis reported, maintained a contradiction *in terminis*, in the face of three hundred persons.

But to return to verse, whether it be natural or not in plays, is a problem which is not demonstrable of either side: 'tis enough for me that he acknowledges he had rather read good verse than prose: for if all the enemies of verse will confess as much, I shall not need to prove that it is natural. I am satisfied if it cause delight: for delight is the chief, if not the only end of poesy; instruction can be admitted but in the second place, for poesy only instructs as it delights. 'Tis true that to imitate well is a poet's work; but to affect the soul, and excite the passions, and above all to move admiration (which is the delight of serious plays) a bare imitation will not serve. The converse therefore which a poet is to imitate, must be heightened with all the arts and ornaments of poesy; and must be such, as, strictly considered, could never be supposed spoken by any without premeditation.

As for what he urges, that a play will still be supposed to be a composition of several persons speaking *ex tempore*; and that good verses are the hardest things which can be imagined to be so spoken, I must crave leave to dissent from his opinion, as to the former part of it; for, if I am not deceived, a play is supposed to be the work of the poet, imitating, or representing the conversation of several persons, and this I think to be as clear, as he thinks the contrary.

But I will be bolder, and do not doubt to make it good, though a paradox, that one great reason why prose is not to be used in serious plays, is because it is too near the nature of converse: there may be too great a likeness, as the most skilful painters affirm, that there may

poet's work: cf. Aristotle, *Poetics* i. 2; iv. 1–5.

be too near a resemblance in a picture; to take every lineament and
feature is not to make an excellent piece, but to take so much only as
will make a beautiful resemblance of the whole, and, with an ingenious flattery of nature, to heighten the beauties of some parts, and
hide the deformities of the rest. For so says Horace,

> Ut pictura poesis erit, etc.—
> Haec amat obscurum, vult haec sub luce videri,
> judicis argutum quae non formidat acumen.
>   —Et quae
> desperat, tractata nitescere posse, relinquit.

In *Bartholomew Fair*, or the lowest kind of comedy, that degree of
heightening is used, which is proper to set off that subject: 'tis true
the author was not there to go out of prose, as he does in his higher
arguments of comedy, *The Fox* and *Alchemist*; yet he does so raise
his matter in that prose, as to render it delightful; which he could
never have performed, had he only said or done those very things that
are daily spoken or practised in the *Fair*: for then the *Fair* itself
would be as full of pleasure to an ingenious person as the play; which
we manifestly see it is not. But he hath made an excellent lazar of it;
the copy is of price, though the original be vile. You see in *Catiline*
and *Sejanus*, where the argument is great, he sometimes ascends to
verse, which shows he thought it not unnatural in serious plays: and
had his genius been as proper for rhyme, as it was for humour; or
had the age in which he lived, attained to as much knowledge in
verse, as ours, 'tis probable he would have adorned those subjects
with that kind of writing.

Thus prose, though the rightful prince, yet is by common consent
deposed, as too weak for the government of serious plays; and he
failing, there now start up two competitors; one the nearer in blood,
which is blank verse; the other more fit for the ends of government,
which is rhyme. Blank verse is, indeed, the nearer prose, but he is
blemished with the weakness of his predecessor. Rhyme (for I will
deal clearly) has somewhat of the usurper in him, but he is brave, and
generous, and his dominion pleasing. For this reason of delight, the
Ancients (whom I will still believe as wise as those who so confidently correct them) wrote all their tragedies in verse, though they
knew it most remote from conversation.

Horace: *Ars Poetica* ll. 361–4, 149–50 ('With a poem as with a painting . . . one
  likes the shade, while another prefers to be seen in the light, not fearing the
  critic's keen judgement'; 'And [the poet] leaves out those things which he
  cannot make attractive by his skill').
lazar: leper.
verse: i.e. rhyme.

But I perceive I am falling into the danger of another rebuke from my opponent: for when I plead that the Ancients used verse, I prove not that they would have admitted rhyme, had it then been written. All I can say is only this, that it seems to have succeeded verse by the general consent of poets in all modern languages, for almost all their serious plays are written in it, which, though it be no demonstration that therefore they ought to be so, yet, at least the practice first, and then the continuation of it, shows that it attained the end, which was to please; and if that cannot be compassed here, I will be the first who shall lay it down. For I confess my chief endeavours are to delight the age in which I live. If the humour of this be for low comedy, small accidents, and raillery, I will force my genius to obey it, though with more reputation I could write in verse. I know I am not so fitted by nature to write comedy. I want that gaiety of humour which is required to it. My conversation is slow and dull, my humour saturnine and reserved. In short, I am none of those who endeavour to break jests in company, or make repartee. So that those who decry my comedies do me no injury, except it be in point of profit: reputation in them is the last thing to which I shall pretend. I beg pardon for entertaining the reader with so ill a subject; but before I quit that argument, which was the cause of this digression, I cannot but take notice how I am corrected for my quotation of Seneca, in my defence of plays in verse. My words are these. Our language is noble, full, and significant, and I know not why he who is master of it, may not clothe ordinary things in it as decently as the Latin, if he use the same diligence in his choice of words. One would think 'unlock a door' was a thing as vulgar as could be spoken; yet Seneca could make it sound high and lofty in his Latin.

Reserate clusos regii postes laris.

But he says of me, that being filled with the precedents of the Ancients who writ their plays in verse, I commend the thing, declaring our language to be full, noble, and significant, and charging all defects upon the ill placing of words, which I prove by quoting Seneca loftily expressing such an ordinary thing as shutting a door.

Here he manifestly mistakes; for I spoke not of the placing, but of the choice of words: for which I quoted that aphorism of Julius Caesar, *delectus verborum est origo eloquentiae*: but *delectus verborum*

---

verse: i.e. blank verse.
Reserate . . .: see 'Of Dramatic Poesy', p. 74 above, and footnote.
delectus verborum . . .: see p. 74 above, and footnote.

is no more Latin for the placing of words, than *reserate* is Latin for shut the door, as he interprets it, which I ignorantly construed unlock or open it.

He supposes I was highly affected with the sound of those words; and I suppose I may more justly imagine it of him, for if he had not been extremely satisfied with the sound, he would have minded the sense a little better.

But these are now to be no faults; for ten days after his book is published, and that his mistakes are grown so famous, that they are come back to him, he sends his *errata* to be printed, and annexed to his play: and desires that instead of shutting you would read opening; which it seems, was the printer's fault. I wonder at his modesty, that he did not rather say it was Seneca's or mine, and that in some authors *reserate* was to shut as well as to open, as the word *barach*, say the learned, is both to bless and curse.

Well, since it was the printer, he was a naughty man to commit the same mistake twice in six lines: I warrant you *delectus verborum* for placing of words was his mistake too, though the author forgot to tell him of it: if it were my book I assure you I should. For those rascals ought to be the proxies of every gentleman author, and to be chastised for him, when he is not pleased to own an error. Yet since he has given the *errata*, I wish he would have enlarged them only a few sheets more, and then he would have spared me the labour of an answer: for this cursed printer is so given to mistakes, that there is scarce a sentence in the preface, without some false grammar, or hard sense in it: which will all be charged upon the poet, because he is so good natured as to lay but three errors to the printer's account, and to take the rest upon himself, who is better able to support them. But he needs not apprehend that I should strictly examine those little faults, except I am called upon to do it. I shall return therefore to that quotation of Seneca, and answer not to what he writes, but to what he means. I never intended it as an argument, but only as an illustration of what I had said before concerning the election of words; and all he can charge me with is only this, that if Seneca could make an ordinary thing sound well in Latin by the choice of words, the same with the like care might be performed in English. If it cannot, I have committed an error on the right hand, by commending too much the copiousness and well sounding of our language, which I hope my countrymen will pardon me. At least the words which follow in my *Dramatic Essay* will plead somewhat in my behalf; for I say there,

curse: in Hebrew: Watson quotes Genesis 9:26 (bless), and Numbers 22:12 (curse).

that this objection happens but seldom in a play, and then too either
the meanness of the expression may be avoided, or shut out from the
verse by breaking it in the midst.

But I have said too much in the defence of verse; for after all 'tis a
very indifferent thing to me, whether it obtain or not. I am content
hereafter to be ordered by his rule, that is, to write it sometimes because it pleases me, and so much the rather, because he has declared
that it pleases him. But he has taken his last farewell of the muses,
and he has done it civilly, by honouring them with the name of his
long acquaintances, which is a compliment they have scarce deserved
from him. For my own part I bear a share in the public loss, and how
emulous soever I may be of his fame and reputation, I cannot but
give this testimony of his style, that it is extreme poetical, even in
oratory; his thoughts elevated, sometimes above common apprehension; his notions politic and grave, and tending to the instruction
of princes, and reformation of states; that they are abundantly interlaced with variety of fancies, tropes, and figures, which the critics
have enviously branded with the name of obscurity and false
grammar.

Well, he is now fettered in business of more unpleasant nature: the
muses have lost him, but the commonwealth gains by it. The
corruption of a poet is the generation of a statesman.

He will not venture again into the civil wars of censure, *ubi—nullos
habitura triumphos*: if he had not told us he had left the muses, we
might have half suspected it by that word, *ubi*, which does not any
way belong to them in that place; the rest of the verse is indeed
Lucan's, but that *ubi* I will answer for it, is his own. Yet he has
another reason for this disgust of poesy; for he says immediately
after, that 'the manner of plays which are now in most esteem, is
beyond his power to perform': to perform the manner of a thing I
confess is new English to me. 'However, he condemns not the satisfaction of others, but rather their unnecessary understanding, who,
like Sancho Panza's doctor, prescribe too strictly to our appetites;
for, says he, in the difference of tragedy and comedy, and of farce
itself, there can be no determination but by the taste, nor in the
manner of their composure.'

We shall see him now as great a critic as he was a poet, and the
reason why he excelled so much in poetry will be evident, for it will
appear to have proceeded from the exactness of his judgement. In

---

statesman: Howard the statesman was, by 1668, merely M.P. for Stockbridge and
  Secretary to the Commissioners of the Treasury.
ubi—: Lucan, *Pharsalia*, i. 12 ('Where no triumphs will be gained': '*ubi*', as
  Dryden says, is Howard's addition).

the difference of tragedy, comedy, and farce itself, there can be no determination but by the taste. I will not quarrel with the obscurity of his phrase, though I justly might; but beg his pardon if I do not rightly understand him: if he means that there is no essential difference betwixt comedy, tragedy, and farce, but what is only made by the people's taste, which distinguishes one of them from the other, that is so manifest an error that I need not lose time to contradict it. Were there neither judge, taste, nor opinion in the world, yet they would differ in their natures; for the action, character, and language of tragedy, would still be great and high; that of comedy lower and more familiar; admiration would be the delight of one, and satire of the other.

I have but briefly touched upon these things, because, whatever his words are, I can scarce imagine, that he who is always concerned for the true honour of reason, and would have no spurious issue fathered upon her, should mean anything so absurd as to affirm, that there is no difference betwixt comedy and tragedy but what is made by the taste only, unless he would have us understand the comedies of my Lord L. where the first act should be pottages, the second fricasses, etc. and the fifth, a *chère entière* of women.

I rather guess he means, that betwixt one comedy or tragedy and another, there is no other difference but what is made by the liking or disliking of the audience. This is indeed a less error than the former, but yet it is a great one. The liking or disliking of the people gives the play the denomination of good or bad, but does not really make, or constitute it such. To please the people ought to be the poet's aim, because plays are made for their delight; but it does not follow that they are always pleased with good plays, or that the plays which please them are always good. The humour of the people is now for comedy, therefore in hope to please them, I write comedies rather than serious plays: and so far their taste prescribes to me. But it does not follow from that reason, that comedy is to be preferred before tragedy in its own nature, for that which is so in its own nature cannot be otherwise; as a man cannot but be a rational creature: but the opinion of the people may alter, and in another age, or perhaps in this, serious plays may be set up above comedies.

This I think a sufficient answer; if it be not, he has provided me of an excuse; it seems in his wisdom, he foresaw my weakness, and has found out this expedient for me. 'That it is not necessary for poets to

---

my Lord L.: it is, following Malone, generally accepted that Dryden is referring
   to the dissolute John Maitland (1616–82), 2nd Earl of Lauderdale.
chère entière: 'whole meal'.

study strict reason, since they are so used to a greater latitude than is allowed by that severe inquisition, that they must infringe their own jurisdiction to profess themselves obliged to argue well.'

I am obliged to him for discovering to me this back door; but I am not yet resolved on my retreat. For I am of opinion that they cannot be good poets who are not accustomed to argue well. False reasonings and colours of speech, are the certain marks of one who does not understand the stage. For moral truth is the mistress of the poet as much as of the philosopher. Poesy must resemble natural truth, but it must *be* ethical. Indeed the poet dresses truth, and adorns nature, but does not alter them:

> Ficta voluptatis causa sint proxima veris.

Therefore that is not the best poesy which resembles notions of things that are not, to things that are: though the fancy may be great and the words flowing, yet the soul is but half satisfied when there is not truth in the foundation. This is that which makes Virgil be preferred before the rest of poets. In variety of fancy and sweetness of expression, you see Ovid far above him, for Virgil rejected many of those things which Ovid wrote. A great wit's great work is to refuse, as my worthy friend Sir John Berkenhead has ingeniously expressed it. You rarely meet with anything in Virgil but truth, which therefore leaves the strongest impression of pleasure in the soul. This I thought myself obliged to say in behalf of poesy: and to declare, though it be against myself, that when poets do not argue well, the defect is in the workmen, not in the art.

And now I come to the boldest part of his discourse, wherein he attacks not me, but all the Ancients and Moderns, and undermines, as he thinks, the very foundations on which dramatic poesy is built. I could wish he would have declined that envy which must of necessity follow such an undertaking, and contented himself with triumphing over me in my opinions of verse, which I will never hereafter dispute with him; but he must pardon me if I have that veneration for Aristotle, Horace, Ben Jonson, and Corneille, that I dare not serve him in such a cause, and against such heroes, but rather fight under their protection, as Homer reports of little Teucer, who shot the Trojans from under the large buckler of Ajax Telamon.

Ficta voluptatis . . .: Horace, *Ars Poetica*, l. 338 ('Fiction made to delight should be close to truth').

Berkenhead: (1616–79) a Fellow of All Souls; editor of a Royalist journal in the Civil War; member of the Royal Society. Dryden is quoting from Berkenhead's poem 'In Memory of Mr. Cartwright', published in Cartwright's *Comedies, Tragi-Comedies with other Poems* (1651).

Ajax Telamon: *Iliad*, viii. 267.

4*

Στῆ δ' ἄρ' ὑπ' Αἴαντος σάκεϊ Τελαμωνιάδαο, etc.
He stood beneath his brother's ample shield;
And, covered there, shot death through all the field.

The words of my noble adversary are these: 'But if we examine the general rules laid down for plays by strict reason, we shall find the errors equally gross; for the great foundation which is laid to build upon, is nothing as it is generally stated, as will appear upon the examination of the particulars.'

These particulars in due time shall be examined. In the mean while let us consider what this great foundation is, which he says is nothing, as it is generally stated. I never heard of any other foundation of dramatic poesy than the imitation of nature; neither was there ever pretended any other by the Ancients or Moderns, or me, who endeavour to follow them in that rule. This I have plainly said in my definition of a play; that it is a just and lively image of human nature, etc. Thus the foundation, as it is generally stated, will stand sure, if this definition of a play be true; if it be not, he ought to have made his exception against it, by proving that a play is not an imitation of nature, but somewhat else which he is pleased to think it.

But 'tis very plain, that he has mistaken the foundation for that which is built upon it, though not immediately: for the direct and immediate consequence is this; if nature be to be imitated, then there is a rule for imitating nature rightly, otherwise there may be an end, and no means conducing to it. Hitherto I have proceeded by demonstration; but as our divines, when they have proved a deity, because there is order, and have inferred that this deity ought to be worshipped, differ afterwards in the manner of the worship; so having laid down, that nature is to be imitated, and that proposition proving the next, that then there are means which conduce to the imitating of nature, I dare proceed no farther positively: but have only laid down some opinions of the Ancients and Moderns, and of my own, as means which they used, and which I thought probable for the attaining of that end. Those means are the same which my antagonist calls the foundations, how properly the world may judge; and to prove that this is his meaning, he clears it immediately to you, by enumerating those rules or propositions against which he makes his particular exceptions; as namely, those of time and place, in these words: 'First we are told the plot should not be so ridiculously contrived, as to crowd two several countries into one stage; secondly, to cramp the accidents of many years or days into the representation of two hours

definition: the definition put forward by Lisideius in the Essay (above, p. 25) is now presented as Dryden's own.

and an half; and lastly, a conclusion drawn, that the only remaining dispute is, concerning time, whether it should be contained in 12 or 24 hours; and the place to be limited to that spot of ground where the play is supposed to begin: and this is called nearest nature; for that is concluded most natural, which is most probable, and nearest to that which it presents.'

Thus he has only made a small mistake of the means conducing to the end, for the end itself, and of the superstructure for the foundation: but he proceeds: 'To show therefore upon what ill grounds they dictate laws for dramatic poesy,' etc. He is here pleased to charge me with being magisterial, as he has done in many other places of his preface. Therefore in vindication of myself, I must crave leave to say, that my whole discourse was sceptical, according to that way of reasoning which was used by Socrates, Plato, and all the academics of old, which Tully and the best of the Ancients followed, and which is imitated by the modest inquisitions of the Royal Society. That it is so, not only the name will show, which is an essay, but the frame and composition of the work. You see it is a dialogue sustained by persons of several opinions, all of them left doubtful, to be determined by the readers in general; and more particularly deferred to the accurate judgement of my Lord Buckhurst, to whom I made a dedication of my book. These are my words in my epistle, speaking of the persons whom I introduced in my dialogue: ''Tis true they differed in their opinions, as 'tis probable they would; neither do I take upon me to reconcile, but to relate them, leaving your Lordship to decide it in favour of that part which you shall judge most reasonable.' And after that in my advertisement to the reader I said this: 'The drift of the ensuing discourse is chiefly to vindicate the honour of our English writers from the censure of those who unjustly prefer the French before them. This I intimate, lest any should think me so exceeding vain, as to teach others an art which they understand much better than myself.' But this is more than necessary to clear my modesty in that point: and I am very confident that there is scarce any man who has lost so much time, as to read that trifle, but will be my compurgator as to that arrogance whereof I am accused. The truth is, if I had been naturally guilty of so much vanity as to dictate my opinions; yet I do not find that the character of a positive or self-

inquisitions: investigations (Dryden was a member of the Royal Society from 1662 to 1666).
an essay: literally 'an attempt'.
myself: see p. 19 above.
compurgator: 'a witness who clears an accused person of a charge by vindicating his character' (Boulton).

conceited person is of such advantage to any in this age, that I should labour to be publicly admitted of that order.

But I am not now to defend my own cause, when that of all the Ancients and Moderns is in question: for this gentleman who accuses me of arrogance, has taken a course not to be taxed with the other extreme of modesty. Those propositions which are laid down in my discourse as helps to the better imitation of nature, are not mine (as I have said) nor were ever pretended so to be, but derived from the authority of Aristotle and Horace, and from the rules and examples of Ben Jonson and Corneille. These are the men with whom properly he contends, and against whom he will endeavour to make it evident, that there is no such thing as what they all pretend.

His argument against the unities of place and time, is this; 'That 'tis as impossible for one stage to present two rooms or houses truly, as two countries or kingdoms: and as impossible that five hours or twenty-four hours should be two hours, as that a thousand hours or years should be less than what they are, or the greatest part of time to be comprehended in the less: for all of them being impossible, they are none of them nearest the truth or nature of what they present; for impossibilities are all equal and admit of no degree.'

This argument is so scattered into parts, that it can scarce be united into a syllogism; yet, in obedience to him, I will abbreviate and comprehend as much of it as I can in few words, that my answer to it may be more perspicuous. I conceive his meaning to be what follows as to the unity of place: (if I mistake, I beg his pardon, professing it is not out of any design to play the argumentative poet). If one stage cannot properly present two rooms or houses, much less two countries or kingdoms, then there can be no unity of place: but one stage cannot properly perform this; therefore there can be no unity of place.

I plainly deny his minor proposition; the force of which, if I mistake not, depends on this; that the stage being one place, cannot be two. This indeed is as great a secret, as that we are all mortal; but to requite it with another, I must crave leave to tell him, that though the stage cannot be two places, yet it may properly represent them, successively, or at several times. His argument is indeed no more than a mere fallacy, which will evidently appear when we distinguish place, as it relates to plays, into real and imaginary. The real place is that theatre, or piece of ground on which the play is acted. The

---

few words: Howard, himself inexact and diffuse in argument, complains of poets' reluctance 'to abbreviate, or endure to hear their reasons reduced into one strict definition'.

imaginary, that house, town, or country where the action of the drama is supposed to be; or more plainly, where the scene of the play is laid. Let us now apply this to that Herculean argument, which if strictly and duly weighed, is to make it evident, that there is no such thing as what they all pretend. 'Tis impossible, he says, for one stage to present two rooms or houses: I answer, 'tis neither impossible, nor improper, for one real place to represent two or more imaginary places, so it be done successively, which in other words is no more than this; that the imagination of the audience, aided by the words of the poet, and painted scenes, may suppose the stage to be sometimes one place, sometimes another, now a garden, or wood, and immediately a camp, which I appeal to every man's imagination, if it be not true. Neither the Ancients nor Moderns, as much fools as he is pleased to think them, ever asserted that they could make one place two; but they might hope by the good leave of this author, that the change of a scene might lead the imagination to suppose the place altered, so that he cannot fasten those absurdities upon this scene of a play, or imaginary place of action, that it is one place and yet two. And this being so clearly proved, that 'tis past any show of a reasonable denial, it will not be hard to destroy that other part of his argument which depends upon it, namely, that 'tis as impossible for a stage to represent two rooms or houses, as two countries or kingdoms: for his reason is already overthrown, which was, because both were alike impossible. This is manifestly otherwise; for 'tis proved, that a stage may properly represent two rooms or houses; for the imagination being judge of what is represented, will in reason be less shocked with the appearance of two rooms in the same house, or two houses in the same city, than with two distant cities in the same country, or two remote countries in the same universe. Imagination in a man, or reasonable creature, is supposed to participate of reason, and when that governs, as it does in the belief of fiction, reason is not destroyed, but misled, or blinded: that can prescribe to the reason, during the time of the representation, somewhat like a weak belief of what it sees and hears; and reason suffers itself to be so hoodwinked, that it may better enjoy the pleasures of the fiction: but it is never so wholly made a captive, as to be drawn head-long into a persuasion of those things which are most remote from probability: 'tis in that case a free-born subject, not a slave, it will contribute willingly its assent, as far as it sees convenient, but will not be forced. Now there is a greater vicinity in nature, betwixt two rooms than betwixt two houses, betwixt two houses than betwixt two cities, and so of the rest: reason therefore can sooner be led by imagination to step from one room into another, than to walk to two distant houses, and yet rather to go thither, than to fly like a witch through the air, and be hurried from one region to another. Fancy and reason go hand in hand, the first cannot leave the last behind; and though fancy, when it sees the wide gulf, would venture over, as the nimbler; yet it is withheld by reason, which will refuse to take the leap, when the distance over it appears too large. If Ben Jonson himself will remove the scene from Rome into Tuscany in the same act, and from thence return to Rome, in the scene which immediately follows; reason will consider there is no proportionable allowance of time to perform the journey, and therefore will choose to stay at home. So then the less change of place there is, the less time is taken up in transporting the persons of the drama, with analogy to reason; and in that analogy, or resemblance of fiction to truth, consists the excellency of the play.

For what else concerns the unity of place, I have already given my opinion of it in my Essay, that there is a latitude to be allowed to it, as several places in the same town or city, or places adjacent to each other in the same country; which may all be comprehended under the larger denomination of one place; yet with this restriction, that the nearer and fewer those imaginary places are, the greater resemblance they will have to truth: and reason which cannot make them one, will be more easily led to suppose them so.

What has been said of the unity of place, may easily be applied to that of time. I grant it to be impossible, that the greater part of time should be comprehended in the less, that twenty-four hours should be crowded into three: but there is no necessity of that supposition. For as place, so time relating to a play, is either imaginary or real; the real is comprehended in those three hours, more or less, in the space of which the play is represented, the imaginary is that which is supposed to be taken up in the representation, as twenty-four hours more or less. Now no man ever could suppose that twenty-four real hours could be included in the space of three: but where is the absurdity of affirming that the feigned business of twenty-four imagined hours, may not more naturally be represented in the compass of three real hours, than the like feigned business of twenty-four years in the same proportion of real time? For the proportions are always real, and much nearer, by his permission, of twenty-four to three, than of four thousand to it.

I am almost fearful of illustrating anything by similitude, lest he should confute it for an argument; yet I think the comparison of a glass will discover very aptly the fallacy of his argument, both concerning time and place. The strength of his reason depends on this, that the less cannot comprehend the greater. I have already answered, that we need not suppose it does. I say not that the less can comprehend the greater, but only that it may represent it. As in a glass or mirror of half a yard diameter, a whole room and many persons in it may be seen at once: not that it can comprehend that room or those persons, but that it represents them to the sight.

But the author of *The Duke of Lerma* is to be excused for his declaring against the unity of time: for if I be not much mistaken, he is an interested person; the time of that play taking up so many years as the favour of the Duke of Lerma continued; nay, the second and third act including all the time of his prosperity, which was a great part of the reign of Philip the Third: for in the beginning of the second act he was not yet a favourite, and before the end of the third, was in disgrace. I say not this with the least design of limiting the stage too servilely to twenty-four hours, however he be pleased to tax me with dogmatizing in that point. In my dialogue, as I before hinted, several persons maintained their several opinions: one of them, indeed, who supported the cause of the French poesy, said how strict they were in that particular: but he who answered in behalf of our nation, was willing to give more latitude to the rule; and cites the words of Corneille himself, complaining against the severity of it, and observing what beauties it banished from the stage, *pag.* 44 of my Essay. In few words my own opinion is this, (and I willingly submit it to my adversary, when he will please impartially to consider it,) that the imaginary time of every play ought to be contrived into as narrow a compass, as the nature of the plot, the quality of the persons, and variety of accidents will allow. In comedy I would not exceed twenty-four or thirty hours: for the plot, accidents, and persons of comedy are small, and may be naturally turned in a little compass: but in tragedy the design is weighty, and the persons great, therefore there will naturally be required a greater space of time in which to move them. And this, though Ben Jonson has not told us, yet 'tis manifestly his opinion: for you see that to his comedies he allows generally but twenty-four hours; to his two tragedies, *Sejanus* and *Catiline*, a much larger time: though he draws both of them into as narrow a compass as he can: for he shows you only the latter end of Sejanus's favour, and the conspiracy of Catiline already ripe, and just breaking out into action.

But as it is an error on the one side, to make too great a disproportion betwixt the imaginary time of the play, and the real time of its representation; so on the other side, 'tis an oversight to compress the accidents of a play into a narrower compass than that in which they could naturally be produced. Of this last error the French

Essay: see pp. 53–4 above.

are seldom guilty, because the thinness of their plots prevents them from it: but few Englishmen, except Ben Jonson, have ever made a plot with variety of design in it, included in twenty-four hours which was altogether natural. For this reason, I prefer *The Silent Woman* before all other plays, I think justly, as I do its author in judgement, above all other poets. Yet of the two, I think that error the most pardonable, which in too strait a compass crowds together many accidents, since it produces more variety, and consequently more pleasure to the audience: and because the nearness of proportion betwixt the imaginary and real time, does speciously cover the compression of the accidents.

Thus I have endeavoured to answer the meaning of his argument; for as he drew it, I humbly conceive that it was none: as will appear by his proposition, and the proof of it. His proposition was this:

'If strictly and duly weighed, 'tis as impossible for one stage to present two rooms or houses, as two countries or kingdoms, etc.', and his proof this: 'For all being impossible, they are none of them nearest the truth or nature of what they present.'

Here you see, instead of a proof or reason, there is only a *petitio principii*: for in plain words, his sense is this; two things are as impossible as one another, because they are both equally impossible: but he takes those two things to be granted as impossible, which he ought to have proved such before he had proceeded to prove them equally impossible: he should have made out first that it was impossible for one stage to represent two houses, and then have gone forward to prove that it was as equally impossible for a stage to present two houses, as two countries.

After all this, the very absurdity to which he would reduce me, is none at all: for he only drives at this, that if his argument be true, I must then acknowledge that there are degrees in impossibilities, which I easily grant him without dispute: and if I mistake not, Aristotle and the School are of my opinion. For there are some things which are absolutely impossible, and others which are only so *ex parte*; as 'tis absolutely impossible for a thing to be, and not be at the same time; but for a stone to move naturally upward, is only impossible *ex parte materiae*; but it is not impossible for the first mover, to alter the nature of it.

His last assault, like that of a Frenchman, is most feeble: for whereas I have observed, that none have been violent against verse, but such only as have not attempted it, or have succeeded ill in their attempt, he will needs, according to his usual custom, improve my observation to an argument, that he might have the glory to confute it. But I lay my observation at his feet, as I do my pen, which I have often employed willingly in his deserved commendations, and now most unwillingly against his judgement. For his person and parts, I honour them as much as any man living, and have had so many particular obligations to him, that I should be very ungrateful, if I did not acknowledge them to the world. But I gave not the first occasion of this difference in opinions. In my Epistle Dedicatory, before my *Rival Ladies*, I had said somewhat in behalf of verse, which he was pleased to answer in his preface to his *Plays*: that occasioned my reply in my *Essay*, and that reply begot this rejoinder of his in his preface to *The Duke of Lerma*. But as I was the last who took up arms, I will be the first to lay them down. For what I have here written, I submit it wholly to him; and if I do not hereafter answer what may be objected against this paper,[n] I hope the world will not impute it to any other reason, than only the due respect which I have for so noble an opponent.

commendations: in 'To my Honoured Friend, Sir Robert Howard' and the 'Account' of *Annus Mirabilis*.

PROLOGUE TO
THE TEMPEST, OR THE ENCHANTED ISLAND
1670

As when a tree's cut down, the secret root
Lives under ground, and thence new branches shoot,
So, from old Shakespeare's honoured dust, this day
Springs up and buds a new reviving play.
Shakespeare, who (taught by none) did first impart
To Fletcher wit, to labouring Jonson art.
He monarch-like gave those his subjects law,
And is that nature which they paint and draw.
Fletcher reached that which on his heights did grow,
Whilst Jonson crept and gathered all below.[n]
This did his love, and this his mirth digest:
One imitates him most, the other best.
If they have since out-writ all other men,
'Tis with the drops which fell from Shakespeare's pen.
The storm which vanished on the neighbouring shore,
Was taught by Shakespeare's Tempest first to roar.
That innocence and beauty which did smile
In Fletcher, grew on this Enchanted Isle.
But Shakespeare's magic could not copied be,
Within that circle none durst walk but he.
I must confess 'twas bold, nor would you now,
That liberty to vulgar wits allow,
Which works by magic supernatural things:
But Shakespeare's power is sacred as a king's.
Those legends from old priest-hood were received,
And he then writ, as people then believed.
But, if for Shakespeare we your grace implore,
We for our theatre shall want it more:
Who by our dearth of youths are forced to employ
One of our women to present a boy.
And that's a transformation you will say
Exceeding all the magic in the play.
Let none expect in the last act to find
Her sex transformed from man to woman-kind.
Whate'er she was before the play began,
All you shall see of her is perfect man.
Or if your fancy will be farther led,
To find her woman, it must be abed.

PREFACE AND PROLOGUE TO *TYRANNIC LOVE, OR THE ROYAL MARTYR: A TRAGEDY*
1670

I WAS moved to write this play by many reasons: amongst others, the commands of some persons of honour, for whom I have a most particular respect, were daily sounding in my ears that it would be of good example to undertake a poem of this nature. Neither was my own inclination wanting to second their desires. I considered that pleasure was not the only end of poesy; and that even the instructions of morality were not so wholly the business of a poet as that the precepts and examples of piety were to be omitted. For to leave that employment altogether to the clergy were to forget that religion was first taught in verse (which the laziness or dullness of succeeding priesthood turned afterwards into prose); and it were also to grant, which I never shall, that representations of this kind may not as well be conducing to holiness as to good manners. Yet far be it from me to compare the use of dramatic poesy with that of divinity: I only maintain, against the enemies of the stage, that patterns of piety, decently represented and equally removed from the extremes of superstition and profaneness, may be of excellent use to second the precepts of our religion. By the harmony of words we elevate the mind to a sense of devotion, as our solemn music, which is inarticulate poesy, does in churches; and by the lively images of piety, adorned by action, through the senses allure the soul: which while it is charmed in a silent joy of what it sees and hears, is struck at the same time with a secret veneration of things celestial, and is wound up insensibly into the practice of that which it admires. Now if, instead of this, we sometimes see on our theatres the examples of vice rewarded, or at least unpunished; yet it ought not to be an argument against the art, any more than the extravagances and impieties of the pulpit in the late times of rebellion can be against the office and dignity of the clergy.

But many times it happens that poets are wrongfully accused; as it is in my own case in this very play, where I am charged by some ignorant or malicious persons with no less crimes than profaneness and irreligion.[n]

The part of Maximin, against which these holy critics so much declaim, was designed by me to set off the character of S. Catherine.

The part of Maximin: Daja Maximinus (or Gaius Valerius Maximinus) was Emperor A.D. 310–11; he condemned Catherine to imprisonment, torture, and death.

And those who have read the Roman history may easily remember
that Maximin was not only a bloody tyrant, *vastus corpore, animo
ferus*, as Herodian describes him, but also a persecutor of the Church,
against which he raised the sixth persecution. So that whatsoever he
speaks or acts in this tragedy is no more than a record of his life and
manners; a picture, as near as I could take it, from the original. If
with much pains and some success I have drawn a deformed piece,
there is as much of art, and as near an imitation of nature, in a lazar
as in a Venus. Maximin was an heathen, and what he speaks against
religion is in contempt of that which he professed. He defies the gods
of Rome, which is no more than S. Catherine might with decency
have done. If it be urged that a person of such principles who scoffs
at any religion ought not to be presented on the stage; why then are
the lives and sayings of so many wicked and profane persons recorded
in the Holy Scriptures? I know it will be answered that a due use may
be made of them; that they are remembered with a brand of infamy
fixed upon them; and set as sea-marks for those who behold them to
avoid. And what other use have I made of Maximin? Have I proposed him as a pattern to be imitated, whom even for his impiety to
his false gods I have so severely punished? Nay, as if I had foreseen
this objection, I purposely removed the scene of the play, which
ought to have been at Alexandria in Egypt (where S. Catherine
suffered) and laid it under the walls of Aquileia in Italy, where
Maximin was slain, that the punishment of his crime might immediately succeed its execution.

This, Reader, is what I owed to my just defence, and the due
reverence of that religion which I profess, to which all men who
desire to be esteemed good or honest are obliged: I have neither
leisure nor occasion to write more largely on this subject, because I
am already justified by the sentence of the best and most discerning
Prince in the world, by the suffrage of all unbiassed judges, and,
above all, by the witness of my own conscience, which abhors the
thought of such a crime; to which I ask leave to add my outward
conversation, which shall never be justly taxed with the note of
atheism or profaneness.

In what else concerns the play, I shall be brief: for the faults of the
writing and contrivance, I leave them to the mercy of the reader. For

---

Herodian: *Roman History*, vii. The Latin quotation ('huge in body, fierce of
    mind') echoes—as Watson notes—Pareus's heading to Book vii of his edition
    of Herodian. Dryden (as he himself remarks later in this essay) is here con-
    fusing Daja with Maximinus Thrax (Emperor A.D. 235–8), to whom Herodian
    is referring.
lazar: leper.

I am as little apt to defend my own errors as to find those of other poets. Only I observe that the great censors of wit and poetry either produce nothing of their own, or what is more ridiculous than anything they reprehend. Much of ill nature, and a very little judgement, go far in the finding the mistakes of writers.

I pretend not that any thing of mine can be correct: this poem, especially, which was contrived and written in seven weeks, though afterwards hindered by many accidents from a speedy representation, which would have been its best excuse.

Yet the scenes are everywhere unbroken, and the unities of place and time more exactly kept than perhaps is requisite in a tragedy; or at least than I have since preserved them in *The Conquest of Granada*.

I have not everywhere observed the equality of numbers in my verse; partly by reason of my haste; but more especially because I would not have my sense a slave to syllables.

'Tis easy to discover that I have been very bold in my alteration of the story, which of itself was too barren for a play; and that I have taken from the Church two martyrs, in the persons of Porphyrius and the Empress, who suffered for the Christian faith under the tyranny of Maximin.

I have seen a French play called *The Martyrdom of S. Catherine*, but those who have read it will soon clear me from stealing out of so dull an author. I have only borrowed a mistake from him, of one Maximin for another: for finding him in the French poet called the son of a Thracian herdsman and an Alane woman, I too easily believed him to have been the same Maximin mentioned in Herodian. Till afterwards consulting Eusebius and Metaphrastes, I found the Frenchman had betrayed me into an error (when it was too late to alter it) by mistaking that first Maximin for a second, the contemporary of Constantine the Great, and one of the usurpers of the Eastern Empire.

But neither was the other name of my play more fortunate: for as some who had heard of a tragedy of S. Catherine imagined I had taken my plot from thence; so others, who had heard of another play called *L'amour tyrannique*, with the same ignorance accused me to have borrowed my design from it, because I have accidentally given my play the same title, not having to this day seen it; and knowing

---

The Martyrdom of S. Catherine: probably a reference to the anonymous *Sainte Catherine* (1649), which has been attributed variously to the Abbé d'Aubignac and to Desfontaines.

Eusebius: (A.D. 265–340), Bk. viii.

Metaphrastes: Symeon Metaphrastes (*fl.* A.D. 960–70), *Menologion*.

only by report that such a comedy is extant in French under the name of Monsieur Scudéry.

As for what I have said of astral or aerial spirits, it is no invention of mine, but taken from those who have written on that subject. Whether there are such beings or not, it concerns not me; 'tis sufficient for my purpose that many have believed the affirmative; and that these heroic representations, which are of the same nature with the epic, are not limited but with the extremest bounds of what is credible.

PROLOGUE

Self-love (which never rightly understood)
Makes poets still conclude their plays are good:
And malice in all critics reigns so high,
That for small errors they whole plays decry;
So that to see this fondness, and that spite,
You'd think that none but madmen judge or write.
Therefore our poet, as he thinks not fit
T'impose upon you what he writes for wit,
So hopes that leaving you your censures free, ⎫
You equal judges of the whole will be: ⎬
They judge but half who only faults will see. ⎭
Poets like lovers should be bold and dare,
They spoil their business with an over-care.
And he who servilely creeps after sense,
Is safe, but ne'er will reach an excellence.
Hence 'tis our poet in his conjuring,
Allowed his fancy the full scope and swing.
But when a tyrant for his theme he had,
He loosed the reins, and bid his Muse run mad:
And though he stumbles in a full career;
Yet rashness is a better fault than fear.
He saw his way; but in so swift a pace,
To choose the ground might be to lose the race.
They then who of each trip th'advantage take
Find but those faults which they want wit to make.

Monsieur Scudéry: Georges de Scudéry wrote a *tragedy* of this name, published in 1639.

PREFACE TO *AN EVENING'S LOVE, OR THE MOCK ASTROLOGER*

1671

I HAD thought, Reader, in this preface to have written somewhat concerning the difference betwixt the plays of our age and those of our predecessors on the English stage: to have shown in what parts of dramatic poesy we were excelled by Ben Jonson, I mean humour and contrivance of comedy; and in what we may justly claim precedence of Shakespeare and Fletcher, namely in heroic plays: but this design I have waived on second considerations; at least deferred it till I publish *The Conquest of Granada*, where the discourse will be more proper. I have also prepared to treat of the improvement of our language since Fletcher's and Jonson's days, and consequently of our refining the courtship, raillery, and conversation of plays: but as I am willing to decline that envy which I should draw on myself from some old opiniatre judges of the stage; so likewise I am pressed in time so much that I have not leisure, at present, to go through with it.

Neither, indeed, do I value a reputation gained from comedy so far as to concern myself about it any more than I needs must in my own defence: for I think it, in its own nature, inferior to all sorts of dramatic writing. Low comedy especially requires, on the writer's part, much of conversation with the vulgar: and much of ill nature in the observation of their follies. But let all men please themselves according to their several tastes: that which is not pleasant to me may be to others who judge better; and, to prevent an accusation from my enemies, I am sometimes ready to imagine that my disgust of low comedy proceeds not so much from my judgement as from my temper; which is the reason why I so seldom write it; and that when I succeed in it (I mean so far as to please the audience), yet I am nothing satisfied with what I have done; but am often vexed to hear the people laugh, and clap, as they perpetually do, where I intended 'em no jest; while they let pass the better things without taking notice of them. Yet even this confirms me in my opinion of slighting popular applause, and of condemning that approbation which those very people give, equally with me, to the zany of a mountebank; or to the appearance of an antic on the theatre, without wit on the poet's part, or any occasion of laughter from the actor besides the ridiculousness of his habit and his grimaces.

But I have descended, before I was aware, from comedy to farce, which consists principally of grimaces. That I admire not any comedy equally with tragedy is, perhaps, from the sullenness of my humour;

opiniatre: a French loan ('stubborn').

but that I detest those farces which are now the most frequent entertainments of the stage, I am sure I have reason on my side. Comedy
consists, though of low persons, yet of natural actions and characters;
I mean such humours, adventures, and designs as are to be found and
met with in the world. Farce, on the other side, consists of forced
humours and unnatural events. Comedy presents us with the imperfections of human nature. Farce entertains us with what is monstrous and chimerical: the one causes laughter in those who can judge
of men and manners, by the lively representation of their folly or
corruption; the other produces the same effect in those who can judge
of neither, and that only by its extravagances. The first works on the
judgement and fancy; the latter on the fancy only: there is more of
satisfaction in the former kind of laughter, and in the latter more of
scorn. But how it happens that an impossible adventure should cause
our mirth, I cannot so easily imagine. Something there may be in the
oddness of it, because on the stage it is the common effect of things
unexpected to surprise us into a delight: and that is to be ascribed to
the strange appetite, as I may call it, of the fancy; which, like that of
a longing woman, often runs out into the most extravagant desires;
and is better satisfied sometimes with loam, or with the rinds of trees,
than with the wholesome nourishments of life. In short, there is the
same difference betwixt farce and comedy as betwixt an empiric and
a true physician: both of them may attain their ends; but what the
one performs by hazard, the other does by skill. And as the artist is
often unsuccessful, while the mountebank succeeds; so farces more
commonly take the people than comedies. For to write unnatural
things is the most probable way of pleasing them, who understand
not nature. And a true poet often misses of applause because he
cannot debase himself to write so ill as to please his audience.

  After all, it is to be acknowledged that most of those comedies
which have been lately written have been allied too much to farce;
and this must of necessity fall out till we forbear the translation of
French plays: for their poets, wanting judgement to make or to
maintain true characters, strive to cover their defects with ridiculous
figures and grimaces. While I say this, I accuse myself as well as
others: and this very play would rise up in judgement against me, if I
would defend all things I have written to be natural: but I confess I
have given too much to the people in it, and am ashamed for them as
well as for myself, that I have pleased them at so cheap a rate: not
that there is anything here which I would not defend to an ill-

---

empiric: one given to prescribing according to observation rather than scientific
    theory—hence, a quack.

natured judge (for I despise their censures, who I am sure would
write worse on the same subject), but because I love to deal clearly
and plainly, and to speak of my own faults with more criticism than
I would of another poet's. Yet I think it no vanity to say that this
comedy has as much of entertainment in it as many other which have
been lately written: and, if I find my own errors in it, I am able at the
same time to arraign all my contemporaries for greater. As I pretend
not that I can write humour, so none of them can reasonably pretend
to have written it as they ought. Jonson was the only man of all ages
and nations who has performed it well, and that but in three or four
of his comedies: the rest are but a *crambe bis cocta*; the same humours
a little varied and written worse. Neither was it more allowable in
him, than it is in our present poets, to represent the follies of particular persons; of which many have accused him. *Parcere personis*,
dicere de vitiis is the rule of plays. And Horace tells you that the Old
Comedy amongst the Grecians was silenced for the too great liberties
of the poets:

> in vitium libertas excidit et vim
> dignam lege regi: lex est accepta, chorusque
> turpiter obticuit, sublato jure nocendi.

Of which he gives you the reason in another place: where, having
given the precept,

> neve immunda crepent, ignominiosaque dicta,

he immediately subjoins,

> offenduntur enim quibus est equus, et pater, et res.

But Ben Jonson is to be admired for many excellencies; and can be
taxed with fewer failings than any English poet. I know I have been
accused as an enemy of his writings; but without any other reason
than that I do not admire him blindly, and without looking into his
imperfections. For why should he only be exempted from those
frailties from which Homer and Virgil are not free? Or why should
there be any *ipse dixit* in our poetry, any more than there is in our

---

crambe bis cocta: Juvenal, *Satires*, vii. 154 ('crambe repetita': 'the same mess
    served up over and again').
Parcere personis, . . .: 'To talk of vices but spare individuals.' Source unknown;
    the sentiment a commonplace defence by satirists and dramatists.
in vitium libertas . . .: *Ars Poetica*, ll. 282–4 ('Liberty fell into excess and into
    outrages meriting legal restraint. A law was passed, and with no right to libel
    anymore the chorus fell shamefully silent').
neve immunda crepent, . . .: ibid. ll. 247–8 ('aut immunda crepent . . .'; 'nor
    speak rude and scurrilous words, for people of standing, birth and wealth are
    offended by them').

philosophy? I admire and applaud him where I ought: those who do
more do but value themselves in their admiration of him: and, by
telling you they extol Ben Jonson's way, would insinuate to you that
they can practise it. For my part, I declare that I want judgement to
imitate him; and should think it a great impudence in myself to
attempt it. To make men appear pleasantly ridiculous on the stage
was, as I have said, his talent; and in this he needed not the acumen
of wit, but that of judgement. For the characters and representations
of folly are only the effects of observation; and observation is an
effect of judgement. Some ingenious men, for whom I have a particular esteem, have thought I have much injured Ben Jonson when I
have not allowed his wit to be extraordinary: but they confound the
notion of what is witty with what is pleasant. That Ben Jonson's plays
were pleasant, he must want reason who denies: but that pleasantness
was not properly wit, or the sharpness of conceit, but the natural
imitation of folly: which I confess to be excellent in its kind, but not
to be of that kind which they pretend. Yet if we will believe Quintilian in his chapter *De movendo risu*, he gives his opinion of both in
these following words: *stulta reprehendere facillimum est; nam per se
sunt ridicula: et a derisu non procul abest risus: sed rem urbanam facit
aliqua ex nobis adjectio.*

And some perhaps would be apt to say of Jonson as it was said of
Demosthenes: *non displicuisse illi jocos, sed non contigisse.*

I will not deny but that I approve most the mixed way of comedy;
that which is neither all wit, nor all humour, but the result of both.
Neither so little of humour as Fletcher shows, nor so little of love and
wit as Jonson; neither all cheat, with which the best plays of the one
are filled, nor all adventure, which is the common practice of the
other. I would have the characters well chosen, and kept distant from
interfering with each other; which is more than Fletcher or Shakespeare did: but I would have more of the *urbana, venusta, salsa,
faceta*, and the rest which Quintilian reckons up as the ornaments of
wit; and these are extremely wanting in Ben Jonson. As for repartee
in particular; as it is the very soul of conversation, so it is the greatest

---

stulta reprehendere . . .: *Institutio oratoria*, VI. iii. 71 (Dryden's 'et a derisu non
procul abest risus' is not in the Quintilian texts examined; 'It is easy to mock
folly, for folly is ridiculous in itself . . . but something of our own improves
the joke').

non displicuisse . . .: ibid. VI. iii. 2 ('not just that he disliked jokes but that he
lacked the power to make them').

urbana, venusta . . .: ibid. VI. iii. 17–20, where the first four 'ornaments of wit'
given are 'urbanitas' (urbane), 'venustus' (graceful), 'salsus' (sharp, salt),
'facetus' (elegant).

grace of comedy, where it is proper to the characters: there may be much of acuteness in a thing well said; but there is more in a quick reply: *sunt enim longe venustiora omnia in respondendo quam in provocando*. Of one thing I am sure, that no man ever will decry wit but he who despairs of it himself; and who has no other quarrel to it but that which the fox had to the grapes. Yet, as Mr Cowley (who had a greater portion of it than any man I know) tells us in his character of wit, rather than all wit let there be none. I think there's no folly so great in any poet of our age as the superfluity and waste of wit was in some of our predecessors: particularly we may say of Fletcher and of Shakespeare what was said of Ovid, *in omni ejus ingenio, facilius quod rejici, quam quod adjici potest, invenies*. The contrary of which was true in Virgil, and our incomparable Jonson.

Some enemies of repartee have observed to us that there is a great latitude in their characters which are made to speak it: and that it is easier to write wit than humour; because, in the characters of humour, the poet is confined to make the person speak what is only proper to it. Whereas all kind of wit is proper in the character of a witty person. But, by their favour, there are as different characters in wit as in folly. Neither is all kind of wit proper in the mouth of every ingenious person. A witty coward and a witty brave must speak differently. Falstaff and the Liar speak not like Don John in *The Chances*, and Valentine in *Wit without Money*. And Jonson's Truewit in *The Silent Woman* is a character different from all of them. Yet it appears that this one character of wit was more difficult to the author than all his images of humour in the play: for those he could describe and manage from his observations of men; this he has taken, at least a part of it, from books: witness the speeches in the first act, translated *verbatim* out of Ovid *De arte amandi*; to omit what afterwards he borrowed from the sixth satire of Juvenal against women.

However, if I should grant that there were a greater latitude in characters of wit than in those of humour; yet that latitude would be of small advantage to such poets who have too narrow an imagination to write it. And to entertain an audience perpetually with

sunt enim . . .: ibid. VI. iii. 13 ('for wit always shows up better in riposte than in attack').

Mr. Cowley: 'Ode: Of wit', stanza 5.

what was said of Ovid: Quintilian, op. cit. VI. iii. 5 ('. . . . possit, invenient'; 'it is easier to find excess than shortage in all his wit').

the Liar: Dorante in Corneille's *Le Menteur*; the two plays mentioned in the following line are by Fletcher.

the speeches in the first act: for Jonson's use of Ovid see *Works*, ed. Herford and Simpson, X. 7 ff. The Collegiate Ladies may owe something to Juvenal.

humour is to carry them from the conversation of gentlemen, and treat them with the follies and extravagances of Bedlam.

I find I have launched out farther than I intended in the beginning of this preface. And that, in the heat of writing, I have touched at something which I thought to have avoided. 'Tis time now to draw homeward: and to think rather of defending myself than assaulting others. I have already acknowledged that this play is far from perfect: but I do not think myself obliged to discover the imperfections of it to my adversaries, any more than a guilty person is bound to accuse himself before his judges. 'Tis charged upon me that I make debauched persons (such as they say my Astrologer and Gamester are) my protagonists, or the chief persons of the drama; and that I make them happy in the conclusion of my play; against the law of comedy, which is to reward virtue and punish vice. I answer first, that I know no such law to have been constantly observed in comedy, either by the ancient or modern poets. Chaerea is made happy in the *Eunuch*, after having deflowered a virgin; and Terence generally does the same through all his plays, where you perpetually see not only debauched young men enjoy their mistresses, but even the courtesans themselves rewarded and honoured in the catastrophe. The same may be observed in Plautus almost everywhere. Ben Jonson himself, after whom I may be proud to err, has given me more than once the example of it. That in *The Alchemist* is notorious, where Face, after having contrived and carried on the great cozenage of the play, and continued in it without repentance to the last, is not only forgiven by his master, but enriched by his consent with the spoils of those whom he had cheated. And, which is more, his master himself, a grave man and a widower, is introduced taking his man's counsel, debauching the widow first, in hope to marry her afterward. In *The Silent Woman*, Dauphine (who, with the other two gentlemen, is of the same character with my Celadon in *The Maiden Queen*, and with Wild-blood in this) professes himself in love with all the Collegiate Ladies: and they likewise are all of the same character with each other, excepting only Madam Otter, who has something singular: yet this naughty Dauphine is crowned in the end with the possession of his uncle's estate, and with the hopes of enjoying all his mistresses. And his friend Mr Truewit (the best character of a gentleman which Ben Jonson ever made) is not ashamed to pimp for him. As for Beaumont and Fletcher, I need not allege examples out of them; for that were to quote almost all their comedies.

But now it will be objected that I patronize vice by the authority of former poets, and extenuate my own faults by recrimination. I answer that, as I defend myself by their example, so that example I defend by reason, and by the end of all dramatic poesy. In the first place, therefore, give me leave to show you their mistake who have accused me. They have not distinguished, as they ought, betwixt the rules of tragedy and comedy. In tragedy, where the actions and persons are great, and the crimes horrid, the laws of justice are more strictly to be observed; and examples of punishment to be made to deter mankind from the pursuit of vice. Faults of this kind have been rare amongst the ancient poets: for they have punished in Oedipus, and in his posterity, the sin which he knew not he had committed. Medea is the only example I remember at present who escapes from punishment after murder. Thus tragedy fulfils one great part of its institution; which is, by example, to instruct. But in comedy it is not so; for the chief end of it is divertisement and delight: and that so much, that it is disputed, I think, by Heinsius, before Horace his *Art of Poetry*, whether instruction be any part of its employment. At least I am sure it can be but its secondary end: for the business of the poet is to make you laugh: when he writes humour he makes folly ridiculous; when wit, he moves you, if not always to laughter, yet to a pleasure that is more noble. And if he works a cure on folly, and the small imperfections in mankind, by exposing them to public view, that cure is not performed by an immediate operation. For it works first on the ill nature of the audience; they are moved to laugh by the representation of deformity; and the shame of that laughter teaches us to amend what is ridiculous in our manners. This being, then, established, that the first end of comedy is delight, and instruction only the second, it may reasonably be inferred that comedy is not so much obliged to the punishment of the faults which it represents, as tragedy. For the persons in comedy are of a lower quality, the action is little, and the faults and vices are but the sallies of youth, and the frailties of human nature, and not premeditated crimes: such to which all men are obnoxious, not such as are attempted only by few, and those abandoned to all sense of virtue: such as move pity and commiseration, not detestation and horror; such, in short, as may be forgiven, not such as must of necessity be punished. But, lest any man should think that I write this to make libertinism amiable, or that I cared not to debase the end and institution of comedy, so I might thereby maintain my own errors, and those of better poets, I must further declare, both for them and for myself, that we make not vicious persons happy, but only as Heaven makes sinners so; that is

---

Heinsius: 'Heinsius appears to have had no scruples such as Dryden here imposes on him. *Delectare enim et docere est Comoediae*: Danielis Heinsius *in Horat. Notae*' (Ker).

by reclaiming them first from vice. For so 'tis to be supposed they are, when they resolve to marry; for then enjoying what they desire in one, they cease to pursue the love of many. So Chaerea is made happy by Terence, in marrying her whom he had deflowered: and so are Wildblood and the Astrologer in this play.

There is another crime with which I am charged, at which I am yet much less concerned, because it does not relate to my manners, as the former did, but only to my reputation as a poet: a name of which I assure the reader I am nothing proud; and therefore cannot be very solicitous to defend it. I am taxed with stealing all my plays, and that by some who should be the last men from whom I would steal any part of 'em. There is one answer which I will not make; but it has been made for me by him to whose grace and patronage I owe all things,

> et spes et ratio studiorum in Caesare tantum,

and without whose command they should no longer be troubled with anything of mine, that he only desired that they who accused me of theft would always steal him plays like mine. But though I have reason to be proud of this defence, yet I should waive it, because I have a worse opinion of my own comedies than any of my enemies can have. 'Tis true, that wherever I have liked any story in a romance, novel, or foreign play, I have made no difficulty, nor ever shall, to take the foundation of it, to build it up, and to make it proper for the English stage. And I will be so vain to say it has lost nothing in my hands: but it always cost me so much trouble to heighten it for our theatre (which is incomparably more curious in all the ornaments of dramatic poesy than the French or Spanish), that when I had finished my play, it was like the hulk of Sir Francis Drake, so strangely altered that there scarcely remained any plank of the timber which first built it. To witness this I need go no farther than this play: it was first Spanish, and called *El astrologo fingido*; then made French by the younger Corneille; and is now translated into English, and in print, under the name of *The Feigned Astrologer*. What I have performed in this will best appear by comparing it with those: you will see that I have rejected some adventures which I judged were not diverting; that I have heightened those which I have chosen, and that I have added others which were neither in the French nor Spanish. And besides, you will easily dis-

---

et spes et ratio . . .: Juvenal, *Satires*, viii. 1 ('All the hopes and prospects of scholars rest on Caesar alone').

it was first Spanish: Thomas Corneille used Calderón's *El astrologo fingido*—with other sources—for *Le feint astrologue* (1651), an anonymous English version of which was published in 1668.

cover that the walk of the Astrologer is the least considerable in my play: for the design of it turns more on the parts of Wildblood and Jacinta, who are the chief persons in it. I have farther to add that I seldom use the wit and language of any romance or play, which I undertake to alter: because my own invention (as bad as it is) can furnish me with nothing so dull as what is there. Those who have called Virgil, Terence, and Tasso plagiaries (though they much injured them) had yet a better colour for their accusation: for Virgil has evidently translated Theocritus, Hesiod, and Homer, in many places; besides what he has taken from Ennius in his own language. Terence was not only known to translate Menander (which he avows also in his prologues), but was said also to be helped in those translations by Scipio the African and Laelius. And Tasso, the most excellent of modern poets, and whom I reverence next to Virgil, has taken both from Homer many admirable things which were left untouched by Virgil, and from Virgil himself where Homer could not furnish him. Yet the bodies of Virgil's and Tasso's poems were their own: and so are all the ornaments of language and elocution in them. The same (if there were anything commendable in this play) I could say for it. But I will come nearer to our own countrymen. Most of Shakespeare's plays, I mean the stories of them, are to be found in the *Hecatommithi* or *Hundred Novels* of Cinthio. I have myself read in his Italian that of *Romeo and Juliet, The Moor of Venice*, and many others of them.[n] Beaumont and Fletcher had most of theirs from Spanish novels: witness *The Chances, The Spanish Curate, Rule a Wife and have a Wife, The Little French Lawyer*, and so many others of them as compose the greatest part of their volume in folio. Ben Jonson, indeed, has designed his plots himself; but no man has borrowed so much from the Ancients as he has done: and he did well in it, for he has thereby beautified our language.

But these little critics do not well consider what is the work of a poet, and what the graces of a poem. The story is the least part of either: I mean the foundation of it, before it is modelled by the art of him who writes it; who forms it with more care, by exposing only the beautiful parts of it to view, than a skilful lapidary sets a jewel. On this foundation of the story the characters are raised: and, since no story can afford characters enough for the variety of the English stage, it follows that it is to be altered and enlarged with new persons, accidents, and designs, which will almost make it new. When this is done, the forming it into acts and scenes, disposing of actions and

The Little French Lawyer: from Guzman; *Chances* from Cervantes; *Spanish Curate* from Gonzales de Céspedes; *Rule a Wife* . . . partly from Cervantes.

passions into their proper places, and beautifying both with descriptions, similitudes, and propriety of language, is the principal employment of the poet; as being the largest field of fancy, which is the principal quality required in him: for so much the word ποιητής implies. Judgement, indeed, is necessary in him; but 'tis fancy that gives the life-touches, and the secret graces to it; especially in serious plays, which depend not much on observation. For to write humour in comedy (which is the theft of poets from mankind) little of fancy is required; the poet observes only what is ridiculous and pleasant folly, and by judging exactly what is so, he pleases in the representation of it.

But in general, the employment of a poet is like that of a curious gunsmith or watchmaker: the iron or silver is not his own; but they are the least part of that which gives the value: the price lies wholly in the workmanship. And he who works dully on a story, without moving laughter in a comedy, or raising concernments in a serious play, is no more to be accounted a good poet than a gunsmith of the Minories is to be compared with the best workman of the town.

But I have said more of this than I intended; and more, perhaps, than I needed to have done. I shall but laugh at them hereafter who accuse me with so little reason; and withal contemn their dullness who, if they could ruin that little reputation I have got, and which I value not, yet would want both wit and learning to establish their own; or to be remembered in after ages for any thing but only that which makes them ridiculous in this.

the Minories: a street near the Tower of London

OF HEROIC PLAYS: AN ESSAY
PREFIXED TO *THE CONQUEST OF GRANADA*
BY THE SPANIARDS, IN TWO PARTS[n]

1672

WHETHER heroic verse ought to be admitted into serious plays is not now to be disputed: 'tis already in possession of the stage, and I dare confidently affirm that very few tragedies, in this age, shall be received without it. All the arguments which are formed against it can amount to no more than this, that it is not so near conversation as prose, and therefore not so natural. But it is very clear to all who understand poetry that serious plays ought not to imitate conversation too nearly. If nothing were to be raised above that level, the foundation of poetry would be destroyed. And, if you once admit of a latitude, that thoughts may be exalted and that images and actions may be raised above the life, and described in measure without rhyme, that leads you insensibly from your own principles to mine: you are already so far onward of your way that you have forsaken the imitation of ordinary converse. You are gone beyond it; and, to continue where you are, is to lodge in the open field, betwixt two inns. You have lost that which you call natural, and have not acquired the last perfection of art. But it was only custom which cozened us so long: we thought, because Shakespeare and Fletcher went no farther, that there the pillars of poetry were to be erected; that, because they excellently described passion without rhyme, therefore rhyme was not capable of describing it. But time has now convinced most men of that error. 'Tis indeed so difficult to write verse that the adversaries of it have a good plea against many who undertake that task, without being formed by art or nature for it. Yet, even they who have written worst in it, would have written worse without it. They have cozened many with their sound, who never took the pains to examine their sense. In fine, they have succeeded: though 'tis true they have more dishonoured rhyme by their good success than they could have done by their ill. But I am willing to let fall this argument: 'tis free for every man to write, or not to write, in verse, as he judges it to be, or not to be, his talent; or as he imagines the audience will receive it.

For heroic plays (in which only I have used it without the mixture of prose), the first light we had of them on the English theatre was from the late Sir William Davenant. It being forbidden him in the rebellious times to act tragedies and comedies, because they contained some matter of scandal to those good people who could more

---

not so natural: Dryden summarizes Howard's arguments against rhyme, which appear in the Preface to *The Great Favourite*, 1668 (Spingarn, II, pp. 105 f.).

5+s.c.

easily dispossess their lawful sovereign than endure a wanton jest, he was forced to turn his thoughts another way, and to introduce the examples of moral virtue writ in verse, and performed in recitative music. The original of this music, and of the scenes which adorned his work, he had from the Italian operas; but he heightened his characters (as I may probably imagine) from the example of Corneille and some French poets. In this condition did this part of poetry remain at his Majesty's return; when, growing bolder, as being now owned by a public authority, he reviewed his *Siege of Rhodes*, and caused it to be acted as a just drama. But as few men have the happiness to begin and finish any new project, so neither did he live to make his design perfect: there wanted the fulness of a plot, and the variety of characters to form it as it ought; and, perhaps, something might have been added to the beauty of the style. All which he would have performed with more exactness, had he pleased to have given us another work of the same nature. For myself and others, who come after him, we are bound, with all veneration to his memory, to acknowledge what advantage we received from that excellent ground-work which he laid: and, since it is an easy thing to add to what already is invented, we ought all of us, without envy to him, or partiality to ourselves, to yield him the precedence in it.

Having done him this justice, as my guide, I may do myself so much as to give an account of what I have performed after him. I observed then, as I said, what was wanting to the perfection of his *Siege of Rhodes*; which was design, and variety of characters. And in the midst of this consideration, by mere accident, I opened the next book that lay by me, which was an Ariosto in Italian; and the very first two lines of that poem gave me light to all I could desire:

> Le donne, i cavalier, l'arme, gli amori,
> Le cortesie, l'audaci imprese io canto, etc.

For the very next reflection which I made was this, that an heroic play ought to be an imitation, in little, of an heroic poem: and, consequently, that Love and Valour ought to be the subject of it. Both these Sir William Davenant had begun to shadow: but it was so, as first discoverers draw their maps, with headlands, and promontories, and some few outlines of somewhat taken at a distance, and which the designer saw not clearly. The common drama obliged him to a plot well formed and pleasant or, as the Ancients called it, one entire and great action. But this he afforded not himself in a story

the Italian operas: see p. 5 above, and footnote.
Le donne, i cavalier, . . .: *Orlando Furioso* i. 1–2 ('I sing of ladies, knights, arms, love, of courtesy, and great deeds').

which he neither filled with persons, nor beautified with characters, nor varied with accidents. The laws of an heroic poem did not dispense with those of the other, but raised them to a greater height, and indulged him a farther liberty of fancy, and of drawing all things as far above the ordinary proportion of the stage as that is beyond the common words and actions of human life; and therefore, in the scanting of his images and design, he complied not enough with the greatness and majesty of an heroic poem.

I am sorry I cannot discover my opinion of this kind of writing without dissenting much from his, whose memory I love and honour. But I will do it with the same respect to him as if he were now alive, and overlooking my paper while I write. His judgement of an heroic poem was this: 'That it ought to be dressed in a more familiar and easy shape; more fitted to the common actions and passions of human life; and, in short, more like a glass of nature, showing us ourselves in our ordinary habits, and figuring a more practicable virtue to us than was done by the Ancients or Moderns.' Thus he takes the image of an heroic poem from the drama, or stage poetry; and accordingly intended to divide it into five books, representing the same number of acts; and every book into several cantos, imitating the scenes which compose our acts.

But this, I think, is rather a play in narration (as I may call it) than an heroic poem; if at least you will not prefer the opinion of a single man to the practice of the most excellent authors both of ancient and latter ages. I am no admirer of quotations; but you shall hear, if you please, one of the Ancients delivering his judgement on this question; 'tis Petronius Arbiter, the most elegant, and one of the most judicious authors of the Latin tongue; who, after he had given many admirable rules for the structure and beauties of an epic poem, concludes all in these following words:

Non enim res gestae versibus comprehendendae sunt, quod longe melius historici faciunt: sed, per ambages, deorumque ministeria, praecipitandus est liber spiritus, ut potius furentis animi vaticinatio appareat, quam religiosae orationis, sub testibus, fides.

In which sentence, and in his own essay of a poem which im-

His judgement of an heroic poem was this: Dryden paraphrases Davenant's Preface to *Gondibert*, 1650 (Spingarn, II p. 17).

Non enim res gestae . . .: *Satyricon*, 118 ('For it is not real events which verse is to record, which historians can do much better. The free spirit must concern himself with allusion and godly interventions . . . so that the prophesies of someone inspired appear rather than the precision of a statement made on oath'). The quotation is a commonplace among critics of the epic at this time. Dryden omits a phrase of Petronius.

mediately he gives you, it is thought he taxes Lucan, who followed too much the truth of history, crowded sentences together, was too full of points, and too often offered at somewhat which had more of the sting of an epigram than of the dignity and state of an heroic poem. Lucan used not much the help of his heathen deities, there was neither the ministry of the gods, nor the precipitation of the soul, nor the fury of a prophet (of which my author speaks), in his *Pharsalia*: he treats you more like a philosopher than a poet, and instructs you, in verse, with what he had been taught by his uncle Seneca in prose. In one word, he walks soberly afoot, when he might fly. Yet Lucan is not always this religious historian. The oracle of Appius, and the witchcraft of Erictho, will somewhat atone for him, who was, indeed, bound up by an ill-chosen and known argument, to follow truth with great exactness. For my part, I am of opinion that neither Homer, Virgil, Statius, Ariosto, Tasso, nor our English Spenser could have formed their poems half so beautiful without those gods and spirits, and those enthusiastic parts of poetry which compose the most noble parts of all their writings. And I will ask any man who loves heroic poetry (for I will not dispute their tastes who do not) if the ghost of Polydorus in Virgil, the Enchanted Wood in Tasso, and the Bower of Bliss in Spenser (which he borrows from that admirable Italian) could have been omitted without taking from their works some of the greatest beauties in them. And if any man object the improbabilities of a spirit appearing or of a palace raised by magic, I boldly answer him that an heroic poet is not tied to a bare representation of what is true, or exceeding probable: but that he may let himself loose to visionary objects, and to the representation of such things as depending not on sense, and therefore not to be comprehended by know-ledge, may give him a freer scope for imagination. 'Tis enough that in all ages and religions the greatest part of mankind have believed the power of magic, and that there are spirits or spectres which have appeared. This, I say, is foundation enough for poetry: and I dare farther affirm that the whole doctrine of separated beings, whether those spirits are incorporeal substances (which Mr. Hobbes, with some reason, thinks to imply a contradiction) or that they are a thinner and more aerial sort of bodies (as some of the Fathers have conjectured) may better be explicated by poets than by philosophers or divines. For their speculations on this subject are wholly poetical;

---

the oracle of Appius . . . Erictho: *Pharsalia*, v. 64 f. and vi. 507 f.
the ghost of Polydorus . . .: Virgil, *Aeneid*, iii. 41 f.; Tasso, *Gerusalemme Liberata*, xvi. 9 f.; Spenser, *Faerie Queene* II. xii. f.
Mr. Hobbes: *Leviathan* (1651), III. xxxiv.

they have only their fancy for their guide, and that, being sharper in an excellent poet than it is likely it should in a phlegmatic, heavy gown-man, will see farther in its own empire, and produce more satisfactory notions on those dark and doubtful problems.

Some men think they have raised a great argument against the use of spectres and magic in heroic poetry by saying they are unnatural: but whether they or I believe there are such things is not material; 'tis enough that, for aught we know, they may be in nature: and whatever is, or may be, is not properly unnatural. Neither am I much concerned at Mr Cowley's verses before *Gondibert* (though his authority is almost sacred to me): 'tis true, he has resembled the old epic poetry to a fantastic fairy land; but he has contradicted himself by his own example. For he has himself made use of angels and visions in his *Davideis*, as well as Tasso in his *Godfrey*.

What I have written on this subject will not be thought a digression by the reader, if he please to remember what I said in the beginning of this Essay, that I have modelled my heroic plays by the rules of an heroic poem. And if that be the most noble, the most pleasant, and the most instructive way of writing in verse, and withal the highest pattern of human life, as all poets have agreed, I shall need no other argument to justify my choice in this imitation. One advantage the drama has above the other, namely that it represents to view what the poem only does relate, and, *segnius irritant animum demissa per aures, quam quae sunt oculis subjecta fidelibus*, as Horace tells us.

To those who object my frequent use of drums and trumpets, and my representations of battles, I answer, I introduced them not on the English stage. Shakespeare used them frequently; and though Jonson shows no battle in his *Catiline*, yet you hear from behind the scenes the sounding of trumpets, and the shouts of fighting armies. But I add farther: that these warlike instruments, and even the representations of fighting on the stage, are no more than necessary to produce the effects of an heroic play; that is, to raise the imagination of the audience, and to persuade them, for the time, that what they behold on the theatre is really performed. The poet is, then, to endeavour an absolute dominion over the minds of the spectators; for, though our fancy will contribute to its own deceit, yet a writer ought to help its operation. And that the Red Bull has formerly done the same, is no more an argument against our practice than it would be for a

---

as Horace tells us: *Ars Poetica*, ll. 180–1 ('. . . aurem . . .'; 'the mind is less strongly stirred by what comes through the ears than by what is brought before its faithful eyes.').

the Red Bull: see p. 41 above, and footnote.

physician to forbear an approved medicine because a mountebank has used it with success.

Thus I have given a short account of heroic plays. I might now, with the usual eagerness of an author, make a particular defence of this. But the common opinion (how unjust soever) has been so much to my advantage that I have reason to be satisfied, and to suffer, with patience, all that can be urged against it.

For, otherwise, what can be more easy for me than to defend the character of Almanzor, which is one great exception that is made against the play? 'Tis said that Almanzor is no perfect pattern of heroic virtue, that he is a contemner of kings, and that he is made to perform impossibilities.

I must therefore avow, in the first place, from whence I took the character. The first image I had of him was from the Achilles of Homer, the next from Tasso's Rinaldo (who was a copy of the former), and the third from the Artaban of Monsieur Calprenède (who has imitated both). The original of these (Achilles) is taken by Homer for his hero; and is described by him as one who in strength and courage surpassed the rest of the Grecian army; but, withal, of so fiery a temper, so impatient of an injury, even from his King and General, that when his mistress was to be forced from him by the command of Agamemnon, he not only disobeyed it, but returned him an answer full of contumely, and in the most opprobrious terms he could imagine. They are Homer's words which follow, and I have cited but some few amongst a multitude:

> οἰνοβαρές, κυνὸς ὄμματ᾽ ἔχων, κραδίην δ᾽ ἐλάφοιο:
> δημοβόρος βασιλεύς, etc.

Nay, he proceeded so far in his insolence as to draw out his sword, with intention to kill him:

> ἕλκετο δ᾽ ἐκ κολεοῖο μέγα ξίφος.

And, if Minerva had not appeared, and held his hand, he had executed his design; and 'twas all she could do to dissuade him from it: the event was that he left the army, and would fight no more. Agamemnon gives his character thus to Nestor:

> ἀλλ᾽ ὅδ᾽ ἀνὴρ ἐθέλει περὶ πάντων ἔμμεναι ἄλλων,
> πάντων μὲν κρατέειν ἐθέλει, πάντεσσι δ᾽ ἀνάσσειν;

Monsieur Calprenède: Gauthier de la Calprenède (1614–63) wrote several plays and romances; Artaban is a character in his *Cléopâtre*.

They are Homer's words which follow: the three quotations are taken from *Iliad*, i (ll. 225, 231, 'You, sodden with wine, with a dog's face but a deer's heart ... a king who devours his subjects ...'; l. 194, '... was drawing his great sword from its scabbard'; ll. 287–8, 'this man feels he must be superior to everyone else; he wants to rule everyone, to be King and give all the orders').

and Horace gives the same description of him in his *Art of Poetry*:

> honoratum si forte reponis Achillem,
> impiger, iracundus, inexorabilis, acer,
> jura neget sibi nata, nihil non arroget armis.

Tasso's chief character, Rinaldo, was a man of the same temper; for when he had slain Gernando in his heat of passion, he not only refused to be judged by Godfrey, his general, but threatened that if he came to seize him, he would right himself by arms upon him; witness these following lines of Tasso:

> Venga egli, o mandi, io terrò fermo il piede:
> Giudici fian tra noi la sorte e l'arme;
> Fera tragedia vuol che s'appresenti,
> Per lor diporto, alle nemiche genti.

You see how little these great authors did esteem the point of honour, so much magnified by the French, and so ridiculously aped by us. They made their heroes men of honour; but so as not to divest them quite of human passions and frailties, they contented themselves to show you what men of great spirits would certainly do when they were provoked, not what they were obliged to do by the strict rules of moral virtue. For my own part I declare myself for Homer and Tasso, and am more in love with Achilles and Rinaldo than with Cyrus and Oroondates. I shall never subject my characters to the French standard, where love and honour are to be weighed by drams and scruples. Yet, where I have designed the patterns of exact virtues, such as in this play are the parts of Almahide, of Ozmyn, and Benzayda, I may safely challenge the best of theirs.

But Almanzor is taxed with changing sides: and what tie has he on him to the contrary? He is not born their subject whom he serves, and he is injured by them to a very high degree. He threatens them, and speaks insolently of sovereign power; but so do Achilles and Rinaldo, who were subjects and soldiers to Agamemnon and

---

in his Art of Poetry: *Ars Poetica*, ll. 120–2 ('If you put the renowned Achilles on the stage let him be tireless, angry, stubborn, fierce. Let him deny that laws relate to him and judge everything by force of arms').

these following lines of Tasso: *Gerusalemme Liberata*, v. 43 ('Whether Godfrey comes or sends someone, I shall not leave here until we know who will regret this bargain, so that what was done lately may be the first act of our tragedy and this the second').

Cyrus and Oroondates: heroes, respectively, of Madame de Scudéry's *Artamène: ou le Grand Cyrus* (1649–53) and of Calprenède's *Cassandre* (1644–50).

Godfrey of Bulloigne. He talks extravagantly in his passion; but, if I would take the pains to quote an hundred passages of Ben Jonson's Cethegus, I could easily show you that the rhodomontades of Almanzor are neither so irrational as his, nor so impossible to be put in execution; for Cethegus threatens to destroy nature, and to raise a new one out of it; to kill all the Senate for his part of the action; to look Cato dead; and a thousand other things as extravagant he says, but performs not one action in the play.

But none of the former calumnies will stick: and, therefore, 'tis at last charged upon me that Almanzor does all things; or if you will have an absurd accusation, in their nonsense who make it, that he performs impossibilities. They say that being a stranger he appeases two fighting factions, when the authority of their lawful sovereign could not. This is indeed the most improbable of all his actions, but 'tis far from being impossible. Their king had made himself contemptible to his people, as the *History of Granada* tells us. And Almanzor, though a stranger, yet was already known to them by his gallantry in the *juego de toros*, his engagement on the weaker side, and, more especially, by the character of his person and brave actions, given by Abdalla just before. And, after all, the greatness of the enterprise consisted only in the daring; for he had the king's guards to second him. But we have read both of Caesar, and many other generals, who have not only calmed a mutiny with a word, but have presented themselves single before an army of their enemies; which upon sight of them has revolted from their own leaders and come over to their trenches. In the rest of Almanzor's actions, you see him for the most part victorious; but the same fortune has constantly attended many heroes who were not imaginary. Yet you see it no inheritance to him. For, in the first part, he is made a prisoner; and, in the last, defeated, and not able to preserve the city from being taken. If the history of the late Duke of Guise be true, he hazarded more and performed not less in Naples than Almanzor is feigned to have done in Granada.

I have been too tedious in this apology; but to make some satisfaction, I will leave the rest of my play, exposed to the critics, without defence.

The concernment of it is wholly passed from me, and ought to be in them who have been favourable to it, and are somewhat obliged

---

Cethegus: in *Catiline* (1611).
the History of Granada: Perez de Hita's *Guerras Civiles* (1595–1619).
juego de toros: bullfight.
Duke of Guise: the *Mémoires* of the Duke were translated into English in 1669.

to defend their own opinions. That there are errors in it, I deny not:

> ast opere in tanto fas est obrepere somnum.

But I have already swept the stakes; and with the common good fortune of prosperous gamesters, can be content to sit quietly; to hear my fortune cursed by some, and my faults arraigned by others, and to suffer both without reply.

---

ast opere . . .: Horace, *Ars Poetica*, l. 360 ('verum operi longo fas est obrepere somnum': 'it is permissible to be overcome by sleep in a long poem').

EPILOGUE TO THE SECOND PART OF
THE CONQUEST OF GRANADA

1672

THEY who have best succeeded on the stage,
Have still conform'd their genius to their age.
Thus Jonson did mechanic humour show,
When men were dull, and conversation low.
Then comedy was faultless, but 'twas coarse:
Cobb's tankard was a jest, and Otter's horse.
And, as their comedy, their love was mean:
Except, by chance, in some one labour'd scene,
Which must atone for an ill-written play.
They rose, but at their height could seldom stay.
Fame then was cheap, and the first comer sped;
And they have kept it since, by being dead.
But, were they now to write, when critics weigh
Each line, and every word, throughout a play,
None of them, no, not Jonson in his height
Could pass without allowing grains for weight.
Think it not envy that these truths are told,
Our poet's not malicious, though he's bold.
'Tis not to brand 'em that their faults are shown,
But, by their errors, to excuse his own.
If love and honour now are higher raised,
'Tis not the poet but the age is praised.
Wit's now arrived to a more high degree;
Our native language more refined and free.
Our ladies and our men now speak more wit
In conversation than those poets writ.
Then one of these is, consequently, true;
That what this poet writes comes short of you,
And imitates you ill (which most he fears),
Or else his writing is not worse than theirs.
Yet, though you judge (as sure the critics will),
That some before him writ with greater skill,
In this one praise he has their fame surpast,
To please an age more gallant than the last.

Cobb's tankard . . . Otter's horse: Cobb appears in Jonson's *Every Man in his Humour* (1601) and Otter in his *Epicoene* (?1609).

DEFENCE OF THE EPILOGUE

OR *AN ESSAY ON THE DRAMATIC POETRY OF THE LAST AGE*

THE promises of authors that they will write again[n] are, in effect, a threatening of their readers with some new impertinence, and they who perform not what they promise will have their pardon on easy terms. 'Tis from this consideration that I could be glad to spare you the trouble which I am now giving you of a preface, if I were not obliged by many reasons to write somewhat concerning our present plays, and those of our predecessors on the English stage. The truth is, I have so far engaged myself in a bold Epilogue to this play, wherein I have somewhat taxed the former writing, that it was necessary for me either not to print it, or to show that I could defend it. Yet I would so maintain my opinion of the present age as not to be wanting in my veneration for the past: I would ascribe to dead authors their just praises in those things wherein they have excelled us; and in those wherein we contend with them for the pre-eminence, I would acknowledge our advantages to the age, and claim no victory from our wit. This being what I have proposed to myself, I hope I shall not be thought arrogant when I inquire into their errors. For we live in an age so sceptical, that as it determines little, so it takes nothing from antiquity on trust. And I profess to have no other ambition in this essay than that poetry may not go backward, when all other arts and sciences are advancing. Whoever censures me for this inquiry, let him hear his character from Horace:

> ingeniis non ille favet, plauditque sepultis,
> nostra sed impugnat; nos nostraque lividus odit.

> He favours not dead wits, but hates the living.

It was upbraided to that excellent poet that he was an enemy to the writings of his predecessor Lucilius, because he had said *Lucilium lutulentum fluere*, that he ran muddy; and that he ought to have retrenched from his satires many unnecessary verses. But Horace makes Lucilius himself to justify him from the imputation of envy, by telling

---

from Horace: *Epistles*, II. i. 88–9.
Lucilium lutulentum fluere: *Satires*, I. x. 50 ('at dixi fluere hunc lutulentum, saepe ferentem': Lucilius, *c.* 180–102 B.C., the reputed originator of Roman satire, is mentioned at l. 53).

you that he would have done the same had he lived in an age which
was more refined:

> si foret hoc nostrum fato delapsus in aevum,
> detraheret sibi multa, recideret omne quod ultra
> perfectum traheretur, etc.

And, both in the whole course of that satire, and in his most admirable Epistle to Augustus, he makes it his business to prove that
antiquity alone is no plea for the excellency of a poem; but that, one
age learning from another, the last (if we can suppose an equality of
wit in the writers) has the advantage of knowing more and better
than the former. And this, I think, is the state of the question in
dispute. It is therefore my part to make it clear that the language, wit,
and conversation of our age are improved and refined above the last;
and then it will not be difficult to infer that our plays have received
some part of those advantages.

In the first place, therefore, it will be necessary to state, in general,
what this refinement is of which we treat: and that, I think, will not
be defined amiss: *an improvement of our wit, language, and conversation; or, an alteration in them for the better.*

To begin with language. That an alteration is lately made in ours,
or since the writers of the last age (in which I comprehend Shakespeare, Fletcher, and Jonson), is manifest. Any man who reads those
excellent poets, and compares their language with what is now
written, will see it almost in every line. But that this is an improvement of the language, or an alteration for the better, will not so easily
be granted. For many are of a contrary opinion, that the English
tongue was then in the height of its perfection; that from Jonson's
time to ours it has been in a continual declination, like that of the
Romans from the age of Virgil to Statius, and so downward to
Claudian: of which not only Petronius, but Quintilian himself, so
much complains, under the person of Secundus, in his famous
dialogue *De causis corruptae eloquentiae.*

But to show that our language is improved, and that those people
have not a just value for the age in which they live, let us consider in
what the refinement of a language principally consists: that is, *either
in rejecting such old words or phrases which are ill sounding, or improper, or in admitting new, which are more proper, more sounding, and
more significant.*

si foret hoc nostrum . . .; ibid. 68–70 (for 'delapsus' read 'dilatus'; 'Had Fate
   reserved him for this our age, he would delete much that he wrote, and remove
   everything that exceeded a finished line').
Epistle to Augustus: Epistles. II. i.
De causis . . .: *De Oratoribus*, attributed both to Quintilian and to Tacitus.

The reader will easily take notice that when I speak of rejecting improper words and phrases, I mention not such as are antiquated by custom only and, as I may say, without any fault of theirs: for in this case the refinement can be but accidental: that is, when the words and phrases which are rejected happen to be improper. Neither would I be understood (when I speak of impropriety in language) either wholly to accuse the last age, or to excuse the present; and least of all myself. For all writers have their imperfections and failings. But I may safely conclude in the general, that our improprieties are less frequent, and less gross than theirs. One testimony of this is undeniable, that we are the first who have observed them. And, certainly, to observe errors is a great step to the correcting of them. But malice and partiality set apart, let any man who understands English read diligently the works of Shakespeare and Fletcher; and I dare undertake that he will find in every page either some solecism of speech, or some notorious flaw in sense; and yet these men are reverenced when we are not forgiven. That their wit is great, and many times their expressions noble, envy itself cannot deny:

> neque ego illi detrahere ausim
> haerentem capiti multa cum laude coronam.

But the times were ignorant in which they lived. Poetry was then, if not in its infancy among us, at least not arrived to its vigour and maturity: witness the lameness of their plots; many of which, especially those which they writ first (for even that age refined itself in some measure), were made up of some ridiculous, incoherent story, which in one play many times took up the business of an age. I suppose I need not name *Pericles, Prince of Tyre*, nor the historical plays of Shakespeare. Besides many of the rest, as the *Winter's Tale*, *Love's Labour Lost*, *Measure for Measure*, which were either grounded on impossibilities, or at least so meanly written that the comedy neither caused your mirth, nor the serious part your concernment. If I would expatiate on this subject, I could easily demonstrate that our admired Fletcher, who writ after him, neither understood correct plotting, nor that which they call the decorum of the stage. I would not search in his worst plays for examples: he who will consider his *Philaster*, his *Humorous Lieutenant*, his *Faithful Shepherdess*, and

---

solecism: abuse, impropriety.
neque ego . . .: Horace, *Satires*, I. x. 48–9 ('Nor should I dare wrench off the wreath which clings with much glory to his head').
Philaster: (?1609) by Beaumont and Fletcher. The other two plays mentioned (respectively ?1619 and ?1608) are probably by Fletcher alone.

many others which I could name, will find them much below the applause which is now given them. He will see Philaster wounding his mistress, and afterwards his boy, to save himself, not to mention the Clown who enters immediately, and not only has the advantage of the combat against the hero, but diverts you from your serious concernment with his ridiculous and absurd raillery. In his *Humorous Lieutenant* you find his Demetrius and Leoncius staying in the midst of a routed army to hear the cold mirth of the Lieutenant; and Demetrius afterwards appearing with a pistol in his hand, in the next age to Alexander the Great. And for his *Shepherd*, he falls twice into the former indecency of wounding women. But these absurdities which those poets committed may more properly be called the age's fault than theirs. For, besides the want of education and learning (which was their particular unhappiness), they wanted the benefit of converse. But of that I shall speak hereafter, in a place more proper for it. Their audiences knew no better: and therefore were satisfied with what they brought. Those who call theirs the Golden Age of poetry have only this reason for it, that they were then content with acorns before they knew the use of bread; or that ἅλις δρυὸς was become a proverb. They had many who admired them, and few who blamed them. And, certainly, a severe critic is the greatest help to good wit. He does the office of a friend, while he designs that of an enemy; and his malice keeps a poet within those bounds which the luxuriancy of his fancy would tempt him to overleap.

But it is not their plots which I meant principally to tax: I was speaking of their sense and language. And I dare almost challenge any man to show me a page together which is correct in both. As for Ben Jonson, I am loth to name him, because he is a most judicious writer; yet he very often falls into these errors. And I once more beg the reader's pardon for accusing him of them. Only let him consider that I live in an age where my least faults are severely censured; and that I have no way left to extenuate my failings but my showing as great in those whom we admire:

> caedimus, inque vicem praebemus crura sagittis.

I cast my eyes but by chance on *Catiline*; and in the three or four first

---

he will see Philaster wounding: IV. v–vi.
Demetrius . . . Alexander the Great: II. ii; IV. iv.
wounding women: III; IV. iv.
ἅλις δρυὸς: see Cicero, *Ad Atticum*, ii. 19 ('enough of acorns').
caedimus, inque vicem . . .: Persius, *Satires*, iv. 42 ('We strike in turn and in turn expose our own legs to the arrows').

pages found enough to conclude that Jonson writ not correctly:

> Let the long-hid seeds
> Of treason, in thee, now shoot forth in deeds
> Ranker than horror.

In reading some bombast speeches of *Macbeth*, which are not to be understood, he used to say that it was horror; and I am much afraid that this is so.

> Thy parricide late on thy only son,
> After his mother, to make empty way
> For thy last wicked nuptials, worse than they
> That blaze that act of thy incestuous life,
> Which gained thee at once a daughter and a wife.

The sense is here extremely perplexed: and I doubt the word *they* is false grammar.

> And be free
> Not heaven itself from thy impiety.

A synchysis, or ill placing of words, of which Tully so much complains in *Oratory*.

> The waves and dens of beasts could not receive
> The bodies that those souls were frighted from.

The preposition in the end of the sentence; a common fault with him, and which I have but lately observed in my own writings.

> What all the several ills that visit earth,
> Plague, famine, fire, could not reach unto,
> The sword, nor surfeits; let thy fury do.

Here are both the former faults: for, besides that the preposition *unto* is placed last in the verse, and at the half period, and is redundant, there is the former synchysis in the words *the sword, nor surfeits*, which in construction ought to have been placed before the other.

Catiline says of Cethegus that for his sake he would

> Go on upon the gods, kiss lightning, wrest
> The engine from the Cyclops, and give fire
> At face of a full cloud, and stand his ire.

Let the long-hid seeds . . .: I. i. 25–7.

Thy parricide . . .: ibid. 32–6 (for the second 'thy' in l. 32 read 'thine', and for 'gained' in l. 36 'got').

And be free . . .: ibid. 59–60.

Tully so much complains: Cicero, *De oratore*, II. lxiv, although the term itself is not used there. 'Synchysis', otherwise named 'confusio', is defined by Peacham as 'A confusion of order in all parts of the construction'.

The waves and dens . . .: *Catiline*, I. i. 250–1 (for 'waves' read 'mawes').

What all the several ills . . .: ibid. 49, 51–2 ('Plagues . . .').

Go on upon the gods, . . .: ibid. 143–5.

To *go on upon* is only to go on twice. To *give fire at face of a full cloud* was not understood in his own time; *and stand his ire*, besides the antiquated word *ire*, there is the article *his*, which makes false construction: and *giving fire at the face of a cloud* is a perfect image of shooting, however it came to be known in those days to Catiline.

> Others there are,
> Whom envy to the state draws and pulls on,
> For contumelies received; and such are sure ones.

Ones in the plural number: but that is frequent with him; for he says, not long after,

> Caesar and Crassus, if they be ill men,
> Are mighty ones.
> Such men, they do not succour more the cause, etc.

They redundant.

> Though Heaven should speak with all his wrath at once,
> We should stand upright and unfeared.

His is ill syntax with *Heaven*; and by *unfeared* he means *unafraid*: words of a quite contrary signification.

> The ports are open.

He perpetually uses ports for gates; which is an affected error in him, to introduce Latin by the loss of the English idiom; as in the translation of Tully's speeches he usually does.

Well placing of words for the sweetness of pronunciation was not known till Mr. Waller introduced it; and therefore 'tis not to be wondered if Ben Jonson has many such lines as these:

But being bred up in his father's needy fortunes, Brought up in's sister's prostitution, etc.

But meanness of expression one would think not to be his error in a tragedy, which ought to be more high and sounding than any other kind of poetry; and yet amongst others in *Catiline* I find these four lines together:

> So Asia, thou art cruelly even
> With us, for all the blows thee given;
> When we, whose virtues conquered thee,
> Thus by thy vices ruined be.

Others there are, . . .: ibid. 146–8 ('. . . puts on . . .').
Caesar and Crassus, . . .: ibid. IV. 530–1, 56.
Though Heaven . . .: ibid. 30, 32.
The ports are open: ibid. 302.
But being bred up . . .: ibid. 122–3 ('. . . bred in's father's . . .').
So Asia, . . .: ibid. I. 587–90.

Be there is false English for *are*; though the rhyme hides it.

But I am willing to close the book, partly out of veneration to the author, partly out of weariness to pursue an argument which is so fruitful in so small a compass. And what correctness, after this, can be expected from Shakespeare or from Fletcher, who wanted that learning and care which Jonson had? I will therefore spare my own trouble of inquiring into their faults; who, had they lived now, had doubtless written more correctly. I suppose it will be enough for me to affirm (as I think I safely may) that these and the like errors which I taxed in the most correct of the last age, are such into which we do not ordinarily fall. I think few of our present writers would have left behind them such a line as this:

> Contain your spirit in more stricter bounds.

But that gross way of two comparatives was then ordinary; and therefore more pardonable in Jonson.

As for the other part of refining, which consists in receiving new words and phrases, I shall not insist much on it. 'Tis obvious that we have admitted many: some of which we wanted, and therefore our language is the richer for them, as it would be by importation of bullion; others are rather ornamental than necessary, yet by their admission the language is become more courtly, and our thoughts are better dressed. These are to be found scattered in the writers of our age, and it is not my business to collect them. They who have lately written with most care have, I believe, taken the rule of Horace for their guide; that is, not to be too hasty in receiving of words, but rather to stay till custom has made them familiar to us:

> quem penes arbitrium est, et jus, et norma loquendi.

For I cannot approve of their way of refining, who corrupt our English idiom by mixing it too much with French: that is a sophistication of language, not an improvement of it; a turning English into French, rather than a refining of English by French. We meet daily with those fops who value themselves on their travelling, and pretend they cannot express their meaning in English because they would put off to us some French phrase of the last edition: without considering that, for aught they know, we have a better of our own. But these are not the men who are to refine us; their talent is to prescribe fashions, not words: at best, they are only serviceable to a writer so as Ennius was to Virgil. He may *aurum ex stercore colligere*. For 'tis hard if,

---

Contain your spirit . . .: *Every Man Out of his Humour*, Induction, l. 46.
quem penes . . .: *Ars Poetica*, l. 72 ('to which belongs the rule, law and government of speech').
aurum ex stercore colligere: 'pick gold out of the dung' (Latin proverb).

amongst many insignificant phrases, there happen not something worth preserving; though they themselves, like Indians, know not the value of their own commodity.

There is yet another way of improving language, which poets especially have practised in all ages: that is, by applying received words to a new signification. And this, I believe, is meant by Horace, in that precept which is so variously construed by expositors:

> dixeris egregie, notum si callida verbum
> reddiderit junctura novum.

And, in this way, he himself had a particular happiness: using all the tropes, and particularly metaphors, with that grace which is observable in his Odes, where the beauty of expression is often greater than that of thought; as in that one example, amongst an infinite number of others: *et vultus nimium lubricus aspici.*

And therefore, though he innovated little, he may justly be called a great refiner of the Roman tongue. This choice of words, and heightening of their natural signification, was observed in him by the writers of the following ages: for Petronius says of him, *et Horatii curiosa felicitas.* By this graffing, as I may call it, on old words, has our tongue been beautified by the three forementioned poets, Shakespeare, Fletcher, and Jonson: whose excellencies I can never enough admire. And in this they have been followed especially by Sir John Suckling and Mr. Waller, who refined upon them. Neither have they who now succeed them been wanting in their endeavours to adorn our mother tongue: but it is not so lawful for me to praise my living contemporaries as to admire my dead predecessors.

I should now speak of the refinement of wit; but I have been so large on the former subject that I am forced to contract myself in this. I will therefore only observe to you that the wit of the last age was yet more incorrect than their language. Shakespeare, who many times has written better than any poet, in any language, is yet so far from writing wit always, or expressing that wit according to the dignity of the subject, that he writes in many places below the dullest writer of ours, or of any precedent age. Never did any author precipitate himself from such heights of thought to so low expressions as he often does. He is the very Janus of poets; he wears almost everywhere two faces; and you have scarce begun to admire the one, ere you despise

---

dixeris egregie, . . .: *Ars Poetica*, ll. 47–8 ('You will speak well if a new setting gives a common word new force').

et vultus nimium . . .: *Odes*, I. xix. 8 ('her face too dangerous to look at').

. . . curiosa felicitas.: *Satyricon*, 118.

the other. Neither is the luxuriance of Fletcher (which his friends have taxed in him) a less fault than the carelessness of Shakespeare. He does not well always, and, when he does, he is a true Englishman; he knows not when to give over. If he wakes in one scene he commonly slumbers in another; and if he pleases you in the first three acts, he is frequently so tired with his labour that he goes heavily in the fourth, and sinks under his burden in the fifth.

For Ben Jonson, the most judicious of poets, he always writ properly, and as the character required; and I will not contest farther with my friends who call that wit: it being very certain that even folly itself, well represented, is wit in a larger signification; and that there is fancy as well as judgement in it, though not so much or noble: because all poetry being imitation, that of folly is a lower exercise of fancy, though perhaps as difficult as the other, for 'tis a kind of looking downward in the poet, and representing that part of mankind which is below him.

In these low characters of vice and folly lay the excellency of that inimitable writer; who, when at any time he aimed at wit in the stricter sense, that is, sharpness of conceit, was forced either to borrow from the Ancients, as to my knowledge he did very much from Plautus; or, when he trusted himself alone, often fell into meanness of expression. Nay, he was not free from the lowest and most grovelling kind of wit, which we call clenches, of which *Every Man in His Humour* is infinitely full. And, which is worse, the wittiest persons in the drama speak them. His other comedies are not exempted from them: will you give me leave to name some few? Asper, in which character he personates himself (and he neither was, nor thought himself, a fool), exclaiming against the ignorant judges of the age, speaks thus:

> How monstrous and detested is't, to see
> A fellow that has neither art nor brain,
> Sit like an Aristarchus, or stark-ass,
> Taking men's lines, with a tobacco face,
> In snuff, etc.

And presently after: 'I mar'le whose wit 'twas to put a prologue in yond sackbut's mouth. They might well think he would be out of tune, and yet you'd play upon him too.' Will you have another of the

---

clenches: puns.
How monstrous . . .: *Every Man Out of his Humour*, Induction, ll. 177–8.
'*I mar'le . . .*': ibid. ll. 322–5.

same stamp? 'O, I cannot abide these limbs of satin, or rather Satan.'

But it may be you will object that this was Asper, Macilente, or Carlo Buffone: you shall, therefore, hear him speak in his own person, and that in the two last lines or sting of an epigram. 'Tis inscribed to Fine Grand who, he says, was indebted to him for many things which he reckons there; and concludes thus:

> Forty things more, dear Grand, which you know true,
> For which, or pay me quickly, or I'll pay you.

This was then the mode of wit, the vice of the age, and not Ben Jonson's. For you see, a little before him, that admirable wit Sir Philip Sidney perpetually playing with his words. In his time, I believe, it ascended first into the pulpit, where (if you will give me leave to clench too) it yet finds the benefit of its clergy. For they are commonly the first corrupters of eloquence, and the last reformed from vicious oratory; as a famous Italian has observed before me, in his *Treatise of the Corruption of the Italian Tongue*, which he principally ascribes to priests and preaching friars.

But, to conclude with what brevity I can, I will only add this in defence of our present writers, that, if they reach not some excellencies of Ben Jonson (which no age, I am confident, ever shall) yet, at least, they are above that meanness of thought which I have taxed, and which is frequent in him.

That the wit of this age is much more courtly may easily be proved by viewing the characters of gentlemen which were written in the last. First, for Jonson, Truewit in *The Silent Woman* was his masterpiece. And Truewit was a scholar-like kind of man, a gentleman with an allay of pedantry, a man who seems mortified to the world, by much reading. The best of his discourse is drawn not from the knowledge of the town, but books. And, in short, he would be a fine gentleman in a university. Shakespeare showed the best of his skill in his Mercutio, and he said himself that he was forced to kill him in the third act, to prevent being killed by him. But, for my part, I cannot find he was so dangerous a person: I see nothing in him but what was so exceeding harmless that he might have lived to the end of the play, and died in his bed, without offence to any man.

Fletcher's Don John is our only bugbear; and yet I may affirm without suspicion of flattery, that he now speaks better, and that his character is maintained with much more vigour in the fourth and

---

'*O, I cannot abide . . .*': ibid. IV. iv. 14–15.
Forty things more, . . .: *Epigrammes*, lxxxiii. 21–2.
a famous Italian: unidentified.   *Don John*: hero of *The Chances* (?1617).

fifth acts than it was by Fletcher in the three former. I have always acknowledged the wit of our predecessors, with all the veneration which becomes me, but, I am sure, their wit was not that of gentlemen; there was ever somewhat that was ill-bred and clownish in it, and which confessed the conversation of the authors.

And this leads me to the last and greatest advantage of our writing, which proceeds from conversation. In the age wherein those poets lived, there was less of gallantry than in ours; neither did they keep the best company of theirs. Their fortune has been much like that of Epicurus, in the retirement of his gardens: to live almost unknown, and to be celebrated after their decease. I cannot find that any of them were conversant in courts, except Ben Jonson: and his genius lay not so much that way as to make an improvement by it. Greatness was not then so easy of access, nor conversation so free, as now it is. I cannot, therefore, conceive it any insolence to affirm that, by the knowledge and pattern of their wit who writ before us, and by the advantage of our own conversation, the discourse and raillery of our comedies excel what has been written by them. And this will be denied by none but some few old fellows who value themselves on their acquaintance with the Blackfriars; who, because they saw their plays, would pretend a right to judge ours. The memory of these grave gentlemen is their only plea for being wits. They can tell a story of Ben Jonson, and perhaps have had fancy enough to give a supper in Apollo that they might be called his sons: and, because they were drawn in to be laughed at in those times, they think themselves now sufficiently entitled to laugh at ours. Learning I never saw in any of them, and wit no more than they could remember. In short, they were unlucky to have been bred in an unpolished age, and more unlucky to live to a refined one. They have lasted beyond their own, and are cast behind ours: and not contented to have known little at the age of twenty, they boast of their ignorance at threescore.

Now, if any ask me whence it is that our conversation is so much refined, I must freely, and without flattery, ascribe it to the Court; and, in it, particularly to the King, whose example gives a law to it. His own misfortunes, and the nation's, afforded him an opportunity which is rarely allowed to sovereign princes, I mean of travelling, and being conversant in the most polished courts of Europe; and, thereby, of cultivating a spirit which was formed by nature to receive the impressions of a gallant and generous education. At his return, he found a nation lost as much in barbarism as in rebellion. And as the excellency of his nature forgave the one, so the excellency of his

---

Apollo: a room in the Devil Tavern, an inn frequented by Jonson and his 'tribe'.

manners reformed the other. The desire of imitating so great a pattern first weakened the dull and heavy spirits of the English from their natural reservedness, loosened them from their stiff forms of conversation, and made them easy and pliant to each other in discourse. Thus, insensibly, our way of living became more free: and the fire of the English wit, which was before stifled under a constrained, melancholy way of breeding, began first to display its force, by mixing the solidity of our nation with the air and gaiety of our neighbours. This being granted to be true, it would be a wonder if the poets, whose work is imitation, should be the only persons in three kingdoms who should not receive advantage by it; or if they should not more easily imitate the wit and conversation of the present age than of the past.

Let us therefore admire the beauties and the heights of Shakespeare, without falling after him into a carelessness and (as I may call it) a lethargy of thought, for whole scenes together. Let us imitate, as we are able, the quickness and easiness of Fletcher, without proposing him as a pattern to us, either in the redundancy of his matter, or the incorrectness of his language. Let us admire his wit and sharpness of conceit; but let us at the same time acknowledge that it was seldom so fixed, and made proper to his characters, as that the same things might not be spoken by any person in the play. Let us applaud his scenes of love; but let us confess that he understood not either greatness or perfect honour in the parts of any of his women. In fine, let us allow that he had so much fancy as when he pleased he could write wit: but that he wanted so much judgement as seldom to have written humour, or described a pleasant folly. Let us ascribe to Jonson the height and accuracy of judgement in the ordering of his plots, his choice of characters, and maintaining what he had chosen to the end. But let us not think him a perfect pattern of imitation; except it be in humour: for love, which is the foundation of all comedies in other languages, is scarcely mentioned in any of his plays. And for humour itself, the poets of this age will be more wary than to imitate the meanness of his persons. Gentlemen will now be entertained with the follies of each other: and though they allow Cob and Tib to speak properly, yet they are not much pleased with their tankard or with their rags: and surely their conversation can be no jest to them on the theatre, when they would avoid it in the street.

To conclude all, let us render to our predecessors what is their due,

---

Cob and Tib: characters in *Every Man in his Humour.*

without confining ourselves to a servile imitation of all they writ: and, without assuming to ourselves the title of better poets, let us ascribe to the gallantry and civility of our age the advantage which we have above them; and to our knowledge of the customs and manners of it, the happiness we have to please beyond them.

PROLOGUE
TO *AURENG-ZEBE*

1676

OUR author by experience finds it true,
'Tis much more hard to please himself than you:
And out of no feigned modesty, this day
Damns his laborious trifle of a play:
Not that it's worse than what before he writ,
But he has now another taste of wit;
And to confess a truth (though out of time)
Grows weary of his long-loved mistress, Rhyme.[n]
Passion's too fierce to be in fetters bound,
And Nature flies him like enchanted ground.
What verse can do, he has performed in this,
Which he presumes the most correct of his:
But spite of all his pride, a secret shame
Invades his breast at Shakespeare's sacred name:
Awed when he hears his godlike Romans rage,
He, in a just despair, would quit the stage.
And to an age less polished, more unskilled,
Does with disdain the foremost honours yield.
As with the greater dead he dares not strive,
He would not match his verse with those who live:
Let him retire, betwixt two ages cast,
The first of this, and hindmost of the last.
A losing gamester, let him sneak away;
He bears no ready money from the play.
The fate which governs poets thought it fit,
He should not raise his fortunes by his wit.
The clergy thrive, and the litigious bar;
Dull heroes fatten with the spoils of war:
All southern vices, Heaven be praised, are here;
But wit's a luxury you think too dear.
When you to cultivate the plant are loth,
'Tis a shrewd sign 'twas never of your growth:
And wit in northern climates will not blow,
Except, like orange-trees, 'tis housed from snow.
There needs no care to put a playhouse down,
'Tis the most desert place of all the town.
We and our neighbours, to speak proudly, are
Like monarchs ruined with expensive war.
While, like wise English, unconcerned, you sit,
And see us play the tragedy of wit.

THE AUTHOR'S APOLOGY FOR HEROIC POETRY AND POETIC LICENCE
PREFIXED TO *THE STATE OF INNOCENCE AN OPERA*

1677

To satisfy the curiosity of those who will give themselves the trouble of reading the ensuing poem, I think myself obliged to render them a reason why I publish an opera which was never acted. In the first place, I shall not be ashamed to own that my chiefest motive was the ambition which I acknowledged in the Epistle. I was desirous to lay at the feet of so beautiful and excellent a Princess a work which I confess was unworthy her, but which I hope she will have the goodness to forgive. I was also induced to it in my own defence; many hundred copies of it being dispersed abroad without my knowledge or consent: so that every one gathering new faults, it became at length a libel against me; and I saw, with some disdain, more nonsense than either I, or as bad a poet, could have crammed into it at a month's warning; in which time 'twas wholly written, and not since revised. After this, I cannot, without injury to the deceased author of *Paradise Lost*, but acknowledge that this poem has received its entire foundation, part of the design, and many of the ornaments, from him. What I have borrowed will be so easily discerned from my mean productions, that I shall not need to point the reader to the places: and truly I should be sorry, for my own sake, that any one should take the pains to compare them together; the original being undoubtedly one of the greatest, most noble, and most sublime poems which either this age or nation has produced. And though I could not refuse the partiality of my friend who is pleased to commend me in his verses, I hope they will rather be esteemed the effect of his love to me than of his deliberate and sober judgement. His genius is able to make beautiful what he pleases: yet, as he has been too favourable to me, I doubt not but he will hear of his kindness from many of our contemporaries. For we are fallen into an age of illiterate, censorious, and detracting people who, thus qualified, set up for critics.

In the first place, I must take leave to tell them that they wholly mistake the nature of criticism who think its business is principally to find fault. Criticism, as it was first instituted by Aristotle, was meant a standard of judging well; the chiefest part of which is to observe those excellencies which should delight a reasonable reader. If the

---

the Epistle: 'To her Royal Highness, the Duchess', i.e. Mary, Duchess of York.
my friend: Nathaniel Lee, who contributed complimentary verses to the 1677 edition of Dryden's 'opera'.

design, the conduct, the thoughts, and the expressions of a poem be generally such as proceed from a true genius of poetry, the critic ought to pass his judgement in favour of the author. 'Tis malicious and unmanly to snarl at the little lapses of a pen from which Virgil himself stands not exempted. Horace acknowledges that honest Homer nods sometimes: he is not equally awake in every line; but he leaves it also as a standing measure for our judgements,

> non, ubi plura nitent in carmine, paucis
> offendar maculis, quas aut incuria fudit,
> aut humana parum cavit natura.

And Longinus, who was undoubtedly, after Aristotle, the greatest critic amongst the Greeks, in his twenty-seventh chapter *ΠΕΡΙ 'ΥΨΟΥΣ*, has judiciously preferred the sublime genius that sometimes errs to the middling or indifferent one which makes few faults, but seldom or never rises to any excellence. He compares the first to a man of large possessions who has not leisure to consider of every slight expense, will not debase himself to the management of every trifle: particular sums are not laid out or spared to the greatest advantage in his economy, but are sometimes suffered to run to waste, while he is only careful of the main. On the other side, he likens the mediocrity of wit to one of a mean fortune, who manages his store with extreme frugality, or rather parsimony; but who, with fear of running into profuseness, never arrives to the magnificence of living. This kind of genius writes indeed correctly. A wary man he is in grammar: very nice as to solecism or barbarism, judges to a hair of little decencies, knows better than any man what is not to be written, and never hazards himself so far as to fall, but plods on deliberately and, as a grave man ought, is sure to put his staff before him; in short, he sets his heart upon it, and with wonderful care makes his business sure; that is, in plain English, neither to be blamed nor praised. I could, says my author, find out some blemishes in Homer; and am, perhaps, as naturally inclined to be disgusted at a fault as another man; but, after all, to speak impartially, his failings are such as are only marks of human frailty: they are little mistakes, or rather negligences, which have escaped his pen in the fervour of his writing; the sublimity of his spirit carries it with me against his carelessness; and though Apollonius's *Argonauts*, and Theocritus'

---

honest Homer nods: Ars Poetica, l. 359.
non, ubi plura nitent . . .: ibid. 351–3 ('Verum ubi plura . . . non ego paucis').
Longinus . . . has judiciously preferred: On the Sublime, xxxiii.
Apollonius . . . Theocritus: Apollonius (c. 295–215 B.C.) was a writer of epic; Theocritus (fl. 270 B.C.) a writer of pastoral.

Eidullia, are more free from errors, there is not any man of so false a judgement who would choose rather to have been Apollonius or Theocritus than Homer.

'Tis worth our consideration a little to examine how much these hypercritics of English poetry differ from the opinion of the Greek and Latin judges of antiquity; from the Italians and French who have succeeded them; and, indeed, from the general taste and approbation of all ages. Heroic poetry, which they contemn, has ever been esteemed, and ever will be, the greatest work of human nature: in that rank has Aristotle placed it, and Longinus is so full of the like expressions that he abundantly confirms the other's testimony. Horace as plainly delivers his opinion, and particularly praises Homer in these verses:

> Trojani Belli scriptorem, Maxime Lolli,
> dum tu declamas Romae, Praeneste relegi:
> qui quid sit pulchrum, quid turpe, quid utile, quid non,
> planius ac melius Chrysippo et Crantore dicit.

And in another place modestly excluding himself from the number of poets, because he only writ odes and satires, he tells you a poet is such a one,

> cui mens divinior, atque os
> magna sonaturum.

Quotations are superfluous in an established truth: otherwise I could reckon up, amongst the moderns, all the Italian commentators on Aristotle's book of poetry; and amongst the French, the greatest of this age, Boileau and Rapin; the latter of which is alone sufficient, were all other critics lost, to teach anew the rules of writing. Any man who will seriously consider the nature of an epic poem, how it agrees with that of poetry in general, which is to instruct and to delight; what actions it describes, and what persons they are chiefly whom it informs, will find it a work which indeed is full of difficulty in the attempt, but admirable when 'tis well performed. I write not this with the least intention to undervalue the other parts of poetry: for comedy is both excellently instructive, and extremely pleasant: satire lashes vice into reformation, and humour represents folly so as to render it ridiculous. Many of our present writers are eminent in both

---

Trojani Belli scriptorem, . . .: Epistles, I. ii. 1–4 ('While, Lollius Maximus, you study the art of speaking in Rome, I have at Praeneste read again the poet of the Trojan War; who shows to better effect and more fully than Chrysippus and Crantor what is noble and what low, what useful and what is not').

cui mens divinior, . . .: Satires, I. iv. 43–4 ('Whose soul is more divine, and whose mouth utters great thoughts').

these kinds; and particularly the author of *The Plain Dealer*, whom I
am proud to call my friend, has obliged all honest and virtuous men
by one of the most bold, most general, and most useful satires which
has ever been presented on the English theatre. I do not dispute the
preference of tragedy; let every man enjoy his taste: but 'tis unjust
that they who have not the least notion of heroic writing should
therefore condemn the pleasure which others receive from it, because
they cannot comprehend it. Let them please their appetites in eating
what they like; but let them not force this dish on all the table. They
who would combat general authority with particular opinion must
first establish themselves a reputation of understanding better than
other men. Are all the flights of heroic poetry to be concluded bombast, unnatural, and mere madness, because they are not affected
with their excellencies? 'Tis just as reasonable as to conclude there is
no day because a blind man cannot distinguish of light and colours.
Ought they not rather, in modesty, to doubt of their own judgements,
when they think this or that expression in Homer, Virgil, Tasso, or
Milton's *Paradise* to be too far strained, than positively to conclude
that 'tis all fustian, and mere nonsense? 'Tis true, there are limits to
be set betwixt the boldness and rashness of a poet; but he must understand those limits who pretends to judge as well as he who undertakes
to write: and he who has no liking to the whole, ought in reason to
be excluded from censuring of the parts. He must be a lawyer before
he mounts the tribunal; and the judicature of one court, too, does
not qualify a man to preside in another. He may be an excellent
pleader in the Chancery, who is not fit to rule the Common Pleas. But
I will presume for once to tell them that the boldest strokes of poetry,
when they are managed artfully, are those which most delight the
reader.

Virgil and Horace, the severest writers of the severest age, have
made frequent use of the hardest metaphors, and of the strongest
hyperboles: and in this case the best authority is the best argument.
For generally to have pleased, and through all ages, must bear the
force of universal tradition. And if you would appeal from thence to
right reason, you will gain no more by it in effect than, first, to set up
your reason against those authors; and, secondly, against all those
who have admired them. You must prove why that ought not to
have pleased, which has pleased the most learned and the most
judicious; and to be thought knowing, you must first put the fool
upon all mankind. If you can enter more deeply than they have done
into the causes and resorts of that which moves pleasure in a reader,

the author of The Plain Dealer: William Wycherley (1640?–1716).

the field is open, you may be heard: but those springs of human nature are not so easily discovered by every superficial judge. It requires philosophy as well as poetry to sound the depth of all the passions; what they are in themselves, and how they are to be provoked; and in this science the best poets have excelled. Aristotle raised the fabric of his *Poetry* from observation of those things in which Euripides, Sophocles, and Aeschylus pleased: he considered how they raised the passions, and thence has drawn rules for our imitation. From hence have sprung the tropes and figures for which they wanted a name who first practised them, and succeeded in them. Thus I grant you that the knowledge of nature was the original rule; and that all poets ought to study her, as well as Aristotle and Horace, her interpreters. But then this also undeniably follows, that those things which delight all ages must have been an imitation of nature; which is all I contend. Therefore is rhetoric made an art; therefore the names of so many tropes and figures were invented: because it was observed they had such and such effect upon the audience. Therefore catachreses and hyperboles have found their place amongst them; not that they were to be avoided, but to be used judiciously, and placed in poetry as heightenings and shadows are in painting, to make the figure bolder, and cause it to stand off to sight.

> nec retia cervis
> ulla dolum meditantur,

says Virgil in his *Eclogues*: and speaking of Leander in his *Georgics*,

> caeca nocte natat serus freta, quem super ingens
> porta tonat coeli, et scopulis inlisa reclamant
> aequora.

In both of these, you see he fears not to give voice and thought to things inanimate.

Will you arraign your master Horace for his hardness of expression when he describes the death of Cleopatra, and says she did *asperos tractare serpentes, ut atrum corpore combiberet venenum*, because the body in that action performs what is proper to the mouth?

As for hyperboles, I will neither quote Lucan, nor Statius, men of an unbounded imagination, but who often wanted the poise of

---

catachreses: misuses of a word or rhetorical figure (otherwise 'abusio').

nec retia cervis . . .: *Eclogues*, v. 60–1 ('nets do not plan snares for stags').

caeca nocte natat . . .: *Georgics*, iii. 260–2 (read 'caeli' for 'coeli': 'Heaven's great portal thunders over him, and the waves, dashing against the cliffs, echo the sound').

asperos tractare . . .: *Odes*, I. xxxvii, 26–8 ('asperas . . .': 'to handle wild snakes, to drink black poison into her body').

judgement. The divine Virgil was not liable to that exception; and yet he describes Polyphemus thus:

> graditurque per aequor
> jam medium; necdum fluctus latera ardua tingit.

In imitation of this place, our admirable Cowley thus paints Goliath:

> The valley, now, this monster seemed to fill;
> And we, methought, looked up to him from our hill,

where the two words *seemed* and *methought* have mollified the figure, and yet if they had not been there, the fright of the Israelites might have excused their belief of the giant's stature.

In the 8th of the Aeneids, Virgil paints the swiftness of Camilla thus:

> illa vel intactae segetis per summa volaret
> gramina, nec teneras cursu laesisset aristas;
> vel mare per medium, fluctu suspensa tumenti,
> ferret iter, celeres nec tingeret aequore plantas.

You are not obliged, as in history, to a literal belief of what the poet says; but you are pleased with the image, without being cozened by the fiction.

Yet even in history, Longinus quotes Herodotus on this occasion of hyperboles. The Lacedemonians, says he, at the straits of Thermopylae, defended themselves to the last extremity; and when their arms failed them, fought it out with their nails and teeth; till at length (the Persians shooting continually upon them) they lay buried under the arrows of their enemies. It is not reasonable (continues the critic) to believe that men could defend themseves with their nails and teeth from an armed multitude; nor that they lay buried under a pile of darts and arrows; and yet there wants not probability for the figure: because the hyperbole seems not to have been made for the sake of the description, but rather to have been produced from the occasion.

'Tis true, the boldness of the figures are to be hidden sometimes by the address of the poet, that they may work their effect upon the mind without discovering the art which caused it. And therefore they are principally to be used in passion; when we speak more warmly,

---

graditurque per aequor . . .: *Aeneid*, iii. 664–5 ('tinxit': 'He marches through the sea; and the wave has not yet wetted his mighty sides').

Cowley: *Davideis*, iii. 385–6 ('. . . methoughts . . .').

illa vel intactae . . .: *Aeneid*, vii. 808–11 ('Outpaced the winds for speed on the plain, and flew over the fields without damaging the wheat; she swept the seas and as she skimmed the waves her feet hung above them without getting wet').

Longinus quotes Herodotus: *On the Sublime*, xxxviii: cf. Herodotus, vii. 225.

and with more precipitation, than at other times: for then, *si vis me
flere, dolendum est primum ipsi tibi*; the poet must put on the passion
he endeavours to represent: a man in such an occasion is not cool
enough, either to reason rightly, or to talk calmly. Aggravations are
then in their proper places; interrogations, exclamations, hyperbata,
or a disordered connection of discourse, are graceful there because
they are natural. The sum of all depends on what before I hinted,
that this boldness of expression is not to be blamed if it be managed
by the coolness and discretion which is necessary to a poet.

Yet before I leave this subject, I cannot but take notice how dis-
ingenuous our adversaries appear: all that is dull, insipid, languishing, and without sinews, in a poem, they call an imitation of nature:
they only offend our most equitable judges, who think beyond them;
and lively images and elocution are never to be forgiven.

What fustian, as they call it, have I heard these gentlemen find out
in Mr. Cowley's *Odes*? I acknowledge myself unworthy to defend so
excellent an author, neither have I room to do it here: only in general
I will say that nothing can appear more beautiful to me than the
strength of those images which they condemn.

Imaging is, in itself, the very height and life of poetry. 'Tis, as
Longinus describes it, a discourse which, by a kind of enthusiasm, or
extraordinary emotion of the soul, makes it seem to us that we behold
those things which the poet paints, so as to be pleased with them, and
to admire them.

If poetry be imitation, that part of it must needs be best which
describes most lively our actions and passions, our virtues and our
vices, our follies and our humours: for neither is comedy without its
part of imaging; and they who do it best are certainly the most
excellent in their kind. This is too plainly proved to be denied. But
how are poetical fictions, how are hippocentaurs and chimeras, or
how are angels and immaterial substances to be imaged; which some
of them are things quite out of nature; others, such whereof we can
have no notion? This is the last refuge of our adversaries; and more
than any of them have yet had the wit to object against us. The
answer is easy to the first part of it. The fiction of some beings which
are not in nature (second notions, as the logicians call them) has been
founded on the conjunction of two natures which have a real separate

---

si vis me flere, . . .: Horace, *Ars Poetica*, ll. 102–3 ('If you want me to mourn, first
    mourn yourself ').
hyperbata: transpositions of words, otherwise known as 'transgressio' (see
    Longinus, xxii).
as Longinus describes it: *On the Sublime*, xv.

being. So hippocentaurs were imagined by joining the natures of a man and horse together; as Lucretius tells us, who has used this word of *image* oftener than any of the poets:

> nam certe ex vivo centauri non fit imago,
> nulla fuit quoniam talis natura animantis:
> verum ubi equi atque hominis, casu, convenit imago,
> haerescit facile extemplo, etc.

The same reason may also be alleged for chimeras and the rest. And poets may be allowed the like liberty for describing things which really exist not, if they are founded on popular belief. Of this nature are fairies, pigmies, and the extraordinary effects of magic; for 'tis still an imitation, though of other men's fancies: and thus are Shakespeare's *Tempest*, his *Midsummer Night's Dream*, and Ben Jonson's *Masque of Witches* to be defended. For immaterial substances, we are authorized by Scripture in their description: and herein the text accommodates itself to vulgar apprehension, in giving angels the likeness of beautiful young men. Thus, after the pagan divinity, has Homer drawn his gods with human faces: and thus we have notion of things above us, by describing them like other beings more within our knowledge.

I wish I could produce any one example of excellent imaging in all this poem: perhaps I cannot; but that which comes nearest it is in these four lines, which have been sufficiently canvassed by my well-natured censors:

> Seraph and cherub, careless of their charge,
> And wanton, in full ease now live at large:
> Unguarded leave the passes of the sky,
> And all dissolved in hallelujahs lie.

I have heard (says one of them) of anchovies dissolved in sauce; but never of an angel in hallelujahs. A mighty witticism (if you will pardon a new word!) but there is some difference between a laugher and a critic. He might have burlesqued Virgil too, from whom I took the image: *invadunt urbem, somno vinoque sepultam*. A city's being buried is just as proper on occasion as an angel's being dissolved in

---

nam certe ex vivo . . .: *De rerum natura*, iv. 739–42 ('Certainly a centaur's image is not drawn from the life, as no creature like it ever existed. Yet where the images of horse and man meet they may combine easily').

Masque of Witches: *The Masque of Queens*, performed in 1609.

Seraph and cherub, . . .: *State of Innocence*, I. i.

invadunt urbem, . . .: *Aeneid*, ii. 265 ('They capture the city, buried in sleep and wine').

ease and songs of triumph. Mr. Cowley lies as open too in many places:

> Where their vast courts the mother waters keep, etc.

For if the mass of waters be the mothers, then their daughters, the little streams, are bound, in all good manners, to make courtesy to them, and ask them blessing. How easy 'tis to turn into ridicule the best descriptions, when once a man is in the humour of laughing, till he wheezes at his own dull jest! But an image which is strongly and beautifully set before the eyes of the reader, will still be poetry when the merry fit is over: and last when the other is forgotten.

I promised to say somewhat of poetic licence, but have in part anticipated my discourse already. Poetic licence I take to be the liberty, which poets have assumed to themselves in all ages, of speaking things in verse which are beyond the severity of prose. 'Tis that particular character which distinguishes and sets the bounds betwixt *oratio soluta* and poetry. This, as to what regards the thought or imagination of a poet, consists in fiction: but then those thoughts must be expressed; and here arise two other branches of it: for if this licence be included in a single word, it admits of tropes; if in a sentence or proposition, of figures; both which are of a much larger extent, and more forcibly to be used in verse than prose. This is that birthright which is derived to us from our great forefathers, even from Homer down to Ben. And they who would deny it to us have, in plain terms, the fox's quarrel to the grapes: they cannot reach it.

How far these liberties are to be extended, I will not presume to determine here, since Horace does not. But it is certain that they are to be varied, according to the language and age in which an author writes. That which would be allowed to a Grecian poet, Martial tells you, would not be suffered in a Roman. And 'tis evident that the English does more nearly follow the strictness of the latter than the freedoms of the former. Connection of epithets, or the conjunction of two words in one, are frequent and elegant in the Greek, which yet Sir Philip Sidney, and the translator of Du Bartas, have unluckily attempted in the English; though this, I confess, is not so proper an instance of poetic licence, as it is of variety of idiom in languages.

Where their vast courts . . .: *Davideis*, i. 79 ('. . . vast court . . .').
oratio soluta: Cicero's term for prose.
Martial tells you: *Epigrams*, ix. 12.
the translator of Du Bartas: Joshua Sylvester (1563–1618).

Horace a little explains himself on this subject of *licentia poetica*, in these verses:

> pictoribus atque poetis
> quidlibet audendi semper fuit aequa potestas:
> sed non, ut placidis coeant immitia, non ut
> serpentes avibus geminentur, tigribus haedi.

He would have a poem of a piece; not to begin with one thing and end with another: he restrains it so far that thoughts of an unlike nature ought not to be joined together. That were indeed to make a chaos. He taxed not Homer, nor the divine Virgil, for interesting their gods in the wars of Troy and Italy; neither, had he now lived, would he have taxed Milton, as our false critics have presumed to do, for his choice of a supernatural argument: but he would have blamed my author, who was a Christian, had he introduced into his poem heathen deities, as Tasso is condemned by Rapin on the like occasion; and as Camoens, the author of the *Lusiads*, ought to be censured by all his readers when he brings in Bacchus and Christ into the same adventure of his fable.

From that which has been said, it may be collected that the definition of wit (which has been so often attempted, and ever unsuccessfully, by many poets) is only this: that it is a propriety of thoughts and words; or, in other terms, thought and words elegantly adapted to the subject. If our critics will join issue on this definition, that we may *convenire in aliquo tertio*; if they will take it as a granted principle, 'twill be easy to put an end to this dispute. No man will disagree from another's judgement concerning the dignity of style in heroic poetry; but all reasonable men will conclude it necessary that sublime subjects ought to be adorned with the sublimest, and (consequently often) with the most figurative expressions. In the meantime, I will not run into their fault of imposing my opinions on other men, any more than I would my writings on their taste: I have only laid down, and that superficially enough, my present thoughts; and shall be glad to be taught better by those who pretend to reform our poetry.

pictoribus atque poetis . . .: *Ars Poetica*, ll. 9–10, 12–13 ('Painters and poets have always had equal rights to be bold. . . . But not to make the savage mate with the tame, nor to put snakes with birds, kids and tigers').

Rapin: in *Réflexions sur la poétique* . . ., II. xiii, Rapin attacks Camoens for this, but not Tasso.

convenire in aliquo tertio: 'agree upon some third position'.

HEADS OF AN ANSWER TO RYMER[n]

1] He who undertakes to answer this excellent critique of Mr. Rymer, in behalf of our English poets against the Greek, ought to do it in this manner.

2] Either by yielding to him the greatest part of what he contends for, which consists in this, that the μῦθος, i.e. the design and conduct of it, is more conducing in the Greeks to those ends of tragedy which Aristotle and he propose, namely to cause terror and pity; yet the granting this does not set the Greeks above the English poets.

3] But the answerer ought to prove two things: first, that the fable is not the greatest masterpiece of a tragedy, tho' it be the foundation of it.

4] Secondly, that other ends as suitable to the nature of tragedy may be found in the English, which were not in the Greek.

5] Aristotle places the fable first; not *quoad dignitatem, sed quoad fundamentum*; for a fable, never so movingly contrived to those ends of his, pity and terror, will operate nothing on our affections, except the characters, manners, thoughts, and words are suitable.

6] So that it remains for Mr. Rymer to prove that in all those, or the greatest part of them, we are inferior to Sophocles and Euripides; and this he has offered at in some measure but, I think, a little partially to the Ancients.

7] To make a true judgement in this competition, between the Greek poets and the English in tragedy, consider

   I. How Aristotle has defined a tragedy.
   II. What he assigns the end of it to be.
   III. What he thinks the beauties of it.
   IV. The means to attain the end proposed.

Compare the Greek and English tragic poets justly and without partiality, according to those rules.

8] Then, secondly, consider whether Aristotle has made a just definition of tragedy, of its parts, of its ends, of its beauties; and whether he, having not seen any others but those of Sophocles, Euripides, etc., had or truly could determine what all the excellencies of tragedy are, and wherein they consist.

9] Next show in what ancient tragedy was deficient: for example, in

---

Aristotle places the fable first: Poetics, vi.
quoad dignitatem, . . .: 'because of its dignity, but because it is basic'.
Then, secondly, consider . . .: comp. 'The Author's Apology for Heroic Poetry', pp. 133–142 above.

the narrowness of its plots, and fewness of persons, and try whether that be not a fault in the Greek poets; and whether their excellency was so great when the variety was visibly so little; or whether what they did was not very easy to do.

10] Then make a judgement on what the English have added to their beauties: as, for example, not only more plot, but also new passions; as namely, that of love, scarce touched on by the Ancients, except in this one example of Phaedra, cited by Mr. Rymer; and in that how short they were of Fletcher.

11] Prove also that love, being an heroic passion, is fit for tragedy, which cannot be denied, because of the example alleged of Phaedra; and how far Shakespeare has outdone them in friendship, etc.

12] To return to the beginning of this enquiry: consider if pity and terror be not enough for tragedy to move; and I believe, upon a true definition of tragedy, it will be found that its work extends farther, and that it is to reform manners by delightful representation of human life in great persons, by way of dialogue. If this be true, then not only pity and terror are to be moved as the only means to bring us to virtue, but generally love to virtue and hatred to vice; by showing the rewards of one, and punishments of the other; at least by rendering virtue always amiable, though it be shown unfortunate; and vice detestable, tho' it be shown triumphant.

13] If then the encouragement of virtue and discouragement of vice be the proper ends of poetry in tragedy: pity and terror, though good means, are not the only. For all the passions in their turns are to be set in a ferment: as joy, anger, love, fear are to be used as the poet's commonplaces; and a general concernment for the principal actors is to be raised, by making them appear such in their characters, their words and actions, as will interest the audience in their fortunes.

14] And if after all, in a large sense, pity comprehends this concernment for the good, and terror includes detestation for the bad, then let us consider whether the English have not answered this end of tragedy as well as the Ancients, or perhaps better.

15] And here Mr. Rymer's objections against these plays are to be impartially weighed, that we may see whether they are of weight enough to turn the balance against our countrymen.

16] 'Tis evident those plays which he arraigns have moved both those passions in a high degree upon the stage.

17] To give the glory of this away from the poet, and to place it upon the actors, seems unjust.

---

those plays which he arraigns: *A King and No King* and *The Maid's Tragedy* (Beaumont and Fletcher), *The Bloody Brother* (*Rollo*) (Fletcher and others).

18] One reason is, because whatever actors they have found, the event has been the same, that is, the same passions have been always moved; which shows that there is something of force and merit in the plays themselves, conducing to the design of raising these two passions: and suppose them ever to have been excellently acted, yet action only adds grace, vigour, and more life upon the stage; but cannot give it wholly where it is not first. But secondly, I dare appeal to those who have never seen them acted, if they have not found those two passions moved within them; and if the general voice will carry it, Mr. Rymer's prejudice will take off his single testimony.

19] This being matter of fact, is reasonably to be established by this appeal; as if one man says 'tis night, when the rest of the world conclude it to be day, there needs no further argument against him that it is so.

20] If he urge that the general taste is depraved, his arguments to prove this can at best but evince that our poets took not the best way to raise those passions; but experience proves against him that those means which they have used have been successful and have produced them.

21] And one reason of that success is, in my opinion, this, that Shakespeare and Fletcher have written to the genius of the age and nation in which they lived; for tho' nature, as he objects, is the same in all places, and reason too the same, yet the climate, the age, the dispositions of the people to whom a poet writes, may be so different that what pleased the Greeks would not satisfy an English audience.

22] And if they proceeded upon a foundation of truer reason to please the Athenians than Shakespeare and Fletcher to please the English, it only shows that the Athenians were a more judicious people; but the poet's business is certainly to please the audience.

23] Whether our English audience have been pleased hitherto with acorns, as he calls it, or with bread, is the next question; that is, whether the means which Shakespeare and Fletcher have used in their plays to raise those passions before named, be better applied to the ends by the Greek poets than by them; and perhaps we shall not grant him this wholly. Let it be yielded that a writer is not to run down with the stream, or to please the people by their own usual methods, but rather to reform their judgements: it still remains to prove that our theatre needs this total reformation.

---

with acorns . . . or with bread: Dryden is echoing Rymer here (*Critical Works*, ed. Zimansky, p. 20), but the image was made widely known by Jonson's 'Ode, to Himself' ('Come leave the loathed stage . . .').

24] The faults which he has found in their designs are rather wittily aggravated in many places than reasonably urged; and as much may be returned on the Greeks by one who were as witty as himself.

25] Secondly, they destroy not, if they are granted, the foundation of the fabric, only take away from the beauty of the symmetry: for example, the faults in the character of the King and No King are not, as he makes them, such as render him detestable, but only imperfections which accompany human nature, and for the most part excused by the violence of his love; so that they destroy not our pity or concernment for him. This answer may be applied to most of his objections of that kind.

26] And Rollo committing many murders, when he is answerable but for one, is too severely arraigned by him; for it adds to our horror and detestation of the criminal: and poetic justice is not neglected neither, for we stab him in our minds for every offence which he commits; and the point which the poet is to gain on the audience is not so much in the death of an offender, as the raising an horror of his crimes.

27] That the criminal should neither be wholly guilty, nor wholly innocent, but so participating of both as to move both pity and terror, is certainly a good rule, but not perpetually to be observed; for that were to make all tragedies too much alike; which objection he foresaw, but has not fully answered.

28] To conclude, therefore: if the plays of the Ancients are more correctly plotted, ours are more beautifully written; and if we can raise passions as high on worse foundations, it shows our genius in tragedy is greater, for in all other parts of it the English have manifestly excelled them.

29] For the fable itself, 'tis in the English more adorned with episodes, and larger than in the Greek poets; consequently more diverting, for, if the action be but one, and that plain, without any counter-turn of design or episode, i.e. under-plot, how can it be so pleasing as the English, which have both under-plot and a turned design, which keeps the audience in expectation of the catastrophe? whereas in the Greek poets we see through the whole design at first.

30] For the characters, they are neither so many nor so various in Sophocles and Euripides as in Shakespeare and Fletcher; only they are more adapted to those ends of tragedy which Aristotle commends to us: pity and terror.

31] The manners flow from the characters, and consequently must partake of their advantages and disadvantages.

32] The thoughts and words, which are the fourth and fifth beauties of tragedy, are certainly more noble and more poetical in the English

than in the Greek, which must be proved by comparing them somewhat more equitably than Mr. Rymer has done.

33] After all, we need not yield that the English way is less conducing
to move pity and terror, because they often show virtue oppressed
and vice punished: where they do not both, or either, they are not to
be defended.

34] That we may the less wonder why pity and terror are not now the
only springs on which our tragedies move, and that Shakespeare may
be more excused, Rapin confesses that the French tragedies now all
run on the *tendre*; and gives the reason, because love is the passion
which most predominates in our souls, and that therefore the passions
represented become insipid, unless they are conformable to the
thoughts of the audience. But it is to be concluded that this passion
works not now among the French so strongly as the other two did
amongst the Ancients: amongst us, who have a stronger genius for
writing, the operations from the writing are much stronger; for the
raising of Shakespeare's passions are more from the excellency of the
words and thoughts than the justness of the occasion; and if he has
been able to pick single occasions, he has never founded the whole
reasonably; yet by the genius of poetry, in writing he has succeeded.

35] The parts of a poem, tragic or heroic, are:

   I. The fable itself.
  II. The order or manner of its contrivance in relation of the parts
      to the whole.
 III. The manners or decency of the characters in speaking or acting
      what is proper for them, and proper to be shown by the poet.
  IV. The thoughts which express the manners.
   V. The words which express those thoughts.

36] In the last of these Homer excels Virgil, Virgil all other ancient
poets, and Shakespeare all modern poets.

37] For the second of these, the order: the meaning is that a fable
ought to have a beginning, middle, and an end, all just and natural,
so that that part which is the middle, could not naturally be the beginning or end, and so of the rest: all are depending on one another, like
the links of a curious chain.

38] If terror and pity are only to be raised, certainly this author
follows Aristotle's rules, and Sophocles's and Euripides's example;
but joy may be raised too, and that doubly, either by seeing a
wicked man punished, or a good man at last fortunate; or perhaps

---

Rapin confesses . . .: *Réflexions sur la poetique* (1674), II. x.
a beginning, middle, and an end: Aristotle, *Poetics*, vii.

indignation, to see wickedness prosperous and goodness depressed: both these may be profitable to the end of tragedy, reformation of manners; but the last improperly, only as it begets pity in the audience: though Aristotle, I confess, places tragedies of this kind in the second form.

39] And, if we should grant that the Greeks performed this better, perhaps it may admit a dispute whether pity and terror are either the prime, or at least the only ends of tragedy.

40] 'Tis not enough that Aristotle has said so, for Aristotle drew his models of tragedy from Sophocles and Euripides; and if he had seen ours, might have changed his mind.

41] And chiefly we have to say (what I hinted on pity and terror in the last paragraph save one) that the punishment of vice and reward of virtue are the most adequate ends of tragedy, because most conducing to good example of life. Now pity is not so easily raised for a criminal (as the ancient tragedy always represents its chief person such) as it is for an innocent man, and the suffering of innocence and punishment of the offender is of the nature of English tragedy: contrary, in the Greek, innocence is unhappy often, and the offender escapes.

42] Then, we are not touched with the sufferings of any sort of men so much as of lovers; and this was almost unknown to the Ancients; so that they neither administered poetical justice (of which Mr. Rymer boasts) so well as we; neither knew they the best commonplace of pity, which is love.

43] He therefore unjustly blames us for not building upon what the Ancients left us, for it seems, upon consideration of the premisses, that we have wholly finished what they began.

44] My judgement on this piece is this; that it is extremely learned; but that the author of it is better read in the Greek than in the English poets; that all writers ought to study this critique as the best account I have ever seen of the Ancients; that the model of tragedy he has here given is excellent and extreme correct; but that it is not the only model of all tragedy, because it is too much circumscribed in plot, characters, etc.; and lastly, that we may be taught here justly to admire and imitate the Ancients, without giving them the preference with this author in prejudice to our own country.

45] Want of method in this excellent treatise makes the thoughts of the author sometimes obscure.

46] His meaning, that pity and terror are to be moved, is that they

---

'Tis not enough that Aristotle has said so . . .: see p. 65 above.
last paragraph save one: the connexion is rather with § 38 above.

are to be moved as the means conducing to the ends of tragedy, which are pleasure and instruction.

47] And these two ends may be thus distinguished. The chief end of the poet is to please; for his immediate reputation depends on it.

48] The great end of the poem is to instruct, which is performed by making pleasure the vehicle of that instruction; for poetry is an art, and all arts are made to profit.

49] The pity which the poet is to labour for is for the criminal, not for those, or him, whom he has murdered, or who have been the occasion of the tragedy. The terror is likewise in the punishment of the same criminal who, if he be represented too great an offender, will not be pitied; if altogether innocent, his punishment will be unjust.

50] Another obscurity is, where he says Sophocles perfected tragedy by introducing the third actor; that is, he meant three kinds of action, one company singing or speaking, another playing on the music, a third dancing.

51] Rapin attributes more to the *dictio*, that is, to the words and discourses of a tragedy, than Aristotle has done, who places them in the last rank of beauties; perhaps only last in order, because they are the last product of the design, of the disposition or connection of its parts; of the characters, of the manners of those characters, and of the thoughts proceeding from those manners.

52] Rapin's words are remarkable: ' 'Tis not the admirable intrigue, the surprising events, and extraordinary incidents that make the beauty of a tragedy; 'tis the discourses when they are natural and passionate.'

53] So are Shakespeare's.

for poetry is an art . . .: cf. Rapin, *Réflexions sur la poétique*, I. ix.
. . . *his punishment will be unjust*: cf. Aristotle, *Poetics*, xiii.
Rapin's words are remarkable: *Réflexions sur la poétique*, I. xxvi.

PREFACE TO *ALL FOR LOVE, OR THE WORLD WELL LOST*

THE death of Antony and Cleopatra is a subject which has been treated by the greatest wits of our nation, after Shakespeare; and by all so variously that their example has given me the confidence to try myself in this bow of Ulysses amongst the crowd of suitors; and, withal, to take my own measures, in aiming at the mark. I doubt not but the same motive has prevailed with all of us in this attempt: I mean the excellency of the moral. For the chief persons represented were famous patterns of unlawful love; and their end accordingly was unfortunate. All reasonable men have long since concluded that the hero of the poem ought not to be a character of perfect virtue, for then he could not, without injustice, be made unhappy; nor yet altogether wicked, because he could not then be pitied. I have therefore steered the middle course; and have drawn the character of Antony as favourably as Plutarch, Appian, and Dion Cassius would give me leave: the like I have observed in Cleopatra. That which is wanting to work up the pity to a greater height was not afforded me by the story: for the crimes of love which they both committed were not occasioned by any necessity, or fatal ignorance, but were wholly voluntary; since our passions are, or ought to be, within our power. The fabric of the play is regular enough, as to the inferior parts of it; and the unities of time, place, and action more exactly observed than, perhaps, the English theatre requires. Particularly, the action is so much one that it is the only of the kind without episode, or underplot; every scene in the tragedy conducing to the main design, and every act concluding with a turn of it. The greatest error in the contrivance seems to be in the person of Octavia: for though I might use the privilege of a poet to introduce her into Alexandria, yet I had not enough considered that the compassion she moved to herself and children was destructive to that which I reserved for Antony and Cleopatra; whose mutual love, being founded upon vice, must lessen the favour of the audience to them when virtue and innocence were oppressed by it. And, though I justified Antony in some measure, by making Octavia's departure to proceed wholly from herself; yet the

---

a subject which has been treated . . .: Dryden is presumably thinking of such plays as Daniel's *Tragedy of Cleopatra* (1594) and the Fletcher–Massinger play *The False One* (c. 1620).

. . . *could not then be pitied*: cf. Aristotle, *Poetics*, xiii.

Plutarch, Appian, and Dion Cassius: in, respectively, *Lives*, *The Civil War*, *Roman History*.

. . . *every act concluding with a turn of it*: Aristotle, ibid.

force of the first machine still remained; and the dividing of pity, like
the cutting of a river into many channels, abated the strength of the
natural stream. But this is an objection which none of my critics have
urged against me; and therefore I might have let it pass, if I could
have resolved to have been partial to myself. The faults my enemies
have found are rather cavils concerning little, and not essential
decencies; which a Master of the Ceremonies may decide betwixt us.
The French poets, I confess, are strict observers of these punctilios:
they would not, for example, have suffered Cleopatra and Octavia to
have met; or, if they had met, there must only have passed betwixt
them some cold civilities, but no eagerness of repartee, for fear of
offending against the greatness of their characters, and the modesty
of their sex. This objection I foresaw, and at the same time contemned: for I judged it both natural and probable that Octavia,
proud of her new-gained conquest, would search out Cleopatra to
triumph over her; and that Cleopatra, thus attacked, was not of a
spirit to shun the encounter: and 'tis not unlikely that two exasperated
rivals should use such satire as I have put into their mouths; for after
all, though the one were a Roman, and the other a queen, they were
both women. 'Tis true, some actions, though natural, are not fit to be
represented; and broad obscenities in words ought in good manners
to be avoided: expressions therefore are a modest clothing of our
thoughts, as breeches and petticoats are of our bodies. If I have kept
myself within the bounds of modesty, all beyond it is but nicety and
affectation; which is no more but modesty depraved into a vice: they
betray themselves who are too quick of apprehension in such cases,
and leave all reasonable men to imagine worse of them than of the
poet.

Honest Montaigne goes yet further: *Nous ne sommes que cérémonie;
la cérémonie nous emporte, et laissons la substance des choses. Nous
nous tenons aux branches, et abandonnons le tronc et le corps. Nous
avons appris aux dames de rougir, oyant seulement nommer ce qu'elles
ne craignent aucunement à faire. Nous n'osons appeler à droit nos
membres, et ne craignons pas de les employer à toute sorte de débauche.
La cérémonie nous défend d'exprimer par paroles les choses licites et
naturelles, et nous l'en croyons; la raison nous défend de n'en faire
point d'illicites et mauvaises, et personne ne l'en croit.* My comfort is
that by this opinion my enemies are but sucking critics, who would
fain be nibbling ere their teeth are come.

Yet in this nicety of manners does the excellency of French poetry
consist: their heroes are the most civil people breathing; but their

Honest Montaigne . . .: Essais (1580), ii. 17, 'De la praesumption'.

good breeding seldom extends to a word of sense. All their wit is in their ceremony; they want the genius which animates our stage; and therefore 'tis but necessary, when they cannot please, that they should take care not to offend. But as the civillest man in the company is commonly the dullest, so these authors, while they are afraid to make you laugh or cry, out of pure good manners make you sleep. They are so careful not to exasperate a critic that they never leave him any work; so busy with the broom, and make so clean a riddance, that there is little left either for censure or for praise: for no part of a poem is worth our discommending where the whole is insipid; as when we have once tasted of palled wine, we stay not to examine it glass by glass. But while they affect to shine in trifles, they are often careless in essentials. Thus their Hippolytus is so scrupulous in point of decency that he will rather expose himself to death than accuse his stepmother to his father; and my critics, I am sure, will commend him for it: but we of grosser apprehensions are apt to think that this excess of generosity is not practicable but with fools and madmen. This was good manners with a vengeance; and the audience is like to be much concerned at the misfortunes of this admirable hero: but take Hippolytus out of his poetic fit, and I suppose he would think it a wiser part to set the saddle on the right horse, and choose rather to live with the reputation of a plain-spoken, honest man, than to die with the infamy of an incestuous villain. In the meantime we may take notice that where the poet ought to have preserved the character as it was delivered to us by antiquity, when he should have given us the picture of a rough young man, of the Amazonian strain, a jolly hunts-man, and both by his profession and his early rising a mortal enemy to love, he has chosen to give him the turn of gallantry, sent him to travel from Athens to Paris, taught him to make love, and trans-formed the Hippolytus of Euripides into Monsieur Hippolyte. I should not have troubled myself thus far with French poets, but that I find our Chedreux critics wholly form their judgements by them. But for my part, I desire to be tried by the laws of my own country; for it seems unjust to me that the French should prescribe here till they have conquered. Our little sonneteers who follow them have too narrow souls to judge of poetry. Poets themselves are the most proper, though I conclude not the only critics. But till some genius as universal as Aristotle shall arise, one who can penetrate into all arts and sciences without the practice of them, I shall think it reason-

---

than accuse his stepmother: Racine, *Phèdre*, IV. ii.
Chedreux: modish, fashionable. Chedreux was a 17th-century wig-maker fre-
    quently mentioned in Restoration literature.

able that the judgement of an artificer in his own art should be preferable to the opinion of another man; at least where he is not bribed by interest, or prejudiced by malice: and this, I suppose, is manifest by plain induction. For first, the crowd cannot be presumed to have more than a gross instinct of what pleases or displeases them: every man will grant me this; but then, by a particular kindness to himself, he draws his own stake first, and will be distinguished from the multitude of which other men may think him one. But, if I come closer to those who are allowed for witty men, either by the advantage of their quality, or by common fame, and affirm that neither are they qualified to decide sovereignly concerning poetry, I shall yet have a strong party of my opinion; for the most of them severally will exclude the rest, either from the number of witty men, or at least of able judges. But here again they are all indulgent to themselves; and every one who believes himself a wit, that is, every man, will pretend at the same time to a right of judging. But to press it yet farther, there are many witty men, but few poets; neither have all poets a taste of tragedy. And this is the rock on which they are daily splitting. Poetry, which is a picture of nature, must generally please; but 'tis not to be understood that all parts of it must please every man; therefore is not tragedy to be judged by a witty man, whose taste is only confined to comedy. Nor is every man who loves tragedy a sufficient judge of it: he must understand the excellencies of it too, or he will only prove a blind admirer, not a critic. From hence it comes that so many satires on poets, and censures of their writings, fly abroad. Men of pleasant conversation (at least esteemed so), and endued with a trifling kind of fancy, perhaps helped out with some smattering of Latin, are ambitious to distinguish themselves from the herd of gentlemen by their poetry:

> rarus enim ferme sensus communis in illa
> fortuna.

And is not this a wretched affectation, not to be contented with what fortune has done for them, and sit down quietly with their estates, but they must call their wits in question, and needlessly expose their nakedness to public view? Not considering that they are not to expect the same approbation from sober men which they have found from their flatterers after the third bottle. If a little glittering in discourse has passed them on us for witty men, where was the necessity

---

those who are allowed for witty men: probably, but not necessarily, a jibe at the Earl of Rochester, whose 'An Allusion to Horace' mocks Dryden.

rarus enim . . .: Juvenal, *Satires*, viii. 73–4 ('Concern for others is very rare in those high places').

of undeceiving the world? Would a man who has an ill title to an
estate, but yet is in possession of it, would he bring it of his own
accord to be tried at Westminster? We who write, if we want the
talent, yet have the excuse that we do it for a poor subsistence; but
what can be urged in their defence who, not having the vocation of
poverty to scribble, out of mere wantonness take pains to make
themselves ridiculous? Horace was certainly in the right where he
said that *no man is satisfied with his own condition*. A poet is not
pleased, because he is not rich; and the rich are discontented, because
the poets will not admit them of their number. Thus the case is hard
with writers: if they succeed not, they must starve; and if they do,
some malicious satire is prepared to level them for daring to please
without their leave. But while they are so eager to destroy the fame of
others, their ambition is manifest in their concernment: some poem
of their own is to be produced, and the slaves are to be laid flat with
their faces on the ground, that the monarch may appear in the greater
majesty.

Dionysius and Nero had the same longings, but with all their
power they could never bring their business well about. 'Tis true,
they proclaimed themselves poets by sound of trumpet; and poets
they were, upon pain of death to any man who durst call them otherwise. The audience had a fine time on it, you may imagine; they sat in
a bodily fear, and looked as demurely as they could: for 'twas a
hanging matter to laugh unseasonably and the tyrants were suspicious, as they had reason, that their subjects had 'em in the wind;
so, every man in his own defence set as good a face upon the business
as he could. 'Twas known beforehand that the monarchs were to be
crowned laureates; but when the show was over, and an honest man
was suffered to depart quietly, he took out his laughter which he had
stifled, with a firm resolution never more to see an Emperor's play,
though he had been ten years a-making it. In the meantime the true
poets were they who made the best markets, for they had wit enough
to yield the prize with a good grace, and not contend with him who
had thirty legions. They were sure to be rewarded if they confessed
themselves bad writers, and that was somewhat better than to be
martyrs for their reputation. Lucan's example was enough to teach
them manners; and after he was put to death, for overcoming Nero,
the Emperor carried it without dispute for the best poet in his
dominions. No man was ambitious of that grinning honour; for if

---

Horace was certainly in the right: *Satires*, I. i.
grinning honour: cf. Shakespeare, *1 Henry IV*, V. iii. 58–9 ('I like not such grinning honour as Sir Walter hath').

he heard the malicious trumpeter proclaiming his name before his
betters, he knew there was but one way with him. Maecenas took
another course, and we know he was more than a great man, for he
was witty too: but finding himself far gone in poetry, which Seneca
assures us was not his talent, he thought it his best way to be well
with Virgil and with Horace; that at least he might be a poet at the
second hand; and we see how happily it has succeeded with him; for
his own bad poetry is forgotten, and their panegyrics of him still
remain. But they who should be our patrons are for no such expensive
ways to fame; they have much of the poetry of Maecenas, but little of
his liberality. They are for persecuting Horace and Virgil, in the
persons of their successors (for such is every man who has any part
of their soul and fire, though in a less degree). Some of their little
zanies yet go further; for they are persecutors even of Horace himself,
as far as they are able, by their ignorant and vile imitations of him; by
making an unjust use of his authority, and turning his artillery against
his friends. But how would he disdain to be copied by such hands! I
dare answer for him, he would be more uneasy in their company than
he was with Crispinus, their forefather, in the Holy Way; and would
no more have allowed them a place amongst the critics than he would
Demetrius the mimic, and Tigellius the buffoon:

> Demetri, teque, Tigelli,
> discipulorum inter jubeo plorare cathedras.

With what scorn would he look down on such miserable translators
who make doggerel of his Latin, mistake his meaning, misapply his
censures, and often contradict their own? He is fixed as a landmark to
set out the bounds of poetry:

> saxum antiquum, ingens, . . .
> limes agro positus, litem ut discerneret arvis.

But other arms than theirs, and other sinews, are required to raise
the weight of such an author; and when they would toss him against
their enemies,

Seneca assures us: Epistulae Morales, 114.
ignorant and vile imitations of him: again probably a reference to Rochester.
Demetri, teque, Tigelli, . . .: Satires, I. x. 90–1 ('discipularum . . .': 'Go Demetrius, and you, Tigellius, and grizzle among your pupils' seats').
saxum antiquum, ingens, . . .: Aeneid, xii. 897–8. Dryden omits half a line:

> An antique stone he saw: the common bound
> Of neighb'ring fields, and barrier of the ground . . .
>   (Dryden's *Aeneis*, xii. 1300–1).

> genua labant, gelidus concrevit frigore sanguis.
> tum lapis ipse, viri vacuum per inane volutus,
> nec spatium evasit totum, nec pertulit ictum.

For my part, I would wish no other revenge, either for myself or the rest of the poets, from this rhyming judge of the twelvepenny gallery, this legitimate son of Sternhold, than that he would subscribe his name to his censure, or (not to tax him beyond his learning) set his mark: for, should he own himself publicly, and come from behind the lion's skin, they whom he condemns would be thankful to him, they whom he praises would choose to be condemned; and the magistrates whom he has elected would modestly withdraw from their employment, to avoid the scandal of his nomination. The sharpness of his satire, next to himself, falls most heavily on his friends, and they ought never to forgive him for commending them perpetually the wrong way, and sometimes by contraries. If he have a friend whose hastiness in writing is his greatest fault, Horace would have taught him to have minced the matter, and to have called it readiness of thought, and a flowing fancy; for friendship will allow a man to christen an imperfection by the name of some neighbour virtue:

> vellem in amicitia sic erraremus; et isti
> errori nomen virtus posuisset honestum.

But he would never have allowed him to have called a slow man hasty, or a hasty writer a slow drudge, as Juvenal explains it:

> canibus pigris, scabieque vetusta
> laevibus, et siccae lambentibus ora lucernae,
> nomen erit, Pardus, Tigris, Leo; si quid adhuc est
> quod fremit in terris violentius.

genua labant, . . .: ibid. 905–7:

> His knocking knees are bent beneath the load:
> And shivering cold congeals his vital blood.
> The stone drops from his arms: and falling short,
> For want of vigour, mocks his vain effort
> > (ibid. 1308–11).

Sternhold: (1500–49) author—with John Hopkins (d. 1570)—of a very popular version of the Psalms.
the magistrates: see Rochester, *Allusion* . . ., ll. 120–4.
vellem in amicitia . . .: *Satires*, I. iii. 41–2 ('I wish that we could in friendship sin like this and that sense had given such errors an honourable name').
a slow man hasty . . .: see Rochester, *Allusion* . . ., ll. 41–3.
canibus pigris, . . .: *Satires*, viii. 34–7 ('. . . fremat . . .': 'slovenly dogs, bald with mange, who lick a dry lamp, will be called "pard", "tiger", or any other animal which roars fiercely').

Yet Lucretius laughs at a foolish lover, even for excusing the imperfections of his mistress:

> nigra μελίχροος est, immunda et foetida ἄκοσμος.
> balba loqui, non quit, τραυλίζει; muta pudens est, etc.

But to drive it *ad Aethiopem cygnum* is not to be endured. I leave him to interpret this by the benefit of his French version on the other side, and without farther considering him than I have the rest of my illiterate censors, whom I have disdained to answer, because they are not qualified for judges. It remains that I acquaint the reader that I have endeavoured in this play to follow the practice of the Ancients, who, as Mr. Rymer has judiciously observed, are and ought to be our masters. Horace likewise gives it for a rule in his art of poetry:

> vos exemplaria Graeca
> nocturna versate manu, versate diurna.

Yet, though their models are regular, they are too little for English tragedy, which requires to be built in a larger compass. I could give an instance in the *Oedipus Tyrannus*, which was the masterpiece of Sophocles; but I reserve it for a more fit occasion, which I hope to have hereafter. In my style I have professed to imitate the divine Shakespeare; which that I might perform more freely, I have disencumbered myself from rhyme.[n] Not that I condemn my former way, but that this is more proper to my present purpose. I hope I need not to explain myself that I have not copied my author servilely: words and phrases must of necessity receive a change in succeeding ages: but 'tis almost a miracle that much of his language remains so pure; and that he who began dramatic poetry amongst us, untaught by any and, as Ben Jonson tells us, without learning, should by the force of his own genius perform so much, that in a manner he has left no praise for any who come after him. The occasion is fair, and the subject would be pleasant to handle: the difference of styles betwixt him and Fletcher, and wherein, and how far, they are both to be

---

nigra μελίχροος . . .: *De rerum natura*, iv. 1160, 1164:

> The sallow skin is for the swarthy put . . .
> She stammers on, oh what grace in lisping lies,
> If she says nothing, to be sure she's wise

(Dryden, from *Sylvae*, 'Concerning the Nature of Love', ll. 145, 151–2).

ad Aethiopem cygnum: Juvenal, *Satires*, viii. 33 (no 'ad' in Juvenal: 'to a deep-black swan').

vos exemplaria Graeca . . .: *Ars Poetica*, ll. 268–9 ('Examine your Grecian models day and night').

Ben Jonson tells us: 'To the Memory of . . . Mr. William Shakespeare', ll. 31 f.

imitated. But since I must not be over-confident of my own performance after him, it will be prudence in me to be silent. Yet I hope I may affirm, and without vanity, that by imitating him I have excelled myself throughout the play; and particularly that I prefer the scene betwixt Antony and Ventidius in the first act to anything which I have written in this kind.

PREFACE TO *TROILUS AND CRESSIDA*, INCLUDING 'THE GROUNDS OF CRITICISM IN TRAGEDY'ⁿ

1679

THE poet Aeschylus was held in the same veneration by the Athenians of after ages as Shakespeare is by us; and Longinus has judged, in favour of him, that he had a noble boldness of expression, and that his imaginations were lofty and heroic; but, on the other side, Quintilian affirms that he was daring to extravagance. 'Tis certain that he affected pompous words, and that his sense too often was obscured by figures; notwithstanding these imperfections, the value of his writings after his decease was such that his countrymen ordained an equal reward to those poets who could alter his plays to be acted on the theatre, with those whose productions were wholly new, and of their own. The case is not the same in England; though the difficulties of altering are greater, and our reverence for Shakespeare much more just, than that of the Grecians for Aeschylus. In the age of that poet, the Greek tongue was arrived to its full perfection; they had then amongst them an exact standard of writing and of speaking. The English language is not capable of such a certainty; and we are at present so far from it that we are wanting in the very foundation of it, a perfect grammar. Yet it must be allowed to the present age that the tongue in general is so much refined since Shakespeare's time that many of his words, and more of his phrases, are scarce intelligible. And of those which we understand, some are ungrammatical, others coarse; and his whole style is so pestered with figurative expressions, that it is as affected as it is obscure. 'Tis true, that in his later plays he had worn off somewhat of the rust; but the tragedy which I have undertaken to correct was, in all probability, one of his first endeavours on the stage.

The original story was written by one Lollius, a Lombard, in Latin verse, and translated by Chaucer into English; intended, I suppose, a satire on the inconstancy of women: I find nothing of it among the Ancients; not so much as the name Cressida once mentioned. Shakespeare (as I hinted) in the apprenticeship of his writing, modelled it into that play which is now called by the name of *Troilus and Cressida*; but so lamely is it left to us, that it is not divided into acts; which fault I ascribe to the actors who printed it after Shakespeare's death; and that too so carelessly, that a more uncorrect copy I never saw.

Longinus has judged: On the Sublime, xv. 5–6.
Quintilian affirms: Institutio, X. i. 66.
one of his first endeavours: it is now generally accepted that *Troilus* is a product of Shakespeare's middle period.

For the play itself, the author seems to have begun it with some fire; the characters of Pandarus and Thersites are promising enough; but as if he grew weary of his task, after an entrance or two, he lets 'em fall: and the later part of the tragedy is nothing but a confusion of drums and trumpets, excursions and alarms. The chief persons, who give name to the tragedy, are left alive: Cressida is false, and is not punished. Yet, after all, because the play was Shakespeare's, and that there appeared in some places of it the admirable genius of the author, I undertook to remove that heap of rubbish under which many excellent thoughts lay wholly buried. Accordingly, I new modelled the plot; threw out many unnecessary persons; improved those characters which were begun and left unfinished, as Hector, Troilus, Pandarus, and Thersites; and added that of Andromache. After this I made, with no small trouble, an order and connection of all the scenes; removing them from the places where they were in-artificially set; and though it was impossible to keep 'em all un-broken, because the scene must be sometimes in the city and sometimes in the camp, yet I have so ordered them that there is a coherence of 'em with one another, and a dependence on the main design: no leaping from Troy to the Grecian tents, and thence back again in the same act; but a due proportion of time allowed for every motion. I need not say that I have refined his language, which before was obsolete; but I am willing to acknowledge that as I have often drawn his English nearer to our times, so I have sometimes con-formed my own to his: and consequently, the language is not al-together so pure as it is significant. The scenes of Pandarus and Cressida, of Troilus and Pandarus, of Andromache with Hector and the Trojans, in the second act, are wholly new; together with that of Nestor and Ulysses with Thersites, and that of Thersites with Ajax and Achilles. I will not weary my reader with the scenes which are added of Pandarus and the lovers, in the third; and those of Thersites, which are wholly altered; but I cannot omit the last scene in it, which is almost half the act, betwixt Troilus and Hector. The occasion of raising it was hinted to me by Mr. Betterton: the contrivance and working of it was my own. They who think to do me an injury by saying that it is an imitation of the scene betwixt Brutus and Cassius, do me an honour by supposing I could imitate the incomparable Shakespeare; but let me add that if Shakespeare's scene, or the faulty copy of it in *Amintor and Melantius*, had never been, yet Euripides had furnished me with an excellent example in his *Iphigenia*, between Agamemnon and Menelaus; and from thence, indeed, the last turn

Agamemnon and Menelaus: in comparing the Agamemnon/Menelaus quarrel in Euripides' *Iphigenia in Aulis* with that of Amintor and Melantius in Beaumont

of it is borrowed. The occasion which Shakespeare, Euripides, and
Fletcher have all taken is the same; grounded upon friendship: and
the quarrel of two virtuous men, raised by natural degrees to the
extremity of passion, is conducted in all three to the declination of
the same passion, and concludes with a warm renewing of their
friendship. But the particular groundwork which Shakespeare has
taken is incomparably the best; because he has not only chosen two
of the greatest heroes of their age, but has likewise interested the
liberty of Rome, and their own honours, who were the redeemers of
it, in this debate. And if he has made Brutus, who was naturally a
patient man, to fly into excess at first, let it be remembered in his
defence that, just before, he has received the news of Portia's death;
whom the poet, on purpose neglecting a little chronology, supposes
to have died before Brutus, only to give him an occasion of being
more easily exasperated. Add to this that the injury he had received
from Cassius had long been brooding in his mind; and that a melancholy man, upon consideration of an affront, especially from a
friend, would be more eager in his passion than he who had given it,
though naturally more choleric.

Euripides, whom I have followed, has raised the quarrel betwixt
two brothers who were friends. The foundation of the scene was this:
the Grecians were windbound at the port of Aulis, and the oracle had
said that they could not sail, unless Agamemnon delivered up his
daughter to be sacrificed: he refuses; his brother Menelaus urges the
public safety; the father defends himself by arguments of natural
affection, and hereupon they quarrel. Agamemnon is at last convinced, and promises to deliver up Iphigenia, but so passionately
laments his loss that Menelaus is grieved to have been the occasion of
it and, by a return of kindness, offers to intercede for him with the
Grecians, that his daughter might not be sacrificed. But my friend
Mr. Rymer has so largely, and with so much judgement, described
this scene, in comparing it with that of Melantius and Amintor, that
it is superfluous to say more of it; I only named the heads of it, that
any reasonable man might judge it was from thence I modelled my
scene betwixt Troilus and Hector. I will conclude my reflexions on it
with a passage of Longinus, concerning Plato's imitation of Homer:
'We ought not to regard a good imitation as a theft, but as a beautiful
idea of him who undertakes to imitate, by forming himself on the

and Fletcher's *The Maid's Tragedy* (III. ii) Dryden is following Rymer (*Critica
Works*, ed. Zimansky, p. 74).
supposes to have died before Brutus: *Julius Caesar*, IV.
with a passage of Longinus: *On the Sublime*, xiii. 4.

invention and the work of another man; for he enters into the lists like a new wrestler, to dispute the prize with the former champion. This sort of emulation, says Hesiod, is honourable, ἀγαθὴ δ᾽ ἔρις ἐστὶ βροτοῖσιν, when we combat for victory with a hero, and are not without glory even in our overthrow. Those great men whom we propose to ourselves as patterns of our imitation serve us as a torch, which is lifted up before us to enlighten our passage; and often elevate our thoughts as high as the conception we have of our author's genius.'

I have been so tedious in three acts that I shall contract myself in the two last. The beginning scenes of the fourth act are either added or changed wholly by me; the middle of it is Shakespeare altered, and mingled with my own; three or four of the last scenes are altogether new. And the whole fifth act, both the plot and the writing, are my own additions.

But having written so much for imitation of what is excellent, in that part of the preface which related only to myself, methinks it would neither be unprofitable nor unpleasant to inquire how far we ought to imitate our own poets, Shakespeare and Fletcher, in their tragedies: and this will occasion another inquiry how those two writers differ between themselves. But since neither of these questions can be solved unless some measures be first taken by which we may be enabled to judge truly of their writings, I shall endeavour, as briefly as I can, to discover the grounds and reason of all criticism, applying them in this place only to tragedy. Aristotle with his interpreters, and Horace, and Longinus, are the authors to whom I owe my lights; and what part soever of my own plays, or of this, which no mending could make regular, shall fall under the condemnation of such judges, it would be impudence in me to defend. I think it no shame to retract my errors, and am well pleased to suffer in the cause, if the art may be improved at my expense: I therefore proceed to

THE GROUNDS OF CRITICISM IN TRAGEDY

Tragedy is thus defined by Aristotle (omitting what I thought unnecessary in his definition). 'Tis an imitation of one entire, great, and probable action; not told, but represented; which, by moving in us fear and pity, is conducive to the purging of those two passions in our minds. More largely thus, tragedy describes or paints an action,

says Hesiod: *Works and Days*, l. 24 ('such rivalry is good for men').
Tragedy . . . Aristotle: a loose paraphrase of *Poetics*, vi, follows.

which action must have all the properties above named. First, it must be one or single, that is, it must not be a history of one man's life; suppose of Alexander the Great, or Julius Caesar, but one single action of theirs. This condemns all Shakespeare's historical plays, which are rather chronicles represented than tragedies, and all double action of plays. As to avoid a satire upon others, I will make bold with my own *Marriage-à-la-Mode*, where there are manifestly two actions, not depending on one another: but in *Oedipus* there cannot properly be said to be two actions, because the love of Adrastus and Eurydice has a necessary dependence on the principal design, into which it is woven. The natural reason of this rule is plain, for two different independent actions distract the attention and concernment of the audience, and consequently destroy the intention of the poet: if his business be to move terror and pity, and one of his actions be comical, the other tragical, the former will divert the people, and utterly make void his greater purpose. Therefore, as in perspective, so in tragedy, there must be a point of sight in which all the lines terminate; otherwise the eye wanders, and the work is false. This was the practice of the Grecian stage. But Terence made an innovation in the Roman: all his plays have double actions; for it was his custom to translate two Greek comedies, and to weave them into one of his, yet so that both the actions were comical, and one was principal, the other but secondary or subservient. And this has obtained on the English stage, to give us the pleasure of variety.

As the action ought to be one, it ought, as such, to have order in it, that is, to have a natural beginning, a middle, and an end. A natural beginning, says Aristotle, is that which could not necessarily have been placed after another thing, and so of the rest. This consideration will arraign all plays after the new model of Spanish plots, where accident is heaped upon accident, and that which is first might as reasonably be last: an inconvenience not to be remedied but by making one accident naturally produce another, otherwise 'tis a farce and not a play. Of this nature is *The Slighted Maid*, where there is no scene in the first act which might not by as good reason be in the fifth. And if the action to be one, the tragedy ought likewise to conclude with the action of it. Thus in *Mustapha*, the play should naturally have ended with the death of Zanger, and not have given us the grace cup after dinner of Solyman's divorce from Roxolana.

---

says Aristotle: *Poetics*, vii.
Spanish plots: see 'Of Dramatic Poesy', above, p. 42.
Slighted Maid: by Sir Robert Stapylton (d. 1669); published 1663.
Mustapha: by Lord Orrery; published 1668.

The following properties of the action are so easy that they need not my explaining. It ought to be great, and to consist of great persons, to distinguish it from comedy, where the action is trivial, and the persons of inferior rank. The last quality of the action is that it ought to be probable, as well as admirable and great. 'Tis not necessary that there should be historical truth in it; but always necessary that there should be a likeness of truth, something that is more than barely possible, *probable* being that which succeeds or happens oftener than it misses. To invent therefore a probability, and to make it wonderful, is the most difficult undertaking in the art of poetry; for that which is not wonderful is not great, and that which is not probable will not delight a reasonable audience. This action, thus described, must be represented and not told, to distinguish dramatic poetry from epic: but I hasten to the end or scope of tragedy, which is, to rectify or purge our passions, fear and pity.

To instruct delightfully is the general end of all poetry. Philosophy instructs, but it performs its work by precept: which is not delightful, or not so delightful as example. To purge the passions by example is therefore the particular instruction which belongs to tragedy. Rapin, a judicious critic, has observed from Aristotle that pride and want of commiseration are the most predominant vices in mankind; therefore, to cure us of these two, the inventors of tragedy have chosen to work upon two other passions, which are fear and pity. We are wrought to fear by their setting before our eyes some terrible example of misfortune, which happened to persons of the highest quality; for such an action demonstrates to us that no condition is privileged from the turns of fortune; this must of necessity cause terror in us, and consequently abate our pride. But when we see that the most virtuous, as well as the greatest, are not exempt from such misfortunes, that consideration moves pity in us, and insensibly works us to be helpful to, and tender over, the distressed, which is the noblest and most God-like of moral virtues. Here 'tis observable that it is absolutely necessary to make a man virtuous, if we desire he should be pitied: we lament not, but detest, a wicked man, we are glad when we behold his crimes are punished, and that poetical justice is done upon him. Euripides was censured by the critics of his time for making his chief characters too wicked: for example, Phaedra, though she loved her son-in-law with reluctancy, and that it

---

the end or scope of tragedy: Aristotle, *Poetics*, xiii.

Rapin . . . has observed: *Réflexions sur la poétique*, II. xvii; Dryden's distinction between poetry and philosophy was commonplace in English from Sidney's *Apology* onwards.

was a curse upon her family for offending Venus, yet was thought too ill a pattern for the stage. Shall we therefore banish all characters of villainy? I confess I am not of that opinion; but it is necessary that the hero of the play be not a villain: that is, the characters which should move our pity ought to have virtuous inclinations, and degrees of moral goodness in them. As for a perfect character of virtue, it never was in nature, and therefore there can be no imitation of it; but there are allays of frailty to be allowed for the chief persons, yet so that the good which is in them shall outweigh the bad, and consequently leave room for punishment on the one side, and pity on the other.

After all, if any one will ask me whether a tragedy cannot be made upon any other grounds than those of exciting pity and terror in us, Bossu, the best of modern critics, answers thus in general: that all excellent arts, and particularly that of poetry, have been invented and brought to perfection by men of a transcendent genius; and that therefore they who practise afterwards the same arts are obliged to tread in their footsteps, and to search in their writings the foundation of them; for it is not just that new rules should destroy the authority of the old. But Rapin writes more particularly thus: that no passions in a story are so proper to move our concernment as fear and pity; and that it is from our concernment we receive our pleasure, is undoubted; when the soul becomes agitated with fear for one character, or hope for another, then it is that we are pleased in tragedy by the interest which we take in their adventures.

Here, therefore, the general answer may be given to the first question, how far we ought to imitate Shakespeare and Fletcher in their plots; namely, that we ought to follow them so far only as they have copied the excellencies of those who invented and brought to perfection dramatic poetry: those things only excepted which religion, customs of countries, idioms of languages, etc., have altered in the superstructures, but not in the foundation of the design.

How defective Shakespeare and Fletcher have been in all their plots, Mr. Rymer has discovered in his criticisms: neither can we who follow them be excused from the same or greater errors; which are the more unpardonable in us, because we want their beauties to countervail our faults. The best of their designs, the most approaching to antiquity, and the most conducing to move pity, is the *King and No King*; which, if the farce of Bessus were thrown away, is of that inferior sort of tragedies which end with a prosperous event.

allays: dilutions.
Bossu: (1631–89) *Du poème épique* (1675).
Rapin writes: *Réflexions sur la poétique*, II. xviii.

'Tis probably derived from the story of Oedipus, with the character of Alexander the Great, in his extravagancies, given to Arbaces. The taking of this play, amongst many others, I cannot wholly ascribe to the excellency of the action; for I find it moving when it is read: 'tis true, the faults of the plot are so evidently proved that they can no longer be denied. The beauties of it must therefore lie either in the lively touches of the passion: or we must conclude, as I think we may, that even in imperfect plots there are less degrees of nature, by which some faint emotions of pity and terror are raised in us: as a less engine will raise a less proportion of weight, though not so much as one of Archimedes's making; for nothing can move our nature, but by some natural reason, which works upon passions. And since we acknowledge the effect, there must be something in the cause.

The difference between Shakespeare and Fletcher in their plotting seems to be this: that Shakespeare generally moves more terror, and Fletcher more compassion. For the first had a more masculine, a bolder and more fiery genius; the second, a more soft and womanish. In the mechanic beauties of the plot, which are the observation of the three unities, time, place, and action, they are both deficient; but Shakespeare most. Ben Jonson reformed those errors in his comedies, yet one of Shakespeare's was regular before him; which is, *The Merry Wives of Windsor*. For what remains concerning the design, you are to be referred to our English critic. That method which he has prescribed to raise it from mistake, or ignorance of the crime, is certainly the best though 'tis not the only: for amongst all the tragedies of Sophocles, there is but one, *Oedipus*, which is wholly built after that model.

After the plot, which is the foundation of the play, the next thing to which we ought to apply our judgement is the manners, for now the poet comes to work above ground: the ground-work indeed is that which is most necessary, as that upon which depends the firmness of the whole fabric; yet it strikes not the eye so much as the beauties or imperfections of the manners, the thoughts, and the expressions.

The first rule which Bossu prescribes to the writer of an heroic poem, and which holds too by the same reason in all dramatic poetry, is to make the moral of the work, that is, to lay down to yourself what that precept of morality shall be, which you would insinuate into the people; as, namely, Homer's (which I have copied in my *Conquest of Granada*) was that union preserves a commonwealth, and

The Merry Wives of Windsor: the time-scheme of this play extends, in fact, over about three days.

discord destroys it; Sophocles, in his *Oedipus*, that no man is to be
accounted happy before his death. 'Tis the moral that directs the
whole action of the play to one centre; and that action or fable is the
example built upon the moral, which confirms the truth of it to our
experience: when the fable is designed with their manners, characters,
and passions.

The manners in a poem are understood to be those inclinations,
whether natural or acquired, which move and carry us to actions,
good, bad, or indifferent, in a play; or which incline the persons to
such or such actions. I have anticipated part of this discourse already,
in declaring that a poet ought not to make the manners perfectly
good in his best persons; but neither are they to be more wicked in
any of his characters than necessity requires. To produce a villain,
without other reason than a natural inclination to villainy is, in
poetry, to produce an effect without a cause; and to make him more
a villain than he has just reason to be, is to make an effect which is
stronger than the cause.

The manners arise from many causes; and are either distinguished
by complexion, as choleric and phlegmatic, or by the differences of
age or sex, of climates, or quality of the persons, or their present condition: they are likewise to be gathered from the several virtues, vices,
or passions, and many other commonplaces which a poet must be
supposed to have learned from natural philosophy, ethics, and
history; of all which whosoever is ignorant, does not deserve the
name of poet.

But as the manners are useful in this art, they may be all comprised
under these general heads: first, they must be apparent; that is, in
every character of the play, some inclinations of the person must
appear; and these are shown in the actions and discourse. Secondly,
the manners must be suitable, or agreeing to the persons; that is, to
the age, sex, dignity, and the other general heads of manners: thus,
when a poet has given the dignity of a king to one of his persons, in
all his actions and speeches, that person must discover majesty,
magnanimity, and jealousy of power, because these are suitable to
the general manners of a king. The third property of manners is
resemblance; and this is founded upon the particular characters of
men, as we have them delivered to us by relation or history; that is,
when a poet has the known character of this or that man before him,
he is bound to represent him such, at least not contrary to that which
fame has reported him to have been. Thus, it is not a poet's choice to
make Ulysses choleric, or Achilles patient, because Homer has
described them quite otherwise. Yet this is a rock on which ignorant
writers daily split; and the absurdity is as monstrous as if a painter

should draw a coward running from a battle, and tell us it was the picture of Alexander the Great.

The last property of manners is that they be constant and equal, that is, maintained the same through the whole design: thus, when Virgil had once given the name of *pious* to Aeneas, he was bound to show him such, in all his words and actions through the whole poem. All these properties Horace has hinted to a judicious observer: 1. *notandi sunt tibi mores*; 2. *aut famam sequere*; 3. *aut sibi convenientia finge*; 4. *servetur ad imum, qualis ab incepto processerit, et sibi constet.*

From the manners, the characters of persons are derived; for indeed the characters are no other than the inclinations, as they appear in the several persons of the poem; a character being thus defined, that which distinguishes one man from another. Not to repeat the same things over again which have been said of the manners, I will only add what is necessary here. A character, or that which distinguishes one man from all others, cannot be supposed to consist of one particular virtue, or vice, or passion only; but 'tis a composition of qualities which are not contrary to one another in the same person: thus the same man may be liberal and valiant, but not liberal and covetous; so in a comical character or humour (which is an inclination to this or that particular folly), Falstaff is a liar, and a coward, and a glutton, and a buffoon, because all these qualities may agree in the same man; yet it is still to be observed that one virtue, vice, and passion ought to be shown in every man, as predominant over all the rest; as covetousness in Crassus, love of his country in Brutus; and the same in characters which are feigned.

The chief character or hero in a tragedy, as I have already shown, ought in prudence to be such a man who has so much more in him of virtue than of vice, that he may be left amiable to the audience, which otherwise cannot have any concernment for his sufferings; and 'tis on this one character that the pity and terror must be principally, if not wholly, founded. A rule which is extremely necessary, and which none of the critics that I know have fully enough discovered to us. For terror and compassion work but weakly when they are divided into many persons. If Creon had been the chief character in *Oedipus*, there had neither been terror nor compassion moved; but only detestation of the man and joy for his punishment; if Adrastus and

---

. . . *the name of* '*pious*' *to Aeneas*: *Aeneid*, i. 378 ('sum pius Aeneas').

Horace has hinted: *Ars Poetica*, ll. 156, 119, 126–7 (1. 'You must note each age's manners'; 2. 'either follow tradition'; 3. 'or make your own convention'; 4. 'let each character be maintained as it started, and stay consistent to itself').

Eurydice had been made more appearing characters, then the pity had been divided, and lessened on the part of Oedipus: but making Oedipus the best and bravest person, and even Jocasta but an under-part to him, his virtues and the punishment of his fatal crime drew both the pity and the terror to himself.

By what had been said of the manners, it will be easy for a reason-able man to judge whether the characters be truly or falsely drawn in a tragedy; for if there be no manners appearing in the characters, no concernment for the persons can be raised; no pity or horror can be moved, but by vice or virtue; therefore, without them, no person can have any business in the play. If the inclinations be obscure, 'tis a sign the poet is in the dark, and knows not what manner of man he presents to you; and consequently you can have no idea, or very im-perfect, of that man; nor can judge what resolutions he ought to take; or what words or actions are proper for him. Most comedies made up of accidents or adventures are liable to fall into this error; and tragedies with many turns are subject to it: for the manners never can be evident where the surprises of fortune take up all the business of the stage; and where the poet is more in pain to tell you what hap-pened to such a man than what he was. 'Tis one of the excellencies of Shakespeare that the manners of his persons are generally apparent, and you see their bent and inclinations. Fletcher comes far short of him in this, as indeed he does almost in everything: there are but glimmerings of manners in most of his comedies, which run upon adventures; and in his tragedies, *Rollo, Otto*, the *King and No King*, *Melantius*, and many others of his best, are but pictures shown you in the twilight; you know not whether they resemble vice or virtue, and they are either good, bad, or indifferent, as the present scene requires it. But of all poets, this commendation is to be given to Ben Jonson, that the manners even of the most inconsiderable persons in his plays are everywhere apparent.

By considering the second quality of manners, which is that they be suitable to the age, quality, country, dignity, etc., of the character, we may likewise judge whether a poet has followed nature. In this kind, Sophocles and Euripides have more excelled among the Greeks than Aeschylus; and Terence more than Plautus among the Romans. Thus Sophocles gives to Oedipus the true qualities of a king, in both those plays which bear his name; but in the latter, which is the *Oedipus Colonoeus*, he lets fall on purpose his tragic style; his hero speaks not in the arbitrary tone; but remembers, in the softness of his

---

Rollo . . . Melantius: Rollo and Otto are characters in *The Bloody Brother*, and Melantius in *The Maid's Tragedy*.

complaints, that he is an unfortunate blind old man; that he is banished from his country, and persecuted by his next relations. The present French poets are generally accused that wheresoever they lay the scene, or in whatsoever age, the manners of their heroes are wholly French. Racine's Bajazet is bred at Constantinople; but his civilities are conveyed to him, by some secret passage, from Versailles into the Seraglio. But our Shakespeare, having ascribed to Henry the Fourth the character of a king and of a father, gives him the perfect manners of each relation, when either he transacts with his son or with his subjects. Fletcher, on the other side, gives neither to Arbaces, nor to his King in *The Maid's Tragedy*, the qualities which are suitable to a monarch; though he may be excused a little in the latter, for the King there is not uppermost in the character; 'tis the lover of Evadne, who is King only in a second consideration; and though he be unjust, and has other faults which shall be nameless, yet he is not the hero of the play. 'Tis true, we find him a lawful prince (though I never heard of any King that was in Rhodes) and therefore Mr. Rymer's criticism stands good; that he should not be shown in so vicious a character. Sophocles has been more judicious in his *Antigona*; for though he represents in Creon a bloody prince, yet he makes him not a lawful king, but an usurper, and Antigona herself is the heroine of the tragedy. But when Philaster wounds Arethusa and the boy; and Perigot his mistress, in *The Faithful Shepherdess*, both these are contrary to the character of manhood. Nor is Valentinian managed much better, for though Fletcher has taken his picture truly, and shown him as he was, an effeminate, voluptuous man, yet he has forgotten that he was an Emperor, and has given him none of those royal marks which ought to appear in a lawful successor of the throne. If it be inquired what Fletcher should have done on this occasion; ought he not to have represented Valentinian as he was? Bossu shall answer this question for me, by an instance of the like nature: Mauritius, the Greek Emperor, was a prince far surpassing Valentinian, for he was endued with many kingly virtues; he was religious, merciful, and valiant, but withal he was noted of extreme covetousness, a vice which is contrary to the character of a hero, or a prince: therefore, says the critic, that emperor was no fit person to be represented in a tragedy, unless his good qualities were only to be shown, and his covetousness (which sullied them all) were slurred over by the artifice of the poet. To return once more to Shakespeare: no man ever drew so many characters, or generally distinguished them better from one another, excepting only Jonson. I will instance

Bossu shall answer . . .: *Du poème épique*, IV. vii.

but in one, to show the copiousness of his invention: 'tis that of Caliban, or the Monster in *The Tempest*. He seems there to have created a person which was not in nature, a boldness which at first sight would appear intolerable; for he makes him a species of himself, begotten by an incubus on a witch; but this, as I have elsewhere proved, is not wholly beyond the bounds of credibility, at least the vulgar still believe it. We have the separated notions of a spirit, and of a witch (and spirits, according to Plato, are vested with a subtle body; according to some of his followers, have different sexes); therefore, as from the distinct apprehensions of a horse, and of a man, imagination has formed a centaur; so from those of an incubus and a sorceress, Shakespeare has produced his monster. Whether or no his generation can be defended, I leave to philosophy; but of this I am certain, that the poet has most judiciously furnished him with a person, a language, and a character, which will suit him, both by father's and mother's side: he has all the discontents and malice of a witch, and of a devil, besides a convenient proportion of the deadly sins; gluttony, sloth, and lust are manifest; the dejectedness of a slave is likewise given him, and the ignorance of one bred up in a desert island. His person is monstrous, as he is the product of unnatural lust; and his language is as hobgoblin as his person; in all things he is distinguished from other mortals. The characters of Fletcher are poor and narrow, in comparison of Shakespeare's; I remember not one which is not borrowed from him; unless you will accept that strange mixture of a man in the *King and No King*; so that in this part Shakespeare is generally worth our imitation; and to imitate Fletcher is but to copy after him who was a copier.

Under this general head of manners, the passions are naturally included as belonging to the characters. I speak not of pity and of terror, which are to be moved in the audience by the plot; but of anger, hatred, love, ambition, jealousy, revenge, etc., as they are shown in this or that person of the play. To describe these naturally, and to move them artfully, is one of the greatest commendations which can be given to a poet: to write pathetically, says Longinus, cannot proceed but for a lofty genius. A poet must be born with this quality; yet, unless he help himself by an acquired knowledge of the passions, what they are in their own nature, and by what springs they are to be moved, he will be subject either to raise them where they ought not to be raised, or not to raise them by the just degrees of

---

that strange mixture of a man: either Arbaces or Bessus would fit this vague description.
says Longinus: *On the Sublime*, viii.

nature, or to amplify them beyond the natural bounds, or not to observe the crisis and turns of them, in their cooling and decay: all which errors proceed from want of judgement in the poet, and from being unskilled in the principles of moral philosophy. Nothing is more frequent in a fanciful writer than to foil himself by not managing his strength; therefore, as in a wrestler, there is first required some measure of force, a well-knit body, and active limbs, without which all instruction would be vain; yet, these being granted, if he want the skill which is necessary to a wrestler, he shall make but small advantage of his natural robustuousness: so, in a poet, his inborn vehemence and force of spirit will only run him out of breath the sooner, if it be not supported by the help of art. The roar of passion, indeed, may please an audience, three parts of which are ignorant enough to think all is moving which is noise, and it may stretch the lungs of an ambitious actor, who will die upon the spot for a thundering clap; but it will move no other passion than indignation and contempt from judicious men. Longinus, whom I have hitherto followed, continues thus: '*If the passions be artfully employed, the discourse becomes vehement and lofty: if otherwise, there is nothing more ridiculous than a great passion out of season*': and to this purpose he animadverts severely upon Aeschylus, who writ nothing in cold blood, but was always in a rapture, and in fury with his audience: the inspiration was still upon him, he was ever tearing it upon the tripos; or (to run off as madly as he does, from one similitude to another) he was always at high flood of passion, even in the dead ebb and lowest water-mark of the scene. He who would raise the passion of a judicious audience, says a learned critic, must be sure to take his hearers along with him; if they be in a calm, 'tis in vain for him to be in a huff: he must move them by degrees, and kindle with them; otherwise he will be in danger of setting his own heap of stubble on fire, and of burning out by himself without warming the company that stand about him. They who would justify the madness of poetry from the authority of Aristotle have mistaken the text, and consequently the interpretation: I imagine it to be false read, where he says of poetry that it is εὐφυοῦς ἢ μανικοῦ, that it had always somewhat in it either of a genius, or of a madman. 'Tis more probable that the original ran thus, that poetry was εὐφυοῦς οὐ μανικοῦ, that it

Longinus . . . continues thus: ibid. iii.
the tripos: the three-legged vessel used by Apollo's priestess at the Delphic shrine in delivering his prophecies.
a learned critic: Le Bossu, *Du poème épique*, III. ix.
where he says of poetry . . .: see *Poetics*, xvii. Dryden is following Rapin, *Réflexions sur la poètique . . .*, I. v.

belongs to a witty man, but not to a madman. Thus then the passions, as they are considered simply and in themselves, suffer violence when they are perpetually maintained at the same height; for what melody can be made on that instrument, all whose strings are screwed up at first to their utmost stretch, and to the same sound? But this is not the worst: for the characters likewise bear a part in the general calamity, if you consider the passions as embodied in them; for it follows of necessity that no man can be distinguished from another by his discourse, when every man is ranting, swaggering, and exclaiming with the same excess: as if it were the only business of all the characters to contend with each other for the prize at Billingsgate; or that the scene of the tragedy lay in Bedlam. Suppose the poet should intend this man to be choleric, and that man to be patient; yet when they are confounded in the writing, you cannot distinguish them from one another: for the man who was called patient and tame is only so before he speaks; but let his clack be set a-going, and he shall tongue it as impetuously, and as loudly, as the errantest hero in the play. By this means, the characters are only distinct in name; but, in reality, all the men and women in the play are the same person. No man should pretend to write who cannot temper his fancy with his judgement: nothing is more dangerous to a raw horseman than a hot-mouthed jade without a curb.

'Tis necessary therefore for a poet who would concern an audience by describing of a passion, first to prepare it, and not to rush upon it all at once. Ovid has judiciously shown the difference of these two ways, in the speeches of Ajax and Ulysses: Ajax, from the very beginning, breaks out into his exclamations, and is swearing by his Maker, *agimus, proh Jupiter, inquit*. Ulysses, on the contrary, prepares his audience with all the submissiveness he can practise, and all the calmness of a reasonable man; he found his judges in a tranquillity of spirit, and therefore set out leisurely and softly with them, till he had warmed them by degrees; and then he began to mend his pace, and to draw them along with his own impetuousness: yet so managing his breath, that it might not fail him at his need, and reserving his utmost proofs of ability even to the last. The success, you see, was answerable; for the crowd only applauded the speech of Ajax:

> vulgique secutum
> ultima murmur erat:

Bedlam: a common 17th-century synonym for a lunatic asylum.
agimus, proh Jupiter, inquit: *Metamorphoses*, xiii. 5.
vulgique secutum . . .: ibid. 123–4.

But the judges awarded the prize for which they contended to Ulysses:

> mota manus procerum est; et quid facundia posset
> tum patuit, fortisque viri tulit arma disertus.

The next necessary rule is to put nothing into the discourse which may hinder your moving of the passions. Too many accidents, as I have said, encumber the poet, as much as the arms of Saul did David; for the variety of passions which they produce are ever crossing and jostling each other out of the way. He who treats of joy and grief together is in a fair way of causing neither of those effects. There is yet another obstacle to be removed, which is pointed wit, and sentences affected out of season; these are nothing of kin to the violence of passion: no man is at leisure to make sentences and similes when his soul is in an agony. I the rather name this fault that it may serve to mind me of my former errors; neither will I spare myself, but give an example of this kind from my *Indian Emperor*. Montezuma, pursued by his enemies, and seeking sanctuary, stands parleying without the fort, and describing his danger to Cydaria, in a simile of six lines:

> As on the sands the frighted traveller
> Sees the high seas come rolling from afar, etc.

My Indian potentate was well skilled in the sea for an inland prince, and well improved since the first act, when he sent his son to discover it. The image had not been amiss from another man, at another time: *sed nunc non erat hisce locus*: he destroyed the concernment which the audience might otherwise have had for him; for they could not think the danger near when he had the leisure to invent a simile.

If Shakespeare be allowed, as I think he must, to have made his characters distinct, it will easily be inferred that he understood the nature of the passions: because it has been proved already that confused passions make undistinguishable characters: yet I cannot deny that he has his failings; but they are not so much in the passions themselves as in his manner of expression: he often obscures his meaning by his words, and sometimes makes it unintelligible. I will not say of so great a poet that he distinguished not the blown puffy

---

mota manus procerum est; . . .: ibid. 382–3 ('re patuit . . .': 'the assembly was greatly moved, and what eloquence could do was shown: the skilled orator carried the hero's arms away').

As on the sands . . .: *The Indian Emperor*, V. ii. 200–1 ('As when upon the sands . . . sea . . .').

sed nunc . . .: *Ars Poetica*, l. 19 (for 'hisce' read 'his': 'but this was not the place').

style from true sublimity; but I may venture to maintain that the fury of his fancy often transported him beyond the bounds of judgement, either in coining of new words and phrases, or racking words which were in use into the violence of a catachresis. 'Tis not that I would explode the use of metaphors from passions, for Longinus thinks 'em necessary to raise it; but to use 'em at every word, to say nothing without a metaphor, a simile, an image, or description, is I doubt to smell a little too strongly of the buskin. I must be forced to give an example of expressing passion figuratively; but that I may do it with respect to Shakespeare, it shall not be taken from anything of his: 'tis an exclamation against Fortune, quoted in his *Hamlet*, but written by some other poet:

> Out, out, thou strumpet Fortune! all you gods,
> In general synod, take away her power;
> Break all the spokes and felleys from her wheel,
> And bowl the round nave down the hill of heaven,
> As low as to the fiends.

And immediately after, speaking of Hecuba, when Priam was killed before her eyes:

> The mobled queen ran up and down, threatening the flame
> With bisson rheum; a clout about that head
> Where late the diadem stood; and for a robe,
> About her lank and all o'er-teemed loins,
> A blanket in the alarm of fear caught up.
> Who this had seen, with tongue in venom steeped
> 'Gainst Fortune's state would treason have pronounced;
> But if the gods themselves did see her then,
> When she saw Pyrrhus make malicious sport
> In mincing with his sword her husband's limbs,
> The instant burst of clamour that she made
> (Unless things mortal move them not at all)
> Would have made milch the burning eyes of heaven,
> And passion in the gods.

What a pudder is here kept in raising the expression of trifling thoughts! Would not a man have thought that the poet had been bound prentice to a wheelwright, for his first rant? and had followed a ragman for the clout and blanket, in the second? Fortune is painted on a wheel, and therefore the writer, in a rage, will have poetical justice done upon every member of that engine: after this execution,

---

catachresis: v. 'Of Dramatic Poesy', p. 21 above, and footnote.
Longinus thinks 'em necessary: *On the Sublime*, xxxii.
in his Hamlet: II. ii. 497–501.
And immediately after: ibid. 507, 509–22.

he bowls the nave down hill, from heaven to the fiends (an unreasonable long mark a man would think); 'tis well there are no solid orbs to stop it in the way, or no element of fire to consume it: but when it came to the earth, it must be monstrous heavy, to break ground as low as to the centre. His making milch the burning eyes of heaven was a pretty tolerable flight too: and I think no man ever drew milk out of eyes before him: yet, to make the wonder greater, these eyes were burning. Such a sight indeed were enough to have raised passion in the gods; but to excuse the effects of it, he tells you, perhaps they did not see it. Wise men would be glad to find a little sense couched under all these pompous words; for bombast is commonly the delight of that audience which loves poetry, but understands it not: and as commonly has been the practice of those writers who, not being able to infuse a natural passion into the mind, have made it their business to ply the ears and to stun their judges by the noise. But Shakespeare does not often thus; for the passions in his scene between Brutus and Cassius are extremely natural, the thoughts are such as arise from the matter, the expression of them not viciously figurative. I cannot leave this subject, before I do justice to that divine poet by giving you one of his passionate descriptions: 'tis of Richard the Second when he was deposed, and led in triumph through the streets of London by Henry of Bullingbrook: the painting of it is so lively, and the words so moving, that I have scarce read anything comparable to it in any other language. Suppose you have seen already the fortunate usurper passing through the crowd, and followed by the shouts and acclamations of the people; and now behold King Richard entering upon the scene: consider the wretchedness of his condition, and his carriage in it; and refrain from pity if you can:

> As in a theatre, the eyes of men,
> After a well-graced actor leaves the stage,
> Are idly bent on him that enters next,
> Thinking his prattle to be tedious:
> Even so, or with much more contempt, men's eyes
> Did scowl on Richard: no man cried, God save him:
> No joyful tongue gave him his welcome home,
> But dust was thrown upon his sacred head,
> Which with such gentle sorrow he shook off,
> His face still combating with tears and smiles
> (The badges of his grief and patience),
> That had not God (for some strong purpose) steeled
> The hearts of men, they must perforce have melted,
> And barbarism itself have pitied him.

one of his passionate descriptions: *Richard II*, V. ii. 23–36.

To speak justly of this whole matter: 'tis neither height of thought that is discommended, nor pathetic vehemence, nor any nobleness of expression in its proper place; but 'tis a false measure of all these, something which is like them, and is not them; 'tis the Bristol-stone, which appears like a diamond; 'tis an extravagant thought, instead of a sublime one; 'tis roaring madness, instead of vehemence; and a sound of words, instead of sense. If Shakespeare were stripped of all the bombast in his passions, and dressed in the most vulgar words, we should find the beauties of his thoughts remaining; if his embroideries were burnt down, there would still be silver at the bottom of the melting-pot: but I fear (at least let me fear it for myself) that we who ape his sounding words have nothing of his thought, but are all outside; there is not so much as a dwarf within our giant's clothes. Therefore, let not Shakespeare suffer for our sakes; 'tis our fault, who succeed him in an age which is more refined, if we imitate him so ill that we copy his failings only, and make a virtue of that in our writings which in his was an imperfection.

For what remains, the excellency of that poet was, as I have said, in the more manly passions; Fletcher's in the softer: Shakespeare writ better betwixt man and man; Fletcher, betwixt man and woman: consequently, the one described friendship better; the other love: yet Shakespeare taught Fletcher to write love: and Juliet, and Desdemona, are originals. 'Tis true, the scholar had the softer soul; but the master had the kinder. Friendship is both a virtue and a passion essentially; love is a passion only in its nature, and is not a virtue but by accident: good nature makes friendship; but effeminacy love. Shakespeare had a universal mind, which comprehended all characters and passions; Fletcher a more confined and limited: for though he treated love in perfection, yet honour, ambition, revenge, and generally all the stronger passions, he either touched not, or not masterly. To conclude all, he was a limb of Shakespeare.

I had intended to have proceeded to the last property of manners, which is that they must be constant, and the characters maintained the same from the beginning to the end; and from thence to have proceeded to the thoughts and expressions suitable to a tragedy: but I will first see how this will relish with the age. 'Tis, I confess, but cursorily written; yet the judgement which is given here is generally founded upon experience: but because many men are shocked at the name of rules, as if they were a kind of magisterial prescription upon poets, I will conclude with the words of Rapin, in his reflections on

Bristol-stone: rock-crystal.
the words of Rapin: *Réflexions sur la poétique* . . ., I. xii.

Aristotle's work of poetry: 'If the rules be well considered, we shall find them to be made only to reduce nature into method, to trace her step by step, and not to suffer the least mark of her to escape us: 'tis only by these that probability in fiction is maintained, which is the soul of poetry. They are founded upon good sense, and sound reason, rather than on authority; for though Aristotle and Horace are produced, yet no man must argue that what they write is true because they writ it; but 'tis evident, by the ridiculous mistakes and gross absurdities which have been made by those poets who have taken their fancy only for their guide, that if this fancy be not regulated, 'tis a mere caprice, and utterly incapable to produce a reasonable and judicious poem'.

PREFACE TO *OVID'S EPISTLES*

Translated by Several Hands[n]

1680

THE life of Ovid being already written in our language before the translation of his *Metamorphoses*, I will not presume so far upon myself, to think I can add anything to Mr. Sandys's undertaking. The English reader may there be satisfied, that he flourished in the reign of Augustus Caesar, that he was extracted from an ancient family of Roman knights; that he was born to the inheritance of a splendid fortune, that he was designed to the study of the law; and had made considerable progress in it, before he quitted that profession for this of poetry, to which he was more naturally formed. The cause of his banishment is unknown; because he was himself unwilling further to provoke the emperor, by ascribing it to any other reason, than what was pretended by Augustus, which was the lasciviousness of his Elegies, and his *Art of Love*. 'Tis true they are not to be excused in the severity of manners, as being able to corrupt a larger empire, if there were any, than that of Rome; yet this may be said in behalf of Ovid, that no man has ever treated the passion of love with so much delicacy of thought, and of expression, or searched into the nature of it more philosophically than he. And the emperor who condemned him, had as little reason as another man to punish that fault with so much severity, if at least he were the author of a certain epigram, which is ascribed to him, relating to the cause of the first Civil War betwixt himself and Mark Anthony the triumvir, which is more fulsome than any passage I have met with in our poet. To pass by the naked familiarity of his expressions to Horace, which are cited in that author's life, I need only mention one notorious act of his in taking Livia to his bed, when she was not only married, but with child by her husband, then living. But deeds, it seems, may be justified by arbitrary power, when words are questioned in a poet. There is another guess of the grammarians, as far from truth as the first from reason; they will have him banished for some favours, which they say he received from Julia, the daughter of Augustus, whom they think he celebrates under the name of Corinna in his Elegies: but he who will observe the verses which are made to that mistress, may gather from the whole contexture of them, that Corinna was not a woman of the highest quality: if Julia were then married to Agrippa, why

---

undertaking: *Ovid's Metamorphosis Englished*, by George Sandys (1578–1644), appeared in 1626.

ascribed to him: Martial, *Epigrams*, xi. 20.

that author's life: by Suetonius.

should our poet make his petition to Isis, for her safe delivery, and afterwards condole her miscarriage; which for aught he knew might be by her own husband? Or indeed how durst he be so bold to make the least discovery of such a crime, which was no less than capital, especially committed against a person of Agrippa's rank? Or if it were before her marriage, he would surely have been more discreet than to have published an accident, which must have been fatal to them both. But what most confirms me against this opinion is, that Ovid himself complains that the true person of Corinna was found out by the fame of his verses to her: which if it had been Julia, he durst not have owned; and besides, an immediate punishment must have followed. He seems himself more truly to have touched at the cause of his exile in those obscure verses,

> Cur aliquid vidi, cur noxia lumina feci? etc.

namely, that he had either seen, or was conscious to somewhat, which had procured him his disgrace. But neither am I satisfied that this was the incest of the emperor with his own daughter, for Augustus was of a nature too vindicative to have contented himself with so small a revenge, or so unsafe to himself, as that of simple banishment, and would certainly have secured his crimes from public notice by the death of him who was witness to them. Neither have histories given us any sight into such an action of this emperor: nor would he (the greatest politician of his time), in all probability, have managed his crimes with so little secrecy, as not to shun the observation of any man. It seems more probable that Ovid was either the confidant of some other passion, or that he had stumbled by some inadvertency upon the privacies of Livia, and seen her in a bath. For the words

> Sine veste Dianam,

agree better with Livia, who had the fame of chastity, than with either of the Julias, who were both noted of incontinency. The first verses which were made by him in his youth, and recited publicly according to the custom were, as he himself assures us, to Corinna. His banishment happened not till the age of fifty; from which it may be deduced, with probability enough, that the love of Corinna did not occasion it. Nay he tells us plainly, that his offence was that of error only, not

---

Isis: *Amores*, II. xiii.
complains: ibid. III. xii. 7–12.
Cur aliquid . . .: *Tristia*, ii. 103 ('Why did I see? Why were harmful rays made to shine?').
Sine veste Dianam: ibid. ii. 105 ('Diana without clothes, naked').

of wickedness: and in the same paper of verses also, that the cause was notoriously known at Rome, though it be left so obscure to after ages.

But to leave conjectures on a subject so uncertain, and to write somewhat more authentic of this poet, that he frequented the court of Augustus, and was well received in it, is most undoubted. All his poems bear the character of a court, and appear to be written as the French call it *cavalièrement*. Add to this, that the titles of many of his elegies, and more of his letters in his banishment, are addressed to persons well known to us, even at this distance, to have been considerable in that court.

Nor was his acquaintance less with the famous poets of his age, than with the noblemen and ladies; he tells you himself, in a particular account of his own life, that Macer, Horace, Tibullus, Propertius, and many others of them were his familiar friends, and that some of them communicated their writings to him, but that he had only seen Virgil.

If the imitation of nature be the business of a poet, I know no author who can justly be compared with ours, especially in the description of the passions. And to prove this, I shall need no other judges than the generality of his readers: for all passions being inborn with us, we are almost equally judges when we are concerned in the representation of them. Now I will appeal to any man who has read this poet, whether he find not the natural emotion of the same passion in himself, which the poet describes in his feigned persons? His thoughts which are the pictures and results of those passions, are generally such as naturally arise from those disorderly motions of our spirits. Yet, not to speak too partially on his behalf, I will confess that the copiousness of his wit was such, that he often writ too pointedly for his subject, and made his persons speak more eloquently than the violence of their passion would admit: so that he is frequently witty out of season, leaving the imitation of nature, and the cooler dictates of his judgement, for the false applause of fancy. Yet he seems to have found out this imperfection in his riper age: for why else should he complain that his *Metamorphosis* was left unfinished? Nothing sure can be added to the wit of that poem, or of the rest, but many things ought to have been retrenched; which I suppose would have been the business of his age, if his misfortunes had not come too fast upon him. But take him uncorrected as he is transmitted to us, and it must be acknowledged in spite of his Dutch friends, the

cavalièrement: offhandedly.
his own life: Tristia, IV. x. 43–54.
    7*

commentators, even of Julius Scaliger himself, that Seneca's censure
will stand good against him;

Nescivit quod bene cessit relinquere:

he never knew how to give over, when he had done well: but continually varying the same sense an hundred ways, and taking up in
another place what he had more than enough inculcated before, he
sometimes cloys his readers instead of satisfying them, and gives
occasion to his translators, who dare not cover him, to blush at the
nakedness of their father. This then is the allay of Ovid's writing,
which is sufficiently recompensed by his other excellencies; nay this
very fault is not without its beauties: for the most severe censor
cannot but be pleased with the prodigality of his wit, though at the
same time he could have wished that the master of it had been a
better manager. Everything which he does becomes him, and if sometimes he appear too gay, yet there is a secret gracefulness of youth,
which accompanies his writings, though the staidness and sobriety of
age be wanting. In the most material part, which is the conduct, 'tis
certain that he seldom has miscarried: for if his elegies be compared
with those of Tibullus and Propertius his contemporaries, it will be
found that those poets seldom designed before they writ. And though
the language of Tibullus be more polished, and the learning of
Propertius, especially in his fourth book, more set out to ostentation, yet their common practice, was to look no further before them
than the next line: whence it will inevitably follow, that they can drive
to no certain point, but ramble from one subject to another, and
conclude with somewhat which is not of a piece with their beginning:

*Purpureus late qui splendeat, unus et alter
assuitur pannus:*

as Horace says, though the verses are golden, they are but patched
into the garment. But our poet has always the goal in his eye, which
directs him in his race, some beautiful design, which he first establishes, and then contrives the means, which will naturally conduct it
to his end. This will be evident to judicious readers in this work of his
Epistles, of which somewhat, at least in general, will be expected.

The title of them in our late editions is *Epistolae Heroidum*, The
Letters of the Heroines. But Heinsius has judged more truly, that the
inscription of our author was barely, *Epistles*, which he concludes
from his cited verses, where Ovid asserts this work as his own in-

---

Nescivit . . .: M. Annaeus Seneca, *Controversiae*, IX. v. 17.
allay: dilution.
Purpureus . . .: *Ars Poetica*, ll. 15–16.

vention, and not borrowed from the Greeks, whom (as the masters of their learning) the Romans usually did imitate. But it appears not from their writers, that any of the Grecians ever touched upon this way, which our poet therefore justly has vindicated to himself. I quarrel not at the word *Heroidum*, because 'tis used by Ovid in his *Art of Love*:

> Jupiter ad veteres supplex Heroidas ibat.

But sure he could not be guilty of such an oversight, to call his work by the name of heroines, when there are divers men or heroes, as namely Paris, Leander, and Acontius, joined in it. Except Sabinus, who writ some answers to Ovid's letters,

> (Quam celer e toto rediit meus orbe Sabinus,)

I remember not any of the Romans who have treated this subject, save only Propertius, and that but once, in his *Epistle of Arethusa to Lycotas*, which is written so near the style of Ovid that it seems to be but an imitation, and therefore ought not to defraud our poet of the glory of his invention.

Concerning this work of the epistles, I shall content myself to observe these few particulars. First, that they are generally granted to be the most perfect piece of Ovid, and that the style of them is tenderly passionate and courtly; two properties well agreeing with the persons which were heroines, and lovers. Yet where the characters were lower, as in Oenone, and Hero, he has kept close to nature in drawing his images after a country life, though perhaps he has romanized his Grecian dames too much, and made them speak sometimes as if they had been born in the city of Rome, and under the Empire of Augustus. There seems to be no great variety in the particular subjects which he has chosen, most of the epistles being written from ladies who were forsaken by their lovers: which is the reason that many of the same thoughts come back upon us in divers letters. But of the general character of women which is modesty, he has taken a most becoming care; for his amorous expressions go no further than virtue may allow, and therefore may be read, as he intended them, by matrons without a blush.

Thus much concerning the poet: whom you find translated by divers hands,[n] that you may at least have that variety in the English, which the subject denied to the author of the Latin. It remains that I should say somewhat of poetical translations in general, and give my

---

Jupiter ad veteres . . .: *Ars Amatoria*, i. 713.
Quam celer . . .: *Amores*, II. xviii. 27–8.
Arethusa: i.e. iv. 3.

opinion (with submission to better judgements) which way of version seems to me most proper.

All translation I suppose may be reduced to these three heads.

First, that of metaphrase, or turning an author word by word, and line by line, from one language into another. Thus, or near this manner, was Horace's *Art of Poetry* translated by Ben Jonson. The second way is that of paraphrase, or translation with latitude, where the author is kept in view by the translator, so as never to be lost, but his words are not so strictly followed as his sense, and that too is admitted to be amplified, but not altered. Such is Mr. Waller's translation of Virgil's fourth *Aeneid*. The third way is that of imitation, where the translator (if now he has not lost that name) assumes the liberty not only to vary from the words and sense, but to forsake them both as he sees occasion: and taking only some general hints from the original, to run division on the groundwork, as he pleases. Such is Mr. Cowley's practice in turning two odes of Pindar, and one of Horace into English.

Concerning the first of these methods, our master Horace has given us this caution,

> Nec verbum verbo curabis reddere, fidus
> interpres—

'Nor word for word too faithfully translate', as the Earl of Roscommon has excellently rendered it. Too faithfully is indeed pedantically: 'tis a faith like that which proceeds from superstition, blind and zealous. Take it in the expression of Sir John Denham, to Sir Rich. Fanshaw, on his version of the *Pastor Fido*.

> That servile path, thou nobly dost decline,
> Of tracing word by word and line by line;
> A new and nobler way thou dost pursue,
> To make translations, and translators too:
> They but preserve the ashes, thou the flame,
> True to his sense, but truer to his fame.

'Tis almost impossible to translate verbally, and well, at the same time; for the Latin (a most severe and compendious language) often

---

Ben Jonson: first published in 1640.

fourth Aeneid: *The Passion of Dido* (1658) by Waller and Godolphin.

groundwork: i.e. to execute a variant or descant of short notes based on a simpler passage of longer notes.

Pindar: Pindar's second Olympic and first Nemean odes; and Horace, *Odes*, IV. ii.

Nec verbum . . .: *Ars Poetica*, ll. 133–4.

That servile path, . . .: from Denham's dedicatory verses to Sir Richard Fanshawe's translation (1647) of Guarini's *Il Pastor Fido* (ll. 15–16, 21–4).

expresses that in one word, which either the barbarity, or the narrowness of modern tongues cannot supply in more. 'Tis frequent also that the conceit is couched in some expression, which will be lost in English.

> Atque iidem venti vela fidemque ferent.

What poet of our nation is so happy as to express this thought literally in English, and to strike wit or almost sense out of it?

In short the verbal copier is encumbered with so many difficulties at once, that he can never disentangle himself from all. He is to consider at the same time the thought of his author, and his words, and to find out the counterpart to each in another language: and besides this he is to confine himself to the compass of numbers, and the slavery of rhyme. 'Tis much like dancing on ropes with fettered legs. A man may shun a fall by using caution, but the gracefulness of motion is not to be expected, and when we have said the best of it, 'tis but a foolish task; for no sober man would put himself into a danger for the applause of escaping without breaking his neck. We see Ben Jonson could not avoid obscurity in his literal translation of Horace, attempted in the same compass of lines: nay Horace himself could scarce have done it to a Greek poet.

> Brevis esse laboro, obscurus fio.

Either perspicuity or gracefulness will frequently be wanting. Horace has indeed avoided both these rocks in his translation of the three first lines of Homer's *Odyssey*, which he has contracted into two.

> Dic mihi Musa virum captae post tempora Trojae
> qui mores hominum multorum vidit et urbes.

> Muse, speak the man, who since the Siege of Troy, ⎫ Earl of
> So many towns, such change of manners saw.   ⎭ *Rosc.*

But then the sufferings of Ulysses, which are a considerable part of that sentence are omitted:

> Ὅς μάλα πολλὰ πλάγχθη.

The consideration of these difficulties, in a servile, literal translation, not long since made two of our famous wits, Sir John Denham, and Mr. Cowley to contrive another way of turning authors into our tongue, called by the latter of them, imitation. As they were friends,

---

Atque iidem . . .: Ovid, *Heroides*, vii. 8.

> While you, with loosened sails and vows, prepare
> To seek a land that flies the searcher's care.
>   (Dryden)

Brevis esse . . .: *Ars Poetica*, ll. 25–6 ('I struggle to be brief and become obscure').
Dic mihi . . .: ibid. ll. 141–2.
Ὅς μάλα: *Odyssey*, i. 1–2.

I suppose they communicated their thoughts on this subject to each
other, and therefore their reasons for it are little different: though the
practice of one is much more moderate. I take imitation of an author
in their sense to be an endeavour of a later poet to write like one who
has written before him on the same subject: that is, not to translate
his words, or to be confined to his sense, but only to set him as a
pattern, and to write as he supposes that author would have done
had he lived in our age, and in our country. Yet I dare not say that
either of them have carried this libertine way of rendering authors (as
Mr. Cowley calls it) so far as my definition reaches. For in the
Pindaric Odes, the customs and ceremonies of ancient Greece are
still preserved, but I know not what mischief may arise hereafter
from the example of such an innovation, when writers of unequal
parts to him shall imitate so bold an undertaking. To add and to
diminish what we please, which is the way avowed by him, ought
only to be granted to Mr. Cowley, and that too only in his translation
of Pindar, because he alone was able to make him amends, by giving
him better of his own, whenever he refused his author's thoughts.
Pindar is generally known to be a dark writer, to want connexion (I
mean as to our understanding) to soar out of sight, and leave his
reader at a gaze. So wild and ungovernable a poet cannot be translated literally; his genius is too strong to bear a chain, and Sampson-
like he shakes it off. A genius so elevated and unconfined as Mr.
Cowley's was but necessary to make Pindar speak English, and that
was to be performed by no other way than imitation. But if Virgil or
Ovid, or any regular intelligible authors be thus used, 'tis no longer
to be called their work, when neither the thoughts nor words are
drawn from the original: but instead of them there is something new
produced, which is almost the creation of another hand. By this way
'tis true, somewhat that is excellent may be invented, perhaps more
excellent than the first design, though Virgil must be still excepted
when that perhaps takes place. Yet he who is inquisitive to know an
author's thoughts will be disappointed in his expectation. And 'tis
not always that a man will be contented to have a present made him,
when he expects the payment of a debt. To state it fairly, imitation of
an author is the most advantageous way for a translator to show
himself, but the greatest wrong which can be done to the memory and
reputation of the dead. Sir John Denham (who advised more liberty
than he took himself,) gives this reason for his innovation, in his

---

practice of one: Denham (see his Preface to *The Destruction of Troy*, 1656, a
version of part of *Aeneid*, ii). Dryden quotes from this Preface on page 187.

admirable preface before the translation of the second *Aeneid*: 'Poetry is of so subtle a spirit, that in pouring out of one language into another, it will all evaporate; and if a new spirit be not added in the transfusion, there will remain nothing but a *caput mortuum*.' I confess this argument holds good against a literal translation, but who defends it? Imitation and verbal version are in my opinion the two extremes, which ought to be avoided: and therefore when I have proposed the mean betwixt them, it will be seen how far his argument will reach.

No man is capable of translating poetry, who besides a genius to that art, is not a master both of his author's language, and of his own. Nor must we understand the language only of the poet, but his particular turn of thoughts, and of expression, which are the characters that distinguish, and as it were individuate him from all other writers. When we are come thus far, 'tis time to look into ourselves, to conform our genius to his, to give his thought either the same turn if our tongue will bear it, or if not, to vary but the dress, not to alter or destroy the substance. The like care must be taken of the more outward ornaments, the words: when they appear (which is but seldom) literally graceful, it were an injury to the author that they should be changed. But since every language is so full of its own proprieties, that what is beautiful in one, is often barbarous, nay sometimes nonsense in another, it would be unreasonable to limit a translator to the narrow compass of his author's words: 'tis enough if he choose out some expression which does not vitiate the sense. I suppose he may stretch his chain to such a latitude, but by innovation of thoughts, methinks he breaks it. By this means the spirit of an author may be transfused, and yet not lost: and thus 'tis plain that the reason alleged by Sir John Denham, has no farther force than to expression: for thought, if it be translated truly, cannot be lost in another language, but the words that convey it to our apprehension (which are the image and ornament of that thought) may be so ill chosen as to make it appear in an unhandsome dress, and rob it of its native lustre. There is therefore a liberty to be allowed for the expression, neither is it necessary that words and lines should be confined to the measure of their original. The sense of an author, generally speaking, is to be sacred and inviolable. If the fancy of Ovid be luxuriant, 'tis his character to be so, and if I retrench it, he is no longer Ovid. It will be replied that he receives advantage by this lopping of his superfluous branches, but I rejoin that a translator has no such right. When a painter copies from the life, I suppose he has no privilege to alter features, and lineaments, under pretence that his picture will look better. Perhaps the face which he has drawn would be more exact, if the eyes, or nose were altered, but 'tis his business to make it resemble the original. In two cases only there may a seeming difficulty arise, that is, if the thought be notoriously trivial or dishonest; but the same answer will serve for both, that then they ought not to be translated.

> —Et quae
> desperes tractata nitescere posse, relinquas.

Thus I have ventured to give my opinion on this subject against the authority of two great men, but I hope without offence to either of their memories, for I both loved them living, and reverence them now they are dead. But if after what I have urged, it be thought by better judges that the praise of a translation consists in adding new beauties to the piece, thereby to recompense the loss which it sustains by change of language, I shall be willing to be taught better, and to recant. In the mean time it seems to me, that the true reason why we have so few versions which are tolerable, is not from the too close pursuing of the author's sense: but because there are so few who have all the talents which are requisite for translation: and that there is so little praise and so small encouragement for so considerable a part of learning.

To apply in short, what has been said, to this present work, the reader will here find most of the translations, with some little latitude or variation from the author's sense. That of Oenone to Paris, is in Mr. Cowley's way of imitation only. I was desired to say that the author who is of the fair sex, understood not Latin. But if she does not, I am afraid she has given us occasion to be ashamed who do.

For my own part I am ready to acknowledge that I have transgressed the rules which I have given; and taken more liberty than a just translation will allow. But so many gentlemen whose wit and learning are well known, being joined in it, I doubt not but that their excellencies will make you ample satisfaction for my errors.

J. DRYDEN

—*Et quae* . . .: *Ars Poetica*, ll. 149–50 ('And abandon these things at which, however you try, you cannot be outstanding').
Oenone to Paris: by Mrs. Behn.

TO THE RIGHT HONOURABLE JOHN, LORD HAUGHTON[n]

PREFIXED TO *THE SPANISH FRIAR*

1681

MY LORD,

WHEN I first designed this play, I found, or thought I found, somewhat so moving in the serious part of it, and so pleasant in the comic, as might deserve a more than ordinary care in both. Accordingly, I used the best of my endeavour, in the management of two plots, so very different from each other, that it was not perhaps the talent of every writer to have made them of a piece. Neither have I attempted other plays of the same nature, in my opinion, with the same judgement; though with like success. And though many poets may suspect themselves for the fondness and partiality of parents to their youngest children, yet I hope I may stand exempted from this rule, because I know myself too well to be ever satisfied with my own conceptions, which have seldom reached to those ideas that I had within me; and consequently, I presume I may have liberty to judge when I write more or less pardonably, as an ordinary marksman may know certainly when he shoots less wide at what he aims. Besides, the care and pains I have bestowed on this beyond my other tragi-comedies may reasonably make the world conclude that either I can do nothing tolerably, or that this poem is not much amiss. Few good pictures have been finished at one sitting; neither can a true just play, which is to bear the test of ages, be produced at a heat, or by the force of fancy, without the maturity of judgement. For my own part, I have both so just a diffidence of myself, and so great a reverence for my audience, that I dare venture nothing without a strict examination; and am as much ashamed to put a loose indigested play upon the public as I should be to offer brass money in a payment. For though it should be taken (as it is too often on the stage), yet it will be found in the second telling; and a judicious reader will discover in his closet that trashy stuff whose glittering deceived him in the action. I have often heard the stationer sighing in his shop, and wishing for those hands to take off his melancholy bargain which clapped its performance on the stage. In a playhouse, everything contributes to impose upon the judgement: the lights, the scenes, the habits, and, above all, the grace of action, which is commonly the best where there is the most need of it, surprise the audience, and cast a mist upon their understandings; not unlike the cunning of a juggler, who is always staring us in the face, and overwhelming us with gibberish, only that he may gain the opportunity of making the cleaner conveyance of his trick. But these false beauties of the stage are no more lasting than a rainbow; when the actor ceases to shine upon them, when he gilds them no longer with his reflection, they vanish in a twinkling.

I have sometimes wondered, in the reading, what was become of those glaring colours which amazed me in *Bussy D'Ambois* upon the theatre; but when I had taken up what I supposed a fallen star, I found I had been cozened with a jelly: nothing but a cold, dull mass, which glittered no longer than it was shooting; a dwarfish thought, dressed up in gigantic words, repetition in abundance, looseness of expression, and gross hyperboles; the sense of one line expanded prodigiously into ten; and, to sum up all, incorrect English, and a hideous mingle of false poetry and true nonsense; or, at best, a scantling of wit which lay gasping for life, and groaning beneath a heap of rubbish. A famous modern poet used to sacrifice every year a Statius to Virgil's Manes; and I have indignation enough to burn a *D'Ambois* annually to the memory of Jonson.

But now, my Lord, I am sensible, perhaps too late, that I have gone too far: for, I remember some verses of my own Maximin and Almanzor which cry vengeance upon me for their extravagance, and which I wish heartily in the same fire with Statius and Chapman. All I can say for those passages, which are I hope not many, is that I knew they were bad enough to please, even when I writ them. But I repent of them amongst my sins; and if any of their fellows intrude by chance into my present writings, I draw a stroke over all those Dalilahs of the theatre; and am resolved I will settle myself no reputation by the applause of fools. 'Tis not that I am mortified to all ambition, but I scorn as much to take it from half-witted judges, as I should to raise an estate by cheating of bubbles. Neither do I discommend the lofty style in tragedy, which is naturally pompous and magnificent; but nothing is truly sublime that is not just and proper. If the Ancients had judged by the same measures which a common

---

Bussy d'Ambois: (1607) by George Chapman; produced several times after the Restoration.

a jelly: 'The alga nostoc, a damp plant, was popularly thought the remains of a falling star' (Watson).

A famous modern poet: Malone refers to the *Prolusiones* (1617) of Strada (1572–1649) as relating that Andrea Navagero used annually to sacrifice a copy of Martial (not Statius) to the memory of Virgil.

Maximin *and* Almanzor: in, respectively, *Tyrannic Love* (1670) and *The Conquest of Granada* (1672).

reader takes, they had concluded Statius to have written higher than
Virgil; for

quae superimposito moles geminata Colosso

carries a more thundering kind of sound than

Tityre tu patulae recubans sub tegmine fagi:

yet Virgil had all the majesty of a lawful prince, and Statius only the
blustering of a tyrant. But when men affect a virtue which they
cannot reach, they fall into a vice which bears the nearest resemblance
to it. Thus an injudicious poet who aims at loftiness runs easily into
the swelling puffy style, because it looks like greatness. I remember,
when I was a boy, I thought inimitable Spenser a mean poet in comparison of Sylvester's *Du Bartas*; and was rapt into an ecstasy when I
read these lines:

> Now, when the Winter's keener breath began
> To crystallize the Baltic Ocean;
> To glaze the lakes, to bridle up the floods,
> And periwig with snow the bald-pate woods.

I am much deceived if this be not abominable fustian, that is, thoughts
and words ill sorted, and without the least relation to each other; yet
I dare not answer for an audience, that they would not clap it on the
stage: so little value there is to be given to the common cry that
nothing but madness can please madmen, and a poet must be of a
piece with the spectators to gain a reputation with them. But as in a
room contrived for state, the height of the roof should bear a proportion to the area; so, in the heightenings of poetry, the strength
and vehemence of figures should be suited to the occasion, the subject, and the persons. All beyond this is monstrous: 'tis out of
nature, 'tis an excrescence, and not a living part of poetry. I had not
said thus much, if some young gallants who pretend to criticism had
not told me that this tragi-comedy wanted the dignity of style; but as
a man who is charged with a crime of which he thinks himself innocent is apt to be too eager in his own defence, so perhaps I have
vindicated my play with more partiality than I ought, or than such a
trifle can deserve. Yet, whatever beauties it may want, 'tis free at least
from the grossness of those faults I mentioned. What credit it has

---

quae superimposito . . .: *Sylvae*, I. i ('a mound doubled by having a colossus on
top of it').

Tityre tu patulae . . .: *Eclogues*, I. i ('You lie, Tityrus, under cover of a spreading
beech tree').

Now, when the Winter's . . .: Joshua Sylvester (1563–1618), *Divine Works and
Days* (from the French of Du Bartas), Part IV, day i, week ii (inaccurately
quoted).

gained upon the stage, I value no farther than in reference to my
profit, and the satisfaction I had in seeing it represented with all the
justness and gracefulness of action. But as 'tis my interest to please
my audience, so 'tis my ambition to be read: that I am sure is the
more lasting and the nobler design: for the propriety of thoughts and
words, which are the hidden beauties of a play, are but confusedly
judged in the vehemence of action. All things are there beheld as in a
hasty motion, where the objects only glide before the eye and dis-
appear. The most discerning critic can judge no more of these silent
graces in the action than he who rides post through an unknown
country can distinguish the situation of places, and the nature of the
soil. The purity of phrase, the clearness of conception and expression,
the boldness maintained to majesty, the significancy and sound of
words, not strained into bombast, but justly elevated; in short, those
very words and thoughts which cannot be changed but for the worse,
must of necessity escape our transient view upon the theatre; and yet
without all these a play may take. For if either the story move us, or
the actor help the lameness of it with his performance, or now and
then a glittering beam of wit or passion strike through the obscurity
of the poem, any of these are sufficient to effect a present liking, but
not to fix a lasting admiration; for nothing but truth can long continue; and time is the surest judge of truth. I am not vain enough to
think I have left no faults in this which that touchstone will not discover; neither indeed is it possible to avoid them in a play of this
nature. There are evidently two actions in it; but it will be clear to
any judicious man that with half the pains I could have raised a play
from either of them; for this time I satisfied my own humour, which
was to tack two plays together; and to break a rule for the pleasure
of variety. The truth is, the audience are grown weary of continued
melancholy scenes; and I dare venture to prophesy that few tragedies
except those in verse shall succeed in this age, if they are not lightened
with a course of mirth. For the feast is too dull and solemn without
the fiddles. But how difficult a task this is, will soon be tried; for a
several genius is required to either way; and, without both of 'em, a
man, in my opinion, is but half a poet for the stage. Neither is it so
trivial an undertaking to make a tragedy end happily; for 'tis more
difficult to save than 'tis to kill. The dagger and the cup of poison are
always in a readiness; but to bring the action to the last extremity,
and then by probable means to recover all, will require the art and
judgement of a writer, and cost him many a pang in the performance.

And now, my Lord, I must confess that what I have written looks
more like a Preface than a Dedication; and truly it was thus far my
design that I might entertain you with somewhat in my own art which

might be more worthy of a noble mind than the stale, exploded trick of fulsome panegyrics. 'Tis difficult to write justly on any thing, but almost impossible in praise. I shall therefore waive so nice a subject; and only tell you that, in recommending a Protestant play to a Protestant patron, as I do myself an honour, so I do your noble family a right, who have been always eminent in the support and favour of our religion and liberties. And if the promises of your youth, your education at home, and your experience abroad, deceive me not, the principles you have embraced are such as will no way degenerate from your ancestors, but refresh their memory in the minds of all true Englishmen, and renew their lustre in your person; which, my Lord, is not more the wish than it is the constant expectation of your Lordship's

Most obedient, faithful servant,
JOHN DRYDEN

PREFACE TO *SYLVAE, OR THE SECOND PART OF POETICAL MISCELLANIES*

1685

FOR this last half year I have been troubled with the disease (as I may call it) of translation; the cold prose fits of it (which are always the most tedious with me) were spent in the *History of the League*; the hot (which succeeded them) in this volume of Verse Miscellanies. The truth is, I fancied to myself a kind of ease in the change of the paroxysm; never suspecting but that the humour would have wasted itself in two or three Pastorals of Theocritus, and as many Odes of Horace. But finding, or at least thinking I found, something that was more pleasing in them, than my ordinary productions, I encouraged myself to renew my old acquaintance with Lucretius and Virgil; and immediately fixed upon some parts of them which had most affected me in the reading. These were my natural impulses for the undertaking. But there was an accidental motive, which was full as forcible, and God forgive him who was the occasion of it. It was my Lord Roscommon's *Essay on translated Verse*, which made me uneasy till I tried whether or no I was capable of following his rules, and of reducing the speculation into practice. For many a fair precept in poetry, is like a seeming demonstration in the mathematics; very specious in the diagram, but failing in the mechanic operation. I think I have generally observed his instructions; I am sure my reason is sufficiently convinced both of their truth and usefulness; which, in other words, is to confess no less a vanity than to pretend that I have at least in some places made examples to his rules. Yet withal, I must acknowledge, that I have many times exceeded my commission; for I have both added and omitted, and even sometimes very boldly made such expositions of my authors, as no Dutch commentator will forgive me. Perhaps, in such particular passages, I have thought that I discovered some beauty yet undiscovered by those pedants, which none but a poet could have found. Where I have taken away some of their expressions, and cut them shorter, it may possibly be on this consideration, that what was beautiful in the Greek or Latin, would not appear so shining in the English. And where I have enlarged them, I desire the false critics would not always think that those thoughts are wholly mine, but that either they are secretly in the poet, or may be fairly deduced from him: or at least, if both those considerations should fail, that my own is of a

---

History of the League: Dryden had translated Maimbourg's *Histoire de la Ligue* at the King's command; it was published in July 1684.
Essay on translated Verse: text in Spingarn, II, pp. 297 ff.

piece with his, and that if he were living, and an Englishman, they are such, as he would probably have written.

For, after all, a translator is to make his author appear as charming as possibly he can, provided he maintains his character, and makes him not unlike himself. Translation is a kind of drawing after the life; where everyone will acknowledge there is a double sort of likeness, a good one and a bad. 'Tis one thing to draw the outlines true, the features like, the proportions exact, the colouring itself perhaps tolerable, and another thing to make all these graceful, by the posture, the shadowings, and chiefly by the spirit which animates the whole. I cannot without some indignation, look on an ill copy of an excellent original. Much less can I behold with patience Virgil, Homer, and some others, whose beauties I have been endeavouring all my life to imitate, so abused, as I may say to their faces by a botching interpreter. What English readers unacquainted with Greek or Latin will believe me or any other man, when we commend those authors, and confess we derive all that is pardonable in us from their fountains, if they take those to be the same poets, whom our Ogilbies have translated? But I dare assure them, that a good poet is no more like himself in a dull translation, than his carcass would be to his living body. There are many who understand Greek and Latin, and yet are ignorant of their mother tongue. The proprieties and delicacies of the English are known to few; 'tis impossible even for a good wit to understand and practice them without the help of a liberal education, long reading, and digesting of those few good authors we have amongst us, the knowledge of men and manners, the freedom of habitudes and conversation with the best company of both sexes; and in short, without wearing off the rust which he contracted, while he was laying in a stock of learning. Thus difficult it is to understand the purity of English, and critically to discern not only good writers from bad, and a proper style from a corrupt, but also to distinguish that which is pure in a good author, from that which is vicious and corrupt in him. And for want of all these requisites, or the greatest part of them, most of our ingenious young men take up some cried up English poet for their model, adore him, and imitate him as they think, without knowing wherein he is defective, where he is boyish and trifling, wherein either his thoughts are improper to his subject, or his expressions unworthy of his thoughts, or the turn of both is unharmonious. Thus it appears necessary that a man should be a nice critic in his mother tongue, before he attempts to translate a foreign

Ogilbies: John Ogilby (1600–76) published his translation of Virgil in 1649, of Homer's *Iliad* in 1660, and of his *Odyssey* in 1665.

language. Neither is it sufficient that he be able to judge of words and
style; but he must be a master of them too. He must perfectly understand his author's tongue, and absolutely command his own, so that
to be a thorough translator, he must be a thorough poet. Neither is it
enough to give his author's sense, in good English, in poetical
expressions, and in musical numbers. For, though all these are
exceeding difficult to perform, there yet remains an harder task; and
'tis a secret of which few translators have sufficiently thought. I have
already hinted a word or two concerning it; that is, the maintaining
the character of an author, which distinguishes him from all others,
and makes him appear that individual poet whom you would interpret. For example, not only the thoughts, but the style and versification of Virgil and Ovid, are very different. Yet I see, even in our best
poets, who have translated some parts of them, that they have confounded their several talents; and by endeavouring only at the sweetness and harmony of numbers, have made them both so much alike,
that if I did not know the originals, I should never be able to judge
by the copies, which was Virgil, and which was Ovid. It was objected
against a late noble painter, that he drew many graceful pictures, but
few of them were like. And this happened to him, because he always
studied himself more than those who sat to him. In such translators I
can easily distinguish the hand which performed the work, but I
cannot distinguish their poet from another. Suppose two authors are
equally sweet, yet there is a great distinction to be made in sweetness,
as in that of sugar, and that of honey. I can make the difference more
plain, by giving you (if it be worth knowing) my own method of
proceeding in my translations out of four several poets in this volume;
Virgil, Theocritus, Lucretius and Horace. In each of these, before I
undertook them, I considered the genius and distinguishing character
of my author. I looked on Virgil, as a succinct and grave majestic
writer; one who weighed not only every thought, but every word and
syllable; who was still aiming to crowd his sense into as narrow a
compass as possibly he could, for which reason he is so very
figurative, that he requires, (I may almost say) a grammar apart to
construe him. His verse is everywhere sounding the very thing in your
ears, whose sense it bears, yet the numbers are perpetually varied, to
increase the delight of the reader; so that the same sounds are never
repeated twice together. On the contrary, Ovid and Claudian,
though they write in styles differing from each other, yet have each
of them but one sort of music in their verses. All the versification, and
little variety of Claudian, is included within the compass of four or

---

painter: probably Sir Peter Lely (1618–80).

five lines, and then he begins again in the same tenor; perpetually
closing his sense at the end of a verse, and that verse commonly which
they call golden, or two substantives and two adjectives with a verb
betwixt them to keep the peace. Ovid with all his sweetness, has as
little variety of numbers and sound as he: he is always as it were
upon the hand-gallop, and his verse runs upon carpet ground. He
avoids like the other all synaloephas, or cutting off one vowel when
it comes before another in the following word, so that minding only
smoothness, he wants both variety and majesty. But to return to
Virgil, though he is smooth where smoothness is required, yet he is so
far from affecting it, that he seems rather to disdain it; frequently
makes use of synaloephas, and concludes his sense in the middle of
his verse. He is everywhere above conceits of epigrammatic wit, and
gross hyperboles. He maintains majesty in the midst of plainness; he
shines, but glares not; and is stately without ambition, which is the
vice of Lucan. I drew my definition of poetical wit from my particular consideration of him. For propriety of thoughts and words are
only to be found in him; and where they are proper, they will be
delightful. Pleasure follows of necessity, as the effect does the cause;
and therefore is not to be put into the definition. This exact propriety
of Virgil, I particularly regarded, as a great part of his character; but
must confess to my shame, that I have not been able to translate any
part of him so well as to make him appear wholly like himself. For
where the original is close, no version can reach it in the same compass. Hannibal Caro's in the Italian, is the nearest, the most poetical,
and the most sonorous of any translation of the *Aeneids*; yet, though
he takes the advantage of blank verse, he commonly allows two lines
for one of Virgil, and does not always hit his sense. Tasso tells us in
his *Letters*, that Sperone Speroni, a great Italian wit, who was his
contemporary, observed of Virgil and Tully that the Latin orator
endeavoured to imitate the copiousness of Homer the Greek poet;
and that the Latin poet, made it his business to reach the conciseness
of Demosthenes the Greek orator. Virgil therefore being so very
sparing of his words, and leaving so much to be imagined by the
reader, can never be translated as he ought, in any modern tongue.
To make him copious is to alter his character; and to translate him

---

hand-gallop: i.e. at an easy gallop.
carpet ground: smooth, easy ground.
synaloepha: e.g. 'th' offspring'; the elision of the first of two juxtaposed vowels.
Hannibal Caro: the translation of the *Aeneid* by Hannibal Caro (1507–66) was
    published in 1581.
Tully: Cicero.
Tasso tells us: *Discorsi del poema eroico*, end of Bk. ii.

line for line is impossible; because the Latin is naturally a more succinct language, than either the Italian, Spanish, French, or even than the English, (which by reason of its monosyllables is far the most compendious of them). Virgil is much the closest of any Roman poet, and the Latin hexameter, has more feet than the English heroic.

Besides all this, an author has the choice of his own thoughts and words, which a translator has not; he is confined by the sense of the inventor to those expressions which are the nearest to it, so that Virgil studying brevity, and having the command of his own language, could bring those words into a narrow compass, which a translator cannot render without circumlocutions. In short they who have called him the torture of grammarians, might also have called him the plague of translators; for he seems to have studied not to be translated. I own that endeavouring to turn his Nisus and Euryalus as close as I was able, I have performed that episode too literally; that giving more scope to Mezentius and Lausus, that version which has more of the majesty of Virgil, has less of his conciseness; and all that I can promise for myself, is only that I have done both, better than Ogilby, and perhaps as well as Caro. So that methinks I come like a malefactor, to make a speech upon the gallows, and to warn all other poets, by my sad example, from the sacrilege of translating Virgil. Yet, by considering him so carefully as I did before my attempt, I have made some faint resemblance of him; and had I taken more time, might possibly have succeeded better; but never so well, as to have satisfied myself.

He who excels all other poets in his own language, were it possible to do him right, must appear above them in our tongue, which, as my Lord Roscommon justly observes, approaches nearest to the Roman in its majesty: nearest indeed, but with a vast interval betwixt them. There is an inimitable grace in Virgil's words, and in them principally consists that beauty, which gives so unexpressible a pleasure to him who best understands their force; this diction of his, I must once again say, is never to be copied, and since it cannot, he will appear but lame in the best translation. The turns of his verse, his breakings, his propriety, his numbers, and his gravity, I have as far imitated, as the poverty of our language, and the hastiness of my performance would allow. I may seem sometimes to have varied from his sense; but I think the greatest variations may be fairly deduced from him;

Euryalus: *Aeneid*, ix. 176 f.
Lausus: ibid. x. 426 f.
Roscommon: see Spingarn, II, p. 309, ll. 13–16.
breakings: elisions.

and where I leave his commentators, it may be I understand him
better. At least I writ without consulting them in many places. But
two particular lines in Mezentius and Lausus, I cannot so easily
excuse; they are indeed remotely allied to Virgil's sense; but they are
too like the trifling tenderness of Ovid; and were printed before I had
considered them enough to alter them. The first of them I have forgotten, and cannot easily retrieve, because the copy is at the press.
The second is this;

> —When Lausus died, I was already slain.

This appears pretty enough at first sight, but I am convinced for
many reasons, that the expression is too bold, that Virgil would not
have said it, though Ovid would. The reader may pardon it, if he
please, for the freeness of the confession; and instead of that, and the
former, admit these two lines which are more according to the author,

> Nor ask I life, nor fought with that design;
> As I had used my fortune, use thou thine.

Having with much ado got clear of Virgil, I have in the next place
to consider the genius of Lucretius, whom I have translated more
happily in those parts of him which I undertook. If he was not of the
best age of Roman poetry, he was at least of that which preceded it;
and he himself refined it to that degree of perfection, both in the
language and the thoughts, that he left an easy task to Virgil, who as
he succeeded him in time, so he copied his excellencies: for the
method of the *Georgics* is plainly derived from him. Lucretius had
chosen a subject naturally crabbed; he therefore adorned it with
poetical descriptions, and precepts of morality, in the beginning and
ending of his books. Which you see Virgil has imitated with great
success, in those four books, which in my opinion are more perfect
in their kind, than even his divine *Aeneids*. The turn of his verse he
has likewise followed, in those places which Lucretius has most
laboured, and some of his very lines he has transplanted into his own
works, without much variation. If I am not mistaken, the distinguishing character of Lucretius (I mean of his soul and genius) is a
certain kind of noble pride, and positive assertion of his opinions. He
is everywhere confident of his own reason, and assuming an absolute
command not only over his vulgar reader, but even his patron
Memmius. For he is always bidding him attend, as if he had the rod
over him; and using a magisterial authority, while he instructs him.
From his time to ours, I know none so like him, as our poet and

---

two particular lines: Dryden corrected himself in the 1697 *Aeneis* (x. 1299–1300).

philosopher of Malmesbury. This is that perpetual dictatorship, which is exercised by Lucretius; who though often in the wrong, yet seems to deal *bona fide* with his reader, and tells him nothing but what he thinks; in which plain sincerity, I believe he differs from our Hobbes, who could not but be convinced, or at least doubt of some eternal truths which he has opposed. But for Lucretius, he seems to disdain all manner of replies, and is so confident of his cause, that he is beforehand with his antagonists; urging for them whatever he imagined they could say, and leaving them as he supposes, without an objection for the future. All this too, with so much scorn and indignation, as if he were assured of the triumph before he entered into the lists. From this sublime and daring genius of his, it must of necessity come to pass that his thoughts must be masculine, full of argumentation, and that sufficiently warm. From the same fiery temper proceeds the loftiness of his expressions, and the perpetual torrent of his verse, where the barrenness of his subject does not too much constrain the quickness of his fancy. For there is no doubt to be made, but that he could have been everywhere as poetical, as he is in his descriptions, and in the moral part of his philosophy, if he had not aimed more to instruct in his system of nature, than to delight. But he was bent upon making Memmius a materialist, and teaching him to defy an invisible power. In short, he was so much an atheist, that he forgot sometimes to be a poet. These are the considerations which I had of that author, before I attempted to translate some parts of him. And accordingly I laid by my natural diffidence and scepticism for a while, to take up that dogmatical way of his, which as I said, is so much his character, as to make him that individual poet. As for his opinions concerning the mortality of the soul, they are so absurd, that I cannot if I would believe them. I think a future state demonstrable even by natural arguments; at least to take away rewards and punishments is only a pleasing prospect to a man who resolves beforehand not to live morally. But on the other side, the thought of being nothing after death is a burden insupportable to a virtuous man, even though a heathen. We naturally aim at happiness, and cannot bear to have it confined to the shortness of our present being, especially when we consider that virtue is generally unhappy in this world, and vice fortunate. So that 'tis hope of futurity alone, that makes this life tolerable, in expectation of a better. Who would not commit all the excesses to which he is prompted by his natural inclinations, if he may do them with security while he is alive, and be incapable of punishment after he is dead! If he be cunning and secret

philosopher of Malmesbury: i.e. Thomas Hobbes.

enough to avoid the laws, there is no band of morality to restrain him, for fame and reputation are weak ties; many men have not the least sense of them: powerful men are only awed by them, as they conduce to their interest, and that not always when a passion is predominant; and no man will be contained within the bounds of duty when he may safely transgress them. These are my thoughts abstractedly, and without entering into the notions of our Christian faith, which is the proper business of divines.

But there are other arguments in this poem (which I have turned into English), not belonging to the mortality of the soul, which are strong enough to a reasonable man, to make him less in love with life, and consequently in less apprehensions of death. Such as are the natural satiety, proceeding from a perpetual enjoyment of the same things; the inconveniencies of old age, which make him incapable of corporeal pleasures; the decay of understanding and memory, which render him contemptible and useless to others; these and many other reasons so pathetically urged, so beautifully expressed, so adorned with examples, and so admirably raised by the prosopopeia of Nature, who is brought in speaking to her children, with so much authority and vigour, deserve the pains I have taken with them, which I hope have not been unsuccessful, or unworthy of my author. At least I must take the liberty to own, that I was pleased with my own endeavours, which but rarely happens to me, and that I am not dissatisfied upon the review, of anything I have done in this author.

'Tis true, there is something, and that of some moment, to be objected against my Englishing the nature of love, from the fourth book of Lucretius. And I can less easily answer why I translated it, than why I thus translated it. The objection arises from the obscenity of the subject; which is aggravated by the too lively and alluring delicacy of the verses. In the first place, without the least formality of an excuse, I own it pleased me: and let my enemies make the worst they can of this confession; I am not yet so secure from that passion, but that I want my author's antidotes against it. He has given the truest and most philosophical account both of the disease and remedy, which I ever found in any author: for which reasons I translated him. But it will be asked why I turned him into this luscious English (for I will not give it a worse word). Instead of an answer, I would ask again of my supercilious adversaries, whether I am not bound when I translate an author, to do him all the right I can, and to translate him to the best advantage? If to mince his meaning, which I am satisfied was honest and instructive, I had either omitted

prosopopeia: otherwise known as *conformatio*, and used to describe various forms of personification.

some part of what he said, or taken from the strength of his expression, I certainly had wronged him; and that freeness of thought and words being thus cashiered, in my hands he had no longer been Lucretius. If nothing of this kind be to be read, physicians must not study nature, anatomies must not be seen, and somewhat I could say of particular passages in books, which to avoid profaneness I do not name. But the intention qualifies the act; and both mine and my author's were to instruct as well as please. 'Tis most certain that barefaced bawdry is the poorest pretence to wit imaginable: if I should say otherwise, I should have two great authorities against me. The one is the *Essay on Poetry*, which I publicly valued before I knew the author of it, and with the commendation of which, my Lord Roscommon so happily begins his *Essay on Translated Verse*. The other is no less than our admired Cowley; who says the same thing in other words: for in his Ode concerning Wit, he writes thus of it;

> Much less can that have any place
> At which a virgin hides her face:
> Such dross the fire must purge away; 'tis just
> The author blush, there where the reader must.

Here indeed Mr. Cowley goes farther than the essay; for he asserts plainly that obscenity has no place in wit; the other only says, 'tis a poor pretence to it, or an ill sort of wit, which has nothing more to support it than bare-faced ribaldry, which is both unmannerly in itself, and fulsome to the reader. But neither of these will reach my case, for in the first place, I am only the translator, not the inventor; so that the heaviest part of the censure falls upon Lucretius, before it reaches me: in the next place, neither he nor I have used the grossest words; but the cleanliest metaphors we could find, to palliate the broadness of the meaning; and to conclude, have carried the poetical part no farther, than the philosophical exacted.

There is one mistake of mine which I will not lay to the printer's charge, who has enough to answer for in false pointings: 'tis in the word 'viper': I would have the verse run thus,

> The scorpion, Love, must on the wound be bruised.

There are a sort of blundering half-witted people, who make a great deal of noise about a verbal slip; though Horace would instruct

Essay on Poetry: by John Sheffield, Lord Mulgrave; published anonymously in 1682 (Spingarn, II, pp. 286 ff.).
Ode concerning Wit: 'Ode of Wit', stanza 6.
The scorpion, . . .: 'Lucretius the Fourth Book', l. 26.
Horace: Ars Poetica ll. 351-3 ('I shall not quarrel with those faults which were caused either by carelessness or human weakness').

them better in true criticism. *Non ego paucis, offendar maculis quas aut incuria fudit, aut humana parum cavit natura.* True judgement in poetry, like that in painting, takes a view of the whole together, whether it be good or not; and where the beauties are more than the faults, concludes for the poet against the little judge; 'tis a sign that malice is hard driven, when 'tis forced to lay hold on a word or syllable; to arraign a man is one thing, and to cavil at him is another. In the midst of an ill-natured generation of scribblers, there is always justice enough left in mankind to protect good writers. And they too are obliged, both by humanity and interest, to espouse each other's cause against false critics, who are the common enemies. This last consideration puts me in mind of what I owe to the ingenious and learned translator of Lucretius; I have not here designed to rob him of any part of that commendation, which he has so justly acquired by the whole author, whose fragments only fall to my portion. What I have now performed, is no more than I intended above twenty years ago. The ways of our translation are very different; he follows him more closely than I have done, which became an interpreter of the whole poem. I take more liberty, because it best suited with my design, which was to make him as pleasing as I could. He had been too voluminous had he used my method in so long a work, and I had certainly taken his, had I made it my business to translate the whole. The preference then is justly his, and I join with Mr. Evelyn in the confession of it, with this additional advantage to him; that his reputation is already established in this poet, mine is to make its fortune in the world. If I have been anywhere obscure in following our common author or if Lucretius himself is to be condemned, I refer myself to his excellent annotations, which I have often read, and always with some new pleasure.

My preface begins already to swell upon me, and looks as if I were afraid of my reader, by so tedious a bespeaking of him; and yet I have Horace and Theocritus upon my hands; but the Greek gentleman shall quickly be dispatched, because I have more business with the Roman.

That which distinguishes Theocritus from all other poets, both Greek and Latin, and which raises him even above Virgil in his *Eclogues*, is the inimitable tenderness of his passions; and the natural expression of them in words so becoming of a pastoral. A simplicity shines through all he writes: he shows his art and learning by disguising both. His shepherds never rise above their country education

---

learned translator: Thomas Creech (1659–1700): his version was published in 1683.
Evelyn: like Tate and Otway, Evelyn admired Creech's translation, for which he wrote some complimentary verses.

in their complaints of love. There is the same difference betwixt him
and Virgil, as there is betwixt Tasso's *Aminta*, and the *Pastor Fido* of
Guarini. Virgil's shepherds are too well read in the philosophy of
Epicurus and of Plato; and Guarini's seem to have been bred in
courts. But Theocritus and Tasso, have taken theirs from cottages
and plains. It was said of Tasso, in relation to his similitudes, *mai
esce del bosco*: that he never departed from the woods, that is, all his
comparisons were taken from the country. The same may be said of
our Theocritus; he is softer than Ovid, he touches the passions more
delicately; and performs all this out of his own fond, without diving
into the arts and sciences for a supply. Even his Doric dialect has an
incomparable sweetness in its clownishness, like a fair shepherdess in
her country russet, talking in a Yorkshire tone. This was impossible
for Virgil to imitate; because the severity of the Roman language
denied him that advantage. Spenser has endeavoured it in his
Shepherds Calendar; but neither will it succeed in English, for which
reason I forbore to attempt it. For Theocritus writ to Sicilians, who
spoke that dialect; and I direct this part of my translations to our
ladies, who neither understand, nor will take pleasure in such homely
expressions. I proceed to Horace.

Take him in parts, and he is chiefly to be considered in his three
different talents, as he was a critic, a satirist, and a writer of odes. His
morals are uniform, and run through all of them; for let his Dutch
commentators say what they will, his philosophy was epicurean; and
he made use of gods and providence only to serve a turn in poetry.
But since neither his criticisms (which are the most instructive of any
that are written in this art) nor his satires (which are incomparably
beyond Juvenal's, if to laugh and rally is to be preferred to railing
and declaiming,) are any part of my present undertaking, I confine
myself wholly to his odes: these are also of several sorts; some of
them are panegyrical, others moral, the rest jovial, or (if I may so call
them) Bacchanalian. As difficult as he makes it, and as indeed it is,
to imitate Pindar, yet in his most elevated flights, and in the sudden
changes of his subject with almost imperceptible connexions, that
Theban poet is his master. But Horace is of the more bounded fancy,
and confines himself strictly to one sort of verse or stanza in every
ode. That which will distinguish his style from all other poets, is the
elegance of his words, and the numerousness of his verse; there is

mai esce . . . : this comment has not been traced.
fond: fund, store.
Shepherds Calendar: Dryden later changed his opinion, see p. 282 below.
Pindar: Odes, IV. ii.
numerousness: i.e. metrical perfection.

nothing so delicately turned in all the Roman language. There appears in every part of his diction, or, (to speak English) in all his expressions, a kind of noble and bold purity. His words are chosen with as much exactness as Virgil's; but there seems to be a greater spirit in them. There is a secret happiness attends his choice, which in Petronius is called *curiosa felicitas*, and which I suppose he had from the *feliciter audere* of Horace himself. But the most distinguishing part of all his character, seems to me, to be his briskness, his jollity, and his good humour. And those I have chiefly endeavoured to copy; his other excellencies, I confess are above my imitation. One ode, which infinitely pleased me in the reading, I have attempted to translate in Pindaric verse: 'tis that which is inscribed to the present Earl of Rochester, to whom I have particular obligations, which this small testimony of my gratitude can never pay. 'Tis his darling in the Latin, and I have taken some pains to make it my masterpiece in English, for which reason I took this kind of verse, which allows more latitude than any other. Everyone knows it was introduced into our language, in this age, by the happy genius of Mr. Cowley. The seeming easiness of it has made it spread; but it has not been considered enough, to be so well cultivated. It languishes in almost every hand but his, and some very few, whom (to keep the rest in countenance) I do not name. He, indeed, has brought it as near perfection as was possible in so short a time. But if I may be allowed to speak my mind modestly, and without injury to his sacred ashes, somewhat of the purity of English, somewhat of more equal of thoughts, somewhat of sweetness in the numbers, in one word, somewhat of a finer turn and more lyrical verse is yet wanting. As for the soul of it, which consists in the warmth and vigour of fancy, the masterly figures, and the copiousness of imagination, he has excelled all others in this kind. Yet, if the kind itself be capable of more perfection, though rather in the ornamental parts of it, than the essential, what rules of morality or respect have I broken, in naming the defects, that they may hereafter be amended? Imitation is a nice point, and there are few poets who deserve to be models in all they write. Milton's *Paradise Lost* is admirable; but am I therefore bound to maintain, that there are no flats amongst his elevations, when 'tis evident he creeps along sometimes, for above an hundred lines together? Cannot I admire the height of his invention, and the

feliciter audere: *Satyricon*, 118; Horace, *Epistles*, II. i. 166.
Pindaric: 'Ode 29, Book 3, Paraphrased in Pindaric verse; and inscribed to the Right Honourable Lawrence, Earl of Rochester': Lawrence Hyde (1641–1711), second son of the Earl of Clarendon, was created Earl of Rochester in 1681.
8+s.c.

strength of his expression, without defending his antiquated words, and the perpetual harshness of their sound? 'Tis as much commendation as a man can bear, to own him excellent; all beyond it is idolatry. Since Pindar was the prince of lyric poets, let me have leave to say, that in imitating him, our numbers should for the most part be lyrical: for variety, or rather where the majesty of the thought requires it, they may be stretched to the English heroic of five feet, and to the French Alexandrine of six. But the ear must preside, and direct the judgement to the choice of numbers. Without the nicety of this, the harmony of Pindaric verse can never be complete; the cadency of one line must be a rule to that of the next; and the sound of the former must slide gently into that which follows; without leaping from one extreme into another. It must be done like the shadowings of a picture, which fall by degrees into a darker colour. I shall be glad if I have so explained myself as to be understood, but if I have not, *quod nequeo dicere et sentio tantum*, must be my excuse. There remains much more to be said on this subject, but to avoid envy, I will be silent. What I have said is the general opinion of the best judges, and in a manner has been forced from me, by seeing a noble sort of poetry so happily restored by one man, and so grossly copied by almost all the rest: a musical ear, and a great genius, if another Mr. Cowley could arise, in another age may bring it to perfection. In the mean time,

> —Fungar vice cotis acutum
> reddere quae ferrum valet, expers ipsa secandi.

I hope it will not be expected from me, that I should say anything of my fellow undertakers in this miscellany. Some of them are too nearly related to me, to be commended without suspicion of partiality. Others I am sure need it not; and the rest I have not perused. To conclude, I am sensible that I have written this too hastily and too loosely; I fear I have been tedious, and which is worse, it comes out from the first draft, and uncorrected. This I grant is no excuse, for it may be reasonably urged, why did he not write with more leisure, or, if he had it not (which was certainly my case) why did he attempt to write on so nice a subject? The objection is unanswerable, but in part of recompense, let me assure the reader, that in hasty productions,

---

quod nequeo . . .: Juvenal, *Satires*, vii. 56 ('qualem nequeo monstrare et sentio tantum': 'what I cannot describe, but only feel').

—Fungar vice . . .: Horace, *Ars Poetica* ll. 304–5 ('I shall act the whetstone, that sharpens steel, though it cannot itself cut').

related: apart from Dryden's son Charles the contributors remain anonymous.

he is sure to meet with an author's present sense, which cooler thoughts would possibly have disguised. There is undoubtedly more of spirit, though not of judgement in these incorrect essays, and consequently though my hazard be the greater, yet the reader's pleasure is not the less.

JOHN DRYDEN

A DISCOURSE CONCERNING THE ORIGINAL AND PROGRESS OF SATIRE

PREFIXED TO *THE SATIRES OF DECIMUS JUNIUS JUVENALIS . . . TOGETHER WITH THE SATIRES OF AULUS PERSIUS FLACCUS*

1693

To The Right Honourable Charles, Earl of Dorset and Middlesex, Lord Chamberlain of Their Majesties Household: Knight of the Most Noble Order of the Garter, etc.

MY LORD,

THE wishes and desires of all good men, which have attended your Lordship from your first appearance in the world, are at length accomplished in your obtaining those honours and dignities, which you have so long deserved. There are no factions, though irreconcilable to one another, that are not united in their affection to you, and the respect they pay you. They are equally pleased in your prosperity, and would be equally concerned in your afflictions. Titus Vespasian was not more the delight of humankind. The universal empire made him only more known, and more powerful, but could not make him more beloved. He had greater ability of doing good, but your inclination to it is not less, and though you could not extend your beneficence to so many persons, yet you have lost as few days as that excellent emperor, and never had his complaint to make when you went to bed, that the sun had shone upon you in vain, when you had the opportunity of relieving some unhappy man. This, my lord, has justly acquired you as many friends, as there are persons who have the honour to be known to you. Mere acquaintance you have none. You have drawn them all into a nearer line, and they who have conversed with you, are for ever after inviolably yours. This is a truth so generally acknowledged, that it needs no proof: 'tis of the nature of a first principle, which is received as soon as it is proposed; and needs not the reformation which Descartes used to his, for we doubt not neither can we properly say we think we admire and love you above all other men. There is a certainty in the proposition, and we know it. With the same assurance I can say you neither have enemies nor can scarce have any, for they who have never heard of you, can

---

To . . . the Earl of Dorset: see 'Of Dramatic Poesy', p. 16 above, and footnote.
humankind: Suetonius (VIII. i) calls Titus 'amor atque deliciae generis humani'.
Descartes: 'Je pense, donc je suis' (*Discours de la méthode*, 1637, IV. ii).

neither love or hate you, and they who have, can have no other notion of you, than that which they receive from the public, that you are the best of men. After this, my testimony can be of no farther use than to declare it to be daylight at high noon. And all who have the benefit of sight, can look up, as well, and see the sun.

'Tis true, I have one privilege which is almost particular to myself, that I saw you in the east at your first arising above the hemisphere. I was as soon sensible as any man of that light, when it was but just shooting out, and beginning to travel upwards to the meridian. I made my early addresses to your Lordship, in my *Essay of Dramatic Poetry*; and therein bespoke you to the world, wherein I have the right of a first discoverer. When I was myself in the rudiments of my poetry, without name or reputation in the world, having rather the ambition of a writer than the skill, when I was drawing the outlines of an art without any living master to instruct me in it; an art which had been better praised than studied here in England, wherein Shakespeare who created the stage among us, had rather written happily, than knowingly and justly; and Jonson, who by studying Horace, had been acquainted with the rules, yet seemed to envy to posterity that knowledge, and like an inventor of some useful art, to make a monopoly of his learning: when thus, as I may say, before the use of the loadstone, or knowledge of the compass, I was sailing in a vast ocean, without other help, than the pole-star of the Ancients, and the rules of the French stage amongst the Moderns, which are extremely different from ours, by reason of their opposite taste; yet even then, I had the presumption to dedicate to your Lordship a very unfinished piece, I must confess, and which only can be excused, by the little experience of the author, and the modesty of the title, *An Essay*. Yet I was stronger in prophecy than I was in criticism. I was inspired to foretell you to mankind, as the restorer of poetry, the greatest genius, the truest judge, and the best patron.

Good sense and good nature, are never separated, though the ignorant world has thought otherwise. Good nature, by which I mean beneficence and candour, is the product of right reason which of necessity will give allowance to the failings of others, by considering that there is nothing perfect in mankind; and by distinguishing that which comes nearest to excellency, though not absolutely free from faults, will certainly produce a candour in the judge. 'Tis incident to an elevated understanding, like your Lordship's, to find out the errors of other men: but 'tis your prerogative to pardon them; to look with pleasure on those things which are somewhat congenial, and of a remote kindred to your own conceptions, and to forgive the many failings of those, who with their wretched art, cannot arrive to those heights that you possess, from a happy, abundant and native genius which are as inborn to you, as they were to Shakespeare; and for aught I know to Homer, in either of whom we find all arts and sciences, all moral and natural philosophy, without knowing that they ever studied them.

There is not an English writer this day living, who is not perfectly convinced, that your Lordship excels all others, in all the several parts of poetry which you have undertaken to adorn. The most vain, and the most ambitious of our age had not dared to assume so much, as the competitors of Themistocles. They have yielded the first place, without dispute; and have been arrogantly content, to be esteemed as second to your Lordship; and even that also, with a *longo, sed proximo intervallo*. If there have been, or are any, who go farther in their self-conceit, they must be very singular in their opinion. They must be like the officer in a play, who was called Captain, Lieutenant, and Company. The world will easily conclude, whether such unattended generals can ever be capable of making a revolution in Parnassus.

I will not attempt in this place to say anything particular of your lyric poems, though they are the delight and wonder of this age, and will be the envy of the next. The subject of this book confines me to satire, and in that, an author of your own quality, (whose ashes I will not disturb,) has given you all the commendation, which his self-sufficiency could afford to any man: the best good man, with the worst-natured muse. In that character, methinks I am reading Jonson's verses to the memory of Shakespeare: an insolent, sparing, and invidious panegyric, where good nature, the most god-like commendation of a man, is only attributed to your person, and denied to your writings: for they are everywhere so full of candour, that like Horace, you only expose the follies of men, without arraigning their vices; and in this excel him, that you add that pointedness of thought, which is visibly wanting in our great Roman. There is more of salt in all your verses, than I have seen in any of the Moderns, or even of the Ancients. But you have been sparing of the gall; by which means you have pleased all readers, and offended none. Donne alone, of all

---

adorn: Dorset's *œuvre* can scarcely justify this eulogy, in terms either of quality or of quantity.

Themistocles: Herodotus, viii. 123: Themistocles's competitors voted first for themselves and only secondly for him.

longo, sed . . .: Virgil, *Aeneid*, v. 320 ('next by a wide margin').

muse: Rochester, *An Allusion to Horace*, ll. 59–60.

panegyric: Dryden does scant justice to the generosity of Jonson's 'To the Memory of my Beloved . . .'.

our countrymen, had your talent; but was not happy enough to arrive at your versification. And were he translated into numbers, and English, he would yet be wanting in the dignity of expression. That which is the prime virtue, and chief ornament of Virgil, which distinguishes him from the rest of writers, is so conspicuous in your verses, that it casts a shadow on all your contemporaries; we cannot be seen, or but obscurely, while you are present. You equal Donne in the variety, multiplicity, and choice of thoughts; you excel him in the manner, and the words. I read you both with the same admiration, but not with the same delight. He affects the metaphysics, not only in his satires, but in his amorous verses, where nature only should reign; and perplexes the minds of the fair sex with nice speculations of philosophy, when he should engage their hearts, and entertain them with the softnesses of love. In this (if I may be pardoned for so bold a truth) Mr. Cowley has copied him to a fault; so great a one, in my opinion, that it throws his *Mistress* infinitely below his Pindarics, and his latter compositions; which are undoubtedly the best of his poems, and the most correct. For my own part, I must avow it freely to the world, that I never attempted anything in satire, wherein I have not studied your writings as the most perfect model. I have continually laid them before me; and the greatest commendation, which my own partiality can give to my productions, is that they are copies, and no farther to be allowed than as they have something more or less of the original. Some few touches of your Lordship, some secret graces which I have endeavoured to express after your manner, have made whole poems of mine to pass with approbation. But take your verses altogether, and they are inimitable. If therefore I have not written better, 'tis because you have not written more. You have not set me sufficient copy to transcribe; and I cannot add one letter of my own invention, of which I have not the example there.

'Tis a general complaint against your Lordship, and I must have leave to upbraid you with it, that, because you need not write, you will not. Mankind that wishes you so well, in all things that relate to your prosperity, have their intervals of wishing for themselves, and are within a little of grudging you the fullness of your fortune. They would be more malicious if you used it not so well, and with so much generosity.

Fame is in itself a real good, if we may believe Cicero, who was perhaps too fond of it. But even fame, as Virgil tells us, acquires strength by going forward. Let Epicurus give indolency as an at-

---

Epicurus: *Cicero, Tusculan Disputations*, v. 16; *Aeneid*, iv. 175; Epicurus; *Kyriai Doxai*, i.

tribute to his gods, and place in it the happiness of the blessed. The divinity which we worship, has given us not only a precept against it, but his own example to the contrary. The world, my Lord, would be content to allow you a seventh day for rest; or if you thought that hard upon you, we would not refuse you half your time. If you came out, like some great monarch, to take a town but once a year, as it were for your diversion, though you had no need to extend your territories: in short, if you were a bad, or which is worse, an indifferent poet, we would thank you for our own quiet, and not expose you to the want of yours. But when you are so great, and so successful, and when we have that necessity of your writing, that we cannot subsist in poetry without it, any more, (I may almost say,) than the world without the daily course of ordinary Providence, methinks this argument might prevail with you, my Lord, to forgo a little of your repose for the public benefit. 'Tis not that you are under any force of working daily miracles, to prove your being; but now and then somewhat of extraordinary, that is anything of your production, is requisite to refresh your character.

This, I think, my Lord, is a sufficient reproach to you; and should I carry it as far as mankind would authorise me, would be little less than satire. And, indeed, a provocation is almost necessary, in behalf of the world, that you might be induced sometimes to write; and in relation to a multitude of scribblers, who daily pester the world with their insufferable stuff, that they might be discouraged from writing any more. I complain not of their lampoons and libels, though I have been the public mark for many years. I am vindictive enough to have repelled force by force, if I could imagine that any of them had ever reached me; but they either shot at rovers, and therefore missed, or their powder was so weak, that I might safely stand them, at the nearest distance. I answered not *The Rehearsal*, because I knew the author sat to himself when he drew the picture, and was the very Bays of his own farce. Because also I knew, that my betters were more concerned than I was in that satire. And lastly, because Mr. Smith, and Mr. Johnson, the main pillars of it, were two such languishing gentlemen in their conversation, that I could liken them to nothing but to their own relations, those noble characters of men of wit and pleasure about the town. The like considerations have hindered me from dealing with the lamentable companions of their prose and doggerel. I am so far from defending my poetry against them, that I

at rovers: at random: strictly, in archery, to shoot at a distant target.
farce: the 2nd Duke of Buckingham (Zimri in *Absalom and Achitophel*) was part-author of the play (1672).
Smith . . . Johnson: characters in *The Rehearsal*.

will not so much as expose theirs. And for my morals, if they are not proof against their attacks, let me be thought by posterity, what those authors would be thought, if any memory of them or of their writings could endure so long as to another age. But these dull makers of lampoons, as harmless as they have been to me, are yet of dangerous example to the public. Some witty men may perhaps succeed to their designs, and mixing sense with malice, blast the reputation of the most innocent amongst men, and the most virtuous amongst women.

Heaven be praised, our common libellers are as free from the imputation of wit as of morality; and therefore whatever mischief they have designed, they have performed but little of it. Yet these ill writers, in all justice ought themselves to be exposed: as Persius has given us a fair example in his first satire, which is levelled particularly at them. And none is so fit to correct their faults, as he who is not only clear from any in his own writings, but is also so just, that he will never defame the good; and is armed with the power of verse, to punish and make examples of the bad. But of this, I shall have occasion to speak further, when I come to give the definition and character of true satires.

In the mean time, as a counsellor bred up in the knowledge of the municipal and statute laws, may honestly inform a just prince how far his prerogative extends, so I may be allowed to tell your Lordship, who by an undisputed title are the king of poets, what an extent of power you have, and how lawfully you may exercise it, over the petulant scribblers of this age. As Lord Chamberlain, I know, you are absolute by your office in all that belongs to the decency and good manners of the stage. You can banish from thence scurrility and profaneness, and restrain the licentious insolence of poets and their actors, in all things that shock the public quiet, or the reputation of private persons, under the notion of humour. But I mean not the authority, which is annexed to your office. I speak of that only which is inborn and inherent to your person. What is produced in you by an excellent wit, a masterly and commanding genius over all writers, whereby you are empowered, when you please, to give the final decision of wit; to put your stamp on all that ought to pass for current; and set a brand of reprobation on clipped poetry, and false coin. A shilling dipped in the bath may go for gold amongst the ignorant, but the sceptres on the guineas show the difference. That your Lordship is formed by nature for this supremacy, I could easily

bath: the alchemist's bath, for gilding. In Charles II's reign some issues of both shillings and guineas had four crowned shields but only the guineas had sceptres.
8*

prove, (were it not already granted by the world) from the distinguishing character of your writing; which is so visible to me, that I never could be imposed on to receive for yours, what was written by any others, or to mistake your genuine poetry for their spurious productions. I can farther add with truth (though not without some vanity in saying it) that in the same paper, written by divers hands, whereof your Lordship's was only part, I could separate your gold from their copper. And though I could not give back to every author his own brass, (for there is not the same rule for distinguishing betwixt bad and bad, as betwixt ill and excellently good) yet I never failed of knowing what was yours, and what was not: and was absolutely certain, that this, or the other part was positively yours, and could not possibly be written by any other.

True it is, that some bad poems, though not all, carry their owner's marks about 'em. There is some peculiar awkwardness, false grammar, imperfect sense, or at the least obscurity; some brand or other on this buttock, or that ear, that 'tis notorious who are the owners of the cattle, though they should not sign it with their names. But your Lordship, on the contrary, is distinguished, not only by the excellency of your thoughts, but by your style and manner of expressing them. A painter judging of some admirable piece, may affirm with certainty, that it was of Holbein, or van Dyck. But vulgar designs, and common drafts, are easily mistaken, and misapplied. Thus, by my long study of your Lordship, I am arrived at the knowledge of your particular manner. In the good poems of other men, like those artists, I can only say, this is like the draft of such a one, or like the colouring of another. In short, I can only be sure, that 'tis the hand of a good master. But in your performances 'tis scarcely possible for me to be deceived. If you write in your strength, you stand revealed at the first view; and should you write under it, you cannot avoid some peculiar graces, which only cost me a second consideration to discover you. For I may say it, with all the severity of truth, that every line of yours is precious. Your Lordship's only fault is that you have not written more, unless I could add another, and that yet greater, but I fear for the public, the accusation would not be true, that you have written, and out of a vicious modesty will not publish.

Virgil has confined his works within the compass of eighteen thousand lines, and has not treated many subjects; yet he ever had, and ever will have the reputation of the best poet. Martial says of him, that he could have excelled Varius in tragedy, and Horace in lyric poetry, but out of deference to his friends he attempted neither.

Martial: *Epigrams*, VIII. xviii. 5–8.

The same prevalence of genius is in your Lordship, but the world cannot pardon your concealing it on the same consideration; because we have neither a living Varius, nor a Horace, in whose excellencies both of poems, odes and satires, you had equalled them, if our language had not yielded to the Roman majesty, and length of time had not added a reverence to the works of Horace. For good sense is the same in all or most ages; and course of time rather improves nature, than impairs her. What has been, may be again. Another Homer, and another Virgil may possibly arise from those very causes which produced the first: though it would be impudence to affirm that any such have yet appeared.

'Tis manifest, that some particular ages have been more happy than others in the production of great men, in all sorts of arts and sciences: as that of Euripides, Sophocles, Aristophanes, and the rest for stage-poetry amongst the Greeks: that of Augustus, for heroic, lyric, dramatic, elegiac, and indeed all sorts of poetry, in the persons of Virgil, Horace, Varius, Ovid, and many others; especially if we take into that century the latter end of the commonwealth, wherein we find Varro, Lucretius, and Catullus. And at the same time lived Cicero, and Sallust, and Caesar. A famous age in modern times, for learning in every kind, was that of Lorenzo de Medici and his son Leo the Tenth, wherein painting was revived and poetry flourished, and the Greek language was restored.

Examples in all these are obvious. But what I would infer, is this: that in such an age 'tis possible some great genius may arise, to equal any of the Ancients; abating only for the language. For great contemporaries whet and cultivate each other, and mutual borrowing and commerce makes the common riches of learning, as it does of the civil government.

But suppose that Homer and Virgil were the only of their species, and that nature was so much worn out in producing them, that she is never able to bear the like again; yet the example only holds in heroic poetry. In tragedy and satire I offer myself to maintain against some of our modern critics, that this age and the last, particularly in England, have excelled the Ancients in both those kinds; and I would instance in Shakespeare of the former, in your Lordship of the latter sort.

Thus I might safely confine myself to my native country. But if I would only cross the seas, I might find in France a living Horace and a Juvenal, in the person of the admirable Boileau, whose numbers are excellent, whose expressions are noble, whose thoughts are just, whose language is pure, whose satire is pointed, and whose sense is close. What he borrows from the Ancients, he repays with usury of

his own: in coin as good, and almost as universally valuable, for
setting prejudice and partiality apart, though he is our enemy, the
stamp of a Louis, the patron of all arts, is not much inferior to the
medal of an Augustus Caesar. Let this be said without entering into
the interests of factions and parties; and relating only to the bounty
of that king to men of learning and merit; a praise so just, that even
we who are his enemies, cannot refuse it to him.

Now if it may be permitted me to go back again, to the consideration of epic poetry, I have confessed, that no man hitherto has
reached, or so much as approached to the excellencies of Homer or of
Virgil. I must farther add, that Statius, the best versificator next to
Virgil, knew not how to design after him, though he had the model
in his eye; that Lucan is wanting both in design and subject, and is
besides too full of heat, and affectation; that amongst the Moderns,
Ariosto neither designed justly, nor observed any unity of action, or
compass of time, or moderation in the vastness of his draught; his
style is luxurious, without majesty, or decency; and his adventures,
without the compass of nature and possibility. Tasso, whose design was
regular, and who observed the rules of unity in time and place more
closely than Virgil, yet was not so happy in his action; he confesses
himself to have been too lyrical, that is, to have written beneath the
dignity of heroic verse, in his episodes of Sophronia, Erminia, and
Armida. His story is not so pleasing as Ariosto's; he is too flatulent
sometimes, and sometimes too dry; many times unequal, and almost
always forced; and besides, is full of conceits, points of epigram and
witticisms; all which are not only below the dignity of heroic verse,
but contrary to its nature. Virgil and Homer have not one of them.
And those who are guilty of so boyish an ambition in so grave a
subject, are so far from being considered as heroic poets, that they
ought to be turned down from Homer to the *Anthologia*, from Virgil
to Martial and Owen's epigrams, and from Spenser to Fleckno; that
is, from the top to the bottom of all poetry. But to return to Tasso,
he borrows from the invention of Boiardo, and in his alteration of
his poem, which is infinitely for the worse, imitates Homer so very
servilely, that (for example) he gives the King of Jerusalem fifty sons,
only because Homer had bestowed the like number on King Priam.
He kills the youngest in the same manner, and has provided his hero
with a Patroclus, under another name, only to bring him back to the
wars, when his friend was killed. The French have performed

---

lyrical: in *Lettere Poetiche* to Scipione Gonzaga (pub. 1587).

Owen: John Owen (*c*. 1560–1622) had a considerable European reputation as a
    result of his eleven books of Latin epigrams, published between 1606 and 1613.

nothing in this kind, which is not far below those two Italians, and subject to a thousand more reflections, without examining their *Saint Lewis*, their *Pucelle*, or their *Alaric*. The English have only to boast of Spenser and Milton, who neither of them wanted either genius, or learning, to have been perfect poets; and yet both of them are liable to many censures. For there is no uniformity in the design of Spenser. He aims at the accomplishment of no one action. He raises up a hero for every one of his adventures; and endows each of them with some particular moral virtue, which renders them all equal, without subordination or preference. Every one is most valiant in his own legend; only we must do him that justice to observe, that magnanimity, which is the character of Prince Arthur, shines throughout the whole poem, and succours the rest, when they are in distress. The original of every knight, was then living in the Court of Queen Elizabeth, and he attributed to each of them that virtue, which he thought was most conspicuous in them, an ingenious piece of flattery, though it turned not much to his account. Had he lived to finish his poem, in the six remaining legends, it had certainly been more of a piece; but could not have been perfect, because the model was not true. But Prince Arthur, or his chief patron, Sir Philip Sidney, whom he intended to make happy, by the marriage of his Gloriana, dying before him, deprived the poet both of means and spirit, to accomplish his design. For the rest, his obsolete language, and the ill choice of his stanza, are faults but of the second magnitude, for notwithstanding the first he is still intelligible, at least, after a little practice; and for the last, he is the more to be admired; that labouring under such a difficulty, his verses are so numerous, so various, and so harmonious, that only Virgil, whom he professedly imitated, has surpassed him, among the Romans; and only Mr. Waller among the English.

As for Mr. Milton, whom we all admire with so much justice, his subject is not that of an heroic poem, properly so called. His design is the losing of our happiness; his event is not prosperous, like that of all other epic works. His heavenly machines are many, and his human persons are but two. But I will not take Mr. Rymer's work out of his hands. He has promised the world a *critique* on that author wherein, though he will not allow his poem for heroic, I hope he will

---

Saint Lewis ... Alaric: Pierre Le Moyne, *Saint Louys* (1653); Jean Chapelain, *La Pucelle* (1656); Georges de Scudéry, *Alaric* (1654).

The original of every knight: Dryden's speculations have no more than the slender support of Spenser's 'Letter to Sir Walter Raleigh' prefacing *The Faerie Queene* (1590).

critique: at the end of his *Tragedies of the Last Age* (Zimansky, p. 76).

grant us that his thoughts are elevated, his words sounding, and that
no man has so happily copied the manner of Homer; or so copiously
translated his Grecisms, and the Latin elegancies of Virgil. 'Tis true,
he runs into a flat of thought, sometimes for a hundred lines together,
but 'tis when he is got into a track of scripture. His antiquated words
were his choice, not his necessity; for therein he imitated Spenser, as
Spenser did Chaucer. And though, perhaps, the love of their masters
may have transported both too far, in the frequent use of them; yet
in my opinion, obsolete words may then be laudably revived, when
either they are more sounding, or more significant than those in
practice, and when their obscurity is taken away, by joining other
words to them which clear the sense; according to the rule of Horace,
for the admission of new words. But in both cases, a moderation is
to be observed, in the use of them. For unnecessary coinage, as well
as unnecessary revival, runs into affectation, a fault to be avoided on
either hand. Neither will I justify Milton for his blank verse, though
I may excuse him, by the example of Hannibal Caro, and other
Italians, who have used it. For whatever causes he alleges for the
abolishing of rhyme (which I have not now the leisure to examine)
his own particular reason is plainly this, that rhyme was not his
talent; he had neither the ease of doing it, nor the graces of it; which
is manifest in his *Juvenilia*, or verses written in his youth, where his
rhyme is always constrained and forced, and comes hardly from him
at an age when the soul is most pliant and the passion of love makes
almost every man a rhymer, though not a poet.

By this time, my Lord, I doubt not but that you wonder, why I
have run off from my bias so long together, and made so tedious a
digression from satire to heroic poetry. But if you will not excuse it,
by the tattling quality of age, which, as Sir William Davenant says, is
always narrative, yet I hope the usefulness of what I have to say on
this subject will qualify the remoteness of it; and this is the last time
I will commit the crime of prefaces, or trouble the world with my
notions of anything that relates to verse. I have then, as you see,
observed the failings of many great wits amongst the Moderns, who
have attempted to write an epic poem. Besides these, or the like
animadversions of them by other men, there is yet a farther reason

sounding: resonant.
Horace: *Ars Poetica* ll. 47–8.
Hannibal Caro: see Preface to *Sylvae*, above, p. 197.
abolishing of rhyme: in the note 'The Verse' prefixed to *Paradise Lost*.
narrative: perhaps an inaccurate recollection of the Preface to *Gondibert* (1651):
   'Old men . . . think [wit] lies . . . in a kind of an alike tinkling of words; or
   else in a grave telling of wonderful things. . . .'

given, why they cannot possibly succeed, so well as the Ancients, even though we could allow them not to be inferior, either in genius or learning, or the tongue in which they write, or all those other wonderful qualifications which are necessary to the forming of a true accomplished heroic poet. The fault is laid on our religion. They say that Christianity is not capable of those embellishments which are afforded in the belief of those ancient heathens.

And 'tis true, that in the severe notions of our faith, the fortitude of a Christian consists in patience, and suffering for the love of God whatever hardships can befall him in the world; not in any great attempt, or in performance of those enterprises which the poets call heroic; and which are commonly the effects of interest, ostentation, pride and worldly honour. That humility and resignation are our prime virtues; and that these include no action, but that of the soul, whenas, on the contrary, an heroic poem requires, to its necessary design, and as its last perfection, some great action of war, the accomplishment of some extraordinary undertaking; which requires the strength and vigour of the body, the duty of a soldier, the capacity and prudence of a general; and, in short, as much or more of the active virtue than the suffering. But to this, the answer is very obvious. God has placed us in our several stations: the virtues of a private Christian are patience, obedience, submission, and the like; but those of a magistrate, or general, or a king, are prudence, counsel, active fortitude, coercive power, awful command, and the exercise of magnanimity, as well as justice. So that this objection hinders not, but that an epic poem, or the heroic action of some great commander, enterprised for the common good, and honour of the Christian cause, and executed happily, may be as well written now, as it was of old by the heathens; provided the poet be endued with the same talents, and the language, though not of equal dignity, yet as near approaching to it, as our modern barbarism will allow, which is all that can be expected from our own or any other now extant, though more refined, and therefore we are to rest contented with that only inferiority, which is not possibly to be remedied.

I wish I could as easily remove that other difficulty which yet remains. 'Tis objected by a great French critic, as well as an admirable poet, yet living, and whom I have mentioned with that honour, which his merit exacts from me, I mean Boileau, that the machines of our Christian religion in heroic poetry, are much more feeble to support that weight than those of heathenism.[n] Their doctrine, grounded as it was on ridiculous fables, was yet the belief of the two victorious monarchies, the Grecian, and Roman. Their gods did not only interest themselves in the event of wars (which is the effect of a

superior Providence) but also espoused the several parties, in a visible
corporeal descent, managed their intrigues, and fought their battles
sometimes in opposition to each other, though Virgil (more discreet
than Homer in that last particular) has contented himself with the
partiality of his deities, their favours, their counsels or commands, to
those whose cause they had espoused, without bringing them to the
outrageousness of blows. Now, our religion (says he) is deprived of
the greatest part of those machines; at least the most shining in epic
poetry. Though St. Michael in Ariosto seeks out Discord, to send her
amongst the pagans, and finds her in a convent of friars, where peace
should reign, which indeed is fine satire; and Satan, in Tasso, excites
Solyman to an attempt by night on the Christian camp, and brings
an host of devils to his assistance; yet the Archangel, in the former
example, when Discord was restive, and would not be drawn from
her beloved monastery with fair words, has the whip-hand of her,
drags her out with many stripes, sets her, on God's name, about her
business; and makes her know the difference of strength betwixt a
nuncio of Heaven, and a minister of Hell. The same angel, in the
latter instance from Tasso (as if God had never another messenger,
belonging to the court, but was confined like Jupiter to Mercury, and
Juno to Iris), when he sees his time, that is, when half of the Christians
are already killed, and all the rest are in a fair way to be routed,
stickles betwixt the remainders of God's host, and the race of fiends,
pulls the Devils backward by their tails, and drives them from their
quarry; or otherwise the whole business had miscarried, and
Jerusalem remained untaken. This, says Boileau, is a very unequal
match for the poor devils; who are sure to come by the worst of it in
the combat; for nothing is more easy than for an almighty power to
bring his old rebels to reason, when he pleases. Consequently, what
pleasure, what entertainment can be raised from so pitiful a machine?
where we see the success of the battle, from the very beginning of it?
Unless that, as we are Christians, we are glad that we have gotten
God on our side, to maul our enemies when we cannot do the work
ourselves. For if the poet had given the faithful more courage, which
had cost him nothing, or at least have made them exceed the Turks
in number, he might have gained the victory for us Christians, without interesting Heaven in the quarrel; and that with as much ease,
and as little credit to the conqueror, as when a party of a hundred
soldiers defeats another which consists only of fifty.

Ariosto . . . Tasso: *Orlando Furioso*, xiv. 75–81; *Gerusalemme Liberata*, ix.
stickles: arbitrates.

This, my Lord, I confess is such an argument against our modern poetry as cannot be answered by those mediums which have been used. We cannot hitherto boast that our religion has furnished us with any such machines, as have made the strength and beauty of the ancient buildings.

But, what if I venture to advance an invention of my own, to supply the manifest defect of our new writers. I am sufficiently sensible of my weakness, and 'tis not very probable, that I should succeed in such a project, whereof I have not had the least hint from any of my predecessors, the poets, or any of their seconds and coadjutors, the critics. Yet we see the art of war is improved in sieges, and new instruments of death are invented daily. Something new in philosophy and the mechanics is discovered almost every year, and the science of former ages is improved by the succeeding. I will not detain you with a long preamble to that, which better judges will, perhaps, conclude to be little worth.

'Tis this, in short, that Christian poets have not hitherto been acquainted with their own strength. If they had searched the Old Testament as they ought, they might there have found the machines which are proper for their work; and those more certain in their effect, than it may be the New Testament is, in the rules sufficient for salvation. The perusing of one chapter in the Prophecy of Daniel, and accommodating what there they find, with the principles of Platonic philosophy, as it is now Christianised, would have made the ministry of angels as strong an engine, for the working up heroic poetry, in our religion, as that of the Ancients has been to raise theirs by all the fables of their gods, which were only received for truths by the most ignorant, and weakest of the people.

'Tis a doctrine almost universally received by Christians, as well Protestants as Catholics, that there are guardian angels appointed by God Almighty, as his vicegerents, for the protection and government of cities, provinces, kingdoms, and monarchies; and those as well of heathens, as of true believers. All this is so plainly proved from those texts of Daniel, that it admits of no farther controversy. The prince of the Persians, and that other of the Grecians, are granted to be the guardians and protecting ministers of those empires. It cannot be denied, that they were opposite, and resisted one another. St. Michael is mentioned by his name, as the patron of the Jews, and is now taken by the Christians, as the protector general of our religion. These tutelar genii, who presided over the several people

---

Daniel: Daniel 10:10 f. The Cambridge Platonists argued that paganism might contain elements of Christian truth.

and regions committed to their charge, were watchful over them for
good, as far as their commissions could possibly extend. The general
purpose and design of all, was certainly the service of their great
Creator. But 'tis an undoubted truth, that for ends best known to the
Almighty Majesty of Heaven, his providential designs for the benefit
of his creatures, for the debasing and punishing of some nations, and
the exaltation and temporal reward of others, were not wholly
known to these his ministers; else why those factious quarrels,
controversies, and battles amongst themselves, when they were all
united in the same design, the service and honour of their common
master? But being instructed only in the general, and zealous of the
main design; and as finite beings, not admitted into the secrets of
government, the last resorts of Providence, or capable of discovering
the final purposes of God, who can work good out of evil as he
pleases; and irresistibly sways all manner of events on earth, direct-
ing them finally for the best, to his creation in general, and to the
ultimate end of his own glory in particular; they must of necessity be
sometimes ignorant of the means conducing to those ends, in which
alone they can jar, and oppose each other. One angel, as we may
suppose the prince of Persia, as he is called, judging that it would be
more for God's honour and the benefit of his people, that the
Median and Persian monarchy, which delivered them from the
Babylonish captivity, should still be uppermost: and the patron of
the Grecians, to whom the will of God might be more particularly
revealed, contending on the other side for the rise of Alexander and
his successors, who were appointed to punish the backsliding Jews
and thereby to put them in mind of their offences, that they might
repent, and become more virtuous, and more observant of the law
revealed. But how far these controversies and appearing enmities of
those glorious creatures may be carried; how these oppositions may
best be managed, and by what means conducted, is not my business
to show or determine. These things must be left to the invention and
judgement of the poet, if any of so happy a genius be now living, or
any future age can produce a man, who being conversant in the
philosophy of Plato, as it is now accommodated to Christian use; for
(as Virgil gives us to understand by his example) that is the only
proper of all others for an epic poem; who to his natural endowments, of a large invention, a ripe judgement, and a strong memory,
has joined the knowledge of the liberal arts and sciences, and
particularly, moral philosophy, the mathematics, geography and
history, and with all these qualifications is born a poet; knows, and

Virgil: probably a reference to *Aeneid*, vi.

can practice the variety of numbers, and is master of the language in which he writes; if such a man, I say, be now arisen, or shall arise, I am vain enough to think that I have proposed a model to him by which he may build a nobler, a more beautiful and more perfect poem than any yet extant since the Ancients.

There is another part of these machines yet wanting; but by what I have said, it would have been easily supplied by a judicious writer. He could not have failed to add the opposition of ill spirits to the good; they have also their design, ever opposite to that of Heaven; and this alone has hitherto been the practice of the Moderns. But this imperfect system, if I may call it such, which I have given, will infinitely advance and carry farther that hypothesis of the evil spirits contending with the good. For being so much weaker since their fall than those blessed beings, they are yet supposed to have a permitted power from God of acting ill, as from their own depraved nature they have always the will of designing it. A great testimony of which we find in Holy Writ, when God Almighty suffered Satan to appear in the Holy Synod of the Angels, (a thing not hitherto drawn into example by any of the poets,) and also gave him power over all things belonging to his servant Job, excepting only life.

Now what these wicked spirits cannot compass, by the vast disproportion of their forces, to those of the superior beings: they may by their fraud and cunning carry farther, in a seeming league, confederacy or subserviency to the designs of some good angel, as far as consists with his purity, to suffer such an aid, the end of which may possibly be disguised, and concealed from his finite knowledge. This is indeed to suppose a great error in such a being. Yet since a devil can appear like an angel of light; since craft and malice may sometimes blind for a while a more perfect understanding; and lastly, since Milton has given us an example of the like nature, when Satan appearing like a cherub to Uriel, the intelligence of the sun, circumvented him even in his own province, and passed only for a curious traveller through those new created regions, that he might observe therein the workmanship of God, and praise him in his works: I know not why, upon the same supposition, or some other, a fiend may not deceive a creature of more excellency than himself, but yet a creature; at least by the connivance, or tacit permission of the Omniscient Being.

Thus, my Lord, I have as briefly as I could, given your Lordship, and by you the world, a rude draft of what I have been long labouring

Job: 1:12.
Milton: *Paradise Lost*, iii. 636–53; 689–90.

in my imagination. And what I had intended to have put in practice, (though far unable for the attempt of such a poem) and to have left the stage, to which my genius never much inclined me, for a work which would have taken up my life in the performance of it. This too, I had intended chiefly for the honour of my native country, to which a poet is particularly obliged. Of two subjects, both relating to it, I was doubtful, whether I should choose that of King Arthur, conquering the Saxons; which being farther distant in time, gives the greater scope to my invention, or that of Edward the Black Prince in subduing Spain, and restoring it to the lawful prince, though a great tyrant, Don Pedro the Cruel, which for the compass of time, including only the expedition of one year, for the greatness of the action, and its answerable event; for the magnanimity of the English hero, opposed to the ingratitude of the person whom he restored; and for the many beautiful episodes, which I had interwoven with the principal design, together with the characters of the chiefest English persons; wherein, after Virgil and Spenser, I would have taken occasion to represent my living friends and patrons of the noblest families, and also shadowed the events of future ages, in the succession of our imperial line. With these helps, and those of the machines, which I have mentioned, I might perhaps have done as well as some of my predecessors; or at least chalked out a way, for others to amend my errors in a like design. But being encouraged only with fair words, by King Charles II, my little salary ill paid, and no prospect of a future subsistence, I was then discouraged in the beginning of my attempt; and now age has overtaken me; and want, a more insufferable evil, through the change of the times, has wholly disenabled me. Though I must ever acknowledge, to the honour of your Lordship, and the eternal memory of your charity, that since this revolution, wherein I have patiently suffered the ruin of my small fortune, and the loss of that poor subsistence which I had from two kings, whom I had served more faithfully than profitably to myself; then your Lordship was pleased, out of no other motive but your own nobleness, without any desert of mine, or the least solicitation from me, to make me a most bountiful present, which at that time, when I was most in want of it, came most seasonably and unexpectedly to my relief. That favour, my Lord, is of itself sufficient to bind any grateful man, to a perpetual acknowledgment, and to all the future service which one of my mean condition can be ever able to perform.

Saxons: cf. Watson, I, p. 191.
salary ill paid: cf. *Threnodia Augustalis*, ll. 377; *The Hind and the Panther*, iii.
    247–50.

May the Almighty God return it for me, both in blessing you here, and rewarding you hereafter. I must not presume to defend the cause for which I now suffer, because your Lordship is engaged against it. But the more you are so, the greater is my obligation to you, for your laying aside all the considerations of factions and parties, to do an action of pure disinterested charity. This is one amongst many of your shining qualities, which distinguish you from others of your rank. But let me add a farther truth, that without these ties of gratitude, and abstracting from them all, I have a most particular inclination to honour you; and if it were not too bold an expression, to say, I love you. 'Tis no shame to be a poet, though 'tis to be a bad one. Augustus Caesar of old, and Cardinal Richelieu of late, would willingly have been such; and David and Solomon were such. You, who without flattery, are the best of the present age in England, and would have been so, had you been born in any other country, will receive more honour in future ages, by that one excellency, than by all those honours to which your birth has entitled you, or your merits have acquired you.

Ne, forte, pudori,
sit tibi Musa lyrae solers, et cantor Apollo.

I have formerly said in this epistle, that I could distinguish your writings from those of any others: 'tis now time to clear myself from any imputation of self-conceit on that subject. I assume not to myself any particular lights in this discovery; they are such only as are obvious to every man of sense and judgement who loves poetry and understands it. Your thoughts are always so remote from the common way of thinking, that they are, as I may say, of another species than the conceptions of other poets; yet you go not out of nature for any of them. Gold is never bred upon the surface of the ground, but lies so hidden, and so deep, that the mines of it are seldom found; but the force of waters casts it out from the bowels of mountains, and exposes it amongst the sands of rivers, giving us of her bounty, what we could not hope for by our search. This success attends your Lordship's thoughts, which would look like chance, if it were not perpetual, and always of the same tenor. If I grant that there is care in it, 'tis such a care as would be ineffectual, and fruitless in other men. 'Tis the *curiosa felicitas* which Petronius ascribes to Horace in his Odes. We have not wherewithal to imagine so strongly, so justly, and so pleasantly: in short, if we have the same knowledge,

Ne, forte, . . .: *Ars Poetica*, ll. 406–7 ('May you never be caused shame by the Muse skilled in the lyre and by the singing Apollo').
Petronius: *Satyricon*, 118.

we cannot draw out of it the same quintessence; we cannot give it such a turn, such a propriety, and such a beauty. Something is deficient in the manner, or the words, but more in the nobleness of our conception. Yet when you have finished all, and it appears in its full lustre, when the diamond is not only found but the roughness smoothed, when it is cut into a form and set in gold, then we cannot but acknowledge, that it is the perfect work of art and nature, and everyone will be so vain to think he himself could have performed the like, till he attempts it. 'Tis just the description that Horace makes of such a finished piece. It appears so easy, *Ut sibi quivis speret idem, sudet multum, frustraque laboret, ausus idem.* And besides all this, 'tis your Lordship's particular talent to lay your thoughts so close together, that were they closer, they would be crowded, and even a due connexion would be wanting. We are not kept in expectation of two good lines, which are to come after a long parenthesis of twenty bad; which is the April poetry of other writers, a mixture of rain and sunshine by fits. You are always bright, even almost to a fault, by reason of the excess. There is continual abundance, a magazine of thought, and yet a perpetual variety of entertainment, which creates such an appetite in your reader, that he is not cloyed with anything, but satisfied with all. 'Tis that which the Romans call *coena dubia*; where there is such plenty, yet withal so much diversity, and so good order, that the choice is difficult betwixt one excellency and another; and yet the conclusion, by a due climax, is evermore the best; that is, as a conclusion ought to be, ever the most proper for its place. See, my Lord, whether I have not studied your Lordship with some application. And since you are so modest that you will not be judge and party, I appeal to the whole world, if I have not drawn your picture to a great degree of likeness, though 'tis but in miniature, and that some of the best features are yet wanting. Yet what I have done is enough to distinguish you from any other, which is the proposition that I took upon me to demonstrate.

And now, my Lord, to apply what I have said to my present business; the satires of Juvenal and Persius, appearing in this new English dress, cannot so properly be inscribed to any man as to your Lordship, who are the first of the age in that way of writing. Your Lordship, amongst many other favours, has given me your permission for this address; and you have particularly encouraged me by your perusal and approbation of the sixth and tenth satires of

---

Horace: *Ars Poetica*, ll. 240–2 ('so anyone may hope to do it, but may toil hard and find his work vain').
coena dubia: Terence, *Phormio*, II. ii. 28; Horace, *Satires*, II. ii. 77.

Juvenal, as I have translated them. My fellow labourers have likewise commissioned me to perform in their behalf this office of a
dedication to you; and will acknowledge with all possible respect and
gratitude your acceptance of their work. Some of them have the
honour to be known to your Lordship already; and they who have
not yet that happiness, desire it now. Be pleased to receive our
common endeavours with your wonted candour, without entitling
you to the protection of our common failings in so difficult an undertaking. And allow me your patience, if it be not already tired with
this long epistle, to give you from the best authors, the origin, the
antiquity, the growth, the change, and the completement of satire
among the Romans; to describe, if not define, the nature of that
poem, with its several qualifications and virtues, together with the
several sorts of it; to compare the excellencies of Horace, Persius
and Juvenal, and show the particular manners of their satires; and
lastly, to give an account of this new way of version which is attempted in our performance. All which, according to the weakness of
my ability, and the best lights which I can get from others, shall be
the subject of my following discourse.

The most perfect work of poetry, says our master Aristotle, is
tragedy. His reason is, because it is the most united; being more
severely confined within the rules of action, time and place. The
action is entire of a piece, and one, without episodes; the time
limited to a natural day, and the place circumscribed at least within
the compass of one town, or city. Being exactly proportioned thus,
and uniform in all its parts, the mind is more capable of comprehending the whole beauty of it without distraction.

But after all these advantages, an heroic poem is certainly the
greatest work of human nature. The beauties and perfections of the
other are but mechanical; those of the epic are more noble; though
Homer has limited his place to Troy, and the fields about it; his
actions to forty-eight natural days, whereof twelve are holy days, or
cessation from business, during the funerals of Patroclus. To proceed,
the action of the epic is greater. The extension of time enlarges the
pleasure of the reader, and the episodes give it more ornament, and
more variety. The instruction is equal; but the first is only instructive,
and the latter forms a hero, and a prince.

If it signifies anything which of them is of the more ancient family,
the best and most absolute heroic poem was written by Homer, long
before tragedy was invented, but, if we consider the natural endowments, and acquired parts which are necessary to make an accom-

Aristotle: *Poetics*, xxvi.

plished writer in either kind, tragedy requires a less and more confined knowledge: moderate learning, and observation of the rules is
sufficient, if a genius be not wanting. But in an epic poet, one who is
worthy of that name, besides a universal genius is required universal
learning, together with all those qualities and acquisitions which I
have named above, and as many more as I have through haste or
negligence omitted. And after all, he must have exactly studied
Homer and Virgil, as his patterns, Aristotle and Horace as his guides,
and Vida and Bossu, as their commentators, with many others both
Italian and French critics, which I want leisure here to recommend.

In a word, what I have to say, in relation to this subject, which
does not particularly concern satire, is that the greatness of an heroic
poem, beyond that of a tragedy, may easily be discovered by observing, how few have attempted that work, in comparison of those who
have written dramas; and of those few, how small a number have
succeeded. But leaving the critics on either side to contend about the
preference due to this or that sort of poetry, I will hasten to my present
business, which is the antiquity and origin of satire, according to
those informations which I have received from the learned Casaubon,
Heinsius, Rigaltius, Dacier, and the Dauphin's Juvenal; to which I
shall add some observations of my own.

There has been a long dispute amongst the modern critics, whether
the Romans derived their satire from the Grecians, or first invented it
themselves. Julius Scaliger and Heinsius, are of the first opinion;
Casaubon, Rigaltius, Dacier, and the publisher of the Dauphin's
Juvenal maintain the latter. If we take satire in the general signification of the word, as it is used in all modern languages, for an invective, 'tis certain that it is almost as old as verse; and though
hymns, which are praises of God, may be allowed to have been before
it, yet the defamation of others was not long after it. After God had
cursed Adam and Eve in Paradise, the husband and wife excused
themselves by laying the blame on one another; and gave a beginning to those conjugal dialogues in prose, which the poets have perfected in verse. The third chapter of *Job* is one of the first instances of
this poem in Holy Scripture, unless we will take it higher, from the
latter end of the second, where his wife advises him to curse his
Maker.

Vida: Marco Girolamo Vida, *De Arte Poetica* (1527) and René le Bossu, *Du
   Poëme épique* (1675).
Casaubon: Dryden's chief source is Casaubon's *De Satyrica Graecorum Poesi et
   Romanorum Satira* (1605). The others referred to are Heinsius's edition of
   Horace (1612), Rigaltius's edition of Juvenal (1616), Dacier's translation of
   Horace (1681–9), and Prateus's Delphin edition of Juvenal and Persius (1684).
Julius Scaliger: *Poetices Libri Septem*, 1561.

This original, I confess, is not much to the honour of satire; but here it was nature, and that depraved. When it became an art, it bore better fruit. Only we have learnt thus much already, that scoffs and revilings are of the growth of all nations; and consequently that neither the Greek poets borrowed from other people their art of railing, neither needed the Romans to take it from them. But considering satire as a species of poetry, here the war begins amongst the critics. Scaliger the father will have it descend from Greece to Rome; and derives the word satire, from *satyrus*, that mixed kind of animal, or, as the Ancients thought him, rural god, made up betwixt a man and a goat; with a human head, hooked nose, pouting lips, a bunch, or struma under the chin, pricked ears, and upright horns; the body shagged with hair, especially from the waist, and ending in a goat, with the legs and feet of that creature. But Casaubon, and his followers, with reason, condemn this derivation; and prove that from *satyrus*, the word *satira*, as it signifies a poem, cannot possibly descend. For satira is not properly a substantive, but an adjective; to which, the word *lanx*, in English a charger, or large platter, is understood: so that the Greek poem made according to the manners of a satyr, and expressing his qualities, must properly be called satyrical, and not satire, and thus far 'tis allowed, that the Grecians had such poems; but that they were wholly different in specie, from that to which the Romans gave the name of satire.

Aristotle divides all poetry, in relation to the progress of it, into nature without art: art begun, and art completed. Mankind, even the most barbarous, have the seeds of poetry implanted in them. The first specimen of it was certainly shown in the praises of the deity, and prayers to him, and as they are of natural obligation, so they are likewise of divine institution, which Milton observing, introduces Adam and Eve every morning adoring God in hymns and prayers. The first poetry was thus begun in the wild notes of nature, before the invention of feet and measures. The Grecians and Romans had no other original of their poetry. Festivals and holidays soon succeeded to private worship, and we need not doubt but they were enjoined by the true God to his own people, as they were afterwards imitated by the heathens, who by the light of reason knew they were to invoke some superior being in their necessities, and to thank him for his benefits. Thus the Grecian holidays were celebrated with offerings to Bacchus and Ceres, and other deities, to whose bounty they supposed they were owing for their corn and wine, and other helps of life. And

---

art completed: the following three paragraphs are derived from Casaubon, op. cit. I. i.

Milton: Paradise Lost, v. 144 f.

the ancient Romans, as Horace tells us, paid their thanks to Mother Earth, or Vesta, to Silvanus, and their Genius, in the same manner. But as all festivals have a double reason of their institution; the first of religion, the other of recreation, for the unbending of our minds, so both the Grecians and Romans agreed, after their sacrifices were performed, to spend the remainder of the day in sports and merriments; amongst which, songs and dances, and that which they called wit, (for want of knowing better,) were the chiefest entertainments. The Grecians had a notion of satyrs, whom I have already described; and taking them, and the Sileni, that is the young satyrs and the old, for the tutors, attendants, and humble companions of their Bacchus, habited themselves like those rural deities, and imitated them in their rustic dances, to which they joined songs, with some sort of rude harmony, but without certain numbers; and to these they added a kind of chorus.

The Romans also (as nature is the same in all places) though they knew nothing of those Grecian demi-gods, nor had any communication with Greece, yet had certain young men, who at their festivals, danced and sung after their uncouth manner, to a certain kind of verse, which they called Saturnian; what it was, we have no very certain light from antiquity to discover, but we may conclude, that, like the Grecian, it was void of art, or at least with very feeble beginnings of it. Those ancient Romans, at these holidays, which were a mixture of devotion and debauchery, had a custom of reproaching each other with their faults, in a sort of extempore poetry, or rather of tunable hobbling verse; and they answered in the same kind of gross raillery; their wit and their music being of a piece. The Grecians, says Casaubon, had formerly done the same, in the persons of their petulant satyrs: but I am afraid he mistakes the matter, and confounds the singing and dancing of the satyrs, with the rustical entertainments of the first Romans. The reason of my opinion is this; that Casaubon finding little light from antiquity of these beginnings of poetry amongst the Grecians, but only these representations of satyrs, who carried canisters and cornucopias full of several fruits in their hands, and danced with them at their public feasts: and afterwards reading Horace, who makes mention of his homely Romans, jesting at one another in the same kind of solemnities, might suppose those wanton satyrs did the same. And especially because Horace possibly might seem to him, to have shown the original of all poetry in general, including the Grecians, as well as Romans, though 'tis plainly otherwise, that he only described the beginning, and first rudiments of poetry in his own country. The verses are

Horace: Epistles, II. i. 143 (quoted below, p. 231).

these, which he cites from the first epistle of the second book, which
was written to Augustus.

> Agricolae prisci, fortes, parvoque beati,
> condita post frumenta, levantes tempore festo
> corpus et ipsum animum spe finis dura ferentem,
> cum sociis operum, et pueris, et conjuge fida,
> tellurem porco, Silvanum lacte piabant;
> floribus et vino Genium memorem brevis aevi:
> fescennina per hunc inventa licentia morem
> versibus alternis, opprobria rustica fudit.

> Our brawny clowns of old, who turned the soil,
> Content with little, and inured to toil,
> At harvest home, with mirth and country cheer
> Restored their bodies for another year:
> Refreshed their spirits, and renewed their hope,
> Of such a future feast, and future crop.
> Then with their fellow-joggers of the ploughs,
> Their little children, and their faithful spouse;
> A sow they slew to Vesta's deity;
> And kindly milk, Silvanus, poured to thee.
> With flowers, and wine, their genius they adored;
> A short life, and a merry, was the word.
> From flowing cups defaming rhymes ensue,
> And at each other homely taunts they threw.

Yet since it is a hard conjecture, that so great a man as Casaubon
should misapply what Horace writ concerning ancient Rome, to the
ceremonies and manners of ancient Greece, I will not insist on this
opinion, but rather judge in general, that since all poetry had its
original from religion, that of the Grecian and Rome had the same
beginning. Both were invented at festivals of thanksgiving, and both
were prosecuted with mirth and raillery, and rudiments of verses,
amongst the Greeks, by those who represented satyrs, and amongst
the Romans by real clowns.

For, indeed, when I am reading Casaubon, on these two subjects,
methinks I hear the same story told twice over with very little alteration. Of which Dacier taking notice, in his interpretation of the Latin
verses which I have translated, says plainly, that the beginning of
poetry was the same, with a small variety in both countries, and that
the mother of it in all nations was devotion. But what is yet more
wonderful, that most learned critic takes notice also, in his illustrations on the first epistle of the second book, that as the poetry of the
Romans, and that of the Grecians, had the same beginning at feasts
of thanksgiving, as it has been observed; and the Old Comedy of the
Greeks which was invective, and the satire of the Romans which was

Agricolae . . .: Epistles, II. i. 139–46.

of the same nature, were begun on the very same occasion, so the fortune of both in process of time was just the same; the Old Comedy of the Grecians was forbidden, for its too much license in exposing of particular persons, and the rude satire of the Romans was also punished by a law of the Decemviri, as Horace tells us, in these words,

> Libertasque recurrentes accepta per annos
> lusit amabiliter, donec jam saevus apertam
> in rabiem verti coepit jocus; et per honestas
> ire domos impune minax: doluere cruento
> dente lacessiti; fuit intactis quoque cura
> conditione super communi: quinetiam lex,
> poenaque; lata, malo quae nollet carmine quemquam
> describi, vertere modum formidine fustis;
> ad benedicendum delectandumque redacti.

The law of the Decemviri was this. *Siquis occentassit malum carmen, sive condidisit, quod infamiam faxit, flagitiumve alteri, capital esto.* A strange likeness, and barely possible, but the critics being all of the same opinion, it becomes me to be silent, and submit to better judgements than my own.

But to return to the Grecians, from whose satirical dramas the elder Scaliger and Heinsius will have the Roman satire to proceed, I am to take a view of them first, and see if there be any such descent from them as those authors have pretended.

Thespis, or whosoever he were that invented tragedy, (for authors differ) mingled with them a chorus and dances of satyrs, which had before been used in the celebration of their festivals; and there they were ever afterwards retained. The character of them was also kept, which was mirth and wantonness, and this was given, I suppose, to the folly of the common audience, who soon grow weary of good sense, and as we daily see, in our own age and country, are apt to forsake poetry, and still ready to return to buffoonery and farce. From hence it came, that in the Olympic Games, where the poets contended for four prizes, the satyric tragedy was the last of them:

Libertasque . . .: ibid. 147–55 ('Greeted as each year came round, liberty became familiar sport, until the joke became abuse, and went freely through decent homes threatening everyone. Some, injured by its brutal edge, were hurt; others, not harmed, were afraid for the public good; until a law was passed with penalties which forbad anyone to be branded with libellous verses. Then they changed their attitude, forced by crude measures to be civil and to please').

Signis . . .: From a note in the Delphin edition of Horace, *Epistles*, II. i ('Delivering or writing verses bringing another person into shame or disrepute shall be a capital offence').

for in the rest, the satyrs were excluded from the chorus. Amongst the plays of Euripides, which are yet remaining, there is one of these satirics, which is called the *Cyclops*, in which we may see the nature of those poems, and from thence conclude, what likeness they have to the Roman satire.

The story of this cyclops, whose name was Polyphemus, so famous in the Grecian fables, was, that Ulysses, who with his company was driven on that coast of Sicily, where those cyclops inhabited, coming to ask relief from Silenus and the satyrs, who were herdsmen to that one-eyed giant, was kindly received by them, and entertained; till being perceived by Polyphemus they were made prisoners, against the rites of hospitality, for which Ulysses eloquently pleaded, were afterwards put down into the den, and some of them devoured, after which, Ulysses having made him drunk, when he was asleep, thrust a great firebrand into his eye, and so revenging his dead followers, escaped with the remaining party of the living. And Silenus and the satyrs were freed from their servitude under Polyphemus, and re- mitted to their first liberty, of attending and accompanying their patron Bacchus.

This was the subject of the tragedy, which being one of those that end with a happy event, is therefore by Aristotle judged below the other sort, whose success is unfortunate. Notwithstanding which, the satyrs, who were part of the *Dramatis Personae*, as well as the whole chorus, were properly introduced into the nature of the poem, which is mixed of farce and tragedy. The adventure of Ulysses was to enter- tain the judging part of the audience, and the uncouth persons of Silenus and the satyrs to divert the common people with their gross railleries.

Your Lordship has perceived, by this time, that this satiric tragedy, and the Roman satire have little resemblance in any of their features. The very kinds are different. For what has a pastoral tragedy to do with a paper of verses satirically written? The character and raillery of the satyrs is the only thing that could pretend to a likeness, were Scaliger and Heinsius alive to maintain their opinion. And the first farces of the Romans, which were the rudiments of their poetry, were written before they had any communication with the Greeks, or, indeed, any knowledge of that people.

And here it will be proper to give the definition of the Greek satiric poem from Casaubon, before I leave this subject. The satiric, says he,

---

Roman satire: This paragraph is derived from Casaubon, op. cit. i. 3.
cyclops: *Odyssey*, ix.
Aristotle: *Poetics*, xiii.
Casaubon: Casaubon, op. cit. i. 3.

is a dramatic poem, annexed to a tragedy, having a chorus which consists of satyrs. The persons represented in it are illustrious men. The action of it is great; the style is partly serious, and partly jocular; and the event of the action most commonly is happy.

The Grecians, besides these satiric tragedies, had another kind of poem, which they called *silli*; which were more of kin to the Roman satire. Those *silli* were indeed invective poems, but of a different species from the Roman poems of Ennius, Pacuvius, Lucilius, Horace, and the rest of their successors. They were so called, says Casaubon in one place, from Silenus, the foster-father of Bacchus; but in another place, bethinking himself better, he derives their name ἀπὸ τοῦ σιλλαίνειν, from their scoffing and petulancy. From some fragments of the *silli*, written by Timon, we may find, that they were satiric poems, full of parodies; that is, of verses patched up from great poets, and turned into another sense than their author intended them. Such amongst the Romans is the famous *cento* of Ausonius, where the words are Virgil's; but by applying them to another sense, they are made a relation of a wedding-night; and the act of consummation fulsomely described in the very words of the most modest amongst all poets. Of the same manner are our songs, which are turned into burlesque; and the serious words of the author perverted into a ridiculous meaning. Thus in Timon's *silli* the words are generally those of Homer, and the tragic poets; but he applies them satirically to some customs and kinds of philosophy which he arraigns. But the Romans not using any of these parodies in their satires, sometimes, indeed, repeating verses of other men, as Persius cites some of Nero's, but not turning them into another meaning, the *silli* cannot be supposed to be the original of Roman satire. To these *silli* consisting of parodies we may properly add the satires which were written against particular persons; such as were the iambics of Archilocus against Lycambes, which Horace undoubtedly imitated in some of his Odes and Epodes, whose titles bear sufficient witness of it. I might also name the invective of Ovid against Ibis; and many others. But these are the under-wood of satire, rather than the timber-trees: they are not of general extension, as reaching only to some individual person. And Horace seems to have purged himself from those splenetic reflections in those Odes and Epodes, before he undertook the noble work of satires, which were properly so called.

Thus, my Lord, I have at length disengaged myself from those antiquities of Greece; and have proved, I hope, from the best critics, that the Roman satire was not borrowed from thence, but of their

---

in one place: Casaubon does not offer this derivation.

own manufacture. I am now almost gotten into my depth; at least by
the help of Dacier, I am swimming towards it. Not that I will promise
always to follow him, any more than he follows Casaubon; but to
keep him in my eye, as my best and truest guide; and where I think
he may possibly mislead me, there to have recourse to my own lights,
as I expect that others should do by me.

Quintilian says, in plain words, *satira quidem tota, nostra est*. And
Horace had said the same thing before him, speaking of his predecessor in that sort of poetry, *Et Graecis intacti carminis auctor*.
Nothing can be clearer than the opinion of the poet, and the orator,
both the best critics of the two best ages of the Roman Empire, that
satire was wholly of Latin growth, and not transplanted from Athens
to Rome. Yet, as I have said, Scaliger, the father, according to his
custom, that is, insolently enough, contradicts them both; and gives
no better reason, than the derivation of *satyrus* from σάθυ *salacitas*;
and so from the lechery of those fauns, thinks he has sufficiently
proved, that satire is derived from them, as if wantonness and
lubricity were essential to that sort of poem, which ought to be
avoided in it. His other allegation, which I have already mentioned,
is as pitiful: that the satyrs carried platters and canisters full of fruit
in their hands. If they had entered empty-handed, had they been ever
the less satyrs? Or were the fruits and flowers which they offered
anything of kin to satire? Or any argument that this poem was
originally Grecian? Casaubon judged better, and his opinion is
grounded on sure authority; that satire was derived from 'satura', a
Roman word, which signifies full, and abundant; and full also of
variety, in which nothing is wanting to its due perfection. 'Tis thus,
says Dacier, that we lay a full colour, when the wool has taken the
whole tincture, and drunk in as much of the dye as it can receive.
According to this derivation, from *satur* comes *satura*, or *satira*.
According to the new spelling; as optumus and maxumus are now
spelled *optimus* and *maximus*. *Satura*, as I have formerly noted, is
an adjective, and relates to the word *lanx*, which is understood. And
this *lanx*, in English a charger, or large platter, was yearly filled with
all sorts of fruits, which were offered to the gods at their festivals, as
the *premices*, or first gatherings. These offerings of several sorts thus
mingled, 'tis true, were not unknown to the Grecians, who called them
πανκαρπὸν θυσίαν, a sacrifice of all sorts of fruits; and πανσπερμίαν,
when they offered all kinds of grain. Virgil has mentioned these

Quintilian: *Institutio oratoria*, X. i. 93 ('at least satire is all our own').
Et Graecis . . .: *Satires*, I. x. 66 ('writer of poetry unmarked by the Greeks').
Scaliger: *Poetices*, i. 12.
Casaubon: op. cit. ii. 4.

sacrifices in his *Georgics, lancibus et pandis, fumantia reddimus exta.* And in another place, *lancesque et liba feremus.* That is, we offer the smoking entrails in great platters; and we will offer the chargers, and the cakes.

This word *satura* has been afterwards applied to many other sorts of mixtures; as Festus calls it a kind of *olla*, or hotch-potch, made of several sorts of meats. Laws were also called *leges saturae*; when they were of several heads and titles; like our tacked Bills of Parliament. And *per saturam legem ferre*, in the Roman Senate, was to carry a law without telling the senators, or counting voices, when they were in haste. Sallust uses the word *per saturam sententias exquirere*, when the majority was visibly on one side. From hence it might probably be conjectured, that the discourses or satires of Ennius, Lucilius, and Horace, as we now call them, took their name, because they are full of various matters, and are also written on various subjects, as Porphyrius says. But Dacier affirms, that it is not immediately from thence that these satires are so called, for that name had been used formerly for other things, which bore a nearer resemblance to those discourses of Horace. In explaining of which, (continues Dacier) a method is to be pursued, of which Casaubon himself has never thought, and which will put all things into so clear a light, that no farther room will be left for the least dispute.

During the space of almost four hundred years, since the building of their city, the Romans had never known any entertainments of the stage. Chance and jollity first found out those verses which they called *saturnian*, and *fescennine*; or rather human nature, which is inclined to poetry, first produced them, rude and barbarous, and un-polished, as all other operations of the soul are in their beginnings, before they are cultivated with art and study. However, in occasions of merriment they were first practised; and this rough-cast unhewn poetry was instead of stage-plays for the space of an hundred and twenty years together. They were made *ex tempore*, and were, as the French call them, impromptus, for which the Tarsians of old were much renowned; and we see the daily examples of them in the Italian farces of Harlequin and Scaramucha. Such was the poetry of that savage people, before it was tuned into numbers, and the

Georgics: *Georgics*, ii. 194, 394.

olla: see p. 43 above, and footnote.

tacked: a 'tack' was an appendix fixed, to ensure its passing, to a bill dealing with a different matter—particularly to a money bill, of which the Commons denied the Lords the right of amendment.

Porphyrius: Porphyrio (2nd cent. A.D.) a Latin grammarian cited by Casaubon, ii. 4.

harmony of verse. Little of the Saturnian verses is now remaining; we only know from authors, that they were nearer prose than poetry, without feet or measure. They were ἐνρύθμοι, but not ἐμμέτροι: perhaps they might be used in the solemn part of their ceremonies, and the *fescennine*, which were invented after them, in their afternoon's debauchery, because they were scoffing, and obscene.

The *fescennine* and *saturnian* were the same; for as they were called *saturnian* from their ancientness, when Saturn reigned in Italy; they were also called *fescennine*, from Fescennia, a town in the same country, where they were first practised. The actors with a gross and rustic kind of raillery reproached each other with their failings; and at the same time were nothing sparing of it to their audience. Somewhat of this custom was afterwards retained in their *saturnalia*, or feasts of Saturn, celebrated in December; at least all kind of freedom in speech was then allowed to slaves, even against their masters; and we are not without some imitation of it in our Christmas gambols. Soldiers also used those *fescennine* verses, after measure and numbers had been added to them, at the triumph of their generals, of which we have an example, in the triumph of Julius Caesar over Gaul, in these expressions: *Caesar Gallias subegit, Nicomedes Caesarem: Ecce Caesar nunc triumphat, qui subegit Gallias; Nicomedes non triumphat, qui subegit Caesarem.* The vapours of wine made those first satirical poets amongst the Romans; which, says Dacier, we cannot better represent, than by imagining a company of clowns on a holiday, dancing lubberly, and upbraiding one another in extempore doggerel with their defects and vices, and the stories that were told of them in bakehouses and barbers' shops.

When they began to be somewhat better bred, and were entering, as I may say, into the first rudiments of civil conversation, they left these hedge notes, for another sort of poem, somewhat polished, which was also full of pleasant raillery, but without any mixture of obscenity. This sort of poetry appeared under the name of satire, because of its variety, and this satire was adorned with compositions of music, and with dances: but lascivious postures were banished from it. In the Tuscan language, says Livy, the word *hister* signifies a player: and therefore those actors, which were first brought from Etruria to Rome, on occasion of a pestilence; when the Romans were admonished to avert the anger of the gods by plays, in the year *ab urbe condita*, CCCXC. Those actors, I say, were therefore called

ἐμμέτροι: i.e. rhythmical but not metrical.
Soldiers: derived from Heinsius, op. cit., p. 21.
Caesar Gallias . . .: *Historia*, vii. 2, quoted by Dacier.

histriones, and that name has since remained, not only to actors Roman born, but to all others of every nation. They played not the former extempore stuff of *fescennine* verses, or clownish jests; but what they acted was a kind of civil cleanly farce, with music and dances, and motions that were proper to the subject.

In this condition Livius Andronicus found the stage, when he attempted first, instead of farces, to supply it with a nobler entertainment of tragedies and comedies. This man was a Grecian born, and being made a slave by Livius Salinator, and brought to Rome, had the education of his patron's children committed to him, which trust he discharged so much to the satisfaction of his master, that he gave him his liberty.

Andronicus thus became a freeman of Rome, added to his own name that of Livius his master; and, as I observed, was the first author of a regular play in that commonwealth. Being already instructed in his native country in the manners and decencies of the Athenian theatre, and conversant in the *Archaea Comoedia*, or Old Comedy of Aristophanes, and the rest of the Grecian poets, he took from that model his own designing of plays for the Roman stage, the first of which was represented in the year 514 since the building of Rome, as Tully, from the commentaries of Atticus, has assured us; it was after the end of the first Punic War, the year before Ennius was born. Dacier has not carried the matter altogether thus far; he only says, that one Livius Andronicus was the first stage-poet at Rome. But I will adventure on this hint to advance another proposition, which I hope the learned will approve. And though we have not anything of Andronicus remaining to justify my conjecture, yet 'tis exceeding probable, that having read the works of those Grecian wits, his countrymen, he imitated not only the groundwork, but also the manner of their writing. And how grave soever his tragedies might be, yet in his comedies he expressed the way of Aristophanes, Eupolis, and the rest, which was to call some persons by their own names, and to expose their defects to the laughter of the people. The examples of which we have in the forementioned Aristophanes, who turned the wise Socrates into ridicule; and is also very free with the management of Cleon, Alcibiades, and other ministers of the Athenian Government. Now if this be granted, we may easily suppose, that the first hint of satirical plays on the Roman stage was given by the Greeks. Not from their satyrica, for that has been reasonably exploded in the former part of this discourse, but from their Old Comedy, which was imitated first by Livius Andronicus.

Tully: Cicero.

And then Quintilian and Horace must be cautiously interpreted, where they affirm that satire is wholly Roman, and a sort of verse which was not touched on by the Grecians. The reconcilement of my opinion to the standard of their judgement is not however very difficult, since they spoke of satire, not as in its first elements, but as it was formed into a separate work, begun by Ennius, pursued by Lucilius, and completed afterwards by Horace. The proof depends only on this postulatum, that the comedies of Andronicus, which were imitations of the Greek, were also imitations of their railleries, and reflections on particular persons. For if this be granted me, which is a most probable supposition, 'tis easy to infer that the first light which was given to the Roman theatrical satire, was from the plays of Livius Andronicus; which will be more manifestly discovered, when I come to speak of Ennius. In the mean time I will return to Dacier.

The people, says he, ran in crowds to these new entertainments of Andronicus, as to pieces which were more noble in their kind, and more perfect than their former satires, which for some time they neglected and abandoned. But not long after they took them up again, and then they joined them to their comedies, playing them at the end of every drama; as the French continue at this day to act their farces, in the nature of a separate entertainment from their tragedies. But more particularly they were joined to the Atellane fables, says Casaubon; which were plays invented by the Osci. Those fables, says Valerius Maximus, out of Livy, were tempered with the Italian severity, and free from any note of infamy, or obsceneness; and as an old commentator on Juvenal affirms, the Exodiarii, which were singers and dancers, entered to entertain the people with light songs, and mimical gestures, that they might not go away oppressed with melancholy from those serious pieces of the theatre. So that the ancient satire of the Romans was in extemporary reproaches. The next was farce, which was brought from Tuscany. To that succeeded the plays of Andronicus, from the Old Comedy of the Grecians. And out of all these, sprung two several branches of new Roman satire; like different scions from the same root, which I shall prove with as much brevity as the subject will allow.

A year after Andronicus had opened the Roman stage with his new dramas, Ennius was born: who, when he was grown to man's estate, having seriously considered the genius of the people, and how eagerly they followed the first satires, thought it would be worth his pains to refine upon the project, and to write satires not to be acted

Valerius Maximus: Valerius Maximus, II. iv. 4 (cf. Casaubon, op. cit. II. i).

on the theatre, but read. He preserved the groundwork of their pleasantry, their venom, and their raillery on particular persons and general vices, and by this means avoiding the danger of any ill success in a public representation, he hoped to be as well received in the cabinet as Andronicus had been upon the stage. The event was answerable to his expectation. He made discourses in several sorts of verse, varied often in the same paper; retaining still in the title their original name of satire. Both in relation to the subjects and the variety of matters contained in them, the satires of Horace are entirely like them; only Ennius, as I said, confines not himself to one sort of verse, as Horace does; but taking example from the Greeks, and even from Homer himself, in his *Margites*, which is a kind of satire, as Scaliger observes, gives himself the licence, when one sort of numbers comes not easily, to run into another as his fancy dictates. For he makes no difficulty to mingle hexameters with iambic trimeters, or with trochaic tetrameters; as appears by those fragments which are yet remaining of him. Horace has thought him worthy to be copied, inserting many things of his into his own satires, as Virgil has done into his *Aeneids*.

Here we have Dacier making out that Ennius was the first satirist in that way of writing, which was of his invention; that is, satire abstracted from the stage, and new modelled into papers of verses, on several subjects. But he will have Ennius take the groundwork of satire from the first farces of the Romans, rather than from the formed plays of Livius Andronicus, which were copied from the Grecian comedies. It may possibly be so; but Dacier knows no more of it than I do. And it seems to me the more probable opinion, that he rather imitated the fine railleries of the Greeks, which he saw in the pieces of Andronicus, than the coarseness of his old countrymen, in their clownish extemporary way of jeering.

But besides this, 'tis universally granted, that Ennius though an Italian, was excellently learned in the Greek language. His verses were stuffed with fragments of it, even to a fault. And he himself believed, according to the Pythagorean opinion, that the soul of Homer was transfused into him, which Persius observes, in his sixth Satire: *postquam destertuit esse Maeonides*. But this being only the private opinion of so inconsiderable a man as I am, I leave it to the farther disquisition of the critics, if they think it worth their notice. Most evident it is, that whether he imitated the Roman farce, or the Greek comedies, he is to be acknowledged for the first author of Roman satire, as it is properly so called, and distinguished from any sort of stage play.

Persius: *Satires*, vi. 10–11.

Of Pacuvius, who succeeded him, there is little to be said, because there is so little remaining of him, only that he is taken to be the nephew of Ennius, his sister's son; that in probability he was instructed by his uncle in his way of satire, which we are told he has copied; but what advances he made we know not.

Lucilius came into the world, when Pacuvius flourished most; he also made satires after the manner of Ennius, but he gave them a more graceful turn, and endeavoured to imitate more closely the *vetus comoedia* of the Greeks, of the which the old original Roman satire had no idea, till the time of Livius Andronicus. And though Horace seems to have made Lucilius the first author of satire in verse amongst the Romans; in these words, *Quid cum est Lucilius ausus primus in hunc operis componere carmina morem*, he is only thus to be understood, that Lucilius had given a more graceful turn to the satire of Ennius and Pacuvius; not that he invented a new satire of his own. And Quintilian seems to explain this passage of Horace in these words; *Satira quidem tota nostra est, in qua primus insignem laudem adeptus est Lucilius.*

Thus, both Horace and Quintilian, give a kind of primacy of honour to Lucilius amongst the Latin satirists. For as the Roman language grew more refined, so much more capable it was of receiving the Grecian beauties in his time; Horace and Quintilian could mean no more, than that Lucilius writ better than Ennius and Pacuvius. And on the same account we prefer Horace to Lucilius; both of them imitated the Old Greek Comedy; and so did Ennius and Pacuvius before them. The polishing of the Latin tongue, in the succession of times, made the only difference. And Horace himself, in two of his satires, written purposely on this subject, thinks the Romans of his age, were too partial in their commendations of Lucilius; who writ not only loosely, and muddily, with little art, and much less care, but also in a time when the Latin tongue was not yet sufficiently purged from the dregs of barbarism; and many significant and sounding words, which the Romans wanted, were not admitted even in the times of Lucretius and Cicero; of which both complain.

But to proceed, Dacier justly taxes Casaubon, for saying, that the satires of Lucilius were wholly different in specie, from those of Ennius and Pacuvius. Casaubon was led into that mistake, by Diomedes the grammarian, who in effect says this. Satire amongst

---

Quid cum . . .: Satires, II. i. 62–3 ('What? When Lucilius first dared write such poems . . .').

Satira quidem . . .: *Institutio oratoria*, X. i. 93 ('at least satire is all our own, in which Lucilius was first to win fame').

Casaubon: Dryden follows Dacier in misinterpreting Casaubon, ii. 3.

the Romans, but not amongst the Greeks, was a biting invective poem, made after the model of the ancient comedy; for the reprehension of vices such as were the poems of Lucilius, of Horace, and of Persius. But in former times the name of satire was given to poems which were composed of several sorts of verses; such as were made by Ennius, and Pacuvius; more fully expressing the etymology of the word satire, from satura, which we have observed. Here 'tis manifest, that Diomedes makes a specifical distinction betwixt the satires of Ennius, and those of Lucilius. But this, as we say in English, is only a distinction without a difference; for the reason of it is ridiculous, and absolutely false. This was that which cozened honest Casaubon, who relying on Diomedes, had not sufficiently examined the origin and nature of those two satires; which were entirely the same, both in the matter and the form. For all that Lucilius performed beyond his predecessors, Ennius and Pacuvius, was only the adding of more politeness, and more salt, without any change in the substance of the poem. And though Lucilius put not together in the same satire several sorts of verses, as Ennius did, yet he composed several satires, of several sorts of verses, and mingled them with Greek verses. One poem consisted only of hexameters, and another was entirely of iambics, a third of trochaics; as is visible by the fragments yet remaining of his works. In short, if the satires of Lucilius are therefore said to be wholly different from those of Ennius, because he added much more of beauty and polishing to his own poems, than are to be found in those before him; it will follow from hence, that the satires of Horace are wholly different from those of Lucilius, because Horace has not less surpassed Lucilius in the elegancy of his writing, than Lucilius surpassed Ennius in the turn and ornament of his. This passage of Diomedes has also drawn Dousa, the son, into the same error of Casaubon, which, I say, not to expose the little failings of those judicious men, but only to make it appear, with how much diffidence and caution we are to read their works, when they treat a subject of so much obscurity, and so very ancient, as is this of satire.

Having thus brought down the history of satire from its original to the times of Horace, and shown the several changes of it, I should here discover some of those graces which Horace added to it, but that I think it will be more proper to defer that undertaking, till I make the comparison betwixt him and Juvenal. In the meanwhile, following the order of time, it will be necessary to say somewhat of another kind of satire, which also was descended from the Ancients:

Dousa: Franciscus, son of Janus Dousa, and editor of the fragments of Lucilius (1597).

'tis that which we call the Varronian satire, but which Varro himself calls the Menippean; because Varro, the most learned of the Romans, was the first author of it, who imitated, in his works, the manners of Menippus the Gadarenian, who professed the philosophy of the cynics.

This sort of satire was not only composed of several sorts of verse, like those of Ennius, but was also mixed with prose; and Greek was sprinkled amongst the Latin. Quintilian, after he had spoken of the satire of Lucilius, adds what follows. 'There is another and former kind of satire, composed by Terentius Varro, the most learned of the Romans, in which he was not satisfied alone, with mingling in it several sorts of verse.' The only difficulty of this passage, is that Quintilian tells us, that this satire of Varro was of a former kind. For how can we possibly imagine this to be, since Varro, who was contemporary to Cicero, must consequently be after Lucilius? But Quintilian meant not, that the satire of Varro was in order of time before Lucilius, he would only give us to understand, that the Varronian satire, with mixture of several sorts of verses, was more after the manner of Ennius and Pacuvius, than that of Lucilius, who was more severe, and more correct, and gave himself less liberty in the mixture of his verses in the same poem.

We have nothing remaining of those Varronian satires, excepting some inconsiderable fragments, and those for the most part much corrupted. The titles of many of them are indeed preserved, and they are generally double, from whence, at least, we may understand, how many various subjects were treated by that author. Tully, in his academics, introduces Varro himself giving us some light concerning the scope and design of those works, wherein, after he had shown his reasons why he did not *ex professo* write of philosophy, he adds what follows. 'Notwithstanding', says he, 'that those pieces of mine, wherein I have imitated Menippus, though I have not translated him, are sprinkled with a kind of mirth, and gaiety, yet many things are there inserted, which are drawn from the very entrails of philosophy, and many things severely argued, which I have mingled with pleasantries on purpose, that they may more easily go down with the common sort of unlearned readers.' The rest of the sentence is so lame, that we can only make thus much out of it; that in the composition of his satires, he so tempered philology with philosophy, that his work was

---

Varronian satire: cf. Casaubon, op. cit. ii. 2.
Varro: (3rd cent. B.C.) his writings are lost.
Quintilian: *Institutio oratoria*, X. i. 95.
unlearned readers: Cicero, *Academics*, I. ii; quoted by Casaubon, op. cit. ii. 2.

a mixture of them both. And Tully himself confirms us in this opinion, when a little after he addresses himself to Varro in these words: 'And you yourself have composed a most elegant and complete poem; you have begun philosophy in many places: sufficient to incite us, though too little to instruct us'. Thus it appears, that Varro was one of those writers whom they called σπουδογελοῖοι, studious of laughter; and that, as learned as he was, his business was more to divert his reader than to teach him. And he entitled his own satires 'Menippean'; not that Menippus had written any satires (for his were either dialogues or epistles) but that Varro imitated his style, his manner, and his facetiousness. All that we know farther of Menippus, and his writings, which are wholly lost is, that by some he is esteemed, as, amongst the rest, by Varro; by others he is noted of cynical impudence, and obscenity; that he was much given to those parodies, which I have already mentioned; that is, he often quoted the verses of Homer and the tragic poets, and turned their serious meaning into something that was ridiculous; whereas Varro's satires are by Tully called absolute, and most elegant and various poems. Lucian, who was emulous of this Menippus, seems to have imitated both his manners and his style in many of his dialogues; where Menippus himself is often introduced as a speaker in them, and as a perpetual buffoon; particularly his character is expressed in the beginning of that dialogue which is called Νεκυομαντεία. But Varro, in imitating him, avoids his impudence and filthiness, and only expresses his witty pleasantry.

This we may believe for certain, that as his subjects were various, so most of them were tales or stories of his own invention, which is also manifest from antiquity, by those authors who are acknowledged to have written Varronian satires, in imitation of his; of whom the chief is Petronius Arbiter, whose satire, they say, is now printing in Holland, wholly recovered, and made complete. When 'tis made public, it will easily be seen by any one sentence, whether it be supposititious, or genuine. Many of Lucian's dialogues may also properly be called Varronian satires; particularly his *True History*, and consequently *The Golden Ass* of Apuleius, which is taken from him. Of the same stamp is the mock deification of Claudius, by Seneca; and the *Symposium* or *Caesars* of Julian the Emperor. Amongst the Moderns we may reckon the *Encomium Moriae* of Erasmus, Barclay's

---

σπουδογελοῖοι: Strabo, xvi, quoted by Casaubon, op. cit. ii. 2.

Petronius Arbiter: *Satyricon cum fragmentis Albae Graecae recuperatis anno 1688*, published 1691, the additions being forgeries by François Nodot.

Seneca: *Apocolocyntosis*, a skit in verse and prose for Nero.

Euphormio, and a volume of German authors, which my ingenious friend Mr. Charles Killigrew once lent me. In the English I remember none which are mixed with prose, as Varro's were. But of the same kind is *Mother Hubbard's Tale* in Spenser; and (if it be not too vain, to mention anything of my own) the poems of *Absalom*, and *Mac Flecknoe*.

This is what I have to say in general of satire: only as Dacier has observed before me, we may take notice, that the word satire is of a more general signification in Latin, than in French, or English. For amongst the Romans it was not only used for those discourses which decried vice, or exposed folly; but for others also, where virtue was recommended. But in our modern languages we apply it only to invective poems, where the very name of satire is formidable to those persons who would appear to the world what they are not in themselves. For in English, to say satire, is to mean reflection, as we use that word in the worst sense; or as the French call it more properly, 'médisance'. In the criticism of spelling, it ought to be with *i* and not with *y*; to distinguish its true derivation from 'satura', not from 'satyrus'. And if this be so, then 'tis false spelled throughout this book; for here 'tis written satyr. Which having not considered at the first, I thought it not worth correcting afterwards. But the French are more nice, and never spell it any other ways than satire.

I am now arrived at the most difficult part of my undertaking, which is, to compare Horace with Juvenal and Persius. 'Tis observed by Rigaltius, in his preface before Juvenal, written to Thuanus, that these three poets have all their particular partisans and favourers. Every commentator, as he has taken pains with any of them, thinks himself obliged to prefer his author to the other two; to find out their failings, and decry them, that he may make room for his own darling. Such is the partiality of mankind, to set up that interest which they have once espoused, though it be to the prejudice of truth, morality, and common justice; and especially in the productions of the brain. As authors generally think themselves the best poets, because they cannot go out of themselves to judge sincerely of their betters, so it is with critics, who, having first taken a liking to one of these poets, proceed to comment on him, and to illustrate him; after which they fall in love with their own labours, to that degree of blind fondness, that at length they defend and exalt their author, not so much for his sake as for their own. 'Tis a folly of the

Euphormio . . . . German authors: *Euphormionis Lusinini Satyricon* (1603–7), by John Barclay (1582–1621); Ker suggests that the German volume was the *Epistolae Obscurorum Virorum* (1515–17).
reflection: i.e. blame.
9*

same nature, with that of the Romans themselves, in their games of
the circus; the spectators were divided in their factions, betwixt the
Veneti and the Prasini. Some were for the charioteer in blue, and
some for him in green. The colours themselves were but a fancy; but
when once a man had taken pains to set out those of his party, and
had been at the trouble of procuring voices for them, the case was
altered. He was concerned for his own labour, and that so earnestly,
that disputes and quarrels, animosities, commotions, and bloodshed,
often happened. And in the declension of the Grecian empire, the
very sovereigns themselves engaged in it, even when the barbarians
were at their doors, and stickled for the preference of colours, when
the safety of their people was in question. I am now, myself, on the
brink of the same precipice; I have spent some time on the translation
of Juvenal, and Persius, and it behoves me to be wary, lest, for that
reason, I should be partial to them, or take a prejudice against
Horace. Yet, on the other side, I would not be like some of our
judges, who would give the cause for a poor man, right or wrong. For
though that be an error on the better hand, yet it is still a partiality;
and a rich man, unheard, cannot be concluded an oppressor. I remember a saying of King Charles the Second, on Sir Matthew Hales,
(who was doubtless an uncorrupt and upright man) that his servants
were sure to be cast on any trial which was heard before him. Not
that he thought the judge was possibly to be bribed; but that his
integrity might be too scrupulous, and that the causes of the Crown
were always suspicious, when the privileges of subjects were concerned.

It had been much fairer, if the modern critics, who have embarked
in the quarrels of their favourite authors, had rather given to each his
proper due, without taking from another's heap, to raise their own.
There is praise enough for each of them in particular, without en-
croaching on his fellows, and detracting from them, or enriching
themselves with the spoils of others. But to come to particulars:
Heinsius and Dacier, are the most principal of those, who raise
Horace above Juvenal and Persius. Scaliger the father, Rigaltius, and
many others debase Horace, that they may set up Juvenal. And
Casaubon, who is almost single, throws dirt on Juvenal and Horace,
that he may exalt Persius, whom he understood particularly well, and
better than any of his former commentators; even Stelluti who succeeded him. I will begin with him, who in my opinion defends the

---

Sir Matthew Hales: Sir Matthew Hale (1609–76) was Lord Chief Justice from
    1671 to 1676.
Stelluti: Casaubon's edition of Persius was published in 1605, Stelluti's in 1630.

weakest cause, which is that of Persius; and labouring, as Tacitus professes of his own writing, to divest myself of partiality, or prejudice, consider Persius, not as a poet, whom I have wholly translated, and who has cost me more labour and time, than Juvenal, but according to what I judge to be his own merit; which I think not equal in the main to that of Juvenal or Horace, and yet in some things to be preferred to both of them.

First, then, for the verse, neither Casaubon himself, nor any for him, can defend either his numbers, or the purity of his Latin. Casaubon gives this point for lost, and pretends not to justify either the measures or the words of Persius. He is evidently beneath Horace and Juvenal in both.

Then, as his verse is scabrous, and hobbling, and his words not everywhere well chosen, the purity of Latin being more corrupted, than in the time of Juvenal, and consequently of Horace, who writ when the language was in the heighth of its perfection; so his diction is hard, his figures are generally too bold and daring, and his tropes, particularly his metaphors, insufferably strained.

In the third place, notwithstanding all the diligence of Casaubon, Stelluti, and a Scotch gentleman (whom I have heard extremely commended for his illustrations of him): yet he is still obscure: whether he affected not to be understood, but with difficulty; or whether the fear of his safety under Nero compelled him to this darkness in some places; or that it was occasioned by his close way of thinking, and the brevity of his style, and crowding of his figures; or lastly, whether after so long a time, many of his words have been corrupted, and many customs, and stories relating to them, lost to us; whether some of these reasons, or all, concurred to render him so cloudy, we may be bold to affirm, that the best of commentators can but guess at his meanings, in many passages; and none can be certain that he has divined rightly.

After all, he was a young man, like his friend and contemporary Lucan, both of them men of extraordinary parts, and great acquired knowledge, considering their youth. But neither of them had arrived to that maturity of judgement, which is necessary to the accomplishing of a formed poet. And this consideration, as on the one hand it lays some imperfections to their charge, so on the other side 'tis a candid excuse for those failings, which are incident to youth and

---

time of Juvenal: Dryden here wrongly places Juvenal before Persius, although he later correctly names the emperors under whom both lived.

Scotch gentleman: David Wedderburn (1580–1646), whose edition of Persius was published in 1664.

inexperience; and we have more reason to wonder, how they, who died before the thirtieth year of their age, could write so well, and think so strongly, than to accuse them of those faults, from which human nature, and more especially in youth, can never possibly be exempted.

To consider Persius yet more closely, he rather insulted over vice and folly, than exposed them, like Juvenal and Horace. And as chaste, and modest as he is esteemed, it cannot be denied, but that in some places, he is broad and fulsome, as the latter verses of the fourth satire, and of the sixth, sufficiently witness. And 'tis to be believed, that he who commits the same crime often, and without necessity, cannot but do it with some kind of pleasure.

To come to a conclusion, he is manifestly below Horace, because he borrows most of his greatest beauties from him; and Casaubon is so far from denying this, that he has written a treatise purposely concerning it; wherein he shows a multitude of his translations from Horace, and his imitations of him, for the credit of his author; which he calls *Imitatio Horatiana*.

To these defects, which I casually observed while I was translating this author, Scaliger has added others. He calls him, in plain terms, a silly writer, and a trifler, full of ostentation of his learning, and after all, unworthy to come into competition with Juvenal and Horace.

After such terrible accusations, 'tis time to hear what his patron Casaubon can allege in his defence. Instead of answering, he excuses for the most part; and when he cannot, accuses others of the same crimes. He deals with Scaliger, as a modest scholar with a master. He compliments him with so much reverence, that one would swear he feared him as much at least as he respected him. Scaliger will not allow Persius to have any wit: Casaubon interprets this in the mildest sense, and confesses his author was not good at turning things into a pleasant ridicule, or in other words, that he was not a laughable writer. That he was *ineptus*, indeed, but that was, *non aptissimus ad jocandum*. But that he was ostentatious of his learning, that, by Scaliger's good favour, he denies Persius showed his learning, but was no boaster of it; he did *ostendere*, but not *ostentare*; and so, he says, did Scaliger; where, methinks, Casaubon turns it handsomely, upon that supercilious critic, and silently insinuates, that he himself was sufficiently vainglorious; and a boaster of his own knowledge. All the writings of this venerable censor, continues Casaubon, which are χρυσοῦ χρυσότερα, more golden than gold itself, are everywhere smelling of that thyme, which, like a bee, he has gathered from ancient authors. But far be ostentation and vainglory from a gentleman, so well born, and so nobly educated as Scaliger. But, says Scaliger, he is so obscure, that he has got himself the name of *scotinus*, a dark writer. Now, says Casaubon, 'tis a wonder to me, that anything could be obscure to the divine wit of Scaliger; from which nothing could be hidden. This is indeed a strong compliment, but no defence. And Casaubon, who could not but be sensible of his author's blind side, thinks it time to abandon a post that was untenable. He acknowledges that Persius is obscure in some places; but so is Plato, so is Thucydides; so are Pindar, Theocritus, and Aristophanes amongst the Greek poets; and even Horace and Juvenal, he might have added, amongst the Romans. The truth is, Persius is not sometimes, but generally, obscure, and therefore Casaubon, at last, is forced to excuse him, by alleging that it was *se defendendo*, for fear of Nero; and that he was commanded to write so cloudily by Cornutus, in virtue of holy obedience to his master. I cannot help my own opinion; I think Cornutus needed not to have read many lectures to him on that subject. Persius was an apt scholar; and when he was bidden to be obscure, in some places, where his life and safety were in question, took the same counsel for all his book, and never afterwards wrote ten lines together clearly. Casaubon, being upon this chapter, has not failed, we may be sure, of making a compliment to his own dear comment. If Persius, says he, be in himself obscure, yet my interpretation has made him intelligible. There is no question, but he deserves that praise, which he has given to himself. But the nature of the thing, as Lucretius says, will not admit of a perfect explanation. Besides many examples which I could urge, the very last verse of his last satire, upon which he particularly values himself in his preface, is not yet sufficiently explicated. 'Tis true, Holyday has endeavoured to justify his construction; but Stelluti is against it: and, for my part, I can have but a very dark notion of it. As for the chastity of his thoughts, Casaubon denies not, but that one particular passage, in the fourth satire, *At, si unctus cesses*, etc. is not only the most obscure, but the most obscene of all his works. I understood it; but for that reason turned it over. In defence of his boisterous metaphors, he quotes Longinus, who accounts them as instruments of the sublime; fit to move and stir up the affections, particularly in narration. To which it may be replied that where the trope is far fetched, and hard, 'tis fit for nothing but to puzzle the understanding, and may be reckoned amongst those things of Demosthenes, which Aeschines, called θαύματα not ῥήματα; that is prodigies, not

---

Cornutus: Persius, *Satires*, v.

Holyday: Barten Holyday (1593–1661), whose translations of Juvenal and Persius appeared together in 1673.

ῥήματα: *Speeches*, 167.

words. It must be granted to Casaubon, that the knowledge of many things is lost in our modern ages, which were of familiar notice to the Ancients, and that satire is a poem of a difficult nature in itself, and is not written to vulgar readers. And through the relation which it has to comedy, the frequent change of persons, makes the sense perplexed; when we can but divine who it is that speaks, whether Persius himself, or his friend and monitor, or, in some places, a third person. But Casaubon comes back always to himself, and concludes that if Persius had not been obscure, there had been no need of him for an interpreter. Yet when he had once enjoined himself so hard a task, he then considered the Greek proverb, that he must χελώνης φαγεῖν ἢ μὴ φαγεῖν; either eat the whole snail, or let it quite alone; and so, he went through with his laborious task, as I have done with my difficult translation.

Thus far, my Lord, you see it has gone very hard with Persius. I think he cannot be allowed to stand in competition, either with Juvenal or Horace. Yet, for once, I will venture to be so vain, as to affirm that none of his hard metaphors, or forced expressions, are in my translation; but more of this in its proper place, where I shall say somewhat in particular of our general performance, in making these two authors English. In the mean time I think myself obliged, to give Persius his undoubted due; and to acquaint the world, with Casaubon, in what he has equalled, and in what excelled his two competitors.

A man who is resolved to praise an author, with any appearance of justice, must be sure to take him on the strongest side, and where he is least liable to exceptions. He is therefore obliged to choose his mediums accordingly. Casaubon, who saw that Persius could not laugh with a becoming grace, that he was not made for jesting, and that a merry conceit was not his talent, turned his feather, like an Indian, to another light, that he might give it the better gloss. Moral doctrine, says he, and urbanity, or well-mannered wit, are the two things which constitute the Roman satire. But of the two, that which is most essential to this poem, and is as it were the very soul which animates it, is the scourging of vice, and exhortation to virtue. Thus wit, for a good reason, is already almost out of doors and allowed only for an instrument, a kind of tool, or a weapon, as he calls it, of which the satirist makes use, in the compassing of his design. The end and aim of our three rivals, is consequently the same. But by what methods they have prosecuted their intention is farther to be considered. Satire is of the nature of moral philosophy; as being instructive: he therefore, who instructs most usefully, will carry the palm from his two antagonists. The philosophy in which Persius was educated, and which he professes through his whole book, is the

Stoic, the most noble, most generous, most beneficial to human kind, amongst all the sects who have given us the rules of ethics, thereby to form a severe virtue in the soul; to raise in us an undaunted courage against the assaults of fortune; to esteem as nothing the things that are without us, because they are not in our power; not to value riches, beauty, honours, fame, or health, any farther than as conveniences, and so many helps to living as we ought, and doing good in our generation. In short, to be always happy, while we possess our minds with a good conscience, are free from the slavery of vices, and conform our actions and conversation to the rules of right reason. See here, my Lord, an epitome of Epictetus; the doctrine of Zeno, and the education of our Persius. And this he expressed, not only in all his satires, but in the manner of his life. I will not lessen this commendation of the Stoic philosophy by giving you an account of some absurdities in their doctrine, and some perhaps impieties, if we consider them by the standard of Christian faith. Persius has fallen into none of them, and therefore is free from those imputations. What he teaches might be taught from pulpits, with more profit to the audience, than all the nice speculations of divinity, and controversies concerning faith; which are more for the profit of the shepherd, than for the edification of the flock. Passion, interest, ambition, and all their bloody consequences of discord and of war, are banished from this doctrine. Here is nothing proposed but the quiet and tranquillity of the mind; virtue lodged at home, and afterwards diffused in her general effects, to the improvement, and good of human kind. And therefore I wonder not, that the present Bishop of Salisbury, has recommended this our author, and the tenth satire of Juvenal, in his Pastoral Letter, to the serious perusal and practice of the divines in his diocese, as the best commonplaces for their sermons, as the store-houses and magazines of moral virtues, from whence they may draw out, as they have occasion, all manner of assistance, for the accomplishment of a virtuous life, which the Stoics have assigned for the great end and perfection of mankind. Herein then it is, that Persius has excelled both Juvenal and Horace. He sticks to his one philosophy: he shifts not sides, like Horace, who is sometimes an Epicurean, sometimes a Stoic, sometimes an eclectic, as his present humour leads him; nor declaims like Juvenal against vices, more like an orator than a philosopher. Persius is everywhere the same: true to the dogmas of his master: what he has learnt, he teaches vehemently; and what he teaches, that he practices himself.

Bishop of Salisbury: Gilbert Burnet (1643–1715), *A Discourse of the Pastoral Care* (1692).

There is a spirit of sincerity in all he says. You may easily discern that he is in earnest, and is persuaded of that truth which he inculcates. In this I am of opinion, that he excels Horace, who is commonly in jest, and laughs while he instructs; and is equal to Juvenal, who was as honest and serious as Persius, and more he could not be.

Hitherto I have followed Casaubon, and enlarged upon him; because I am satisfied that he says no more than truth; the rest is almost all frivolous. For he says that Horace being the son of a tax-gatherer, or a collector, as we call it, smells everywhere of the meanness of his birth and education. His conceits are vulgar, like the subjects of his satires; that he does *plebeium sapere*, and writes not with that elevation, which becomes a satirist; that Persius being nobly born, and of an opulent family, had likewise the advantage of a better master; Cornutus being the most learned of his time, a man of a most holy life, the chief of the Stoic sect at Rome, and not only a great philosopher, but a poet himself, and in probability a coadjutor of Persius; that, as for Juvenal, he was long a declaimer, came late to poetry, and had not been much conversant in philosophy.

'Tis granted that the father of Horace was *libertinus*, that is one degree removed from his grandfather, who had been once a slave. But Horace, speaking of him, gives him the best character of a father, which I ever read in history. And I wish a witty friend of mine now living had such another. He bred him in the best school, and with the best company of young noblemen. And Horace, by his gratitude to his memory, gives a certain testimony that his education was ingenuous. After this, he formed himself abroad, by the conversation of great men. Brutus found him at Athens, and was so pleased with him, that he took him thence into the army, and made him *Tribunus militum*, a colonel in a legion, which was the preferment of an old soldier. All this was before his acquaintance with Maecenas, and his introduction into the Court of Augustus, and the familiarity of that great Emperor; which, had he not been well-bred before, had been enough to civilise his conversation, and render him accomplished, and knowing in all the arts of complacency and good behaviour; and, in short, an agreeable companion for the retired hours and privacies of a favourite, who was first minister. So that, upon the whole matter, Persius may be acknowledged to be equal with him, in those respects, though better born, and Juvenal inferior to both. If the advantage be anywhere, 'tis on the side of Horace; as much as the Court of Augustus Caesar, was superior to that of Nero. As for the subjects

plebeium sapere: 'taste of the common mob'.
character of a father . . . . *witty friend*: Horace, *Satires*, I. vi; Dryden's friend was
   the dramatist Wycherley, whose father refused him financial help.

which they treated, it will appear hereafter, that Horace writ not vulgarly on vulgar subjects; nor always chose them. His style is constantly accommodated to his subject, either high or low. If his fault be too much lowness, that of Persius is the fault of the hardness of his metaphors, and obscurity; and so they are equal in the failings of their style; where Juvenal manifestly triumphs over both of them.

The comparison betwixt Horace and Juvenal is more difficult; because their forces were more equal. A dispute has always been, and ever will continue, betwixt the favourers of the two poets. *Non nostrum est tantas componere lites.* I shall only venture to give my own opinion, and leave it for better judges to determine. If it be only argued in general, which of them was the better poet, the victory is already gained on the side of Horace. Virgil himself must yield to him in the delicacy of his turns, his choice of words, and perhaps the purity of his Latin. He who says that Pindar is inimitable, is himself inimitable in his *Odes*. But the contention betwixt these two great masters, is for the prize of satire. In which controversy, all the *Odes* and *Epodes* of Horace are to stand excluded. I say this, because Horace has written many of them satirically, against his private enemies; yet these, if justly considered, are somewhat of the nature of the Greek *silli*, which were invectives against particular sects and persons. But Horace had purged himself of this choler, before he entered on those discourses, which are more properly called the Roman satire. He has not now to do with a Lyce, a Canidia, a Cassius Severus, or a Menas; but is to correct the vices and the follies of his time, and to give the rules of a happy and virtuous life. In a word, that former sort of satire, which is known in England by the name of lampoon, is a dangerous sort of weapon, and for the most part unlawful. We have no moral right on the reputation of other men. 'Tis taking from them, what we cannot restore to them. There are only two reasons, for which we may be permitted to write lampoons; and I will not promise that they can always justify us. The first is revenge, when we have been affronted in the same nature, or have been any ways notoriously abused, and can make ourselves no other reparation. And yet we know, that, in Christian charity, all offences are to be forgiven; as we expect the like pardon for those which we daily commit against Almighty God. And this consideration has often made me tremble when I was saying our Saviour's prayer; for the plain condition of the forgiveness which we beg, is the

Non nostrum . . .: Virgil, *Eclogues*, iii. 108 ('. . . nostrum inter vos tantas . . .': 'It is not my part to settle such a question').
Pindar: Horace, *Odes*, IV. ii. 1–4.

pardoning of others the offences which they have done to us, for
which reason I have many times avoided the commission of that
fault, even when I have been notoriously provoked. Let not this, my
Lord, pass for vanity in me: for 'tis truth. More libels have been
written against me, than almost any man now living, and I had reason
on my side, to have defended my own innocence. I speak not of my
poetry, which I have wholly given up to the critics; let them use it, as
they please; posterity, perhaps, may be more favourable to me, for
interest and passion will lie buried in another age, and partiality and
prejudice be forgotten. I speak of my morals, which have been
sufficiently aspersed: that only sort of reputation ought to be dear to
every honest man, and is to me. But let the world witness for me, that
I have been often wanting to myself in that particular; I have seldom
answered any scurrilous lampoon when it was in my power to have
exposed my enemies, and being naturally vindicative, have suffered in
silence, and possessed my soul in quiet.

Anything, though never so little, which a man speaks of himself, in
my opinion, is still too much, and therefore I will waive this subject;
and proceed to give the second reason, which may justify a poet,
when he writes against a particular person; and that is, when he is
become a public nuisance. All those, whom Horace in his satires, and
Persius and Juvenal have mentioned in theirs, with a brand of infamy,
are wholly such. 'Tis an action of virtue to make examples of vicious
men. They may and ought to be upbraided with their crimes and
follies, both for their own amendment, if they are not yet incorrigible;
and for the terror of others, to hinder them from falling into those
enormities, which they see are so severely punished, in the persons
of others. The first reason was only an excuse for revenge; but this
second is absolutely of a poet's office to perform. But how few lam-
pooners are there now living, who are capable of this duty! When
they come in my way, 'tis impossible sometimes to avoid reading
them. But, good God, how remote they are in common justice, from
the choice of such persons as are the proper subject of satire! And
how little wit they bring, for the support of their injustice! The
weaker sex is their most ordinary theme; and the best and fairest are
sure to be the most severely handled. Amongst men, those who are
prosperously unjust, are entitled to a panegyric. But afflicted virtue is
insolently stabbed with all manner of reproaches. No decency is
considered, no fulsomeness omitted; no venom is wanting, as far as
dullness can supply it. For there is a perpetual dearth of wit; a barrenness of good sense, and entertainment. The neglect of the readers
will soon put an end to this sort of scribbling. There can be no
pleasantry where there is no wit. No impression can be made, where

there is no truth for the foundation. To conclude, they are like the
fruits of the earth in this unnatural season. The corn which held up
its head, is spoiled with rankness; but the greater part of the harvest
is laid along; and little of good income and wholesome nourishment
is received into the barns. This is almost a digression, I confess to
your Lordship; but a just indignation forced it from me. Now I have
removed this rubbish, I will return to the comparison of Juvenal and
Horace.

I would willingly divide the palm betwixt them, upon the two heads
of profit and delight, which are the two ends of poetry in general. It
must be granted by the favourers of Juvenal, that Horace is the more
copious and profitable in his instructions of human life. But in my
particular opinion, which I set not up for a standard to better judgements, Juvenal is the more delightful author. I am profited by both, I
am pleased with both; but I owe more to Horace for my instruction,
and more to Juvenal, for my pleasure. This, as I said, is my particular
taste of these two authors. They who will have either of them to excel
the other in both qualities, can scarce give better reasons for their
opinion, than I for mine. But all unbiased readers will conclude, that
my moderation is not to be condemned. To such impartial men I
must appeal, for they who have already formed their judgement, may
justly stand suspected of prejudice; and though all who are my
readers, will set up to be my judges, I enter my *caveat* against them,
that they ought not so much as to be of my jury. Or, if they be admitted, 'tis but reason, that they should first hear what I have to
urge in the defence of my opinion.

That Horace is somewhat the better instructor of the two, is proved
from hence, that his instructions are more general, Juvenal's more
limited. So that granting that the counsels which they give are
equally good for moral use, Horace, who gives the most various
advice, and most applicable to all occasions which can occur to us
in the course of our lives; as including in his discourses, not only all
the rules of morality, but also of civil conversation, is, undoubtedly,
to be preferred to him, who is more circumscribed in his instructions,
makes them to fewer people, and on fewer occasions, than the other.
I may be pardoned for using an old saying, since 'tis true, and to the
purpose, *bonum quo communius, eo melius*. Juvenal, excepting only
his first satire, is in all the rest confined, to the exposing of some
particular vice; that he lashes, and there he sticks. His sentences are
truly shining and instructive. But they are sprinkled here and there.

---

the more delightful author: contrast the Preface to *Sylvae*, above, p. 204.
bonum quo . . .: 'the more general the better'.

Horace is teaching us in every line, and is perpetually moral; he had
found out the skill of Virgil, to hide his sentences, to give you the
virtue of them, without showing them in their full extent, which is the
ostentation of a poet, and not his art. And this Petronius charges on
the authors of his time, as a vice of writing, which was then growing
on the age; *ne sententiae extra corpus orationis emineant.* He would
have them weaved into the body of the work, and not appear
embossed upon it, and striking directly on the reader's view. Folly
was the proper quarry of Horace, and not vice, and, as there are but
few notoriously wicked men, in comparison with a shoal of fools,
and fops; so 'tis a harder thing to make a man wise, than to make
him honest, for the will is only to be reclaimed in the one, but the
understanding is to be informed in the other. There are blind-sides
and follies, even in the professors of moral philosophy; and there is
not any one sect of them that Horace has not exposed, which, as it
was not the design of Juvenal, who was wholly employed in lashing
vices, some of them the most enormous that can be imagined; so
perhaps, it was not so much his talent. *Omne vafer vitium ridenti
Flaccus amico, tangit, et admissus circum praecordia ludit.* This was
the commendation which Persius gave him, where by *vitium*, he
means those little vices, which we call follies, the defects of human
understanding, or at most the peccadilloes of life, rather than the
tragical vices, to which men are hurried by their unruly passions and
exorbitant desires. But in the word *omne*, which is universal, he
concludes, with me, that the divine wit of Horace, left nothing untouched; that he entered into the inmost recesses of nature; found
out the imperfections even of the most wise and grave, as well as of
the common people, discovering, even in the great Trebatius, to
whom he addresses the first satire, his hunting after business, and following the court, as well as in the persecutor Crispinus, his impertinence and importunity. 'Tis true, he exposes Crispinus openly,
as a common nuisance, but he rallies the other, as a friend, more
finely. The exhortations of Persius are confined to noblemen. And the
Stoic philosophy is that alone which he recommends to them.
Juvenal exhorts to particular virtues, as they are opposed to those
vices against which he declaims, but Horace laughs to shame all
follies, and insinuates virtue rather by familiar examples than by the
severity of precepts.

Ne sententiae . . .: *Satyricon,* 118 ('Do not allow maxims to stick out from the
    body of the work').
Omne vafer . . .: Persius, *Satires,* i. 116–17.
Crispinus: *Satires,* I. ix.

This last consideration seems to incline the balance on the side of
Horace, and to give him the preference to Juvenal, not only in profit,
but in pleasure. But, after all, I must confess, that the delight which
Horace gives me, is but languishing. Be pleased still to understand,
that I speak of my own taste only. He may ravish other men, but I
am too stupid and insensible to be tickled. Where he barely grins
himself, and, as Scaliger says, only shows his white teeth, he cannot
provoke me to any laughter. His urbanity, that is, his good manners,
are to be commended, but his wit is faint, and his salt, if I may dare
to say so, almost insipid. Juvenal is of a more vigorous and masculine
wit, he gives me as much pleasure as I can bear. He fully satisfies my
expectation, he treats his subject home. His spleen is raised, and he
raises mine. I have the pleasure of concernment in all he says; he
drives his reader along with him; and when he is at the end of his
way, I willingly stop with him. If he went another stage, it would be
too far, it would make a journey of a progress, and turn delight into
fatigue. When he gives over, 'tis a sign the subject is exhausted, and
the wit of man can carry it no farther. If a fault can be justly found in
him 'tis that he is sometimes too luxuriant, too redundant; says more
than he needs, like my friend the *Plain Dealer*, but never more than
pleases. Add to this, that his thoughts are as just as those of Horace,
and much more elevated. His expressions are sonorous and more
noble; his verse more numerous, and his words are suitable to his
thoughts, sublime and lofty. All these contribute to the pleasure of
the reader, and the greater the soul of him who reads, his transports
are the greater. Horace is always on the amble, Juvenal on the gallop,
but his way is perpetually on carpet ground. He goes with more
impetuosity than Horace, but as securely; and the swiftness adds a
more lively agitation to the spirits. The low style of Horace is according to his subject; that is generally grovelling. I question not but he
could have raised it. For the first epistle of the second book, which he
writes to Augustus, (a most instructive satire concerning poetry,) is of
so much dignity in the words, and of so much elegancy in the
numbers, that the author plainly shows, the *sermo pedestris*, in his
other satires, was rather his choice than his necessity. He was a rival
to Lucilius his predecessor; and was resolved to surpass him in his
own manner. Lucilius, as we see by his remaining fragments, minded
neither his style nor his numbers, nor his purity of words, nor his run
of verse. Horace therefore copes with him in that humble way of

---

Plain Dealer: Wycherley's comedy *The Plain Dealer* was acted in 1676 and pub-
    lished 1677.
sermo pedestris: *Ars Poetica*, l. 95 ('pedestrian manner').

satire, writes under his own force, and carries a dead weight, that he
may match his competitor in the race. This I imagine was the chief
reason, why he minded only the clearness of his satire, and the clean-
ness of expression, without ascending to those heights, to which his
own vigour might have carried him. But limiting his desires only to
the conquest of Lucilius, he had his ends of his rival, who lived before
him; but made way for a new conquest over himself, by Juvenal his
successor. He could not give an equal pleasure to his reader, because
he used not equal instruments. The fault was in the tools, and not in
the workman. But versification, and numbers, are the greatest
pleasures of poetry. Virgil knew it, and practised both so happily;
that for aught I know, his greatest excellency is in his diction. In all
other parts of poetry, he is faultless; but in this he placed his chief
perfection. And give me leave, my Lord, since I have here an apt
occasion, to say, that Virgil, could have written sharper satires than
either Horace or Juvenal, if he would have employed his talent that
way. I will produce a verse and half of his, in one of his *Eclogues*, to
justify my opinion; and with commas after every word, to show that
he has given almost as many lashes, as he has written syllables. 'Tis
against a bad poet; whose ill verses he describes. *Non tu, in triviis,
indocte, solebas, stridenti, miserum, stipula, disperdere carmen*? But to
return to my purpose, when there is anything deficient in numbers
and sound, the reader is uneasy, and unsatisfied; he wants something
of his complement, desires somewhat which he finds not. And this
being the manifest defect of Horace, 'tis no wonder, that finding it
supplied in Juvenal, we are more delighted with him. And besides
this, the sauce of Juvenal is more poignant, to create in us an
appetite of reading him. The meat of Horace is more nourishing; but
the cookery of Juvenal more exquisite; so that, granting Horace to
be the more general philosopher, we cannot deny that Juvenal was
the greater poet, I mean in satire. His thoughts are sharper, his indignation against vice is more vehement; his spirit has more of the
commonwealth genius; he treats tyranny, and all the vices attending
it, as they deserve, with the utmost rigour, and consequently, a noble
soul is better pleased with a zealous vindicator of Roman liberty,
than with a temporizing poet, a well mannered court slave, and a man
who is often afraid of laughing in the right place, who is ever decent,
because he is naturally servile. After all, Horace had the disadvantage
of the times in which he lived; they were better for the man, but
worse for the satirist. 'Tis generally said, that those enormous vices,

---

Non tu . . . .: *Eclogues*, iii. 26–7 ('Wasn't it you, you fool, who used to destroy
  wretched song on a pipe at the cross-roads?').

which were practised under the reign of Domitian, were unknown in the time of Augustus Caesar, that therefore Juvenal had a larger field, than Horace. Little follies were out of doors, when oppression was to be scourged instead of avarice. It was no longer time to turn into ridicule the false opinions of philosophers, when the Roman liberty was to be asserted. There was more need of a Brutus in Domitian's days, to redeem or mend, than of a Horace, if he had then been living, to laugh at a fly-catcher. This reflection at the same time excuses Horace, but exalts Juvenal. I have ended, before I was aware, the comparison of Horace and Juvenal, upon the topics of instruction and delight; and indeed I may safely here conclude that commonplace, for if we make Horace our minister of state in satire, and Juvenal of our private pleasures, I think the latter has no ill bargain of it. Let profit have the preeminence of honour, in the end of poetry. Pleasure, though but the second in degree, is the first in favour. And who would not choose to be loved better, rather than to be more esteemed? But I am entered already upon another topic, which concerns the particular merits of these two satirists. However, I will pursue my business where I left it, and carry it farther than that common observation of the several ages, in which these authors flourished. When Horace writ his satires, the monarchy of his Caesar was in its newness; and the government but just made easy to the conquered people. They could not possibly have forgotten the usurpation of that prince upon their freedom, nor the violent methods which he had used, in the compassing of that vast design. They yet remembered his proscriptions, and the slaughter of so many noble Romans, their defenders. Amongst the rest, that horrible action of his, when he forced Livia from the arms of her husband, who was constrained to see her married, as Dion relates the story; and, big with child as she was, conveyed to the bed of his insulting rival. The same Dion Cassius gives us another instance of the crime before mentioned: that Cornelius Sisenna, being reproached in full Senate with the licentious conduct of his wife, returned this answer; that he had married her by the counsel of Augustus, intimating, says my author, that Augustus had obliged him to that marriage, that he might, under that covert, have the more free access to her. His adulteries were still before their eyes, but they must be patient, where they had not power. In other things that emperor was moderate enough. Propriety was generally secured; and the people entertained with public shows, and donatives, to make them more easily digest their lost liberty. But Augustus, who was conscious to himself, of so

as Dion relates: *Historia*, liv. 27.

many crimes which he had committed, thought in the first place to provide for his own reputation, by making an edict against lampoons and satires, and the authors of those defamatory writings, which my author Tacitus, from the law-term, calls *famosos libellos*.

In the first book of his *Annals*, he gives the following account of it, in these words: *Primus Augustus cognitionem de famosis libellis specie legis ejus, tractavit; commotus Cassii Severi libidine, qua viros foeminasque inlustres, procacibus scriptis diffamaverat.* Thus in English: 'Augustus was the first, who under the colour of that law took cognisance of lampoons; being provoked to it, by the petulancy of Cassius Severus, who had defamed many illustrious persons of both sexes, in his writings.' The law to which Tacitus refers, was *lex laesae majestatis*; commonly called, for the sake of brevity, *majestas*; or as we say, high treason. He means not that this law had not been enacted formerly, for it had been made by the *Decemviri*, and was inscribed amongst the rest in the Twelve Tables. To prevent the aspersion of the Roman Majesty, either of the people themselves, or their religion, or their magistrates; and the infringement of it was capital; that is, the offender was whipped to death, with the *fasces*, which were borne before their chief officers of Rome. But Augustus was the first who restored that intermitted law. By the words, *under colour of the law*, he insinuates that Augustus caused it to be executed, on pretence of those libels, which were written by Cassius Severus, against the nobility; but in truth, to save himself from such defamatory verses. Suetonius likewise makes mention of it thus: *sparsos de se in Curia famosos libellos, nec expavit, et magna cura redarguit: ac ne requisitis quidem auctoribus, id modo censuit, cognoscendum post hac, de iis qui libellos aut carmina ad infamiam cujuspiam sub alieno nomine edant.* Augustus was not afraid of libels, says that author, yet he took all care imaginable to have them answered; and then decreed that for the time to come, the authors of them should be punished. But Aurelius makes it yet more clear, according to my sense, that this emperor for his own sake durst not permit them. *Fecit id Augustus in speciem; et quasi gratificaretur populo Romano, et primoribus urbis; sed revera ut sibi consuleret. Nam habuit in animo, comprimere nimiam quorundam procacitatem in loquendo, a qua nec ipse exemptus fuit. Nam suo nomine compescere erat invidiosum, sub alieno facile et utile. Ergo specie legis tractavit, quasi populi Romani majestas*

Annals: *Annals*, i. 72.
Suetonius: 'Augustus Caesar', lv.
Fecit id Augustus . . .: Watson points out that this is not in Sextus Aurelius Victor and suggests that it comes from a Renaissance commentary.

infamaretur. This, I think is a sufficient comment on that passage of Tacitus. I will add only by the way, that the whole family of the Caesars, and all their relations, were included in the law, because the majesty of the Romans in the time of the empire was wholly in that house: *Omnia Caesar erat*. They were all accounted sacred, who belonged to him. As for Cassius Severus, he was contemporary with Horace; and was the same poet against whom he writes in his *Epodes*, under this title, *In Cassium Severum Maledicum Poetam*, perhaps intending to kill two crows, according to our proverb, with one stone, and revenge both himself and his emperor together.

From hence I may reasonably conclude that Augustus, who was not altogether so good as he was wise, had some by-respect, in the enacting of this law, for to do anything for nothing was not his maxim. Horace, as he was a courtier, complied with the interest of his master, and avoiding the lashing of greater crimes, confined himself to the ridiculing of petty vices, and common follies; excepting only some reserved cases, in his *Odes* and *Epodes*, of his own particular quarrels; which either with permission of the magistrate or without it, every man will revenge, though I say not that he should; for *prior laesit*, is a good excuse in the civil law, if Christianity had not taught us to forgive. However, he was not the proper man to arraign great vices, at least if the stories which we hear of him are true, that he practised some, which I will not here mention, out of honour to him. It was not for a Clodius to accuse adulterers, especially when Augustus was of that number; so that though his age was not exempted from the worst of villainies, there was no freedom left to reprehend them, by reason of the edict. And our poet was not fit to represent them in an odious character, because himself was dipped in the same actions. Upon this account, without farther insisting on the different tempers of Juvenal and Horace, I conclude, that the subjects which Horace chose for satire, are of a lower nature than those of which Juvenal has written.

Thus I have treated in a new method, the comparison betwixt Horace, Juvenal, and Persius; somewhat of their particular manner belonging to all of them is yet remaining to be considered. Persius was grave, and particularly opposed his gravity to lewdness, which was the predominant vice in Nero's Court, at the time when he published his satires, which was before that emperor fell into the excess of cruelty. Horace was a mild admonisher, a Court satirist, fit for the gentle times of Augustus, and more fit, for the reasons which I have already given. Juvenal was as proper for his times, as they for theirs.

Epodes: *Epodes*, vi.

His was an age that deserved a more severe chastisement. Vices were more gross and open, more flagitious, more encouraged by the example of a tyrant, and more protected by his authority. Therefore, wheresoever Juvenal mentions Nero, he means Domitian, whom he dares not attack in his own person, but scourges him by proxy. Heinsius urges in praise of Horace, that according to the ancient art and law of satire, it should be nearer to comedy than to tragedy, not declaiming against vice, but only laughing at it. Neither Persius, nor Juvenal were ignorant of this, for they had both studied Horace. And the thing itself is plainly true. But as they had read Horace, they had likewise read Lucilius, of whom Persius says *secuit urbem; et genuinum fregit in illis*; meaning Mutius and Lupus. And Juvenal also mentions him in these words, *Ense velut stricto, quoties Lucilius ardens infremuit*, etc. so that they thought the imitation of Lucilius was more proper to their purpose than that of Horace. They changed satire, says Holyday; but they changed it for the better; for the business being to reform great vices, chastisement goes farther than admonition; whereas a perpetual grin, like that of Horace, does rather anger than amend a man.

Thus far that learned critic Barten Holyday, whose interpretation and illustrations of Juvenal are as excellent, as the verse of his translation and his English are lame and pitiful. For 'tis not enough to give us the meaning of a poet, which I acknowledge him to have performed most faithfully; but he must also imitate his genius, and his numbers, as far as the English will come up to the elegance of the original. In few words, 'tis only for a poet to translate a poet. Holyday and Stapylton had not enough considered this, when they attempted Juvenal. But I forbear reflections; only I beg leave to take notice of this sentence, where Holyday says, 'A perpetual grin, like that of Horace, rather angers than amends a man'. I cannot give him up the manner of Horace in low satire so easily. Let the chastisements of Juvenal be never so necessary for his new kind of satire; let him declaim as wittily and sharply as he pleases, yet still the nicest and most delicate touches of satire consist in fine raillery. This, my Lord, is your particular talent, to which even Juvenal could not arrive. 'Tis not reading, 'tis not imitation of an author, which can produce this fineness. It must be inborn, it must proceed from a genius, and particular way of thinking, which is not to be taught; and therefore not to be imitated by him who has it not from nature. How easy it is

---

Lucilius: Persius, *Satires*, i. 114–15; Juvenal, *Satires*, i. 165–6 ('Lucilius flogged the town and chewed them up'; 'when Lucilius rages in passion, as if with sword drawn').

to call rogue and villain, and that wittily! But how hard to make a
man appear a fool, a blockhead, or a knave, without using any of
those opprobrious terms! To spare the grossness of the names, and
to do the thing yet more severely, is to draw a full face, and to make
the nose and cheeks stand out, and yet not to employ any depth of
shadowing. This is the mystery of that noble trade, which yet no
master can teach to his apprentice. He may give the rules, but the
scholar is never the nearer in his practice. Neither is it true, that this
fineness of raillery is offensive. A witty man is tickled while he is hurt
in this manner; and a fool feels it not. The occasion of an offence
may possibly be given, but he cannot take it. If it be granted that in
effect this way does more mischief; that a man is secretly wounded,
and though he be not sensible himself, yet the malicious world will
find it for him; yet there is still a vast difference betwixt the slovenly
butchering of a man, and the fineness of a stroke that separates the
head from the body, and leaves it standing in its place. A man may
be capable, as Jack Ketche's wife said of his servant, of a plain piece
of work, a bare hanging; but to make a malefactor die sweetly, was
only belonging to her husband. I wish I could apply it to myself, if
the reader would be kind enough to think it belongs to me. The
character of Zimri in my *Absalom*, is, in my opinion, worth the whole
poem: 'tis not bloody, but 'tis ridiculous enough. And he for whom
it was intended, was too witty to resent it as an injury. If I had railed,
I might have suffered for it justly. But I managed my own work more
happily, perhaps more dextrously. I avoided the mention of great
crimes, and applied myself to the representing of blind-sides, and
little extravagancies: to which, the wittier a man is, he is generally
the more obnoxious. It succeeded as I wished; the jest went round,
and he was laughed at in his turn who began the frolic.

And thus, my Lord, you see I have preferred the manner of
Horace, and of your Lordship, in this kind of satire, to that of
Juvenal; and I think, reasonably. Holyday ought not to have arraigned
so great an author, for that which was his excellency and his merit.
Or if he did, on such a palpable mistake, he might expect, that someone might possibly arise, either in his own time, or after him, to
rectify his error, and restore to Horace that commendation, of
which he has so unjustly robbed him. And let the Manes of Juvenal
forgive me, if I say, that this way of Horace was the best, for amend-
ing manners, as it is the most difficult. His was, an *ense rescindendum*;
but that of Horace was a pleasant cure, with all the limbs preserved

---

Jack Ketche: public hangman under Charles II and James II, until 1685.
ense rescindendum: Ovid, *Metamorphoses*, i. 191 ('to be cut through by a sword').

entire; and as our mountebanks tell us in their bills, without keeping
the patient within doors for a day. What they promise only, Horace
has effectually performed; yet I contradict not the proposition which
I formerly advanced. Juvenal's times required a more painful kind of
operation; but if he had lived in the age of Horace, I must needs
affirm, that he had it not about him. He took the method which was
prescribed him by his own genius, which was sharp and eager; he
could not rally, but he could declaim; and as his provocations were
great, he has revenged them tragically. This notwithstanding, I am to
say another word, which, as true as it is, will yet displease the partial
admirers of our Horace. I have hinted it before; but 'tis time for me
now to speak more plainly.

This manner of Horace is indeed the best; but Horace has not
executed it altogether so happily, at least not often. The manner of
Juvenal is confessed to be inferior to the former; but Juvenal has
excelled him in his performance. Juvenal has railed more wittily than
Horace has railed. Horace means to make his reader laugh; but he is
not sure of his experiment. Juvenal always intends to move your indignation; and he always brings about his purpose. Horace, for
aught I know, might have tickled the people of his age; but amongst
the Moderns he is not so successful. They who say he entertains so
pleasantly, may perhaps value themselves on the quickness of their
own understandings, that they can see a jest farther off than other
men. They may find occasion of laughter, in the wit-battle of the two
buffoons, Sarmentus and Cicerrus, and hold their sides for fear of
bursting, when Rupilius and Persius are scolding. For my own part,
I can only like the characters of all four, which are judiciously given,
but for my heart I cannot so much as smile at their insipid raillery. I
see not why Persius should call upon Brutus, to revenge him on his
adversary, and that because he had killed Julius Caesar, for endeavouring to be a King, therefore he should be desired to murder Rupilius,
only because his name was Mr. King. A miserable clench, in my
opinion, for Horace to record. I have heard honest Mr. Swan make
many a better, and yet have had the grace to hold my countenance.
But it may be puns were then in fashion, as they were wit in the
sermons of the last age, and in the Court of King Charles the Second.
I am sorry to say it, for the sake of Horace; but certain it is, he has
no fine palate who can feed so heartily on garbage.

But I have already wearied myself, and doubt not but I have tired
your Lordship's patience, with this long rambling, and I fear, trivial

Sarmentus and Cicerrus: Horace, *Satires*, I, v. 52; I, vii. 1–2.
Mr. Swan: a contemporary punster.

discourse. Upon the one half of the merits, that is, pleasure, I cannot but conclude that Juvenal was the better satirist. They who will descend into his particular praises, may find them at large in the dissertation of the learned Rigaltius to Thuanus. As for Persius, I have given the reasons why I think him inferior to both of them. Yet I have one thing to add on that subject.

Barten Holyday, who translated both Juvenal and Persius, has made this distinction betwixt them, which is no less true than witty; that, in Persius the difficulty is to find a meaning; in Juvenal, to choose a meaning: so crabbed is Persius, and so copious is Juvenal; so much the understanding is employed in one; and so much the judgement in the other. So difficult it is to find any sense in the former, and the best sense of the latter.

If, on the other side, anyone suppose I have commended Horace below his merit, when I have allowed him but the second place, I desire him to consider, if Juvenal, a man of excellent natural endowments, besides the advantages of diligence and study, and coming after him, and building upon his foundations, might not probably, with all these helps, surpass him? And whether it be any dishonour to Horace, to be thus surpassed; since no art, or science, is at once begun and perfected, but that it must pass first through many hands, and even through several ages? If Lucilius could add to Ennius, and Horace to Lucilius, why, without any diminution to the fame of Horace, might not Juvenal give the last perfection to that work? Or rather, what disreputation is it to Horace, that Juvenal excels in the tragical satire, as Horace does in the comical? I have read over attentively, both Heinsius and Dacier, in their commendations of Horace, but I can find no more in either of them, for the preference of him to Juvenal, than the instructive part; the part of wisdom, and not that of pleasure; which therefore is here allowed him, not withstanding what Scaliger and Rigaltius have pleaded to the contrary for Juvenal. And to show I am impartial, I will here translate what Dacier has said on that subject.

'I cannot give a more just idea of the two books of satires made by Horace, than by comparing them to the statues of the Sileni, to which Alcibiades compares Socrates, in the *Symposium*. They were figures which had nothing of agreeable, nothing of beauty on their outside: but when anyone took the pains to open them, and search into them, he there found the figures of all the deities. So, in the shape that Horace presents himself to us, in his satires, we see nothing at the first view which deserves our attention. It seems that he is rather an

Symposium: *Symposium*, 215.

amusement for children than for the serious consideration of men. But when we take away his crust, and that which hides him from our sight; when we discover him to the bottom, then we find all the divinities in a full assembly; that is to say, all the virtues, which ought to be the continual exercise of those, who seriously endeavour to correct their vices.'

'Tis easy to observe, that Dacier, in this noble similitude, has confined the praise of his author wholly to the instructive part; the commendation turns on this, and so does that which follows.

'In these two books of satire, 'tis the business of Horace to instruct us how to combat our vices, to regulate our passions, to follow nature, to give bounds to our desires, to distinguish betwixt truth and falsehood, and betwixt our conceptions of things, and things themselves; to come back from our prejudicate opinions, to understand exactly the principles and motives of all our actions; and to avoid the ridicule, into which all men necessarily fall, who are intoxicated with those notions which they have received from their masters; and which they obstinately retain, without examining whether or no they are founded on right reason.

'In a word, he labours to render us happy in relation to ourselves, agreeable and faithful to our friends, and discreet, serviceable, and well bred in relation to those with whom we are obliged to live, and to converse. To make his figures intelligible, to conduct his readers through the labyrinth of some perplexed sentence, or obscure parenthesis, is no great matter. And as Epictetus says, there is nothing of beauty in all this, or what is worthy of a prudent man. The principal business, and which is of most importance to us, is to show the use, the reason, and the proof of his precepts.

'They who endeavour not to correct themselves, according to so exact a model, are just like the patients, who have open before them a book of admirable receipts for their diseases, and please themselves with reading it, without comprehending the nature of the remedies; or how to apply them to their cure.'

Let Horace go off with these encomiums, which he has so well deserved.

To conclude the contention betwixt our three poets, I will use the words of Virgil, in his fifth *Aeneid* where Aeneas proposes the rewards of the foot-race to the three first who should reach the goal. *Tres proemia primi accipient; flavaque caput nectentur oliva*: let these three Ancients be preferred to all the Moderns, as first arriving at the goal: let them all be crowned as victors, with the wreath that properly belongs to satire. But, after that, with this distinction amongst themselves, *Primus equum phaleris insignem, victor habeto.*

Let Juvenal ride first in triumph. *Alter Amazoniam pharetram plenamque sagittis Threiciis, lato quam circumplectitur auro balteus, et tereti subnectit fibula gemma.* Let Horace who is the second, and but just the second, carry off the quivers and the arrows, as the badges of his satire; and the golden belt and the diamond button. *Tertius, Argolico hoc clypeo contentus abito.* And let Persius, the last of the first three worthies, be contented with this Grecian shield, and with victory not only over all the Grecians, who were ignorant of the Roman satire, but over all the Moderns in succeeding ages; excepting Boileau and your Lordship.

And thus, I have given the history of satire, and derived it as far as from Ennius, to your Lordship; that is, from its first rudiments of barbarity, to its last polishing and perfection: which is, with Virgil, in his address to Augustus;

> —nomen fama tot ferre per annos,
> Tithoni prima quot abest ab origine Caesar.

I said only from Ennius; but I may safely carry it higher, as far as Livius Andronicus; who, as I have said formerly, taught the first play at Rome in the year *ab urbe condita*, 514. I have since desired my learned friend, Mr. Maidwell, to compute the difference of times, betwixt Aristophanes, and Livius Andronicus; and he assures me, from the best chronologers, that *Plutus*, the last of Aristophanes' plays, was represented at Athens, in the year of the 97th Olympiad, which agrees with the year *urbis conditae* 364: so that the difference of years betwixt Aristophanes and Andronicus is 150; from whence I have probably deduced, that Livius Andronicus, who was a Grecian, had read the plays of the Old Comedy, which were satirical, and also of the New; for Menander was fifty years before him, which must needs be a great light to him, in his own plays; that were of the

---

Tres proemia . . . abito: . . .: *Aeneid*, v. 308–14:

> The foremost three have olive wreaths decreed;
> The first of these obtains a stately steed
> Adorned with trappings; and the next in Fame,
> The quiver of an Amazonian dame;
> With feathered Thracian arrows well supplied,
> A golden belt shall gird his manly side;
> Which with a sparkling diamond shall be tied:
> The third this Grecian helmet shall content
>   (Dryden, *Aeneis*, V, 405–12).

—*nomen fama* . . .: *Georgics*, iii. 47–8 ('to carry his name in fame, through as many years as Caesar is from the distant birth of Tithonus').

Mr. Maidwell: Lewis Maidwell (1650–1715), schoolmaster-grammarian.

satirical nature. That the Romans had farces before this, 'tis true; but then they had no communication with Greece, so that Andronicus was the first who wrote after the manner of the Old Comedy, in his plays; he was imitated by Ennius, about thirty years afterwards. Though the former writ fables, the latter, speaking properly, began the Roman satire. According to that description, which Juvenal gives of it in his first; *Quicquid agunt homines, votum, timor, ira, voluptas, gaudia, discursus, nostri est farrago libelli.* This is that in which I have made bold to differ from Casaubon, Rigaltius, Dacier, and indeed, from all the modern critics, that not Ennius, but Andronicus was the first, who by the *Archaea Comedia* of the Greeks, added many beauties to the first rude and barbarous Roman satire; which sort of poem, though we had not derived from Rome, yet nature teaches it mankind, in all ages, and in every country.

'Tis but necessary, that after so much has been said of satire, some definition of it should be given. Heinsius, in his dissertations on Horace, makes it for me, in these words: Satire is a kind of poetry, without a series of action, invented for the purging of our minds; in which human vices, ignorance, and errors, and all things besides, which are produced from them, in every man, are severely reprehended; partly dramatically, partly simply, and sometimes in both kinds of speaking; but for the most part figuratively, and occultly; consisting in a low familiar way, chiefly in a sharp and pungent manner of speech; but partly, also, in a facetious and civil way of jesting; by which, either hatred, or laughter, or indignation is moved. —Where I cannot but observe, that this obscure and perplexed definition, or rather description of satire, is wholly accommodated to the Horatian way; and excluding the works of Juvenal and Persius, as foreign from that kind of poem. The clause in the beginning of it (without a series of action) distinguishes satire properly from stage plays, which are all of one action, and one continued series of action. The end or scope of satire is to purge the passions; so far it is common to the satires of Juvenal and Persius. The rest which follows, is also generally belonging to all three; till he comes upon us, with the excluding clause (consisting in a low familiar way of speech) which is the proper character of Horace; and from which, the other two, for their honour be it spoken, are far distant. But how come lowness of style, and the familiarity of words to be so much the propriety of satire, that without them a poet can be no more a satirist than without risibility he can be a man? Is the fault of Horace to be made the

---

Quicquid . . .: Satires, i. 85–6 ('Whatsoever men do—their vows, terror, rage, desire, joy, movements—is the various subject of my book').

virtue, and standing rule of this poem? Is the *grande sophos* of
Persius, and the sublimity of Juvenal to be circumscribed with the
meanness of words and vulgarity of expression? If Horace refused
the pains of numbers, and the loftiness of figures, are they bound to
follow so ill a precedent? Let him walk afoot with his pad in his
hand, for his own pleasure; but let not them be accounted no poets
who choose to mount, and show their horsemanship. Holyday is not
afraid to say that there was never such a fall, as from his odes to his
satires, and that he, injuriously to himself, untuned his harp. The
majestic way of Persius and Juvenal was new when they began it; but
'tis old to us; and what poems have not, with time, received an
alteration in their fashion? Which alteration, says Holyday, is to
after-times as good a warrant as the first. Has not Virgil changed the
manners of Homer's heroes in his *Aeneis*? Certainly he has, and for
the better. For Virgil's age was more civilized, and better bred; and
he writ according to the politeness of Rome, under the reign of
Augustus Caesar, not to the rudeness of Agamemnon's age, or the
times of Homer. Why should we offer to confine free spirits to one
form, when we cannot so much as confine our bodies to one fashion
of apparel? Would not Donne's satires, which abound with so much
wit, appear more charming, if he had taken care of his words, and of
his numbers? But he followed Horace so very close, that of necessity
he must fall with him. And I may safely say it of this present age, that
if we are not so great wits as Donne, yet, certainly, we are better poets.

But I have said enough, and it may be, too much on this subject.
Will your Lordship be pleased to prolong my audience, only so far,
till I tell you my own trivial thoughts, how a modern satire should be
made. I will not deviate in the least from the precepts and examples
of the Ancients, who were always our best masters. I will only illustrate them, and discover some of the hidden beauties in their designs,
that we thereby may form our own in imitation of them. Will you
please but to observe, that Persius, the least in dignity of all the three,
has, notwithstanding, been the first who has discovered to us this
important secret in the designing of a perfect satire; that it ought
only to treat of one subject; to be confined to one particular theme,
or, at least, to one principally. If other vices occur in the management
of the chief, they should only be transiently lashed, and not be
insisted on, so as to make the design double. As in a play of the
English fashion, which we call a tragicomedy, there is to be but one
main design. And though there be an under-plot, or second walk of

grande sophos: 'great wisdom': phrase from Rigaltius, op. cit.
pad: saddle.
10+s.c.

comical characters and adventures, yet they are subservient to the
chief fable, carried along under it, and helping to it; so that the
drama may not seem a monster with two heads. Thus the Copernican
system of the planets makes the moon to be moved by the motion of
the earth, and carried about her orb, as a dependent of hers. Mascardi
in his discourse of the *doppia favola*, or double-tale in plays, gives an
instance of it in the famous pastoral of Guarini, called *Il Pastor
Fido*; where Corisca and the satyr are the under-parts. Yet we may
observe, that Corisca is brought into the body of the plot, and made
subservient to it. 'Tis certain, that the divine wit of Horace was not
ignorant of this rule, that a play, though it consists of many parts,
must yet be one in the action, and must drive on the accomplishment
of one design; for he gives this very precept, *sit quodvis simplex
duntaxat et unum*; yet he seems not much to mind it in his satires,
many of them consisting of more arguments than one; and the second
without dependence on the first. Casaubon has observed this before
me, in his preference of Persius to Horace, and will have his own
beloved author to be the first who found out and introduced this
method of confining himself to one subject. I know it may be urged
in defence of Horace, that this unity is not necessary; because the
very word *satura* signifies a dish plentifully stored with all variety of
fruits and grains. Yet Juvenal, who calls his poems a *farrago*, which
is a word of the same signification with *satura*, has chosen to follow
the same method of Persius, and not of Horace. And Boileau, whose
example alone is a sufficient authority, has wholly confined himself,
in all his satires, to this unity of design. That variety which is not to
be found in any one satire, is, at least, in many, written on several
occasions. And if variety be of absolute necessity in every one of
them, according to the etymology of the word, yet it may arise
naturally from one subject, as it is diversely treated, in the several
subordinate branches of it, all relating to the chief. It may be illus-
trated accordingly with variety of examples in the subdivisions of it;
and with as many precepts as there are members of it; which altogether may complete that *olla*, or hotchpotch, which is properly a
satire.

Under this unity of theme, or subject, is comprehended another
rule for perfecting the design of true satire. The poet is bound, and
that *ex officio*, to give his reader some one precept of moral virtue;
and to caution him against some one particular vice or folly. Other

Mascardi: Agostino Mascardi (1590–1640), *Prose Vulgari* (1630): 'Discorso . . .
dell' Unità della Favola Drammatica' (Ker).
sit quodvis . . .: *Ars Poetica*, l. 23 ('have what aim you wish, provided it is one
and simple').

virtues, subordinate to the first, may be recommended, under that chief head; and other vices or follies may be scourged, besides that which he principally intends. But he is chiefly to inculcate one virtue, and insist on that. Thus Juvenal in every satire, excepting the first, ties himself to one principal instructive point, or to the shunning of moral evil. Even in the sixth, which seems only an arraignment of the whole sex of womankind, there is a latent admonition to avoid ill women, by showing how very few who are virtuous and good, are to be found amongst them. But this, though the wittiest of all his satires, has yet the least of truth or instruction in it. He has run himself into his old declamatory way, and almost forgotten, that he was now setting up for a moral poet.

Persius is never wanting to us in some profitable doctrine, and in exposing the opposite vices to it. His kind of philosophy is one which is the Stoic; and every satire is a comment on one particular dogma of that sect, unless we will except the first, which is against bad writers; and yet even there he forgets not the precepts of the Porch. In general, all virtues are everywhere to be praised, and recommended to practice, and all vices to be reprehended, and made either odious or ridiculous; or else there is a fundamental error in the whole design.

I have already declared who are the only persons that are the adequate object of private satire, and who they are that may properly be exposed by name for public examples of vices and follies; and therefore I will trouble your Lordship no farther with them. Of the best and finest manner of satire, I have said enough in the comparison betwixt Juvenal and Horace: 'tis that sharp, well-mannered way, of laughing a folly out of countenance, of which your Lordship is the best master in this age. I will proceed to the versification, which is most proper for it, and add somewhat to what I have said already on that subject. The sort of verse which is called burlesque, consisting of eight syllables, or four feet, is that which our excellent *Hudibras* has chosen. I ought to have mentioned him before, when I spoke of Donne; but by a slip of an old man's memory he was forgotten. The worth of his poem is too well known to need my commendation, and he is above my censure. His satire is of the Varronian kind, though unmixed with prose. The choice of his numbers is suitable enough to his design, as he has managed it. But in any other hand, the shortness of his verse, and the quick returns of rhyme, had debased the dignity of style. And besides, the double rhyme (a necessary companion of

precept of the Porch: i.e. of the Stoic philosophers.
Hudibras: Samuel Butler (1612–80), *Hudibras* (1663–78).

burlesque writing) is not so proper for manly satire, for it turns earnest too much to jest, and gives us a boyish kind of pleasure. It tickles awkwardly with a kind of pain, to the best sort of readers; we are pleased ungratefully, and, if I may say so, against our liking. We thank him not for giving us that unseasonable delight, when we know he could have given us a better, and more solid. He might have left that task to others, who not being able to put in thought, can only make us grin with the excrescence of a word of two or three syllables in the close. 'Tis, indeed, below so great a master to make use of such a little instrument. But his good sense is perpetually shining through all he writes; it affords us not the time of finding faults. We pass through the levity of his rhyme, and are immediately carried into some admirable useful thought. After all, he has chosen this kind of verse; and has written the best in it. And had he taken another, he would always have excelled. As we say of a court favourite, that whatsoever his office be, he still makes it uppermost, and most beneficial to himself.

The quickness of your imagination, my Lord, has already prevented me, and you know before-hand, that I would prefer the verse of ten syllables, which we call the English heroic, to that of eight. This is truly my opinion. For this sort of number is more roomy. The thought can turn itself with greater ease in a larger compass. When the rhyme comes too thick upon us, it straitens the expression; we are thinking of the close, when we should be employed in adorning the thought. It makes a poet giddy with turning in a space too narrow for his imagination. He loses many beauties without gaining one advantage. For a burlesque rhyme, I have already concluded to be none; or if it were, 'tis more easily purchased in ten syllables than in eight. In both occasions 'tis as in a tennis court, when the strokes of greater force are given, when we strike out and play at length. Tassone and Boileau have left us the best examples of this way, in the *Secchia Rapita*, and the *Lutrin*. And next them Merlin Coccajus in his *Baldus*. I will speak only of the two former, because the last is written in Latin verse. The *Secchia Rapita*, is an Italian poem, a satire of the Varronian kind. 'Tis written in the stanza of eight, which is their measure for heroic verse. The words are stately, the numbers smooth, the turn both of thoughts and words is happy. The first six lines of the stanza seem majestical and severe: but the

---

Tassone and Boileau: Alessandro Tassoni (1565–1635), *La Secchia Rapita* (1622); Boileau, *Le Lutrin* (1674–83).
Coccajus: otherwise Teofilo Folengo (c. 1496–1554), *Poema Macaronicum de gestis . . . Baldi* (1517).
stanza of eight: i.e. 'ottava rima'.

two last turn them all into a pleasant ridicule. Boileau, if I am not much deceived, has modelled from hence his famous *Lutrin*. He had read the burlesque poetry of Scarron, with some kind of indignation, as witty as it was, and found nothing in France that was worthy of his imitation. But he copied the Italian so well, that his own may pass for an original. He writes it in the French heroic verse, and calls it an heroic poem. His subject is trivial, but his verse is noble. I doubt not but he had Virgil in his eye, for we find many admirable imitations of him, and some parodies; as particularly this passage in the fourth of the *Aeneids*.

> Nec tibi diva parens; generis nec Dardanus auctor,
> perfide; sed duris genuit te cautibus horrens
> Caucasus; Hyrcanaeque admorunt ubera tigres.

Which he thus translates, keeping to the words, but altering the sense.

> Non, ton père à Paris, ne fut point boulanger:
> Et tu n'es point du sang de Gervais horloger:
> Ta mere ne fut point la maitresse d'un coche:
> Caucase dans ses flancs, te forma d'une roche:
> Une tigresse affreuse, en quelque antre écarté
> Te fit, avec son laict, succer sa cruauté.

And, as Virgil in his fourth *Georgic* of the bees, perpetually raises the lowness of his subject by the loftiness of his words, and ennobles it by comparisons drawn from empires, and from monarchs;

> Admiranda tibi levium spectacula rerum,
> magnanimosque duces, totiusque ordine gentis
> mores et studia, et populos, et proelia dicam.

And again,

> Sed genus immortale manet; multosque per annos
> stat fortuna domus, et avi numerantur avorum.

We see Boileau pursuing him in the same flights, and scarcely yielding to his master. This, I think, my Lord, to be the most beautiful, and most noble kind of satire. Here is the majesty of the heroic, finely mixed with the venom of the other, and raising the delight which otherwise would be flat and vulgar, by the sublimity of the

---

Scarron: Paul Scarron (1610–60), *Typhon, ou la Gigantomachie* (1644) and *Vergile travesti* (1648–59). For Boileau's criticism of the burlesque style see *L'Art poétique*, i. 79 ff.

Nec tibi . . .: Aeneid, iv. 365–7.

Admiranda . . .: Georgics, iv. 3–5; 208–9 ('I shall tell you about the marvellous parade of minute things—great leaders, the nature, studies, tribes, and wars of an entire nation. . . . But the eternal race remains, the house's fortune endures for many a year, and the grandfathers of grandfathers are recorded').

expression. I could say somewhat more of the delicacy of this and some other of his satires; but it might turn to his prejudice, if 'twere carried back to France.

I have given your Lordship but this bare hint, in what verse, and in what manner this sort of satire may best be managed. Had I time, I could enlarge on the beautiful turns of words and thoughts, which are as requisite in this as in heroic poetry itself; of which this satire is undoubtedly a species. With these beautiful turns I confess myself to have been unacquainted, till about twenty years ago, in a conversation which I had with that noble wit of Scotland, Sir George Mackenzie. He asked me why I did not imitate in my verses the turns of Mr. Waller and Sir John Denham, of which, he repeated many to me. I had often read with pleasure, and with some profit, those two fathers of our English poetry; but had not seriously enough considered those beauties which give the last perfection to their works. Some sprinklings of this kind I had also formerly in my plays, but they were casual, and not designed. But this hint, thus seasonably given me, first made me sensible of my own wants, and brought me afterwards to seek for the supply of them in other English authors. I looked over the darling of my youth, the famous Cowley; there I found instead of them, the points of wit, and quirks of epigram, even in the *Davideis*, a heroic poem, which is of an opposite nature to those puerilities; but no elegant turns, either on the word, or on the thought. Then I consulted a greater genius (without offence to the Manes of that noble author) I mean Milton. But as he endeavours everywhere to express Homer, whose age had not arrived to that fineness, I found in him a true sublimity, lofty thoughts, which were clothed with admirable Grecisms, and ancient words, which he had been digging from the mines of Chaucer and of Spenser, and which, with all their rusticity, had somewhat of venerable in them. But I found not there neither that for which I looked. At last I had recourse to his master, Spenser, the author of that immortal poem, called *The Faerie Queene*; and there I met with that which I had been looking for so long in vain. Spenser had studied Virgil to as much advantage as Milton had done Homer; and amongst the rest of his excellencies had copied that. Looking farther into the Italian, I found Tasso had done the same; nay more, that all the sonnets in that language are on the turn of the first thought; which Mr. Walsh, in his late ingenious preface to his poems, has observed. In short, Virgil, and Ovid are the

Mackenzie: Sir George Mackenzie of Rosehaugh (1636–91), Lord Advocate, scholar, founder of the Advocates' Library (1682).

Mr. Walsh: Walsh says nothing of Italian 'turns' in the Preface to *Letters and Poems Amorous and Gallant*.

two principal fountains of them in Latin poetry. And the French at this day are so fond of them, that they judge them to be the first beauties. Delicate, and *bien tourné*, are the highest commendations which they bestow, on somewhat which they think a masterpiece.

An example of the turn on words amongst a thousand others is that, in the last book of Ovid's *Metamorphoses*.

> Heu quantum scelus est, in viscera, viscera condi!
> Congestoque avidum pinguescere corpore corpus;
> alteriusque animantem, animantis vivere leto.

An example of the turn both on thoughts and words, is to be found in Catullus, in the complaint of Ariadne, when she was left by Theseus.

> Tum jam nulla viro juranti foemina credat;
> nulla viri speret sermones esse fideles:
> qui dum aliquid cupiens animus praegestit apisci,
> nil metuunt jurare; nihil promittere parcunt.
> Sed simul ac cupidae mentis satiata libido est,
> dicta nihil metuere; nihil perjuria curant.

An extraordinary turn upon the words, is that in Ovid's *Epistolae Heroidum*, of Sappho to Phaon.

> Si nisi quae forma poterit te digna videri,
> nulla futura tua est; nulla futura tua est.

Lastly, a turn which I cannot say is absolute on words, for the thought turns with them, is in the fourth *Georgic* of Virgil; where Orpheus is to receive his wife from hell, on express condition not to look on her till she was come on earth.

> Cum subita incautum dementia cepit amantem;
> ignoscenda quidem, scirent si ignoscere Manes.

I will not burden your Lordship with more of them; for I write to a master, who understands them better than myself. But I may safely

---

Metamorphoses: xv. 88–90 ('Alas, how wicked it is to swallow flesh into our own greedy bodies by forcing in other bodies, to feed one live creature with another's death').

Catullus: lxiv. 143–8 ('No woman, then, believes a man's word, or expects that he will keep promises. Aching with desire and unaccomplished hopes, men swear without qualm and never spare promises. But just as soon as the heart's lust is satisfied, they have no fear of their words, and no care about breaking their promises').

Ovid: *Heroides*, xv. 39–40. ('If no one is to be yours unless you think her beauty worthy, no one, no one shall be yours').

Virgil: *Georgics*, iv. 488–9 ('When the rash lover was seized by sudden madness, a madness fit for pardoning, the Fates knew how to pardon').

conclude them to be great beauties. I might descend also to the mechanic beauties of heroic verse; but we have yet no English *Prosodia*, not so much as a tolerable dictionary, or a grammar; so that our language is in a manner barbarous; and what government will encourage any one, or more, who are capable of refining it, I know not. But nothing under a public expense can go through with it. And I rather fear a declination of the language, than hope an advancement of it in the present age.

I am still speaking to you, my Lord; though in all probability, you are already out of hearing. Nothing which my meanness can produce, is worthy of this long attention. But I am come to the last petition of Abraham; if there be ten righteous lines, in this vast preface, spare it for their sake; and also spare the next city, because it is but a little one.

I would excuse the performance of this translation, if it were all my own; but the better, though not the greater part being the work of some gentlemen who have succeeded very happily in their undertaking, let their excellencies atone for my imperfections, and those of my sons. I have perused some of the satires, which are done by other hands, and they seem to me as perfect in their kind, as anything I have seen in English verse. The common way which we have taken, is not a literal translation, but a kind of paraphrase; or somewhat which is yet more loose, betwixt a paraphrase and imitation. It was not possible for us, or any men, to have made it pleasant any other way. If rendering the exact sense of these authors, almost line for line, had been our business, Barten Holyday had done it already to our hands. And, by the help of his learned notes and illustrations, not only of Juvenal and Persius, but what yet is more obscure, his own verses might be understood.

But he wrote for fame, and wrote to scholars. We write only for the pleasure and entertainment of those gentlemen and ladies, who though they are not scholars, are not ignorant: persons of understanding and good sense, who not having been conversant in the original, or at least not having made Latin verse so much their business as to be critics in it, would be glad to find, if the wit of our two great authors be answerable to their fame and reputation in the world. We have therefore endeavoured to give the public all the satisfaction we are able in this kind.

And if we are not altogether so faithful to our author, as our predecessors Holyday and Stapylton, yet we may challenge to ourselves this praise, that we shall be far more pleasing to our readers. We have followed our authors at greater distance, though not step by step, as they have done. For oftentimes they have gone so close, that they have trod on the heels of Juvenal and Persius; and hurt them by their too near approach. A noble author would not be pursued too close by a translator. We lose his spirit, when we think to take his body. The grosser part remains with us, but the soul is flown away, in some noble expression or some delicate turn of words, or thought. Thus Holyday, who made this way his choice, seized the meaning of Juvenal; but the poetry has always scaped him.

They who will not grant me that pleasure is one of the ends of poetry, but that it is only a means of compassing the only end, which is instruction, must yet allow that without the means of pleasure the instruction is but a bare and dry philosophy: a crude preparation of morals, which we may have from Aristotle and Epictetus, with more profit than from any poet. Neither Holyday nor Stapylton, have imitated Juvenal, in the poetical part of him, his diction and his elocution. Nor had they been poets, as neither of them were, yet in the way they took, it was impossible for them to have succeeded in the poetic part.

The English verse, which we call heroic, consists of no more than ten syllables; the Latin hexameter sometimes rises to seventeen; as for example, this verse in Virgil,

> Pulverulenta putrem sonitu quatit ungula campum.

Here is the difference, of no less than seven syllables in a line, betwixt the English and the Latin. Now the medium of these is about fourteen syllables; because the dactyl is a more frequent foot in hexameters than the spondee.

But Holyday, without considering that he writ with the disadvantage of four syllables less in every verse, endeavours to make one of his lines to comprehend the sense of one of Juvenal's. According to the falsity of the proposition, was the success. He was forced to crowd his verse with ill-sounding monosyllables, of which our barbarous language affords him a wild plenty. And by that means he arrived at his pedantic end, which was to make a literal translation. His verses have nothing of verse in them, but only the worst part of it, the rhyme, and that, into the bargain, is far from good. But which is more intolerable, by cramming his ill-chosen and worse sounding monosyllables so close together, the very sense which he endeavours to explain, is become more obscure than that of his author. So that

---

Pulverulenta . . .: *Aeneid*, viii. 596: 'quadripedante . . .':

> The neighing coursers answer to the sound;
> And shake with horny hoofs the solid ground
> (Dryden, *Aeneis*, VIII. 789–90).

Holyday himself cannot be understood, without as large a commentary, as that which he makes on his two authors. For my own part, I can make a shift to find the meaning of Juvenal without his notes: but his translation is more difficult than his author. And I find beauties in the Latin to recompense my pains; but in Holyday and Stapylton, my ears, in the first place, are mortally offended; and then their sense is so perplexed, that I return to the original, as the more pleasing task, as well as the more easy.

This must be said for our translation, that if we give not the whole sense of Juvenal, yet we give the most considerable part of it. We give it, in general, so clearly, that few notes are sufficient to make us intelligible. We make our author at least appear in a poetic dress. We have actually made him more sounding, and more elegant, than he was before in English; and have endeavoured to make him speak that kind of English, which he would have spoken had he lived in England, and had written to this age. If sometimes any of us (and 'tis but seldom) make him express the customs and manners of our native country, rather than of Rome; 'tis, either when there was some kind of analogy betwixt their customs and ours; or when, to make him more easy to vulgar understandings, we gave him those manners which are familiar to us. But I defend not this innovation, 'tis enough If I can excuse it. For to speak sincerely, the manners of nations and ages are not to be confounded. We should either make them English, or leave them Roman. If this can neither be defended, nor excused, let it be pardoned, at least, because it is acknowledged; and so much the more easily, as being a fault which is never committed without some pleasure to the reader.

Thus, my Lord, having troubled you with a tedious visit, the best manners will be shown in the least ceremony. I will slip away while your back is turned, and while you are otherwise employed, with great confusion, for having entertained you so long with this discourse; and for having no other recompense to make you, than the worthy labours of my fellow undertakers in this work; and the thankful acknowledgments, prayers, and perpetual good wishes of,

> *MY LORD,*
> *Your Lordship's most obliged, most humble,*
> *and most obedient servant,*
>
> JOHN DRYDEN

Aug. 18 1692

TO THE RIGHT HONOURABLE HUGH
LORD CLIFFORD, BARON OF CHUDLEIGH[n]

PREFIXED TO THE PASTORALS IN
THE WORKS OF VERGIL . . . TRANSLATED
INTO ENGLISH VERSE

1697

MY LORD,

I HAVE found it not more difficult to translate Virgil, than to find such patrons as I desire for my translation. For though England is not wanting in a learned nobility, yet such are my unhappy circumstances, that they have confined me to a narrow choice. To the greater part, I have not the honour to be known; and to some of them I cannot show at present, by any public act, that grateful respect which I shall ever bear them in my heart. Yet I have no reason to complain of fortune, since in the midst of that abundance I could not possibly have chosen better than the worthy son of so illustrious a father. He was the patron of my manhood, when I flourished in the opinion of the world; though with small advantage to my fortune, till he awakened the remembrance of my royal master. He was that Pollio, or that Varus, who introduced me to Augustus: and though he soon dismissed himself from state affairs, yet in the short time of his administration he shone so powerfully upon me, that like the heat of a Russian summer, he ripened the fruits of poetry in a cold climate; and gave me wherewithal to subsist at least, in the long winter which succeeded. What I now offer to your Lordship, is the wretched remainder of a sickly age, worn out with study, and oppressed by fortune: without other support than the constancy and patience of a Christian. You, my Lord, are yet in the flower of your youth, and may live to enjoy the benefits of the peace which is promised Europe. I can only hear of that blessing: for years, and, above all things, want of health, have shut me out from sharing in the happiness. The poets, who condemn their Tantalus to hell, had added to his torments, if they had placed him in Elysium, which is the proper emblem of my condition. The fruit and the water may reach my lips, but cannot enter; and if they could, yet I want a palate as well as a digestion. But it is some kind of pleasure to me, to please those whom I respect. And I am not altogether out of hope, that these pastorals of Virgil may give your Lordship some delight, though made English by one,

---

Varus: C. Asinius Pollio was patron to Virgil and Horace. The former dedicated his fourth eclogue to Pollio and his sixth to the general Alfenus Varus.

who scarce remembers that passion which inspired my author when
he wrote them. These were his first essay in poetry (if the Ciris was
not his) and it was more excusable in him to describe love when he
was young, than for me to translate him when I am old. He died at
the age of fifty-two, and I began this work in my great climacteric.
But having perhaps a better constitution than my author, I have
wronged him less, considering my circumstances, than those who
have attempted him before, either in our own, or any modern language. And though this version is not void of errors, yet it comforts
me that the faults of others are not worth finding. Mine are neither
gross nor frequent in those *Eclogues*, wherein my master has raised
himself above that humble style in which pastoral delights, and which
I must confess is proper to the education and converse of shepherds:
for he found the strength of his genius betimes, and was even in his
youth preluding to his *Georgics*, and his *Aeneis*. He could not forbear
to try his wings, though his pinions were not hardened to maintain a
long laborious flight. Yet sometimes they bore him to a pitch as lofty
as ever he was able to reach afterwards. But when he was admonished
by his subject to descend, he came down gently circling in the air, and
singing to the ground. Like a lark, melodious in her mounting, and
continuing her song till she alights: still preparing for a higher flight
at her next sally, and tuning her voice to better music. The fourth, the
sixth, and the eighth *Pastorals*, are clear evidences of this truth. In the
three first he contains himself within his bounds; but addressing to
Pollio, his great patron, and himself no vulgar poet, he no longer
could restrain the freedom of his spirit, but began to assert his native
character, which is sublimity, putting himself under the conduct of
the same Cumaean Sybil, whom afterwards he gave for a guide to his
Aeneas. 'Tis true he was sensible of his own boldness; and we know
it by the *paulo majora*, which begins his fourth *Eclogue*. He remembered, like young Manlius, that he was forbidden to engage; but
what avails an express command to a youthful courage, which pre-
sages victory in the attempt? Encouraged with success, he proceeds
farther in the sixth, and invades the province of philosophy. And
notwithstanding that Phoebus had forewarned him of singing wars,
as he there confesses, yet he presumed that the search of nature was
as free to him as to Lucretius, who at his age explained it according

Ciris: its authenticity remains unsettled.
climacteric: i.e. at 63 years.
Aeneas: *Aeneid*, iii. 44 f.
paulo majora: 'a little loftier'.
Manlius: this Manlius was killed by his dictator-father, Manlius Torquatus, for
    challenging and killing an enemy without seeking his prior permission.

to the principles of Epicurus. In his eighth *Eclogue*, he has innovated nothing; the former part of it being the complaint and despair of a forsaken lover: the latter, a charm of an enchantress, to renew a lost affection. But the complaint perhaps contains some topics which are above the condition of his persons; and our author seems to have made his herdsmen somewhat too learned for their profession. The charms are also of the same nature, but both were copied from Theocritus, and had received the applause of former ages in their original. There is a kind of rusticity in all those pompous verses; somewhat of a holiday shepherd strutting in his country buskins. The like may be observed, both in the Pollio, and the Silenus; where the similitudes are drawn from the woods and meadows. They seem to me to represent our poet betwixt a farmer, and a courtier, when he left Mantua for Rome, and dressed himself in his best habit to appear before his patron, somewhat too fine for the place from whence he came, and yet retaining part of its simplicity. In the ninth *Pastoral* he collects some beautiful passages which were scattered in Theocritus, which he could not insert into any of his former *Eclogues*, and yet was unwilling they should be lost. In all the rest he is equal to his Sicilian master, and observes like him a just decorum, both of the subject, and the persons; as particularly in the third *Pastoral*, where one of his shepherds describes a bowl, or mazer, curiously carved.

> In medio duo signa: Conon, et quis fuit alter,
> descripsit radio, totum qui gentibus orbem.

He remembers only the name of Conon, and forgets the other on set purpose (whether he means Anaximander or Eudoxus I dispute not), but he was certainly forgotten to show his country swain was no great scholar.

After all, I must confess that the boorish dialect of Theocritus has a secret charm in it, which the Roman language cannot imitate, though Virgil has drawn it down as low as possibly he could; as in the *cujum pecus*, and some other words, for which he was so unjustly blamed by the bad critics of his age, who could not see the beauties of that *merum rus*, which the poet described in those expressions. But Theocritus may justly be preferred as the original, without injury to

---

Pollio . . . Silenus: *Eclogues*, iv, vi respectively.

mazer: see *Eclogues*, iii. 36 f.

In medio . . .: ibid. 40–1 ('There are two figures in between: Conon is one, and who was the other who mapped out the whole sphere for mankind?').

Theocritus: cf. Preface to *Sylvae*, p. 203 above.

cujum pecus: *Eclogues*, iii. i ('Whose flock?').

merum rus: i.e. mere countryside.

Virgil, who modestly contents himself with the second place, and
glories only in being the first who transplanted pastoral into his own
country; and brought it there to bear as happily as the cherry trees
which Lucullus brought from Pontus.

Our own nation has produced a third poet in this kind, not inferior to the two former. For the *Shepherds Calendar* of Spenser is
not to be matched in any modern language; not even by Tasso's
Amynta, which infinitely transcends Guarini's *Pastor Fido*, as having
more of nature in it, and being almost wholly clear from the wretched
affectation of learning. I will say nothing of the *Piscatory Eclogues*,
because no modern Latin can bear criticism. 'Tis no wonder that
rolling down through so many barbarous ages, from the spring of
Virgil, it bears along with it the filth and ordures of the Goths and
Vandals. Neither will I mention Monsieur Fontinelle, the living
glory of the French. 'Tis enough for him to have excelled his master
Lucian, without attempting to compare our miserable age with that
of Virgil, or Theocritus. Let me only add, for his reputation,

> —Si Pergama dextra
> Defendi possint, etiam hac defensa fuissent.

But Spenser being master of our northern dialect, and skilled in
Chaucer's English, has so exactly imitated the Doric of Theocritus,
that his love is a perfect image of that passion which God infused into
both sexes, before it was corrupted with the knowledge of arts, and
the ceremonies of what we call good manners.

My Lord, I know to whom I dedicate; and could not have been
induced by any motive to put this part of Virgil, or any other, into
unlearned hands. You have read him with pleasure, and, I dare say,
with admiration in the Latin, of which you are a master. You have
added to your natural endowments, which without flattery are
eminent, the superstructures of study, and the knowledge of good
authors. Courage, probity, and humanity are inherent in you. These
virtues have even been habitual to the ancient house of Cumberland,
from whence you are descended, and of which our chronicles make

---

Lucullus: Pliny (*Nat. Hist.* xv. 30) says that Lucullus brought the cherry to Italy
after he defeated Mithridates in 63 B.C.
Shepherds Calendar: for Dryden's earlier opinion see p. 204 above.
Piscatory Eclogues: (1526), by Jacopo Sannazaro (*c.* 1455–1530).
Monsieur Fontinelle: Bernard le Bovier de Fontenelle (1657–1757) attacked
   Theocritus and Virgil in his *Discours sur l'Églogue*.
Si Pergama . . .: *Aeneid* ii. 291–2:

> If by a mortal hand my father's throne
> Could be defended, 'twas by mine alone
>   (Dryden, *Aeneis*, II, 387–8).

so honourable mention in the long wars betwixt the rival families of York and Lancaster. Your forefathers have asserted the party which they chose till death, and died for its defence in the fields of battle. You have besides the fresh remembrance of your noble father, from whom you never can degenerate.

> —Nec imbellem, feroces
> progenerant aquilae columbam.

It being almost morally impossible for you to be other than you are by kind, I need neither praise nor incite your virtue. You are acquainted with the Roman history, and know without my information that patronage and clientship always descended from the fathers to the sons; and that the same plebeian houses, had recourse to the same patrician line, which had formerly protected them, and followed their principles and fortunes to the last. So that I am your Lordship's by descent, and part of your inheritance. And the natural inclination which I have to serve you, adds to your paternal right, for I was wholly yours from the first moment, when I had the happiness and honour of being known to you. Be pleased therefore to accept the rudiments of Virgil's poetry, coarsely translated I confess, but which yet retains some beauties of the author, which neither the barbarity of our language, nor my unskilfulness could so much sully, but that they appear sometimes in the dim mirror which I hold before you. The subject is not unsuitable to your youth, which allows you yet to love, and is proper to your present scene of life. Rural recreations abroad, and books at home, are the innocent pleasures of a man who is early wise; and gives fortune no more hold of him, than of necessity he must. 'Tis good on some occasions to think beforehand as little as we can; to enjoy as much of the present as will not endanger our futurity; and to provide ourselves of the virtuoso's saddle, which will be sure to amble, when the world is upon the hardest trot. What I humbly offer to your Lordship, is of this nature. I wish it pleasant, and am sure 'tis innocent. May you ever continue your esteem for Virgil; and not lessen it, for the faults of his translator, who is with all manner of respect, and sense of gratitude,

> *MY LORD,*
> *Your Lordship's most humble, and most*
> *obedient servant,*
>
> JOHN DRYDEN

Nec imbellem . . .: Horace, *Odes*, IV. iv. 31–2 ('nor do fierce eagles beget the timid dove').

PREFACE TO *FABLES, ANCIENT AND MODERN*

1700

Translated into Verse from Horace, Ovid, Boccace, and Chaucer

'TIS with a poet, as with a man who designs to build, and is very exact, as he supposes, in casting up the cost beforehand. But, generally speaking, he is mistaken in his account, and reckons short of the expense he first intended. He alters his mind as the work proceeds, and will have this or that convenience more, of which he had not thought when he began. So has it happened to me; I have built a house, where I intended but a lodge. Yet with better success than a certain nobleman, who beginning with a dog kennel, never lived to finish the palace he had contrived.

From translating the first of Homer's *Iliads*, (which I intended as an essay to the whole work) I proceeded to the translation of the twelfth book of Ovid's *Metamorphoses*, because it contains, among other things, the causes, the beginning, and ending, of the Trojan War. Here I ought in reason to have stopped; but the speeches of Ajax and Ulysses lying next in my way, I could not balk 'em. When I had compassed them, I was so taken with the former part of the fifteenth book, (which is the masterpiece of the whole *Metamorphoses*) that I enjoined myself the pleasing task of rendering it into English. And now I found, by the number of my verses, that they began to swell into a little volume; which gave me an occasion of looking backward on some beauties of my author, in his former books. There occurred to me the hunting of the boar, Cinyras and Myrrha, the good-natured story of Baucis and Philemon, with the rest, which I hope I have translated closely enough, and given them the same turn of verse, which they had in the original; and this, I may say without vanity, is not the talent of every poet. He who has arrived the nearest to it is the ingenious and learned Sandys, the best versifier of the former age, if I may properly call it by that name, which was the former part of this concluding century. For Spenser and Fairfax both flourished in the reign of Queen Elizabeth: great masters in our language, and who saw much farther into the beauties of our numbers, than those who immediately followed them. Milton was the poetical son of Spenser, and Mr. Waller of Fairfax; for we have our lineal descents and clans, as well as other families. Spenser

---

a certain nobleman: probably George Villiers, 2nd Duke of Buckingham (1628–87).
speeches . . . Ulysses: *Metamorphoses*, xiii.
hunting . . . Baucis and Philemon: ibid., viii, x, viii.
Sandys: see 'Of Dramatic Poesy', p. 70 above, and footnote.

more than once insinuates, that the soul of Chaucer was transfused
into his body; and that he was begotten by him two hundred years
after his decease. Milton has acknowledged to me, that Spenser was
his original; and many besides myself have heard our famous Waller
own, that he derived the harmony of his numbers from the *Godfrey of
Bulloigne*, which was turned into English by Mr. Fairfax. But to
return, having done with Ovid for this time, it came into my mind,
that our old English poet Chaucer in many things resembled him,
and that with no disadvantage on the side of the modern author, as I
shall endeavour to prove when I compare them. And as I am, and
always have been studious to promote the honour of my native
country, so I soon resolved to put their merits to the trial, by turning
some of the *Canterbury Tales* into our language, as it is now refined.
For by this means both the poets being set in the same light, and
dressed in the same English habit, story to be compared with story, a
certain judgment may be made betwixt them by the reader, without
obtruding my opinion on him. Or if I seem partial to my countryman,
and predecessor in the laurel, the friends of antiquity are not few;
and besides many of the learned, Ovid has almost all the *beaux*, and
the whole fair sex, his declared patrons. Perhaps I have assumed
somewhat more to myself than they allow me; because I have
adventured to sum up the evidence. But the readers are the jury; and
their privilege remains entire to decide according to the merits of the
cause. Or, if they please to bring it to another hearing, before some
other court. In the mean time, to follow the thread of my discourse
(as thoughts, according to Mr. Hobbes, have always some connexion), so from Chaucer I was led to think on Boccaccio, who was
not only his contemporary, but also pursued the same studies; wrote
novels in prose, and many works in verse; particularly is said to have
invented the octave rhyme, or stanza of eight lines, which ever since
has been maintained by the practice of all Italian writers, who are,
or at least assume the title of heroic poets. He and Chaucer, among
other things, had this in common, that they refined their mother-
tongues; but with this difference, that Dante had begun to file their
language, at least in verse, before the time of Boccaccio, who likewise
received no little help from his master Petrarch. But the reformation
of their prose was wholly owing to Boccaccio himself; who is yet the

soul of Chaucer: *Faerie Queene*, IV. ii. 32–4.
Mr. Fairfax: Edward Fairfax (?1580–1635); his translation of Tasso's *Godfrey of
    Bulloigne* was published in 1600.
Mr. Hobbes: *Leviathan* (1651), I. iii, 'By Consequence, or train of thoughts' etc.
octave rhyme: *Ottava rima* was not invented by Boccaccio but he established it in
    Italian.
11+s.c.

standard of purity in the Italian tongue; though many of his phrases are become obsolete, as in process of time it must needs happen. Chaucer (as you have formerly been told by our learned Mr. Rymer) first adorned and amplified our barren tongue from the Provençal, which was then the most polished of all the modern languages. But this subject has been copiously treated by that great critic, who deserves no little commendation from us his countrymen. For these reasons of time, and resemblance of genius, in Chaucer and Boccaccio, I resolved to join them in my present work; to which I have added some original papers of my own; which whether they are equal or inferior to my other poems, an author is the most improper judge; and therefore I leave them wholly to the mercy of the reader. I will hope the best, that they will not be condemned; but if they should, I have the excuse of an old gentleman, who mounting on horseback before some ladies, when I was present, got up somewhat heavily, but desired of the fair spectators, that they would count fourscore and eight before they judged him. By the mercy of God, I am already come within twenty years of his number, a cripple in my limbs, but what decays are in my mind, the reader must determine. I think myself as vigorous as ever in the faculties of my soul, excepting only my memory, which is not impaired to any great degree; and if I lose not more of it, I have no great reason to complain. What judgement I had, increases rather than diminishes; and thoughts, such as they are, come crowding in so fast upon me, that my only difficulty is to choose or to reject; to run them into verse, or to give them the other harmony of prose. I have so long studied and practised both, that they are grown into a habit, and become familiar to me. In short, though I may lawfully plead some part of the old gentleman's excuse, yet I will reserve it till I think I have greater need, and ask no grains of allowance for the faults of this my present work, but those which are given of course to human frailty. I will not trouble my reader with the shortness of time in which I writ it; or the several intervals of sickness. They who think too well of their own performances, are apt to boast in their prefaces how little time their works have cost them, and what other business of more importance interfered. But the reader will be as apt to ask the question, why they allowed not a longer time to make their works more perfect? and why they had so despicable an opinion of their judges, as to thrust their indigested stuff upon them, as if they deserved no better?

With this account of my present undertaking, I conclude the first part of this discourse: in the second part, as at a second sitting, though I alter not the draft, I must touch the same features over

Mr. Rymer: in *A Short View of Tragedy*, Ch. vi (Zimansky, pp. 126–7).

again, and change the dead-colouring of the whole. In general I will only say that I have written nothing which savours of immorality or profaneness; at least, I am not conscious to myself of any such intention. If there happen to be found an irreverent expression, or a thought too wanton, they are crept into my verses through my inadvertency. If the searchers find any in the cargo, let them be staved or forfeited, like contrabanded goods; at least, let their authors be answerable for them, as being but imported merchandise, and not of my own manufacture. On the other side, I have endeavoured to choose such fables, both ancient and modern, as contain in each of them some instructive moral, which I could prove by induction, but the way is tedious; and they leap foremost into sight, without the reader's trouble of looking after them. I wish I could affirm with a safe conscience, that I had taken the same care in all my former writings; for it must be owned, that supposing verses are never so beautiful or pleasing, yet if they contain anything which shocks religion, or good manners, they are at best, what Horace says of good numbers without good sense, *versus inopes rerum, nugaeque canorae.* Thus far, I hope, I am right in court, without renouncing to my other right of self-defence, where I have been wrongfully accused, and my sense wire-drawn into blasphemy or bawdry, as it has often been by a religious lawyer, in a late pleading against the stage; in which he mixes truth with falsehood, and has not forgotten the old rule of calumniating strongly, that something may remain.

I resume the thread of my discourse with the first of my translations, which was the first *Iliad* of Homer. If it shall please God to give me longer life, and moderate health, my intentions are to translate the whole *Iliad*; provided still, that I meet with those encouragements from the public, which may enable me to proceed in my undertaking with some cheerfulness. And this I dare assure the world beforehand, that I have found by trial Homer a more pleasing task than Virgil, (though I say not the translation will be less laborious.) For the Grecian is more according to my genius, than the Latin poet. In the works of the two authors we may read their manners, and natural inclinations, which are wholly different. Virgil was of a quiet, sedate temper; Homer was violent, impetuous, and full of fire.

---

dead-colouring: a preparatory layer of colour.
staved: crushed inwards.
Horace: *Ars Poetica*, l. 322 ('verses which while pleasing lack substance').
religious lawyer: Jeremy Collier (1650–1726) was a lecturer at Gray's Inn who attacked contemporary drama in his *Short View of the Immorality, and Profaneness of the English Stage* (1698).

The chief talent of Virgil was propriety of thoughts, and ornament of words: Homer was rapid in his thoughts, and took all the liberties both of numbers, and of expressions, which his language and the age in which he lived allowed him. Homer's invention was more copious, Virgil's more confined; so that if Homer had not led the way, it was not in Virgil to have begun heroic poetry. For, nothing can be more evident, than that the Roman poem is but the second part of the *Iliad*; a continuation of the same story; and the persons already formed. The manners of Aeneas, are those of Hector super-added to those which Homer gave him. The adventures of Ulysses in the *Odyssey*, are imitated in the first six books of Virgil's *Aeneid*. And though the accidents are not the same (which would have argued him of a servile, copying, and total barrenness of invention) yet the seas were the same, in which both the heroes wandered; and Dido cannot be denied to be the poetical daughter of Calypso. The six latter books of Virgil's poem, are the four and twenty *Iliads* con-tracted: a quarrel occasioned by a lady, a single combat, battles fought, and a town besieged. I say not this in derogation to Virgil, neither do I contradict anything which I have formerly said in his just praise; for his episodes are almost wholly of his own invention; and the form which he has given to the telling makes the tale his own, even though the original story had been the same. But this proves, however, that Homer taught Virgil to design: and if invention be the first virtue of an epic poet, then the Latin poem can only be allowed the second place. Mr. Hobbes, in the preface to his own bald transla-tion of the *Iliad*, (studying poetry as he did mathematics, when it was too late) Mr. Hobbes, I say, begins the praise of Homer where he should have ended it. He tells us that the first beauty of an epic poem consists in diction, that is, in the choice of words, and harmony of numbers. Now, the words are the colouring of the work, which in the order of nature is last to be considered. The design, the disposi-tion, the manners, and the thoughts, are all before it; where any of those are wanting or imperfect, so much wants or is imperfect in the imitation of human life; which is in the very definition of a poem. Words indeed, like glaring colours, are the first beauties that arise, and strike the sight; but if the draft be false or lame, the figures ill disposed, the manners obscure or inconsistent, or the thoughts un-natural, then the finest colours are but daubing, and the piece is a beautiful monster at the best. Neither Virgil nor Homer were de-ficient in any of the former beauties; but in this last, which is

Mr. Hobbes: Hobbes translated Homer into quatrains (whole version 1677), with Preface 'Concerning the Virtues of an Heroic Poem'.

expression, the Roman poet is at least equal to the Grecian, as I have said elsewhere; supplying the poverty of his language, by his musical ear, and by his diligence. But to return: our two great poets, being so different in their tempers, one choleric and sanguine, the other phlegmatic and melancholic; that which makes them excel in their several ways, is, that each of them has followed his own natural inclination, as well in forming the design, as in the execution of it. The very heroes show their authors: Achilles is hot, impatient, revengeful, *impiger, iracundus, inexorabilis, acer,* etc., Aeneas patient, considerate, careful of his people, and merciful to his enemies; ever submissive to the will of heaven, *quo fata trahunt retrahuntque, sequamur.* I could please myself with enlarging on this subject, but am forced to defer it to a fitter time. From all I have said, I will only draw this inference, that the action of Homer being more full of vigour than that of Virgil, according to the temper of the writer, is of consequence more pleasing to the reader. One warms you by degrees; the other sets you on fire all at once, and never intermits his heat. 'Tis the same difference which Longinus makes betwixt the effects of eloquence in Demosthenes, and Tully. One persuades; the other commands. You never cool while you read Homer, even not in the second book, (a graceful flattery to his countrymen;) but he hastens from the ships, and concludes not that book till he has made you an amends by the violent playing of a new machine. From thence he hurries on his action with variety of events, and ends it in less compass than two months. This vehemence of his, I confess, is more suitable to my temper: and therefore I have translated his first book with greater pleasure than any part of Virgil. But it was not a pleasure without pains. The continual agitations of the spirits must needs be a weakening of any constitution, especially in age: and many pauses are required for refreshment betwixt the heats, the *Iliad* of itself being a third part longer than all Virgil's works together.

This is what I thought needful in this place to say of Homer. I proceed to Ovid, and Chaucer; considering the former only in relation to the latter. With Ovid ended the golden age of the Roman tongue: from Chaucer the purity of the English tongue began. The manners of the poets were not unlike: both of them were well-bred, well-natured, amorous, and libertine, at least in their writings, it may be also in their lives. Their studies were the same, philosophy, and philology. Both of them were knowing in astronomy, of which Ovid's

impiger, ...: Horace, *Ars Poetica*, l. 121.
quo fata ...: *Aeneid*, v. 709 ('Wherever the Fates urge us, let us follow').
Longinus: *On the Sublime*, xii. 4–5.

books of the Roman feasts, and Chaucer's treatise of the Astrolabe, are sufficient witnesses. But Chaucer was likewise an astrologer, as were Virgil, Horace, Persius, and Manilius. Both writ with wonderful facility and clearness; neither were great inventors. For Ovid only copied the Grecian fables; and most of Chaucer's stories were taken from his Italian contemporaries, or their predecessors: Boccaccio's *Decameron* was first published, and from thence our Englishman has borrowed many of his *Canterbury Tales*. Yet that of Palamon and Arcite was written in all probability by some Italian wit, in a former age, as I shall prove hereafter. The tale of Griselda was the invention of Petrarch; by him sent to Boccaccio; from whom it came to Chaucer: *Troilus and Cressida* was also written by a Lombard author, but much amplified by our English translator, as well as beautified; the genius of our countrymen in general being rather to improve an invention, than to invent themselves; as is evident not only in our poetry, but in many of our manufactures. I find I have anticipated already, and taken up from Boccaccio before I come to him. But there is so much less behind; and I am of the temper of most kings, who love to be in debt, are all for present money, no matter how they pay it afterwards. Besides, the nature of a preface is rambling; never wholly out of the way, nor in it. This I have learned from the practice of honest Montaigne, and return at my pleasure to Ovid and Chaucer, of whom I have little more to say. Both of them built on the inventions of other men; yet since Chaucer had something of his own, as *The Wife of Bath's Tale, The Cock and the Fox,* which I have translated, and some others, I may justly give our countryman the precedence in that part, since I can remember nothing of Ovid which was wholly his. Both of them understood the manners, under which name I comprehend the passions and, in a larger sense, the descriptions of persons and their very habits. For an example, I see Baucis and Philemon as perfectly before me, as if some ancient painter had drawn them; and all the pilgrims in the *Canterbury Tales*, their humours, their features, and the very dress, as distinctly as if I had supped with them at the Tabard in Southwark. Yet even there too the figures of Chaucer are much more lively, and set in

Palamon and Arcite: in fact *The Knight's Tale* is based on Boccaccio's *Teseide*.

Griselda: Petrarch translated Griselda's story from *Decamerone*, x. 10 into Latin and it is Petrarch's Latin which is the source of *The Clerk's Tale*.

Lombard author: Dryden does not know that Chaucer's source is Boccaccio's *Filostrato*.

The Wife of Bath's Tale: although a source for this tale is not known the *motif* is common and no invention of Chaucer's.

The Cock and the Fox: based on a number of French sources.

a better light, which though I have not time to prove, yet I appeal to
the reader, and am sure he will clear me from partiality. The thoughts
and words remain to be considered, in the comparison of the two
poets; and I have saved myself one half of that labour by owning that
Ovid lived when the Roman tongue was in its meridian, Chaucer, in
the dawning of our language. Therefore that part of the comparison
stands not on an equal foot, any more than the diction of Ennius and
Ovid, or of Chaucer and our present English. The words are given
up as a post not to be defended in our poet, because he wanted the
modern art of fortifying. The thoughts remain to be considered, and
they are to be measured only by their propriety; that is, as they flow
more or less naturally from the persons described, on such and such
occasions. The vulgar judges, which are nine parts in ten of all
nations, who call conceits and jingles wit, who see Ovid full of them,
and Chaucer altogether without them, will think me little less than
mad for preferring the Englishman to the Roman. Yet, with their
leave, I must presume to say, that the things they admire are only
glittering trifles, and so far from being witty, that in a serious poem
they are nauseous, because they are unnatural. Would any man who
is ready to die for love describe his passion like Narcissus? Would
he think of *inopem me copia fecit*, and a dozen more of such expressions, poured on the neck of one another, and signifying all the
same thing? If this were wit, was this a time to be witty, when the
poor wretch was in the agony of death? This is just John Littlewit in
Bartholomew Fair, who had a conceit (as he tells you) left him in his
misery, a miserable conceit. On these occasions the poet should
endeavour to raise pity. But instead of this, Ovid is tickling you to
laugh. Virgil never made use of such machines, when he was moving
you to commiserate the death of Dido. He would not destroy what he
was building. Chaucer makes Arcite violent in his love, and unjust in
the pursuit of it. Yet when he came to die, he made him think more
reasonably; he repents not of his love, for that had altered his
character, but acknowledges the injustice of his proceedings, and
resigns Emilia to Palamon. What would Ovid have done on this
occasion? He would certainly have made Arcite witty on his death-
bed. He had complained he was farther off from possession, by being
so near, and a thousand such boyisms, which Chaucer rejected as
below the dignity of the subject. They who think otherwise, would by
the same reason prefer Lucan and Ovid to Homer and Virgil, and
Martial to all four of them. As for the turn of words, in which Ovid

inopem me . . .: Ovid, *Metamorphoses*, iii. 466 ('my riches make me poor').
a miserable conceit: I. i.

particularly excels all poets, they are sometimes a fault, and sometimes a beauty, as they are used properly or improperly; but in strong passions always to be shunned, because passions are serious, and will admit no playing. The French have a high value for them, and I confess, they are often what they call delicate, when they are introduced with judgement; but Chaucer writ with more simplicity, and followed nature more closely, than to use them. I have thus far, to the best of my knowledge, been an upright judge betwixt the parties in competition, not meddling with the design nor the disposition of it; because the design was not their own, and in the disposing of it they were equal. It remains that I say somewhat of Chaucer in particular.

In the first place, as he is the Father of English poetry, so I hold him in the same degree of veneration as the Grecians held Homer, or the Romans Virgil. He is a perpetual fountain of good sense; learned in all sciences; and therefore speaks properly on all subjects. As he knew what to say, so he knows also when to leave off; a continence which is practised by few writers, and scarcely by any of the Ancients, excepting Virgil and Horace. One of our late great poets is sunk in his reputation, because he could never forgive any conceit which came in his way; but swept like a dragnet, great and small. There was plenty enough, but the dishes were ill sorted; whole pyramids of sweetmeats, for boys and women, but little of solid meat for men; all this proceeded not from any want of knowledge, but of judgement; neither did he want that in discerning the beauties and faults of other poets; but only indulged himself in the luxury of writing; and perhaps knew it was a fault, but hoped the reader would not find it. For this reason, though he must always be thought a great poet, he is no longer esteemed a good writer. And for ten impressions, which his works have had in so many successive years, yet at present a hundred books are scarcely purchased once a twelvemonth; for, as my last Lord Rochester said, though somewhat profanely, not being of God, he could not stand.

Chaucer followed nature everywhere; but was never so bold to go beyond her. And there is a great difference of being *poeta* and *nimis poeta*, if we may believe Catullus, as much as betwixt a modest behaviour and affectation. The verse of Chaucer, I confess, is not harmonious to us; but 'tis like the eloquence of one whom Tacitus

---

our late great poets: Cowley.

Catullus: in fact Martial, *Epigrams*, iii. 44.

Tacitus: *Orat.* xxi ('auribus iudicum accommodata': 'suited to the ears of another age').

commends, it was *auribus istius temporis accommodata*; they who
lived with him, and some time after him, thought it musical; and it
continues so even in our judgement, if compared with the numbers
of Lydgate and Gower his contemporaries. There is the rude sweetness of a Scotch tune in it, which is natural and pleasing, though not
perfect. 'Tis true, I cannot go so far as he who published the last
edition of him; for he would make us believe the fault is in our ears,
and that there were really ten syllables in a verse where we find but
nine. But this opinion is not worth confuting; 'tis so gross and
obvious an error, that common sense (which is a rule in everything
but matters of faith and revelation) must convince the reader that
equality of numbers in every verse which we call heroic, was either
not known, or not always practised in Chaucer's age. It were an easy
matter to produce some thousands of his verses, which are lame for
want of half a foot, and sometimes a whole one, and which no pronunciation can make otherwise. We can only say that he lived in the
infancy of our poetry, and that nothing is brought to perfection at the
first. We must be children before we grow men. There was an Ennius,
and in process of time a Lucilius, and a Lucretius, before Virgil and
Horace; even after Chaucer there was a Spenser, a Harington, a
Fairfax, before Waller and Denham were in being. And our numbers
were in their nonage till these last appeared. I need say little of his
parentage, life, and fortunes. They are to be found at large in all the
editions of his works. He was employed abroad, and favoured by
Edward the Third, Richard the Second, and Henry the Fourth, and
was poet, as I suppose, to all three of them. In Richard's time, I
doubt, he was a little dipped in the Rebellion of the Commons; and
being brother-in-law to John of Gaunt, it was no wonder if he followed the fortunes of that family; and was well with Henry the
Fourth when he had deposed his predecessor. Neither is it to be
admired, that Henry, who was a wise as well as a valiant prince, who
claimed by succession, and was sensible that his title was not sound,
but was rightfully in Mortimer, who had married the heir of York; it
was not to be admired, I say, if that great politician should be pleased
to have the greatest wit of those times in his interests, and to be the

---

last edition: Thomas Speght's second edition of Chaucer (1602) contains a note
   which states that, contrary to common contemporary belief, Chaucer's lines
   are consistently scannable.

Rebellion of the Commons: Dryden follows Speght, who, thinking Usk's *Testament of Love* to be Chaucer's, assumed that Chaucer had had political difficulties in Richard II's reign.

brother-in-law to John of Gaunt: Speght again: the identity of Chaucer's wife is in
   fact obscure.

11*

trumpet of his praises. Augustus had given him the example, by the advice of Maecenas, who recommended Virgil and Horace to him, whose praises helped to make him popular while he was alive, and after his death have made him precious to posterity. As for the religion of our poet, he seems to have some little bias towards the opinions of Wyclif, after John of Gaunt his patron; somewhat of which appears in the tale of *Piers Plowman*. Yet I cannot blame him for inveighing so sharply against the vices of the clergy in his age. Their pride, their ambition, their pomp, their avarice, their worldly interest, deserved the lashes which he gave them, both in that, and in most of his *Canterbury Tales*. Neither has his contemporary Boccaccio spared them. Yet both those poets lived in much esteem with good and holy men in orders. For the scandal which is given by particular priests, reflects not on the sacred function. Chaucer's Monk, his Canon, and his Friar, took not from the character of his Good Parson. A satirical poet is the check of the laymen on bad priests. We are only to take care that we involve not the innocent with the guilty in the same condemnation. The good cannot be too much honoured, nor the bad too coarsely used; for the corruption of the best, becomes the worst. When a clergyman is whipped, his gown is first taken off, by which the dignity of his order is secured. If he be wrongfully accused, he has his action of slander; and 'tis at the poet's peril, if he transgress the law. But they will tell us, that all kind of satire, though never so well deserved by particular priests, yet brings the whole order into contempt. Is then the Peerage of England anything dishonoured, when a peer suffers for his treason? If he be libelled, or any way defamed, he has his *Scandalum Magnatum* to punish the offender. They who use this kind of argument seem to be conscious to themselves of somewhat which has deserved the poet's lash; and are less concerned for their public capacity, than for their private. At least, there is pride at the bottom of their reasoning. If the faults of men in orders are only to be judged among themselves, they are all in some sort parties. For, since they say the honour of their order is concerned in every member of it, how can we be sure, that they will be impartial judges? How far I may be allowed to speak my opinion in this case, I know not; but I am sure a dispute of this nature caused mischief in abundance betwixt a king of England and an Archbishop of Canterbury, one standing up for the laws of his land, and the other for the honour (as he called it) of God's Church, which ended in the murder of the prelate, and in the whipping of his

---

Piers Plowman: This anonymous poem was considered Chaucer's until Tyrwhitt's edition of 1775.

Archbishop of Canterbury: the reference is to Becket and Henry II.

Majesty from post to pillar for his penance. The learned and ingenious Dr. Drake has saved me the labour of inquiring into the
esteem and reverence which the priests have had of old; and I would
rather extend than diminish any part of it. Yet I must needs say, that
when a priest provokes me without any occasion given him, I have no
reason, unless it be the charity of a Christian, to forgive him. *Prior
laesit* is justification sufficient in the civil law. If I answer him in his
own language, self-defence, I am sure, must be allowed me; and if I
carry it farther, even to a sharp recrimination, somewhat may be
indulged to human frailty. Yet my resentment has not wrought so far,
but that I have followed Chaucer in his character of a holy man, and
have enlarged on that subject with some pleasure, reserving to myself
the right, if I shall think fit hereafter, to describe another sort of
priests, such as are more easily to be found than the Good Parson,
such as have given the last blow to Christianity in this age, by a practice so contrary to their doctrine. But this will keep cold till another
time. In the meanwhile, I take up Chaucer where I left him. He must
have been a man of a most wonderful comprehensive nature, because,
as it has been truly observed of him, he has taken into the compass of
his *Canterbury Tales* the various manners and humours (as we now
call them) of the whole English nation in his age. Not a single
character has escaped him. All his pilgrims are severally distinguished
from each other; and not only in their inclinations, but in their very
physiognomies and persons. Baptista Porta could not have described
their natures better than by the marks which the poet gives them. The
matter and manner of their tales, and of their telling, are so suited
to their different educations, humours, and callings, that each of them
would be improper in any other mouth. Even the grave and serious
characters are distinguished by their several sorts of gravity. Their
discourses are such as belong to their age, their calling, and their
breeding; such as are becoming of them, and of them only. Some of
his persons are vicious, and some virtuous; some are unlearned, or
(as Chaucer calls them) lewd, and some are learned. Even the ribaldry
of the low characters is different. The Reeve, the Miller, and the
Cook, are several men, and distinguished from each other, as much
as the mincing Lady Prioress, and the broad-speaking gap-toothed
Wife of Bath. But enough of this; there is such a variety of game
springing up before me, that I am distracted in my choice, and know

Dr. Drake: James Drake (1667–1707), Tory pamphleteer.
Prior laesit: Terence, *Eunuch*, prol. 6.
Baptista Porta: Giovanni Battista della Porta (*c.* 1538–1615), whose *De humana
    physiognomonia* (1586) discussed the relationship between emotion and facial
    expression.

not which to follow. 'Tis sufficient to say according to the proverb, that here is God's plenty. We have our forefathers and great grand-dames all before us as they were in Chaucer's days; their general characters are still remaining in mankind, and even in England, though they are called by other names than those of Monks, and Friars, and Canons, and Lady Abbesses, and Nuns. For mankind is ever the same, and nothing lost out of nature, though everything is altered. May I have leave to do myself the justice, (since my enemies will do me none, and are so far from granting me to be a good poet, that they will not allow me so much as to be a Christian, or a moral man) may I have leave, I say, to inform my reader, that I have con-fined my choice to such tales of Chaucer as savour nothing of im-modesty. If I had desired more to please than to instruct, the Reeve, the Miller, the Shipman, the Merchant, the Sumner, and above all, the Wife of Bath, in the prologue to her tale, would have procured me as many friends and readers, as there are *beaux* and ladies of pleasure in the town. But I will no more offend against good manners. I am sensible as I ought to be of the scandal I have given by my loose writings; and make what reparation I am able, by this public acknowledgment. If anything of this nature, or of profaneness, be crept into these poems, I am so far from defending it, that I disown it. *Totum hoc indictum volo.* Chaucer makes another manner of apology for his broad-speaking, and Boccaccio makes the like; but I will follow neither of them. Our countryman, in the end of his characters, before the *Canterbury Tales,* thus excuses the ribaldry, which is very gross, in many of his novels.

> But first, I pray you, of your courtesy,
> That ye ne arrete it nought my villany,
> Though that I plainly speak in this mattere
> To tellen you her words, and eke her chere:
> Ne though I speak her words properly,
> For this ye knowen as well as I,
> Who shall tellen a tale after a man
> He mote rehearse as nye, as ever he can:
> Everich word of it been in his charge,
> All speak he, never so rudely, ne large.
> Or else he mote tellen his tale untrue,
> Or feine things, or find words new:
> He may not spare, although he were his brother,
> He mote as well say o word as another.
> Christ spake himself full broad in Holy Writ,
> And well I wote no villany is it.
> Eke Plato saith, who so can him rede,
> The words mote been cousin to the deed.

But first . . .: Prologue, A. ll. 725–42.

Yet if a man should have enquired of Boccaccio or of Chaucer, what need they had of introducing such characters, where obscene words were proper in their mouths, but very undecent to be heard, I know not what answer they could have made. For that reason, such tales shall be left untold by me. You have here a specimen of Chaucer's language, which is so obsolete that his sense is scarce to be understood; and you have likewise more than one example of his unequal numbers, which were mentioned before. Yet many of his verses consist of ten syllables, and the words not much behind our present English as for example, these two lines, in the description of the carpenter's young wife:

> Wincing she was, as is a jolly colt,
> Long as a mast, and upright as a bolt.

I have almost done with Chaucer, when I have answered some objections relating to my present work. I find some people are offended that I have turned these tales into modern English; because they think them unworthy of my pains, and look on Chaucer as a dry, old-fashioned wit, not worth receiving. I have often heard the late Earl of Leicester say, that Mr. Cowley himself was of that opinion; who having read him over at my Lord's request, declared he had no taste of him. I dare not advance my opinion against the judgement of so great an author, but I think it fair, however, to leave the decision to the public. Mr. Cowley was too modest to set up for a dictator; and being shocked perhaps with his old style, never examined into the depth of his good sense. Chaucer, I confess, is a rough diamond, and must first be polished ere he shines. I deny not likewise, that living in our early days of poetry, he writes not always of a piece, but sometimes mingles trivial things, with those of greater moment. Sometimes also, though not often, he runs riot, like Ovid, and knows not when he has said enough. But there are more great wits, beside Chaucer, whose fault is their excess of conceits, and those ill sorted. An author is not to write all he can, but only all he ought. Having observed this redundancy in Chaucer, (as it is an easy matter for a man of ordinary parts to find a fault in one of greater) I have not tied myself to a literal translation; but have often omitted what I judged unnecessary, or not of dignity enough to appear in the company of better thoughts. I have presumed farther in some places, and added somewhat of my own where I thought my author was deficient, and had not given his thoughts their true lustre, for want of

carpenter's young wife: *Miller's Tale*, A. ll. 3263–4.
late Earl of Leicester: Philip Sidney (1619–89), 3rd Earl.

words in the beginning of our language. And to this I was the more
emboldened, because (if I may be permitted to say it of myself) I
found I had a soul congenial to his, and that I had been conversant
in the same studies. Another poet, in another age, may take the same
liberty with my writings; if at least they live long enough to deserve
correction. It was also necessary sometimes to restore the sense of
Chaucer, which was lost or mangled in the errors of the press. Let
this example suffice at present; in the story of Palamon and Arcite,
where the Temple of Diana is described, you find these verses, in all
the editions of our author:

> There saw I Danè turned unto a tree,
> I mean not the goddess Diane,
> But Venus daughter, which that hight Danè.

Which after a little consideration I knew was to be reformed into this
sense, that Daphne the daughter of Peneus was turned into a tree. I
durst not make thus bold with Ovid, lest some future Milbourne
should arise, and say I varied from my author, because I understood
him not.

But there are other judges who think I ought not to have translated Chaucer into English, out of a quite contrary notion. They
suppose there is a certain veneration due to his old language; and
that it is little less than profanation and sacrilege to alter it. They are
farther of opinion, that somewhat of his good sense will suffer in this
transfusion, and much of the beauty of his thoughts will infallibly be
lost, which appear with more grace in their old habit. Of this opinion
was that excellent person, whom I mentioned, the late Earl of
Leicester, who valued Chaucer as much as Mr. Cowley despised him.
My Lord dissuaded me from this attempt, (for I was thinking of it
some years before his death) and his authority prevailed so far with
me, as to defer my undertaking while he lived, in deference to him.
Yet my reason was not convinced with what he urged against it. If
the first end of a writer be to be understood, then as his language
grows obsolete, his thoughts must grow obscure, *multa renascentur*
quae nunc cecidere; cadentque quae nunc sunt in honore vocabula,
si volet usus, quem penes arbitrium est et jus et norma loquendi.
When an ancient word for its sound and significancy deserves to be

Temple of Diana: *Knight's Tale*, A. ll. 2062–4.
Milbourne: Luke Milbourne (1649–1720) had attacked Dryden's 1697 Virgil in
   'Notes . . . In a letter to a Friend' (1698).
multa renascentur . . .: Horace, *Ars Poetica*, ll. 70–2 ('Many terms now obsolete
   shall be reborn, and those now in favour shall fall, if usage decrees, in whose
   hands lies the judgement, the law and the rule of speech').

revived, I have that reasonable veneration for antiquity, to restore it.
All beyond this is superstition. Words are not like landmarks, so
sacred as never to be removed. Customs are changed, and even
statutes are silently repealed, when the reason ceases for which they
were enacted. As for the other part of the argument, that his thoughts
will lose of their original beauty by the innovation of words; in the
first place, not only their beauty, but their being is lost, where they
are no longer understood, which is the present case. I grant, that
something must be lost in all transfusion, that is, in all translations;
but the sense will remain, which would otherwise be lost, or at least
be maimed, when it is scarce intelligible, and that but to a few. How
few are there who can read Chaucer, so as to understand him perfectly? And if imperfectly, then with less profit, and no pleasure.
'Tis not for the use of some old Saxon friends, that I have taken these
pains with him. Let them neglect my version, because they have no
need of it. I made it for their sakes who understand sense and poetry,
as well as they; when that poetry and sense is put into words which
they understand. I will go farther, and dare to add that what beauties
I lose in some places, I give to others which had them not originally.
But in this I may be partial to myself; let the reader judge, and I
submit to his decision. Yet I think I have just occasion to complain of
them, who because they understand Chaucer, would deprive the
greater part of their countrymen of the same advantage, and hoard
him up, as misers do their grandam gold, only to look on it themselves, and hinder others from making use of it. In sum, I seriously
protest that no man ever had, or can have, a greater veneration for
Chaucer than myself. I have translated some part of his works, only
that I might perpetuate his memory, or at least refresh it, amongst
my countrymen. If I have altered him anywhere for the better, I must
at the same time acknowledge, that I could have done nothing without him: *facile est inventis addere*, is no great commendation; and I
am not so vain to think I have deserved a greater. I will conclude
what I have to say of him singly, with this one remark: A lady of my
acquaintance, who keeps a kind of correspondence with some
authors of the fair sex in France, has been informed by them, that
Mademoiselle de Scudéry, who is as old as Sibyl, and inspired like
her by the same God of Poetry, is at this time translating Chaucer
into modern French. From which I gather, that he has been formerly
translated into the old Provençal, (for, how she should come to
understand Old English, I know not.) But the matter of fact being

facile est . . .: 'It is easy to add to what has been already discovered.'
Mlle de Scudéry: there is no evidence that Mme de Scudéry was translating
   Chaucer.

true, it makes me think, that there is something in it like fatality; that after certain periods of time, the fame and memory of great wits should be renewed, as Chaucer is both in France and England. If this be wholly chance, 'tis extraordinary; and I dare not call it more, for fear of being taxed with superstition.

Boccaccio comes last to be considered, who living in the same age with Chaucer, had the same genius, and followed the same studies. Both writ novels, and each of them cultivated his mother tongue; but the greatest resemblance of our two modern authors being in their familiar style, and pleasing way of relating comical adventures, I may pass it over, because I have translated nothing from Boccaccio of that nature. In the serious part of poetry, the advantage is wholly on Chaucer's side; for though the Englishman has borrowed many tales from the Italian, yet it appears, that those of Boccaccio were not generally of his own making, but taken from authors of former ages, and by him only modelled. So that what there was of invention in either of them, may be judged equal. But Chaucer has refined on Boccaccio, and has mended the stories which he has borrowed, in his way of telling; though prose allows more liberty of thought, and the expression is more easy, when unconfined by numbers. Our country-man carries weight, and yet wins the race at disadvantage. I desire not the reader should take my word; and therefore I will set two of their discourses on the same subject in the same light, for every man to judge betwixt them. I translated Chaucer first, and amongst the rest, pitched on *The Wife of Bath's Tale*; not daring, as I have said, to adventure on her prologue, because 'tis too licentious: there Chaucer introduces an old woman of mean parentage, whom a youthful knight of noble blood was forced to marry, and consequently loathed her. The crone being in bed with him on the wedding night, and finding his aversion, endeavours to win his affection by reason, and speaks a good word for herself, (as who could blame her?) in hope to mollify the sullen bridegroom. She takes her topics from the benefits of poverty, the advantages of old age and ugliness, the vanity of youth, and the silly pride of ancestry and titles without inherent virtue, which is the true nobility. When I had closed Chaucer, I returned to Ovid, and translated some more of his fables; and by this time had so far forgotten *The Wife of Bath's Tale*, that when I took up Boccaccio, unawares I fell on the same argument of prefer-ring virtue to nobility of blood, and titles, in the story of Sigismonda; which I had certainly avoided for the resemblance of the two discourses, if my memory had not failed me. Let the reader weigh them both; and if he thinks me partial to Chaucer, 'tis in him to right Boccaccio.

I prefer in our countryman, far above all his other stories, the noble poem of Palamon and Arcite, which is of the epic kind, and perhaps not much inferior to the *Iliad* or the *Aeneid*. The story is more pleasing than either of them, the manners as perfect, the diction as poetical, the learning as deep and various, and the disposition full as artful: only it includes a greater length of time, as taking up seven years at least; but Aristotle has left undecided the duration of the action, which yet is easily reduced into the compass of a year, by a narration of what preceded the return of Palamon to Athens. I had thought for the honour of our nation, and more particularly for his, whose laurel, though unworthy, I have worn after him, that this story was of English growth, and Chaucer's own. But I was un-deceived by Boccaccio, for casually looking on the end of his seventh *Giornata*, I found Dioneo (under which name he shadows himself) and *Fiametta* (who represents his mistress, the natural daughter of Robert King of Naples) of whom these words are spoken. *Dioneo e Fiametta gran pezza cantarono insieme d'Arcita, e di Palamone*: by which it appears that this story was written before the time of Boccaccio; but the name of its author being wholly lost, Chaucer is now become an original; and I question not but the poem has re-ceived many beauties by passing through his noble hands. Besides this tale, there is another of his own invention, after the manner of the Provençals, called *The Flower and the Leaf*; with which I was so particularly pleased, both for the invention and the moral, that I cannot hinder myself from recommending it to the reader.

As a corollary to this preface, in which I have done justice to others, I owe somewhat to myself: not that I think it worth my time to enter the lists with one M——, or one B——, but barely to take notice, that such men there are who have written scurrilously against me without any provocation. M——, who is in orders, pretends amongst the rest this quarrel to me, that I have fallen foul on priesthood; if I have, I am only to ask pardon of good priests, and am afraid his part of the reparation will come to little. Let him be satisfied that he shall not be able to force himself upon me for an adversary. I contemn him too much to enter into competition with him. His own transla-tions of Virgil have answered his criticisms on mine. If (as they say,

---

Dioneo e Fiametta . . .: *Decamerone*, vii. 10, epilogue ('Dioneo and Fiametta told a long story of Palamon and Arcite').

The Flower and the Leaf: Tyrwhitt's edition (1775–78) excluded this anony-mous 15th-century poem, previously regarded as Chaucer's.

M—— . . . B——: Luke Milbourne and Richard Blackmore (*c.* 1655–1729).

translations of Virgil: Milbourne's translation of *Aeneid*, i, was published in 1687.

he has declared in print) he prefers the version of Ogilby to mine, the world has made him the same compliment. For 'tis agreed on all hands, that he writes even below Ogilby. That, you will say, is not easily to be done; but what cannot M—— bring about? I am satisfied however, that while he and I live together, I shall not be thought the worst poet of the age. It looks as if I had desired him underhand to write so ill against me. But upon my honest word I have not bribed him to do me this service, and am wholly guiltless of his pamphlet. 'Tis true I should be glad, if I could persuade him to continue his good offices, and write such another critique on any thing of mine: for I find by experience he has a great stroke with the reader, when he condemns any of my poems to make the world have a better opinion of them. He has taken some pains with my poetry; but nobody will be persuaded to take the same with his. If I had taken to the Church (as he affirms, but which was never in my thoughts) I should have had more sense, if not more grace, than to have turned myself out of my benefice by writing libels on my parishioners. But his account of my manners and my principles, are of a piece with his cavils and his poetry; and so I have done with him for ever.

As for the city bard, or knight physician, I hear his quarrel to me is, that I was the author of *Absalom and Achitophel*, which he thinks is a little hard on his fanatic patrons in London.

But I will deal the more civilly with his two poems, because nothing ill is to be spoken of the dead. And therefore peace be to the Manes of his Arthurs. I will only say that it was not for this noble knight that I drew the plan of an epic poem on King Arthur in my preface to the translation of Juvenal. The guardian angels of kingdoms were machines too ponderous for him to manage; and therefore he rejected them as Dares did the whirl-bats of Eryx when they were thrown before him by Entellus. Yet from that preface he plainly took his hint; for he began immediately upon the story, though he had the baseness not to acknowledge his benefactor, but instead of it, to traduce me in a libel.

I shall say the less of Mr. Collier, because in many things he has taxed me justly; and I have pleaded guilty to all thoughts and

---

Ogilby: see Preface to *Sylvae*, p. 195 above, and footnote.

knight physician: Blackmore was knighted by William III and made Court Physician in 1697.

Arthurs: i.e. *Prince Arthur* (1695) and *King Arthur* (1697).

Juvenal: see above, 'A Discourse concerning . . . Satire', p. 224.

Entellus: *Aeneid*, v. 400.

expressions of mine, which can be truly argued of obscenity, profaneness, or immorality; and retract them. If he be my enemy, let him triumph; if he be my friend, as I have given him no personal occasion to be otherwise, he will be glad of my repentance. It becomes me not to draw my pen in the defence of a bad cause, when I have so often drawn it for a good one. Yet it were not difficult to prove, that in many places he has perverted my meaning by his glosses; and interpreted my words into blasphemy and bawdry, of which they were not guilty. Besides that, he is too much given to horseplay in his raillery; and comes to battle, like a dictator from the plough. I will not say, *The zeal of God's House has eaten him up*; but I am sure it has devoured some part of his good manners and civility. It might also be doubted, whether it were altogether zeal, which prompted him to this rough manner of proceeding; perhaps it became not one of his function to rake into the rubbish of ancient and modern plays; a divine might have employed his pains to better purpose, than in the nastiness of Plautus and Aristophanes, whose examples, as they excuse not me, so it might be possibly supposed, that he read them not without some pleasure. They who have written commentaries on those poets, or on Horace, Juvenal, and Martial, have explained some vices, which without their interpretation had been unknown to modern times. Neither has he judged impartially betwixt the former age and us.

There is more bawdry in one play of Fletcher's, called *The Custom of the Country*, than in all ours together. Yet this has been often acted on the stage in my remembrance. Are the times so much more reformed now, than they were five and twenty years ago? If they are, I congratulate the amendment of our morals. But I am not to prejudice the cause of my fellow poets, though I abandon my own defence. They have some of them answered for themselves, and neither they nor I can think Mr. Collier so formidable an enemy, that we should shun him. He has lost ground at the latter end of the day, by pursuing his point too far, like the Prince of Condé at the Battle of Senef. From immoral plays, to no plays; *ab abusu ad usum, non valet consequentia*. But being a party, I am not to erect myself into a judge. As for the rest of those who have written against me, they are such scoundrels, that they deserve not the least notice to be

The zeal of God's House . . .: Psalms 69:9; John 2:17.
The Custom of the Country: (*c*. 1620) by Fletcher and Massinger.
Senef: at Senef in Flanders, on 11 August 1674, the Prince of Condé pressed his advantage over the Prince of Orange's vanguard too far and suffered heavy losses.
ab abusu . . .: 'abuses do not necessarily lead to good uses.'

taken of them. B—— and M—— are only distinguished from the crowd, by being remembered to their infamy.

> —Demetri, teque Tigelli
> discipularum inter jubeo plorare cathedras.

Demetri, . . .: Horace, *Satires*, I. x. 90–1 ('I command you, Demetrius and Tigellus, to go and grizzle where your female students sit').

Notes

p. 1.   Roger Boyle, Earl of Orrery (1621–79) wrote a romance, *Parthenissa*, and several plays, of which *The General* is the first true heroic play in English, although not acted until after Dryden and Howard's *Indian Queen* had established the genre.

p. 4.   Shakespeare did not, of course, invent blank verse: other English dramatists used the form before him (including the authors of *Gorboduc*, whom Dryden uses to support his defence of rhyme), and Surrey's blank verse translations from the *Aeneid* had appeared in 1554 and 1557.

p. 5.   It becomes a commonplace of Restoration and Augustan criticism that Waller and Denham first brought polish and metrical regularity to English poetry. Denham's *Cooper's Hill* (1642) is not an epic but a long descriptive couplet poem in the Horatian tradition of Jonson's *To Penshurst*.

p. 6.   Dryden maintains this position on rhyme's superiority over blank verse in *Of Dramatic Poesy*, *A Defence of an Essay of Dramatic Poesy*, and *Of Heroic Plays*. In the Prologue to *Aureng Zebe* and the Preface to *All for Love*, however, he defends blank verse in drama.

p. 8.   Quintilian (*Institutio Oratoria*, X. i. 90) distinguishes between 'poetis' and 'oratoribus'. The other reference usually cited in this context is Petronius, *Satyricon* 118. Although Lucan is not mentioned, Quintilian's allusion to 'anyone who attempts the vast theme of the Civil War' is normally taken to refer to him, and the remark from *Satyricon* is a commonplace of 17th-century criticism.

p. 12.   Kinsley, iv, pp. 1827–8, gives references for Dryden's 'most direct reminiscences and imitations of Virgil'. These are largely from the *Aeneid* and relate to about 60 lines of Dryden's poem.

p. 16.   Charles Sackville (1638–1706) became Earl of Middlesex in 1675 and of Dorset in 1677. He was William III's Lord Chamberlain from 1689 to 1697, and is commonly identified with the Eugenius of this essay, although known to have been at the battle which is its formal motivation.

p. 16.   The Great Plague of 1665 kept the theatres closed from May 1665 to November 1666. During this time Dryden stayed with his father-in-law, the Earl of Berkshire, at Charlton Park in Wiltshire.

p. 20.   The four characters of Dryden's dialogue are usually identified as, respectively, Sackville, Sir Robert Howard (1626–98, Dryden's brother-in-law), Sir Charles Sedley (1639?–1701), and Dryden himself. See, however, F. L. Huntley in *MLN* 63 (1948), who attacks these traditional identifications.

p. 24.   If Howard is Crites, his argument here is rather different from that in his Preface to *Four New Plays* (1665): if Crites is in any sense a dramatic character, no problems arise, nor are they of real importance anyway.

p. 25.   As Neander notes later, Lisideius's 'description' fails to define the specific generic qualities of drama. It could, therefore, be as well applied to other genres, especially the epic.

p. 25   i.e. the schoolmen; those medieval philosophers who taught largely under the influence of Aristotle and the Church Fathers. Their influence came under attack in the 16th century, and Bacon viewed them as men who had abandoned 'the commerce of the mind with things', but Dryden here seems to assimilate the Renaissance to the Middle Ages.

p. 27   Aristotle stresses the importance of the unity of action and speaks of the desirability of restricting the period of time a play purports to cover, but he says nothing of unity of place. Both the establishment of the Three Unities and their erection as rules are neo-classical developments.

p. 31   Aristotle (*Poetics*, xii) does give four divisions of tragedy, but those stated by Dryden derive rather from Scaliger's *Poetices* (1561).

p. 40   Under Richelieu's supervision L'Académie Française (founded 1635) required the observance of the Three Unities. Although Corneille is mentioned here in connexion with Richelieu, his *Le Cid* (1637) was disapproved of by the Academy for not conforming to this requirement.

p. 41   Ker suggests Dryden may be referring to Ménage, but the more probable reference is to Howard, who, in his Preface to *Four New Plays*, says that the ancients chose as subject-matter 'usually the most known stories and fables'.

p. 56   Dryden may well have Jonson in mind, but, although Jonson occasionally gibes at Shakespeare's comparative lack of learning. it is often not realized what a magnanimous tribute Jonson's elegy 'To the Memory of my Beloved . . .' is.

p. 57   There is some rather uncertain evidence that Jonson had been involved, at least as a collaborator, in dramatic writing before this, his first success.

p. 58   As Neumann (*PMLA*, vol. 54 (1939)) has shown, this charge is largely unfair, based on a superficial impression rather than any hard evidence.

p. 60   But Molière's early plays show characters moved by extravagance of 'habit, passion, or affection' in a way which suggests that *humeur* could mean something close to Jonsonian humour.

p. 64   Since the conversation which forms this essay is supposed to have taken place on 3 June 1665, when the plague had just begun, this is obviously an anachronism.

p. 64   As Boulton points out, Crites' speech from this point on closely resembles Howard's Preface to *Four New Plays*.

p. 77   This Defence was published in the second edition of *The Indian Emperor* and is the last blow in the Dryden–Howard debate about rhyme in drama. The earlier stages are Dryden's Preface to *The Rival Ladies* (1664), Howard's Preface to *Four New Plays* (1665), Dryden's 'Of Dramatic Poesy', and Howard's Preface to *The Great Favourite* (1668).

p. 93   The Dryden–Howard controversy did end here and the Defence was not printed in later editions of *The Indian Emperor* during Dryden's lifetime.

p. 94   Dryden's distinction between Shakespeare and Jonson was already a critical cliché. Jonson's own comments on Shakespeare (in his conversations with Drummond and his poem 'To the Memory of my Beloved . . . Mr. William Shakespeare') provide the *locus classicus* for the 'natural' Shakespeare, while his own contemporaries stress Jonson's careful artistry and learning.

p. 95   Dryden's remarks about morality here are relevant to the long 17th- and 18th-century argument about the function and responsibility of drama (see J. W. Krutch, *Comedy and Conscience after the Renaissance*, for a full discussion).

p. 107   Dryden exaggerates: *Othello* is based on Cinthio's *Hecatommithi* (Dec. iii Nov. 7); and for several other Shakespeare plays, but not *Romeo and Juliet*, and certainly not 'most of Shakespeare's plays', Cinthio was used.

p. 109   Here and in the Defence of the Epilogue to Part II of *The Conquest of Granada* Dryden comes nearest to fulfilling the promise made in the Preface to *An Evening's Love* to write 'somewhat concerning the difference betwixt the plays of our age and those of our predecessors'.

p. 119   See the Preface to *An Evening's Love* and 'To the Reader' prefixed to 'Of Dramatic Poesy'.

p. 132   Dryden, of course, is here reneging on the position he had held in a number of earlier essays, notably 'Of Dramatic Poesy' and 'Of Heroic Plays'.

p. 143   Rymer sent Dryden a copy of his book *The Tragedies of the Last Age* in 1677, and these notes were written on the end-papers of this copy. The Heads are a kind of draft for 'The Grounds of Criticism in Tragedy', but are superior to that essay in directness and force. They were first printed by Tonson (1711), and in 1779 Samuel Jonson appended them—in an inferior order—to his Life of Dryden.

p. 157   For other of Dryden's views on rhyme see 'Of Dramatic Poesy', 'Of Heroic Plays', 'Prologue to *Aureng-Zebe*'.

p. 159   This essay relates closely to the 'Heads of an Answer to Rymer'. As an answer the essay is less effective than the notes, being more cautious, more deferential to authority, more respectful to Rymer.

p. 179   Dryden also discusses translation at length in the prefaces to *Sylvae* and the *Fables*. Here he calls for a method of translation between the extremes of 'Jonsonian' metaphrastic literalism and the freedom of Cowley's Pindarique Odes, the debate being in some ways a continuation of Elizabethan controversy. Dryden's contribution to this version of Ovid was *Epistles* ii and xviii, together with xiii in collaboration with Mulgrave.

p. 183   Among the fourteen contributors were Dryden, Mulgrave, Mrs. Behn, Otway, Butler, Tate, Rymer, and Settle.

p. 189   John Holles (1662–1711), Lord Haughton, was created Duke of Newcastle in 1694 for services to William III.

p. 219   Boileau, *L'Art Poétique* (1674), iii. 193–236. Dryden is contributing here to a then-active controversy: for other relevant remarks see 'Of Heroic Plays' (p. 111 f.) and a letter of 1694 to Dennis (Watson, II, p. 178).

p. 279   Thomas, Lord Clifford (1630–73), had been a patron of Dryden; he relinquished the Treasurership because of the 1673 Test Act. Dryden's tragedy *Amboyna* (1673) was dedicated to him. Hugh, his son, lived from 1663 to 1730.

Index